NOV 1 3 2009

W9-BDT-125

Abroad
for Her Country

An ADST-DACOR Diplomats and Diplomacy Book

Jean M. Wilkowski

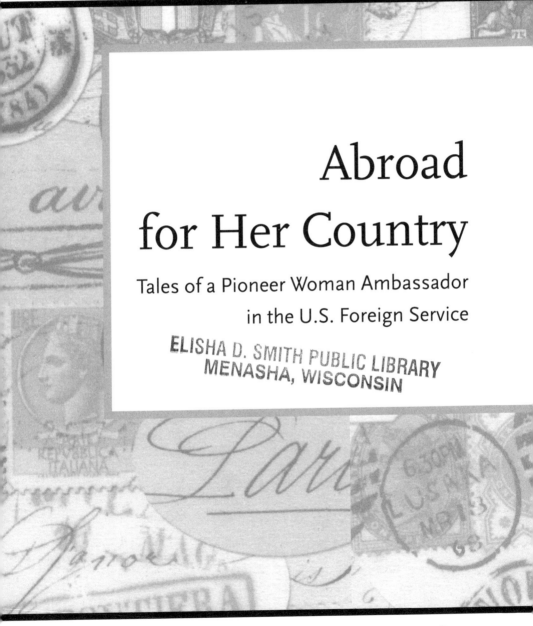

Abroad for Her Country

Tales of a Pioneer Woman Ambassador
in the U.S. Foreign Service

ELISHA D. SMITH PUBLIC LIBRARY
MENASHA, WISCONSIN

University of Notre Dame Press   Notre Dame, Indiana

Copyright © 2008 by University of Notre Dame
Notre Dame, Indiana 46556
www.undpress.nd.edu
All Rights Reserved

Manufactured in the United States of America

Title Page art courtesy of Cavallini Papers & Co., Inc.

The views and opinions in this book are solely those of the author and do not
necessarily reflect those of the Association for Diplomatic Studies and Training,
Diplomatic and Consular Officers, Retired, Inc., or the United States Government.

Library of Congress Cataloging-in-Publication Data

Wilkowski, Jean M., 1919–
    Abroad for her country : tales of a pioneer woman ambassador in the U.S.
Foreign Service / Jean M. Wilkowski.
        p.   cm. — (An ADST-DACOR diplomats and diplomacy book)
    Includes bibliographical references and index.
    ISBN-13: 978-0-268-04413-8 (cloth : alk. paper)
    ISBN-10: 0-268-04413-9 (cloth : alk. paper)
    1. Wilkowski, Jean M., 1919– 2. Ambassadors—United States—Biography.
3. Women ambassadors—United States—Biography.   4. United States—
Foreign relations—1945–1989.   I. Title.
    E748.W683A3   2008
    327.730092—dc22
    [B]

                                                                    2007051042

∞ *The paper in this book meets the guidelines for permanence and durability of
the Committee on Production Guidelines for Book Longevity of the Council on
Library Resources.*

This work is dedicated to all the new and coming generations of Foreign Service officers of the twenty-first century, the roughly three hundred intelligent young men and women carefully selected from among 20,000 applicants each year to be sent abroad to represent their country throughout the world. They are among the best of America's government servants. The foreign posts they go to—Moscow, Prague, Manila, Bujumbura, Jidda, Seoul, Pretoria, and Kinshasa—are as diverse as their own family names, home states, backgrounds, education, and experience. They will observe, analyze, report, and act in defense of their country's vital national interests overseas.

May these young officers be helped by the experiences of all those who went before them, remain true to the principles upon which this great country was founded, and find support under the wing of that Great Spirit who watches over and protects those on missions of justice and peace.

Contents

Preface   ix

ONE
Early Years, 1926–44   3

TWO
Trinidad, BWI, 1944–46 (Vice Consul)   18

THREE
Bogotá, Colombia, 1947–48 (Third Secretary—Economic)   44

FOUR
Milan, Italy, 1949–51 (Vice Consul)   71

FIVE
Paris, France, 1953–56 (Deputy Commercial Attaché)   99

SIX
Santiago, Chile, 1957–59 (Second Secretary)   132

SEVEN
Interim Assignments: GATT Tariff Negotiations, 1960–61; Senior
Seminar, 1962–63; Diplomat in Residence in California, 1976–77   151

EIGHT
Rome, Italy, 1963–66 (Second Secretary), 1969–72 (Commercial
Counselor; Minister/Counselor for Economic Affairs)   172

NINE
Tegucigalpa, Honduras, 1966–69 (Deputy Chief of Mission;
Chargé d'Affaires a.i.)   201

TEN
Lusaka, Zambia, 1972–76 (U.S. Ambassador, Chief of Mission)   234

ELEVEN
To State and the United Nations, 1977–80
(Father Ted, China, and Vienna)   300

TWELVE
Later Years, 1980–2000   319

Epilogue   340

Index   341

PREFACE

The following thoughts are said to have been drafted by Bishop Ken Untener of Saginaw, Michigan, and first spoken by John Cardinal Dearden of Detroit, though they are often incorrectly attributed to Salvadoran Archbishop Oscar Romero. These words have become a prayer ("The Long View," cited in part below). It reminds us of how little can be accomplished in life without our Creator's assistance.

> The kingdom is not only beyond our efforts,
>   it is even beyond our vision.
> We accomplish in our lifetime only a tiny fraction of
>   the magnificent enterprise that is God's work.
> Nothing we do is complete.
>   .   .   .   .
> This is what we are about.
> We plant the seeds that will one day grow.
> We water seeds already planted,
>   knowing that they hold future promise.
> We lay foundations that will need further development.
> We provide yeast that produces effects beyond our capabilities.
> We cannot do everything, and
>   there is a sense of liberation in knowing that.

This enables us to do something
    and to do it very well.
It may be incomplete,
    but it is a beginning,
    a step along the way, an opportunity
    for the Lord's grace to enter and do the rest.
We may never see the end results.
But that is the difference
    between the master builder and the worker.
We are workers, not master builders,
    ministers, not messiahs.
We are prophets of a future that is not our own.

———

To tell the story of one's life and work is obviously a highly egocentric, if not egotistical endeavor. I shied away from it for those reasons, and because I never took myself that seriously nor felt that my professional experiences were of such timeless significance they needed to be part of the recorded history of U.S. foreign relations. Nonetheless, I was persuaded by friends to take pen in hand, or rather to try to master the computer. These same supportive friends seemed to find many of my experiences amusing and worth telling as a part of the continuum of U.S. social and diplomatic history in the twentieth century. I know I dined out on many of these stories, enjoying the hospitality and generosity of good friends, even strangers.

So, taking Bishop Untener's sage advice, I stepped back and took a long view of my past. I realized that I had played a minor but catalytic role in pressing for justice and peace in a number of professional circumstances, as when I challenged the consciences of some leaders in Central America on human rights abuses, or jiggled other consciences at the United Nations when it seemed to some that gaining power and narrow control of financing were more important than programming and delivering actual development projects to needy countries. My most important accomplishment in Africa may have been in advocating and gaining acceptance of a more understanding and humane change in U.S. policy toward southern Africa during the liberation struggles for independence and majority rule there in the mid-1970s. This change helped the United States move beyond the largely rhetorical to a sounder, more realistic course of diplomatic interaction.

I also took pride in being a symbol of social equality that helped enable many highly capable African women to move into government and positions of leadership while I was in Africa, even in the diplomatic service—though it may have taken Zambia another twenty-five years to appoint a woman ambassador to the United States.

I derive special pride and satisfaction from helping to implement U.S. foreign policies on economic development in the poorer nations, particularly in Africa and Latin America. Mine was never a solo performance; work in the Foreign Service is always a collaborative, team effort. Instinctively we followed Untener's counsel. We tried to do the job well, and we recognized that our work was only a beginning, never complete. We liked to think, as Untener suggested, that in our life and work we might have been prophets of the future, however insignificant our endeavors and remote our assignments.

The main purpose of these chapters is to inform and entertain and perhaps incidentally to show how government—to which employees swear allegiance and whose Constitution they swear to defend—deeply influences its employees' personal lives, at least in the era of my service.

I found Bishop Untener's reflections helpful in informing the story of my life and work, especially in reminding me that grace is needed to give meaning, even a sense of achievement, to any life and work. I hope that the parts of my life delineated here reflect the Master's constant protection, support, and forgiveness, for which I am eternally grateful.

I am also grateful to the following people who urged me to undertake this work and helped along the way, though never fully understanding why it took me so long: Frank and Barbara Cain, dear friends in Potomac, Maryland, and Naples, Florida, who, with the Rev. Liam Bergin, Rector, Irish College, Rome, were the primary prompters that I undertake this project; Margery Boichel Thompson, my patient, able, and experienced editor, who also saw me through my earlier publication on conference diplomacy; many dear and close friends in Washington and Florida who encouraged and supported me in many ways; and an international stable of computer "techies," who kept finding text I had lost and making the computer work—Olabode Thomas Akins from Nigeria, Roberto Cotugno from Italy, Carolina Nieviera from the Philippines, and Antonia Abu-Matar from Romania.

Abroad
for Her Country

ONE

Early Years, 1926–44

Who would have thought that a young girl born in Rhinelander, Wisconsin, in the early part of the twentieth century, the tallest in her class and always in the back row so the other children could see the teacher, would become a United States ambassador and travel around the world? Never, in my wildest dreams while growing up did I have any such aspirations. Thoughts of foreign countries never entered my head in grammar school, high school, or college. Whatever hopes my parents may have had for me were focused on health, happiness, and fear of the Lord. But such aspirations may have suffered when I was expelled from first grade. Some might even have wondered in those days if I was headed for a life of delinquency rather than diplomacy.

Expelled from First Grade

I attended first grade at St. Mary's parochial school in Rhinelander, a small village of 7,000 that survived on a paper mill and a modest tourist industry. I can't recall the name of the nun who expelled me, but it should have been Sister Mary Hard Knuckles or Sister Mary of the Roving Eyes. She used to parade around the classroom with a ruler in one hand that she would tap either on the other hand or the head of a misbehaving student. She was tall and thin, a Franciscan from some place near La Crosse, Wisconsin.

One fine day, my little boy chum, baptized James but nicknamed Jimzie by his family, was caught shooting spitballs at someone in class. He was promptly told by Sister Mary-Never-Miss-a-Thing, or whatever her name was, that he was grounded and confined to the classroom during the lunch break. No one, but no one, the nun insisted, her eyes sweeping the entire classroom, was to tell anyone that Jimzie was being punished.

It was my bad fortune to have been invited that day to Jimzie's home for lunch as my mother was visiting Jimzie's mother. That put me on the spot. When I arrived at midday alone at Jimzie's home, the mothers wanted to know where Jimzie was. I told them I couldn't tell.

Jimzie's mother, being something of a policewoman in appearance, manner, and voice, lacking only a badge on her ample Irish bosom and a billy club in her hand, said, "What do you MEAN you can't tell?" She seemed ready to take me by the scruff of the neck when I wailed, "I can't tell; the nun won't let me tell!" She said, "You TELL ME what's going on!" So I did, thereby violating the nun's injunction. I was given a sandwich to take back to Jimzie, the mothers agreeing they would deal with the matter later.

When I returned to class after lunch we were all asked if "anyone had told about Jimzie's detention." Of course I had to raise my hand and confess. At that point the nun totally lost her cool and expelled the two of us from her class and the school. I can still see Jimzie's face all scrunched up with tears as he nibbled away on his tired sandwich, which was becoming increasingly wet and limp as we shuffled lazily back to his home.

Jimzie's mother was enraged. The two mothers promptly put on their hats and marched us back to school. Jimzie developed a serious case of hiccups while I tried to bolt free from yet another round trip to school. I was tired not only of walking but of trouble-prone Jimzie.

The mothers' showdown with the nun was worth the trip back. Jimzie's mother nearly reduced the poor religious to rubble right in front of the entire class. There was loud talk of "abuse of little children." My mother kept giving frequent nods of approval as Jimzie's mother held the floor.

One nun down, the two mothers then swept off to take on the school principal and the pastor. As Jimzie's large family were strong supporters of both church and school, our expulsion was short-lived on recourse to higher authority, thus relieving both of us from carrying the shame through life.

From then on I gave Jimzie a wide berth. I wanted no happenings through association. Before shunning him I told him I thought his name was silly as it rhymed with Chimpanzee. Jimzie thereupon got even by nicknaming me "Squirrel," which stuck through grade school.

My troubled friendship with Jimzie taught me a lesson early in life about the importance of the company one keeps, as well as the kinds of secrets one has to keep—some worthy, others not. It also put me on guard in future relations with religious. Later in life as I looked back on the expulsion from first grade, I concluded that the nun who had expelled us might well have been having a difficult monthly period, going through change of life, or was just one of those control freaks one occasionally encounters in life.

I wasn't at St. Mary's long—only into fifth grade to be exact—when in 1929 my parents decided to move from northern Wisconsin to the south in search of greater economic opportunity.

Long-Distance Travel

Thus when I was ten my brother and I were loaded into the family car and driven from Wisconsin down through the heart of the United States and on into Florida, a distance of some 2,000 miles, on two-lane roads not always paved. It was the longest trip I had ever made and it presaged a life of many journeys. We called Georgia the Black-Eyed Pea State because the item seemed always to be on every menu we encountered along the way.

We were pioneers in our day, being among the first to traverse the Tamiami Trail across the Florida Everglades soon after its completion. Heavy construction equipment and dredges lined the drainage canals on either side of the road. When we took a break from driving, we observed alligators and beautiful tropical birds. We were pioneers also in being among the first to spend our winters in Florida and our summers up north.

What a fortune we could have made—like the Colliers on the West Coast or the Flagers on the East—had we invested in real estate, which was booming in those days. But security rather than speculation seemed the family hallmark. Perhaps that is why in later years a job in government had subconscious appeal.

On arrival in Miami Beach, we immediately checked into a hotel right on the sandy beach, where we stayed nearly a week. Later my parents rented an apartment in Miami and promptly enrolled my brother and me in a grade school connected with Gesu, the Jesuit Church in the middle of downtown Miami. The church had a shrine to Saint Theresa of Lisieux, the Little Flower. My mother frequently prayed there, probably that my father would soon be reestablished and that we children might get through school. Nearby was a wonderful corner bar, where my mother enjoyed the occasional beer and free lunch, which she extended to her ten- and twelve-year-old children, who shared a sip or two of beer to wash down the corned beef and rye.

I shared my fifth grade class at Gesu with the son of Al Capone, the Chicago gangster, who had recently moved his family to one of the fashionable islands between Miami and the Beach. I immediately pegged the Capone boy for another Jimzie, though his name was Sonny. He would arrive at school in a big black limousine accompanied by two swarthy males in dark suits ("hoods"?), who would see to his safe delivery and collection every day. Later he transferred to St. Patrick's on the Beach, a high-tuition parochial school operated by the Dominican nuns from Adrian, Michigan. Years later I heard that Sonny Capone made something of a name for himself in high school with his fast sports car, fast girls, and frequent tippling, reportedly to the despair of the local pastor.

Not long after our arrival in Florida my father joined a business partner from Iowa in a resort hotel venture on Miami Beach. So we too moved across Biscayne Bay to the Beach. The parents promptly enrolled us in school, but this time in the public school, St. Patrick's being too pricey for a family with two youngsters in the waning hard times of the mid-1930s.

Florida—A Whole New World

Coming from the backwoods of northern Wisconsin, our family was continually amazed by differences, not only the change of weather, but the natives—a mix of poor white people from Georgia, blacks in service jobs, high-powered speculators, and investors from all over the North, plus a galaxy of tourists from Latin America, especially Cuba, and also from Europe.

The tourists wore loud and colorful summer clothing, something new to us. Fashion and high-end articles like jewelry, cars, mansions, and yachts were all big business, as were hotels. Lincoln Road on Miami Beach was the place to see and be seen. The wealthy and famous of the Northeast were conspicuously represented, with their chauffeur-driven cars and island villas, as well as the racetrack crowd and gangsters like the Capones ("the mob") from New York and Chicago.

I remember hearing about the notorious gangster "Bugsy" Siegel. Gypsy Rose Lee appeared at a nightclub just a few blocks from our hotel. Further down the street across from our garage, Jack Dempsey, the prize-fighting champion, opened a beachside restaurant. New and fancy nightclubs seemed to spring up all over the beach. Bouchet's Villa Venice (pronounced "Ven–eese") featured nude dancers fresh from Paris's Champs Elysées. Coming from the Northwoods of Wisconsin, we were dazzled.

The gift shop and bookstore at our church were run by the divorced wife of former New York mayor Jimmy Walker. Anyone who wanted to watch the "sport of kings" on Sunday afternoons could visit the nearby polo grounds. Local street gossip focused on whether the latest beach-front hotel under construction—a new skyscraper went up every year—was more elegant, outrageous, or higher priced than last year's leader. Many of the investors shuttled between Miami Beach and Las Vegas.

My early memories of growing up in the Midwest were soon forgotten once we were installed in the South and continued growing up there over our high school years. For entertainment my brother and I would ride the "Aerocar" from the famous Roney Plaza Hotel on Miami Beach over to the grand, Spanish-style Biltmore Hotel in Coral Gables. We seemed to have passes to everything—swimming pools, dog races, and movies included.

My father was intrigued with this whole new southern resort style of life, inspired perhaps by a flood of Hollywood movies he continued to follow closely—especially *The Thin Man*, starring William Powell. He bought a wire-haired fox terrier, more for self-image, I think, than protection. He named it Bugsy, after the gangster, and took to holding the dog on a leash just like Powell in the movie. He also took to copying the tailor-made suits, shirts, and fancy ties of his new business contacts and associates. I suppose it was appropriate for someone in the resort hotel business in Miami Beach, which attracted such a colorful and lively segment of society. At night after dinner the family would listen on the radio to Walter Winchell, *Amos 'n Andy*, or the fireside chats of President Franklin D. Roosevelt. It was a fast-changing era and for me an impressionable age.

One day our dog disappeared. When Bugsy didn't turn up for meals, we assumed she had been stolen. My father was distraught. Luckily, he found her a few weeks later seated alongside a chauffeur, looking anxiously out the window of a Rolls Royce parked around the corner from the nearby Roney Plaza Hotel. With the help of the police, my father quickly retrieved her.

Counterfeiters and Bootleggers

My father had become something of a favorite with the local police and FBI because he had discovered and helped break up a counterfeit ring that was printing $100 bills in its hotel suite, then passing them off at the Hialeah race track. The investigation resulted from my father's having detected a strange chemical odor in one of the hotel hallways.

My father also got involved with another ring of opportunists. This gang was smuggling in liquor from the nearby Bahama Islands. It was in the days of Prohibition. Whenever the rum runners spotted a Coast Guard patrol boat on the Atlantic Ocean, they would throw their illegal caches overboard, carefully recording the spot in relation to either the Gulf Stream, the heavens, or whatever mariners do to fix their locations They would return later when the coast was clear to fish out their shipments and land them at some hidden private docks, perhaps even on the Indian River alongside the fabulous estates of the wealthy, such as Capone's place on Palm Island off the causeway to Miami.

Perhaps to buy my father's allegiance or protection, the rum runners would occasionally gift him with booty, usually a wooden case or two of liquor wrapped in heavy burlap. It would arrive at our apartment soaking wet, with seaweed dangling from it. Many a night I slept with a case or two hidden under my bed. My father certainly didn't consume it all, but he became very popular with friends up north when he would pass them some of the stash during our summer trips north.

Things Foreign and Professional

My family stayed in Miami Beach throughout my high school and college years. I took two years of high school Latin and two years of French, with some vague obligatory connections to the Alliance Française in Coral Gables. I was certainly meeting some school requirement rather than thinking of a trip to Paris in those days. Moreover, I thought I had to keep an eye on my brother, who seemed taken with the French teacher with the flaming red-hair and loose chiffon blouses, despite her being "a woman of a certain age," as the French say.

During my junior and senior years, I developed a taste, though not much of a deep interest, in things foreign when I twice traveled on one-week trips to Cuba with an all-star basketball team! Most of my travel in those days was back and forth to Wisconsin to vacation at our home on a lake and play golf at a course my father had helped develop along the Wisconsin River. Travel thus became second nature to me with the family's spring and fall cross-country junkets.

I graduated from Miami Beach High School in 1937. The school had changed its name that year from Ida M. Fisher High School, having been named for the wife of Carl Fisher, one of the foremost real estate developers of Miami Beach. He had come down from Montauk on Long Island and made a fortune developing Miami Beach by filling in what was then a vast mangrove swamp. In those early days of development the construction people would reportedly joke with prospective buyers by saying, "See that wave out there 100 yards from the shore here? Well, your property will commence there as soon as we dredge the ocean floor or bay bottom and make the land."

While in high school I worked on the school newspaper, became its editor, and developed an interest in journalism. In my sophomore year, I attended a special course at Northwestern University's Medill School of Journalism. We visited newspapers like the *Chicago Tribune*, made numerous field trips, wrote news articles, and pretended we were on the city desk of a metropolitan daily. I liked the novelty and stimulation of the work, following news in the making, meeting interesting people, and writing about it all. One day I saw a movie with Rosalind Russell portraying a foreign correspondent. I thought the character might be a role model worth exploring.

College Bound

When it came time for college, I wasn't at all sure where I would go. I wanted a location that wouldn't be too far from home. I also wanted a Catholic school to make up for what I missed while attending public high school in Florida. Midway between Florida and Wisconsin was Indiana, home of Saint Mary-of-the-Woods College (just north of Terre Haute). Believe it or not, Jimzie's sister had gone there. It was founded by nuns who came over from France in 1840, like the Holy Cross priests who arrived a year later and founded the University of Notre Dame at South Bend. Both religious groups had been invited to the United States by Bishop Bruté, a Frenchman who headed the Diocese of Vincennes, Indiana.

My parents disagreed about my going to college. My father doubted its necessity, believing it would be a waste of money, contending that I "would only get married right after graduation." My mother saw it differently and was willing to use some of her wages as a working mother to underwrite my room and board. She knew that college was important to me, and she tended to indulge her children in things important to them. She believed I would work hard to succeed.

I obtained a tuition scholarship to Saint Mary-of-the-Woods and contributed to my expenses by working. In one job I worked as correspondent for the National Catholic Welfare Conference in Washington, which collected regional news for Catholic newspapers throughout the country. Neither Saint Mary-of-the-Woods College nor western Indiana were hotspots for breaking news, but I scoured about for subjects and wrote any number of stories that were accepted. Sometimes the story was about an important speaker on campus or nearby. Sometimes it concerned college activities or visitors of note. When I wasn't working on news, I was teaching swimming or serving as a lifeguard at the campus pool. I also worked summers, sometimes babysitting, sometimes as a counselor at summer camps. One summer I worked on a daily newspaper owned by the family of a college friend in Laconia, New Hampshire.

In contrast to Notre Dame, which gained fame for its football teams and later for the quality of its faculty and academic excellence, Saint Mary-of-the-Woods just loped along through the twentieth century, catering mainly to good, upper middle-class Catholic families in Chicago, Indianapolis, and Kansas City.

In 1941 I graduated from "the Woods" with a B.A. degree in journalism and a minor in French, still wondering about being a foreign correspondent, like Roz Russell in the movie, and notwithstanding some unexpected entreaties that I consider a religious vocation! Becoming a nun, however, was the furthest thing from my mind. I had achieved my main objectives—a sound liberal arts education while reaffirming and deepening my faith. I also learned there was something very special—even mystical—about my experience at the Woods in the heart of America.

It was not until sixty-five years later that I fully understood that it was the soul, spirit, and being of its foundress that animated the place and continues today. She was Mother Theodore Guerin, who left France in 1840 to establish schools for young women. She had braved rough seas in a trans-Atlantic crossing in a primitive sailing vessel, and then endured the rigors and privations of frontier life to teach not only about God but about how to live in the world in relation to God. Through her intercession, ordinary people were miraculously cured. She was canonized a saint in the Roman Catholic Church in October 2006. I realized I had lived with a saint and benefited from a special protection and intercession from her and her followers throughout my adult life.

Looking for a Real Job

After four years, with a bachelor's degree from a little-known college in the backwoods of Indiana and with lifelong friends, I set out to look for a job to support myself. Yet I did not consider myself highly competitive in the national job market. World War II was just beginning when I returned to Miami Beach. I sought help in my job search from my parish priest, one Monsignor William Barry of St. Patrick's Church and School, explaining that I had done some practice teaching in college. I had my eye on the new Barry College in Miami Shores, which had just been opened under the sponsorship of the monsignor's Irish family—including his brother, the bishop of St. Augustine, Florida; his sister, the head of a Dominican Order of religious in Michigan that would do the core teaching at Barry; and another brother, an architect in Chicago, who designed the campus.

Monsignor Barry recalled my competitive performance on the public high school basketball team, which, he sadly lamented, had always "creamed" St. Patrick's. He felt I should have been playing on "his" team. We didn't go into the cost factor. The recollection prompted him to suggest that I might teach physical education at Barry College! I was appalled at the idea, insisting my interests lay elsewhere. I felt I was capable of helping with the new college's public relations, even of teaching journalism. He recommended me to the dean of Barry. After interviewing me, the dean offered me employment at the not-very-handsome salary of $2,500 a year, including room and board.

The Joys of the Job

My job entailed teaching newswriting and editing in the English Department, setting up a public relations office, and (probably at the insistence of the monsignor) "looking after" the health and recreation needs of the students, of whom there were fewer than a hundred at the time. The recreational aspect of my assignment morphed into my teaching swimming at a beautiful campus pool, horseback riding at a nearby stable, and tennis, archery, and badminton on campus. When it was too cold in February for outdoor activity, I met indoors with the students. And if the Home Economics Department was not using its workroom, we would push back the sewing machines and do calisthenics. First jobs develop initiative and versatility.

This three-sided job at Barry was exhausting. I had to change clothes several times a day, what with any number of swimming classes. As the monsignor observed my feverish activities during his frequent visits to the campus, I assume he must have enjoyed his revenge (if priests indulge in revenge) for all the St. Patrick's basketball defeats to which I had contributed. He knew I hated being even a part-time physical education teacher, but it was a job, indeed my first, and I had to be grateful.

On the other hand, I was pleased and satisfied at the frequency with which the *Miami Herald* used the news stories I was generating about Barry. It must have been their sense of obligation to community development. For my part, nothing was too minor for me to report about Barry if I could find the right angle. Often it was the accompanying photos of the lovely young student mermaids in the pool that helped sell the stories.

I had two quite remarkable students in my newswriting class— British-born girls whose godfather was none other than G. K. Chesterton. They brought their personal cachet to my class, which may have been why it became one of the most popular on campus. Or was it because I was one of the few lay teachers in a sea of religious? Both girls were intelligent and talented writers. One went on after graduation to work for the publisher Farrar & Rinehart, her sister to the Associated Press as AP correspondent in Tallahassee. Their postgraduate accomplishments gave me a sense—merited or not—that I may have contributed something to their future. Teachers, however short-lived their careers, like to think such things.

The Door to Diplomacy Opens

During my two-year stint at Barry, a group of American Catholic historians visited the campus. Just back from a summer at the University of San Marco in Lima, Peru, they were taking a break in Miami to assess their Latin American experience. Would Barry give their findings some local and national publicity and undertake a few radio broadcasts to Latin America? Naturally I obliged, little knowing that this chance encounter would prove pivotal to a career in diplomacy.

The group's work in Latin America intrigued me, particularly a phrase the academics kept using on the significance of "the brotherhood of man and the fatherhood of God." It was new for me to think of other countries, even the world, in such a context.

Before leaving Barry the leader of the visiting group referred to how helpful they had found my "special interest in foreign affairs." I smiled doubtfully at this remark. At the University of Wisconsin at Madison, where I had picked up a master's degree during summer vacations, I had taken a couple of graduate political science courses linked to my journalism studies. One was on Latin America, the other on the Far East. That was about as far foreign as I had ever ventured, except for Cuba.

I told the visiting group's leader about my four or five basketball trips to Havana during high school and college. I had also chaperoned a group of Barry and other students to the University of Havana one summer for Spanish-language training. However, these experiences had in no way led me to consider a career in foreign relations. But the visiting leader, who was also a priest, urged me to consider a career in the U.S. diplomatic service. This surprised me, as I had no intention of spending a lifetime outside the United States. I was uncomfortable, even repelled, by some of the cultural differences I had encountered in Cuba, while admiring other facets of Cuban culture, like art, music, and architecture, and some of the people. Maybe I'd take to short-term assignments as a foreign correspondent, but not to a life abroad. No, thank you.

The priest asked me to think seriously about the idea. He reminded me that I had a Catholic college education and was currently employed by a Catholic college. "Your education has given you a firm sense of morality and ethics, and that is very much needed in government and international affairs today," he said. He recommended that I visit Washington, D.C., and apply for a job in the government. "You could do well in foreign affairs."

I had serious doubts about the man's rather quick assessment of my long-term potential, even though he had been a chaplain in the U.S. Congress and was a distinguished sociologist and historian. But after pondering his remarks in private, I thought, why not at least investigate? I had been at Barry College for two years and concluded that was enough for a starting job. Perhaps it was the three jobs in one that I wanted to escape. Most important, I was intent on following up on a University of Wisconsin–posted job lead as correspondent with the United Press in Chicago.

I bade the priest goodbye, assuring him I would indeed stop off in Washington en route to Chicago. We would see what came of it. Soon thereafter, I traveled to Washington, stayed with family friends, and visited the Department of State. I never made it to Chicago.

Old State by the White House

I did not use the priest's letter of introduction, as I found such introductions awkward for both parties. Once at the Department of State, I thought nothing of asking for an appointment with the assistant secretary of state, the priest's friend. I explained the circumstances and asked for his advice. Such an entry, even a brief meeting would be unheard of today. In the first place, one could never get past security at the front door. Second, appointments at that level are not easy to obtain and certainly not on the spot.

Though cordial, my meeting with the assistant secretary was brief. He directed me to the department's recruiting office. On my way there, I passed by the office of the acting secretary of state, then Edward Stettinius, who was holding a press conference. I stood on the outer fringe of the group, listened, and found it fascinating. I decided to look for the press office. In those days there was little or no security.

Once at the press office, I inquired of the person in charge if the government had press officers in missions overseas. The man smiled indulgently and replied, "Young lady, we have one press officer, and *he* is in London." I said, "Oh, but would he need an assistant?" I don't know where I got the brass in those days—lack of experience presumably. "No, he does not," came the prompt answer, followed by, "but I understand Recruiting is looking for people to do general consular work, vice consuls, that is." "What are they?" I asked. "You'll find out from Recruiting," he replied.

"Scraping the Bottom of the Barrel"

Recruiting confirmed that there were indeed openings because of World War II. The man who interviewed me said, "Let me tell you, young lady, you don't know how lucky you are; it's wartime, and all the men have gone into the services. We are literally scraping the bottom of the barrel and taking in 4-Fs and women!"

Should I have been offended that he placed women after the physically handicapped? No, because in those days men always took precedence over women, and I had by then learned to take no offense. I asked him to tell me more about opportunities for women. Although I wanted to serve my country in time of war, I frankly preferred a civilian role over the military. Attractive as were the uniforms of the Army WACs, Navy WAVEs, and Coast Guard SPARs, they did not seem right for me, given my height. A tight uniform with brass buttons and billed cap would probably make me look even more intimidating.

The recruiting officer proceeded to explain what vice consuls were and did. I learned the job had to do with American citizenship cases overseas, visas for immigrants to the United States, and possibly writing economic and political reports from other countries. If I was interested in this kind of work overseas, I could fill out an application form and return in a month for interviews and possible assignment; a new class of trainees would be forming soon.

I quickly looked for a temporary job to wait out the month and pay for my room and board, then let the city of Washington and its museums and parks work their charms on me. After my first encounter with world-class paintings at the National Gallery of Art, I became captivated and excited over the prospects of an overseas assignment. At the end of the month I reported back to the Department of State and was promptly assigned to a new vice consul's class of about twenty-five people, all around my age, all men except for three women, including me. We were to become Foreign Service auxiliaries.

An experienced retiree taught us the basics of consular work. A Harvard graduate with an annoying habit of flipping his Phi Beta Kappa key from a chain on his waistcoat, his last post had been as consul general in South Africa. I pegged him as a vain old fuddy-duddy, perhaps even irrelevant to the times. Our class was held in a basement room of the old State, War, and Navy Building on Pennsylvania Avenue, next to the White House, since renamed the Executive Office Building and now an integral part of the White House Office. Its dark Victorian architecture made it a haunt for pigeons and other birds. People called it the Starling's Roost.

I had taken a temporary job at the Catholic University library, where I was assigned to sorting out the Church's prohibited books—the Index, just right for a twenty-year-old woman! I rented a very inexpensive room nearby in the northeast section of town. By streetcar it took me nearly an hour to reach Old State. About the second time I was late for my training class, the consul general seemed to flip his Phi Beta key even more vigorously than usual. He announced in a loud voice that effective immediately there would be a penalty for late arrivals.

He instructed me to entertain the class with a quotation from Shakespeare! I wanted to ask if we weren't a little too old for this sort of thing; after all, it wasn't high school all over again; it was training of adults for the wartime Foreign Service. Fortunately, memory kept me company and I recalled a line from Shakespeare: "Sweet are the uses of adversity which like the toad, ugly and venomous, wears yet a precious jewel in its head." I dragged out the word "toad" but seriously doubted that the old goat caught it. He was more than likely focused on "precious jewel in its head," possibly interpreting it as a salute to his superior intelligence.

Enough of this fooling around, I concluded. It was a training session, not a Shakespeare quiz. And indeed we weren't getting much training. Instead, the class was irrelevant to the times, as so often happens when retirees age. I can't remember a single lesson he taught us other than vanity, pride, and a superior if not snobbish bearing, all of which I considered setting a bad example.

During the final week of training the secretary posted a lined sheet of yellow legal paper on the bulletin board, showing our assignments. My heart skipped a beat when I read: *Wilkowski—Port of Spain, Trinidad, British West Indies*. I was outward bound into the vast unknown. So began a thirty-five-year career in the Foreign Service.

Two

Trinidad, BWI, 1944–46 (Vice Consul)

Flying Down to Trinidad

As I prepared to take off for my first Foreign Service post, I was strangely reminded of the time my mother drove me off to first grade! Nearly two decades later, here she was driving me from our apartment in Miami Beach over the Causeway on Biscayne Bay to the Miami International Airport to put me on a plane for an overseas government job. Just as she wanted to be sure I made it into primary school (I must have skipped kindergarten), she proudly wanted to be a part of this new and exciting venture.

Our family's apartment in Miami Beach was special. It had a little balcony hanging over the bay facing west. At sunset, when the tide was going out to the Atlantic Ocean, we would playfully toss apple peelings and the like into the bay (biodegradable, of course) and watch them glide away on the water before disappearing. With each toss off the balcony my mother would shout, "Down to Trinidad!" Just why she chose Trinidad and not the closer and more familiar places like Cuba or Puerto Rico I do not know. But she was a woman with prescience that only the Irish seem to have. It is a sort of sixth sense that comes out of that mysterious Emerald Island, with its Druids and priestesses, ancient folklore, and even "fay-rees" of sorts. And the Irish could be such dreamers, or at least were before the European Common Market entered their lives.

My Irish mother had scraped and saved from her limited earnings to underwrite the essentials of my four years of college, while I worked part of my way. Then I worked all of my way through graduate school at the University of Wisconsin. With two degrees I was able to teach at the college level and also do public relations, but I was not fully satisfied with the work. My mother respected the government and thought the Foreign Service would be just right for me. But then government service had a bit more cachet back in the 1940s.

The prospect of a totally different job outside the country for an indefinite period of time was still a bit daunting. To hide our real feelings, we made our farewells as joyous as possible with little sentimentality. Had there been tears, my mother would have surely admonished, "Let's not make a holy show of ourselves!"

Her final guidance as we parted was to mind my manners and write often. It never seemed to have occurred to her that protocol and communications were basic to the diplomatic work I was entering. Ah, well, that's parents—even very caring ones—in their complicated relations with children, whether in their teens or twenties. But then my mother had always been alternately strict and permissive. She had only recently bade my brother farewell as he went off to some air base in England from which he was to fly sixty-five bomber missions over Germany. Obviously, he had little time to write and this clearly distressed my mother. With a firm promise to write, I said goodbye just as my flight was being called on the loudspeaker. It was in the days before jets and jetways. So I climbed up the stairs of a trustworthy old Pan American Airways DC-3 twin-engine propeller job.

As I entered the plane, I hesitated when I saw there were only eight passenger seats, all of them unoccupied, while the rest of the cabin was filled with stacks of priority air cargo, securely lashed down with heavy canvas tapes. There were enormous truck and tractor tires, long rods, and panels of this and that, a multitude of assorted boxes, some marked, "Electronics," others "Spare Parts." At least we didn't seem to be transporting ammunition to U.S. military bases in the Caribbean. I took my chances. I was greeted by a male steward nattily dressed in black slacks, a short white dinner jacket, and a bow tie. He seemed out of place for what was essentially a cargo flight. I was humbled by the thought that here I was just another piece of government property before even getting on the job.

Once aboard and airborne, the heavy drone of the motors put me into a semisleep until the steward tapped me on the shoulder. We were nearing a rest stop in San Juan, Puerto Rico, and would I please excuse him, he had to black out the windows for landing "for security reasons." Being a bit claustrophobic since childhood, I dreaded the thought of landing without some reference to the ground. Then, all of a sudden, resounding thumps assured me that the wheels had hit the tarmac and we were safely down.

I was allowed to step out and stretch my legs and saw absolutely nothing that might win or lose the war for us or cause us to be blacked out from the air, but then who was I to judge? I saw a couple of parked U.S. Navy planes backed by a tropical setting of swaying palm trees, any number of crowing roosters and braying dogs, plus some hangars and a scruffy-looking terminal. The searing breeze blowing in from the Caribbean was almost unbearable. The crew did what they had to do in a forty-five-minute stopover and filed back into the aircraft, and off we flew, again with shuttered windows. I was relieved when we gained altitude and the shutters came off as we headed for Trinidad. Below the wings was a lovely view of the southern sea with its tiny reefs of white coral surrounded by foaming blue and green waters. Between the clouds we got occasional glimpses of the Windward and Leeward Islands.

Then we spotted Trinidad and its smaller adjunct island of Tobago, lying off the coast of South America and separated by a body of water the steward explained was the Gulf of Paria. German submarines had worked these waters even up to a few months before, he said. Some even daringly entered the narrow northern mouth of the gulf, called the Bocas, only to be sunk by allied military defenses. I thought if the German subs could be sighted by bathers off Palm Beach, Florida, they could certainly be active here. I wondered how they were being fueled and supplied. The steward didn't know the answer to that one. I thought we would both make lousy spies.

Undiplomatic Landing

We touched down at our final destination (mercifully without shutters) and rolled up alongside a tiny terminal marked "Port of Spain, Trinidad,

British West Indies." There was absolutely no one in sight. But as soon as the door of the plane opened, I saw a tall, lanky man in shirtsleeves and boots. Past middle age with leathery skin, he looked straight out of central casting for a western movie. Surely he was not the sophisticated diplomat and new boss I had anticipated, but I could take no chances.

So I pulled on my white gloves, adjusted my small hat, and went primly down the stairs and over to the man the steward pointed out, saying "There's someone waiting for you." With my warmest of smiles, I approached him and gushed, "Oh, Mr. Hall, I am so pleased to be here and to be your new vice consul."

"Aw, shucks," came a Texas drawl from the man. "I ain't the consul, I'm jes' the driver. Name's George. C'mon, I'll git yer bags and drive yuh into town. But maybe you'd first like to have a cool drink in the bar?" He led me over to a small shed that served as the terminal.

With fans but no air conditioning; at least we were out of the sun. "What will Madam have to drink—a rum punch?" asked the reedy little man tending bar. Behind him was a life-sized wall-hanging of none other than Carmen Miranda, hands on hips, artfully done in colorful native cloth, with several layers of ruffles. She smiled leeringly underneath a big straw hat complete with lush but fake tropical fruits and flowers. I timidly asked if it would be possible to have the punch "without the rum." This struck George and the bartender as hilarious. But it was the middle of the afternoon, and I hesitated to have alcohol on my breath when I met the real boss and consul. Little did I know that he had become a world-class alcoholic during his seven years marooned in Trinidad before and during World War II; but more on that later.

My "lime cooler" came topped with a heavy pink froth from a dash or two of Angostura Bitters, which like the rum was produced locally and shipped all over the world. With its exotic taste, I guessed the Bitters were made from native tree barks, spices, and herbs, perhaps even a tiny bit of alcohol for blending. Later I learned directly from the Seigert family who made the stuff that the recipe was a big trade secret.

In that special lilting English so characteristic of speech in the Islands, the bartender said, "Allow me to show Madam something," as he approached Carmen on the wall. With a quick flourish he boldly lifted up her many ruffled skirts to reveal a sign that seemed to shout: "It's quicker by Clipper." It was either Pan Am's own saucy advertisement or someone else's bawdy joke. I humored the bartender with a laugh and tried not to look too prudish.

George loaded me into the car, and we pulled onto the island's main north-south highway, then headed west toward the colony's main town of Port of Spain. Our route took us into a veritable sea of sugar cane fields, occasionally broken by small clusters of incredibly dilapidated housing. Shacks of a sun-bleached shade of sickening pea green alternated with others of weathered natural wood. Aged black people sat on sagging porches in rickety chairs. Small, poorly clad children ran aimlessly around bare ground that passed for front yards. It was a scene of stark and disturbing poverty. Presumably the able-bodied and middle aged were either working in the cane fields or cleaning and cooking in someone else's house in town.

Off to the right on a low mountain range I spied a church and some buildings. "That's a Benedictine monastery," George offered. Surprised, I wondered how he would know. (Much later I visited the place, first for afternoon tea and scones, later for an Easter weekend pilgrimage, not sleeping a wink on that venture because of so much singing and processing up and down the hillside.) As we rode along, George resumed his unofficial tour guide spiel: "Ya should see the scarlet ibis in the early evening as they fly in by the thousands from Ven-zuh-way-luh. And if yer watchin' 'em from the water on the Gulf and enjoyin' a rum punch or two, you can see twice as many." He laughed at his own joke. Further apropos of nothing George blurted out, "They got oil here, too"; I knew that Trinidad produced pitch and some oil from my Washington briefings. "I know sumpin' about oil," George went on, "cuz I worked the oil fields in Ven-zuh-way-luh." That marked George as a drifter. I wondered how long he would be working at the American Consulate in Trinidad. I need not have bothered—it was not for long.

Port of Spain

As we entered the capital city of Port of Spain, we passed an impressive old Anglican Cathedral, whose architecture was obviously copied from England. We moved along the public square by the harbor, with its rows of ships' chandlers and nondescript shops. George pointed to the location of the old Consulate, close by the docks for easy handling of our shipping business, like crew visas and seamen sign-offs, tasks I was to inherit in my work as vice consul.

We passed the cable and wireless company, where George said we transmitted and received cable traffic with Washington. I wondered: cables about what? So far, everything I had seen in Trinidad was sleepy and life-less, but I realized there must be more to the island than first appearances. Whatever minor bilateral economic interests the United States might have with Trinidad, there surely must be some important political problems related to our many U.S. military bases here. I was yet to learn about the many representational and social interests.

As we drove on, we came to a large green open space formally named Queen's Park but known as the Savannah. It covered some twenty or more acres in the heart of the city, complete with racetrack and grand-stand. Fronting the park in great tropical splendor stood the many-spired Government House, befitting the British colonial governor who lived and worked there, according to George, when he wasn't parading about in his white pith helmet and ostrich plumes.

Almost directly opposite Government House stood the town's leading hotel, the Queen's Park, the name also of the large residential area sur-rounding it. A circular boulevard bordered the Savannah and gave access to any number of elegant old two-story, white-frame buildings with spacious verandas. They reminded me of our Deep South in the States, but without the oaks and Spanish moss. Blooming flowers and shrubs abounded and delighted the eye. Also bordering the Savannah were several impressive, nonresidential buildings: an enormous red stone school (attended by the still young and not yet famous writer-to-be V. S. Naipaul), the Roman Catholic archbishop's stately palace, the British Council library and cul-tural center, another church, and a scattering of foreign consulates with colorful flags fluttering in the breeze.

Among these was the American Consulate. George explained that this was the residence of the consul and his wife and that the Consulate itself was a small, garage-like cement building in the rear, in a garden of mango trees. Then came George's surprise: I was to stay with the consul and his wife until I found my own place!

Madam Consul, My Mentor

George dropped me off at the Consulate, where a maid received me. I entered a long, high-ceilinged hall flanked by two enormous reception rooms with huge, overhead fans whirling about—the secret to keeping cool in the tropics. I noticed two smaller rooms behind these and a broad stairway leading upstairs, all very grand and somewhat antebellum in American terms.

"Madam," the consul's wife, appeared to welcome me. She was a short, plumpish woman with a quick manner and a decided Brooklyn accent. She was accompanied by two romping little cocker spaniels, which I later learned she bred and raised on the premises—in the consul's bedroom, to be exact. They had no children.

I was assigned one of four large bedrooms upstairs, dominated by a huge four-poster mahogany bed swathed in mosquito netting. While the housing arrangement might be convenient as an interim measure, I feared it might be controlling if not confining. However, I tried to be my most gracious self in accepting and thanking Madam for her hospitality and minding my manners.

Madam was very much mistress of her domain—the Residence, as the home of the senior officer at Foreign Service posts is called, from consul to ambassador. As time went on I saw her rule her roost like a drill sergeant. Entertaining was frequent. She made up elaborate menus for guests. She shopped herself at the local markets with the maids and cook in tow, and by herself at the U.S. Naval Commissary, where staples, liquors, and frozen foods from the States were available. It was from Madam that I learned how important entertaining was in the diplomatic business—getting to know the right people, picking up local gossip in exchange for giving as little of the same as possible, and, whenever appropriate, keeping guests informed on life and culture in the United States and matters of U.S. foreign policy—all part of good U.S. public diplomacy.

Madam made it clear that I would be paying for my room and board, an arrangement that struck me as a bit odd, since the house was government-owned and provided free to the consul and his wife. But then where could I get such fine food without having to hustle for it and organize and manage a household staff? Might I be paying a little extra for the dog food and veterinarian fees? I had to brush that unkind thought from my head.

I hardly knew this woman, and here I was, passing harsh judgment on her. But she was a bit of a "sharpie," as they called them in Brooklyn.

I later learned she had made good friends with the U.S. Army medic (also from Brooklyn) at the Army's dockside facility. Medical attention there for Foreign Service colleagues and even one's pets was without fee. Eventually I too became friends of the medic, not for pet services like Madam's, but mostly for recreation. The medic had become adept at night spear-fishing by searchlight off a launch in the Gulf. Besides keeping me well supplied with fresh fish, he also offered Siamese cats, which he was breeding on the side. Unfortunately, there was too much inbreeding, and I had to keep exchanging cats with the friendly vet every time one of them flew through the air, miscalculated his jump, and broke his leg. Trying to make it from my second-story window to the street was a favorite aerial course, but proved disastrous to cat after cat.

When not ruling her roost or breeding and training dogs, Madam was bound and determined to make a respectable if not a model Foreign Service officer out of me, advising on what I should wear, what to say, how to steer conversation at table, how to plan, prepare, and carry out formal receptions and dinners, and above all, whom to see and know in the local community and whom not to see or be seen with. Unassigned by Washington and strictly at her own initiative, Madam taught me Protocol 101 because she felt I needed it. And I did, of course. She even chided me once for continuing to wear my college ring! Was this her way of suggesting I should be on a more serious hunt for a diamond, or did she honestly think college rings were childish? But I never argued the point with her. On reflection, she may never have gone to college!

(Not long after I arrived in Port of Spain, my old training-days consul general and his wife—a welcome counterbalance—appeared in Trinidad off their cruise ship to visit me. Apparently no hard feelings, and no one mentioned Shakespeare. Nor was I in any position to offer even tea, living in a rented room. So we just exchanged pleasantries in my tiny office.)

British Rules in a Very Mixed Society

Given that Trinidad was a British Crown Colony in the 1940s (and did not become an independent nation until the 1960s), the British colonials reigned supreme over the predominately black populace. As it was such a mixed society, Madam wanted to be sure I understood and related properly to its many ins and outs and various skin colorations. Trinidadian society then and now still has large segments of Indians and Chinese whom the British originally brought in from Asia in the mid-nineteenth century as indentured servants to work the sugar cane fields. Over time, with their indenture worked off, the Chinese drove themselves hard to become the dominant commercial and trading class, residing primarily in Port of Spain and other urban areas. Many of the early East Indians tended to accept land in Trinidad rather than return passage to India when their indenture was over. Much of the property they acquired was in the interior and found to be oil-bearing. International petroleum companies started buying in. The East Indians built up considerable capital for undertaking larger enterprises on the island. The society also held many remnants from previous centuries of British, French, Dutch, and Portuguese days of exploration, discovery, and occupation. It was claimed that there was more miscegenation in Trinidad than in Hawaii.

Stand Up and Salute the U.S. of A.

While Madam's Protocol 101 course on social relations was strongly color-coded, it also took account of a person's education, position, and rank. Paramount, she would explain, was understanding the importance of the U.S. role in relation to the broader local community. The U.S. official presence in Trinidad was explained by America's having negotiated a crucial World War II agreement with the British in which we exchanged some forty-odd overage destroyers for a number of strategic military bases in the Caribbean, including four in Trinidad.

An enormous U.S. naval base called Macqueripe on the north coast served as a ship repair and training facility and recreation area. The Army had a supply-docking facility (Dockside) on the Gulf side of Port of Spain, a headquarters and command post on some hills in Port of Spain, and an enormous air base in the center of the island, called Waller Field. This air base held what was reputed to be the longest aircraft maintenance line in the world and was the jumping-off place for our warplanes flying to North

Africa and the European theater of war. My brother had flown his Martin Marauder bomber through Waller to Europe, but before I arrived.

There was one U.S. Army general and one U.S. admiral in residence on the island. As the war scaled down, a commodore replaced the admiral. Yet it was the American consul who was the principal diplomatic representative on the island and outranked the military brass in official relations with the British. I began to wonder if I could ever carry the responsibilities of my new station in life! God forbid that anything would ever happen to my boss, the consul.

We Americans came about as close as you could—but without the label—to being an occupying military force in a foreign land, to say nothing about being significant employers in the Trinidad economy. In sum, Americans in Trinidad were important not only politically, militarily, and economically but also socially. And thus, according to Madam, our prominent position commanded great respect. But with it came obligations. Our closest social relations were, of course, with the top-dog British governor himself, Sir Bede Clifford, and his personal secretary, Sir Edward Cunard (of the famous steamship line family). Our relations with the top Brits extended to their official entourage of British civil servants, many with previous experience in India.

Madam allowed as how we dared venture beyond this hierarchy, going into the ranks of the chief justices, some of whom, she did not fail to note, had been "struck by the tar brush." But never you mind, they were ever so acceptable, having been schooled in London at Gray's Inn and beyond, also at Oxford and Cambridge; as were other "coloreds" and ranking civil servants, having married white English schoolmarms, etc., etc. From there the list of acceptables for social contact went on down through some of the British line administrators at Red House—but only the top drawer, you were to understand. And then we might even venture "into the trades," but only at the top.

Sometimes these protocol distinctions were laughable. There were, for example, a local distributor of American automobiles, a bit beige in skin tone, married to an American, and a British heiress to a large food chain throughout the islands, married to the American local bottler and distributor of Coca Cola (credited with having inspired and helped write one of the most famous calypsos, "Rum and Coca Cola," which was all the rage during World War II). I was often amazed when, after meeting some rather important person in business or government, Madam would tell me, "But you know, he has 'a touch of the brush,'" when I was almost certain the person was as lily-white as myself. What difference did it make?

As for other members of the consular corps, Madam held them in virtual disdain. She pointed out that only one or two were career diplomatic service like us. Some of them were even "honorary consuls." And so we had little to do with them except on their national holidays, when we would dutifully attend their functions and they ours. Madam was always indignant when some of these lower-ranking guests would show their "lack of breeding" by swiping scarce duty-free cigarettes from her side tables and stuffing them into their pockets or purses.

As a graduate of Madam's protocol course in the most impressionable early days of my career, it is a wonder I did not become a first-class snob. Perhaps I owe it to my brother, who always managed to take me down a peg or two whenever I returned to the States on home leave from a foreign assignment, especially if I had, as the Irish mother would say, "acquired airs."

My Boss, the Consul

One might at this juncture wonder who was really in charge of the U.S. Consulate in Trinidad toward the end of World War II, Madam or her husband the consul. The day I arrived Madam explained that her husband would meet me within the hour for informal drinks and dinner there in the Residence.

What a surprise when we met. He was rather slightly built, of average height, and rather unimpressive, even a bit awkward. His manner of speech was startling, sounding almost like a muffled machine gun going off. He was obviously brilliant, with a fantastic mind and memory, and was probably the only person I ever knew who could actually speak shorthand! He spoke so fast that he often had to repeat himself.

The consulate files held only the most basic data on the involved bilateral negotiations concerning the military bases the United States had acquired from the British: the land descriptions, the building projects,

eports, there had been no tip-off
dmissible. Perhaps she had cal-
facilitate matters. Frankly, I had
und papers. I brazenly phoned
the issuance of her visas and
. When she did, I took posses-
in the passports, and returned
er she could not travel to the
tion we had received. She did
never saw her again. But I have
Polish, "Hello, how are you?"
een dead wrong in seizing and
ration and Naturalization Ser-
the United States, assuming
d received.

inidadians claiming to be ca-
king visas to cut discs in the
mentation from impresarios
if business was slow and the
ll conference room for "per-
ppropriate and certainly not
emed to catch on or object. I
welcome break from office
ade friends among the Port
tage names like Raging Lion,

ness

a and passport work, I did
merchant vessels would call
alth certificates, and some-
disputes. Again, consider-
nsular stamps and, yes, still

and the legal conditions under which the bases would operate. All the fine points and details of these arrangements remained in the consul's head; but he could extract them immediately and accurately whenever the occasion demanded. Washington never seemed to object to this highly personalized filing system until the consul was eventually transferred. Then there was great fluttering in the dovecote for the details that had gone with him to his job as administrative officer in Warsaw.

I learned that the consul was a graduate physicist who had been on some scientific assignment in South Africa when the U.S. government decided it needed him for the Trinidad job at the start of World War II. He must have been involved in negotiations with the British in both London and Washington before going to Trinidad. There was no question that he was a brilliant man, perhaps even a genius. But he had obviously been in Trinidad too long and was badly in need of a change by the time I arrived. He could not have been less suited for breaking in a green vice consul and a woman.

While we communicated poorly and he gave me little guidance, we both determined to make the most of it. With the fewest of words and briefest of instructions ("Look it up in the Foreign Service Regulations"), he assigned me to all consular duties—passport issuance and renewals, births and deaths of U.S. citizens, and immigration and nonimmigration visas for foreigners (Trinidadians and other non-U.S. nationals) seeking entry to the United States. He also asked me to do the occasional economic or commercial report. Researching and writing on the coconut and lime industries was fun and interesting. These were scarce commodities in those days, as trade with the Philippines was cut off, and we had U.S. candy manufacturers coming to visit us at the Consulate.

Within a week of assigning me my duties, I overheard a very loud exchange with a sea captain in the consul's office. At its conclusion, the boss barged into my dark little cubicle to say, "You'll also do all the shipping. I don't ever want to see another sea captain!" It was then I realized the consul really didn't like people, especially if they were the least bit aggressive. He seemed to tolerate people only when he was quietly playing bridge or engaged in some deeply intellectual conversation (he kept those brief). And he had a quirky way of ferreting out and enjoying local gossip, the raunchier the better. The consul was just not a guy with whom a brand-new woman vice consul could ever feel completely comfortable. In her own authoritarian way, Madam tried to make up for some of these shortcomings.

The Boss's daily routine and appearance were noteworthy. He always wore leather sandals in the office, wearing shoes only when dressed for dinner in the evenings. His office dress never departed from khaki slacks and a crisp white shirt with sleeves rolled part way up, and no tie. Madam bought most of this sparse wardrobe for him at the Navy Commissary. He probably had no patience for shopping. He would eat a hearty breakfast, usually with eggs, occasionally with something I had never seen except as dog food—hamburger meat, broken up and fried loose and scattered over toast. And coffee, lots of coffee. After a few tries, I avoided joining him for breakfast; he would never talk, just feed himself behind an open newspaper. Madam never came down in the morning.

At about 10 a.m. he would leave the house and, in his quick little step, cross the small garden, enter the Consulate, and go immediately to his large office at the back of the building. He shared this room with an American secretary, the wife of an American businessman. At 11 a.m. one of the maids would come across the garden and deliver a large glass of tomato juice to his desk. He needed it. Did anyone else want anything? Juice? Coffee? We were never asked, and he never suggested it. Precisely at 12 noon, the consul would recross the garden to a small family room or library in the rear of the house. There for a half hour before lunch he would make himself a couple of pink Angostura-flavored gins, while he listened to shortwave radio news broadcasts from the States.

Lunch at 12:30 or 1:00 p.m. was usually an awkward affair at home during my three months of residency there. Madam was usually present. Except for the occasional argument between the two (short and inconclusive), they talked very little. The consul usually had a couple of beers with lunch, after which he would retire for a short nap, then reappear at the office at 3 p.m. for a brief shuffling of papers at his desk. Then promptly at 4:00, he would take off for his bridge club a few blocks away on the Savannah. This went on without deviation day after day.

He once admitted to having a couple of whiskeys while playing bridge at the club. He returned home around 6 for the usual shower and change. Cocktails were served from 7 to 8. He and Madam preferred martinis.

certain degree on local police and other [...] that this woman, a Polish refugee, was in [...] culated that the "ski" in my name might [...] found nothing derogatory in her backgr[...] her, explaining there was a small error i[...] asking that she return with all her paper[...] sion of them, voided the visa and entries [...] them to her. Even more brazenly, I told [...] United States because of adverse inform[...] not question me, merely walked out, and I [...] memories. She taught me two phrases in [...] and "Goodbye." I later learned that I had b[...] destroying the visas; only the U.S. Immig[...] vice could legally deny entry upon arrival i[...] they had the same negative information I h[...]

On several occasions small groups of T[...] lypso singers would visit the Consulate se[...] United States. Some had supporting docu[...] and recording studios. Others did not. But[...] work dull, I would invite them into our sm[...] formances." Such "auditions" were hardly [...] a prerequisite for a visa. The Boss never se[...] found the singers highly entertaining and [...] routine, learned a lot of bawdy songs, and [...] of Spain demimonde. They had fascinating s[...] Big Man, King Faroh, and the like.

Shipping: A Difficult and Dangerous Bus[...]

When I wasn't floundering around with vi[...] what was called "shipping." The captains of [...] at the Consulate to request crew list visas, h[...] times government assistance in settling labo[...] able documentation was required involving c[...] more signatures.

When the consul assigned this work to me, he must have slyly thought that a woman vice consul would "tame" the generally rough and surly seamen. He was right. The sea captains seemed pleased to encounter an American woman after being at sea for a long time. Many of the ships came to Trinidad from as far as Lourenço Marques (now Maputo), Mozambique. I found it helped if I merely smiled, even flirted a wee bit with them, keeping it very low key.

When seamen were sick and had to be signed off their ships for treatment, it was often because they had contracted some venereal disease. As this proved a bit awkward, I worked out a sort of code with the captains to save us both embarrassment. I would simply ask if this was the "usual case requiring hospitalization." If the captain said "Yes," I would sign the seaman off and send him on his way to the U.S. naval base, which had agreed to treat them. It was wartime, and the government wanted its merchant ships kept on the move. When these seamen were discharged, they would return to the Consulate, and we would try through the local agents to find them other ships to sign on so they could return to the States.

Sometimes problems arose when seamen remained for any length of time "on the beach." They would steal sheets from the ships, and foodstuffs or other gear, which they would then sell locally, buy rum, get drunk, and usually end up in the local jail. After a time I would get them released and then help them find another ship back to the States. How many illegitimate children these sailors may have spawned in their cavorting on shore I will never know, nor did I want to.

One particularly friendly sea captain ran one of Alcoa's fleet of smaller vessels that sailed from Trinidad down to the rivers in then British Guiana to load up on bauxite. They would return to Port of Spain to transship the ore in larger vessels bound for the United States. This captain insisted I accompany him on his trips to see the "wonders of the jungle in BG." There, on the narrow rivers, the monkeys would leap from the trees onto the ships' decks. Naturally I wondered if that was all the sea captain wanted to show me. But in my best convent school manner, I declined with thanks but no thanks.

Shipping presented me with continuous problems. One day we received a message from a captain via a local agent urgently insisting that the "American consul remove a man in irons from a ship in the stream."

This meant the vessel was anchored offshore in the Gulf of Paria. Someone had to row out, get the man aboard the small dinghy, and bring him into Port of Spain for incarceration by the local authorities. The ship's captain refused to sail with the man on board. It was nighttime when I got the call. Surely my boss would not consider doing this, so I didn't even bother to call him.

What to do? I remembered a mysterious American guy, tall and thin, whose name I believe was Milton. He had some vague but unexplained connection with the Consulate, would float in, have a few words with the consul, and leave. He was clearly not on our payroll but was somehow mysteriously linked to our office. Neither he nor the consul ever discussed his business with me, but I suspected he was FBI with ties to local British intelligence. Throwing caution to the winds, I phoned Milton, knowing only that he lived "somewhere in the neighborhood." He immediately caught the drift of my dilemma and agreed to accompany me on the rowing expedition in the dark of night to pick up "the man in irons." He had enough gallantry and common sense to realize it was no job for a woman alone.

We called the shipping agent to radio the ship's captain we were coming and to prepare to assist us with the transfer. Out we rowed into the Gulf in the dark. As we came alongside the ship, the prisoner was led to the deck, climbed with obvious difficulty down the ladder, and stepped into our boat. I was very uneasy. My companion and I took turns at the oars but I almost preferred rowing to sitting there facing the handcuffed man, never knowing if he would fling those cuffs first around my neck and then Milton's.

The prisoner was obviously much smarter than that. Any struggle might have risked somebody losing their footing and falling overboard. Besides the seaman seemed quite comfortable sitting there like a Roman emperor being rowed by a woman galley slave, perhaps for the first and only time in his life. It certainly was a first for me and never to be repeated.

Free Rides Are Never Quite Free

Casting good judgment to the winds because I was anxious to return home for Christmas, I signed on as a "work-away" for a dollar a day to get a free ride on one of our merchant vessels returning to the United States. As if I hadn't had enough of the shipping business! And with all those troublesome seamen? Nonetheless, I accepted the offer of such a free ride on an Alcoa ship sailing from Trinidad to Mobile, Alabama.

I was the only woman on board a vessel that took more than a week to reach port, a very long week indeed. I was billeted below the water line, gratefully alone, in a cabin meant for eight, at the start of the passageway to the crew's quarters—not the greatest location. I had brought along a Siamese cat in a cage as a present to my family. The room assignment proved unworkable. The ventilation was so poor I had to leave my door open from time to time. That invited all sorts of comments from crew members as they passed my room to theirs.

When I explained the problem to the captain, he reassigned me to a room that the gunnery crew had used during the worst of World War II, located one deck up and across the hall from the so–called Slop Shop, where the crew bought cigarettes, toiletries, and supplies. While the traffic was less, I still received anonymous notes slipped under my door, but at least I had more privacy. Would I recommend such a voyage? Perhaps only for a girl who feels neglected. From that experience I learned that a single woman traveling alone on an all-male freighter leaves herself open to question regarding her motivation. Was I really innocently trying to save money, or was I looking for adventure and a good time? I was learning the hard way and would use better judgment in the future, I consoled myself.

Pan American Airways Plane Crash

Brief as was my Christmas vacation with family in Miami Beach, I returned to Trinidad refreshed and ready for work, even to my old shipping problems. But the familiar routine was abruptly broken with the tragic crash of a Pan American Airways Clipper plane (Flying Boat) in the Gulf of Paria. The Consulate was immediately notified of the crash by the British port authorities and told to stand by for details. They came soon enough. While there were only six or eight passengers on the flight, all were lost together with an American crew of three or four. This was the very same plane Charles Lindbergh had inaugurated for Pan Am with a historic flight around the world. Though considered virtually crashproof, it seems to have struck some hidden object in the waters of the Gulf.

The British authorities brought what salvageable personal items they found to my office to pass on to nearest of kin, some of whom had flown down from the States. The bodies and remains recovered were handed over to the local undertaker to be identified by Pam Am people. Fortunately, I was relieved of that grizzly task (although it was a duty I was unable to avoid at my next post, in Colombia, when a young American died and the embassy had to ship his body back to the States).

The Pan Am tragedy required paperwork and contact with the local undertaker, an East Indian by the name of Battoo. He was the blackest man I had ever seen. The sight of him in the black suit he always wore to the Consulate remains indelible in my mind. There was something haunting about him. Moreover, he insisted I review the photos of the crash and the remains of the victims. As ridiculous as it is to admit, because of my experience with Battoo, I had trouble throughout my life being comfortable when introduced to a very dark-skinned East Indian.

Life Could Be Beautiful

It was not all work and no play in Trinidad. Life could be beautiful. At the many parties at our own Consulate, Madam was at her very best playing the gracious hostess with her superb four- and even five-course dinners, which always had a Cordon Bleu touch.

And then there was Government House. I remember how intimidating my first dinner there was. Guests were met at the door by a liveried servant and escorted into one of the Great Halls, where they were announced. Cocktails were served on the enormous veranda overlooking the mansion's lush gardens, where the scent of night-blooming jasmine and other tropical flowers always hung heavily in the air. Dinner was served in yet another large and dazzling room. The long, heavy mahogany table was polished to an inky blackness. With neither vases nor baskets to hold them, flower blossoms without stems, often orchids, were scattered randomly about the table to appear as though floating on a pond of still, black water.

and the legal conditions under which the bases would operate. All the fine points and details of these arrangements remained in the consul's head; but he could extract them immediately and accurately whenever the occasion demanded. Washington never seemed to object to this highly personalized filing system until the consul was eventually transferred. Then there was great fluttering in the dovecote for the details that had gone with him to his job as administrative officer in Warsaw.

I learned that the consul was a graduate physicist who had been on some scientific assignment in South Africa when the U.S. government decided it needed him for the Trinidad job at the start of World War II. He must have been involved in negotiations with the British in both London and Washington before going to Trinidad. There was no question that he was a brilliant man, perhaps even a genius. But he had obviously been in Trinidad too long and was badly in need of a change by the time I arrived. He could not have been less suited for breaking in a green vice consul and a woman.

While we communicated poorly and he gave me little guidance, we both determined to make the most of it. With the fewest of words and briefest of instructions ("Look it up in the Foreign Service Regulations"), he assigned me to all consular duties—passport issuance and renewals, births and deaths of U.S. citizens, and immigration and nonimmigration visas for foreigners (Trinidadians and other non-U.S. nationals) seeking entry to the United States. He also asked me to do the occasional economic or commercial report. Researching and writing on the coconut and lime industries was fun and interesting. These were scarce commodities in those days, as trade with the Philippines was cut off, and we had U.S. candy manufacturers coming to visit us at the Consulate.

Within a week of assigning me my duties, I overheard a very loud exchange with a sea captain in the consul's office. At its conclusion, the boss barged into my dark little cubicle to say, "You'll also do all the shipping. I don't ever want to see another sea captain!" It was then I realized the consul really didn't like people, especially if they were the least bit aggressive. He seemed to tolerate people only when he was quietly playing bridge or engaged in some deeply intellectual conversation (he kept those brief). And he had a quirky way of ferreting out and enjoying local gossip, the raunchier the better. The consul was just not a guy with whom a brand-new woman vice consul could ever feel completely comfortable. In her own authoritarian way, Madam tried to make up for some of these shortcomings.

The Boss's daily routine and appearance were noteworthy. He always wore leather sandals in the office, wearing shoes only when dressed for dinner in the evenings. His office dress never departed from khaki slacks and a crisp white shirt with sleeves rolled part way up, and no tie. Madam bought most of this sparse wardrobe for him at the Navy Commissary. He probably had no patience for shopping. He would eat a hearty breakfast, usually with eggs, occasionally with something I had never seen except as dog food—hamburger meat, broken up and fried loose and scattered over toast. And coffee, lots of coffee. After a few tries, I avoided joining him for breakfast; he would never talk, just feed himself behind an open newspaper. Madam never came down in the morning.

At about 10 a.m. he would leave the house and, in his quick little step, cross the small garden, enter the Consulate, and go immediately to his large office at the back of the building. He shared this room with an American secretary, the wife of an American businessman. At 11 a.m. one of the maids would come across the garden and deliver a large glass of tomato juice to his desk. He needed it. Did anyone else want anything? Juice? Coffee? We were never asked, and he never suggested it. Precisely at 12 noon, the consul would recross the garden to a small family room or library in the rear of the house. There for a half hour before lunch he would make himself a couple of pink Angostura-flavored gins, while he listened to shortwave radio news broadcasts from the States.

Lunch at 12:30 or 1:00 p.m. was usually an awkward affair at home during my three months of residency there. Madam was usually present. Except for the occasional argument between the two (short and inconclusive), they talked very little. The consul usually had a couple of beers with lunch, after which he would retire for a short nap, then reappear at the office at 3 p.m. for a brief shuffling of papers at his desk. Then promptly at 4:00, he would take off for his bridge club a few blocks away on the Savannah. This went on without deviation day after day.

He once admitted to having a couple of whiskeys while playing bridge at the club. He returned home around 6 for the usual shower and change. Cocktails were served from 7 to 8. He and Madam preferred martinis.

Trinidad, BWI, 1944–46

With dinner at 8 there was always wine and often liqueurs after dinner, especially with guests. And before retiring there would usually be a few more whiskeys while playing a round or two of bridge. How the consul kept up this daily routine without collapsing, or worse, over his seven years in Trinidad without a break I do not know. It would certainly have made me just as nervous as he was if not do me in with cirrhosis of the liver. Perhaps his daily routine and the heavy alcohol intake were the secret to his speaking shorthand.

What Does a Vice Consul Do?

When news came of President Franklin D. Roosevelt's death, I was not surprised that the consul announced he would not attend the British memorial service for the American president in the huge Anglican cathedral downtown. But American diplomatic representation at the service was clearly an imperative. As the consul seemed to want nothing to do with churches or religion and eschewed events where drinks were not served, I was assigned cathedral duty.

As this was my first such experience, I entered the cathedral with slightly shaky knees and was led to a special prie-dieu in the front on the left side of the sanctuary. Sir Edward Cunard occupied the matching prie-dieu on the right side. I wondered if my boss had worked out a prior deal with Governor Sir Bede Clifford not to participate. I vaguely recall having to say a very few words.

After that heady experience I returned to my mundane duties seeing to passports, visas, and shipping. Before long I developed calluses on two of my right fingers as each official document required a total of twenty-five signatures. In addition, there were fingerprint forms to sign. Eventually I dropped my middle name, Mary, to shorten the signing process. I should have changed my last name to Wills, which my father occasionally used in business.

One day in the course of my duties I had a phone call from British Intelligence. They learned that I had granted an immigration visa to a well-known prostitute, who was trying to support her three children and hoping they might have a better life in the States. Although we relied to a certain degree on local police and other reports, there had been no tip-off that this woman, a Polish refugee, was inadmissible. Perhaps she had calculated that the "ski" in my name might facilitate matters. Frankly, I had found nothing derogatory in her background papers. I brazenly phoned her, explaining there was a small error in the issuance of her visas and asking that she return with all her papers. When she did, I took possession of them, voided the visa and entries in the passports, and returned them to her. Even more brazenly, I told her she could not travel to the United States because of adverse information we had received. She did not question me, merely walked out, and I never saw her again. But I have memories. She taught me two phrases in Polish, "Hello, how are you?" and "Goodbye." I later learned that I had been dead wrong in seizing and destroying the visas; only the U.S. Immigration and Naturalization Service could legally deny entry upon arrival in the United States, assuming they had the same negative information I had received.

On several occasions small groups of Trinidadians claiming to be calypso singers would visit the Consulate seeking visas to cut discs in the United States. Some had supporting documentation from impresarios and recording studios. Others did not. But if business was slow and the work dull, I would invite them into our small conference room for "performances." Such "auditions" were hardly appropriate and certainly not a prerequisite for a visa. The Boss never seemed to catch on or object. I found the singers highly entertaining and a welcome break from office routine, learned a lot of bawdy songs, and made friends among the Port of Spain demimonde. They had fascinating stage names like Raging Lion, Big Man, King Faroh, and the like.

Shipping: A Difficult and Dangerous Business

When I wasn't floundering around with visa and passport work, I did what was called "shipping." The captains of merchant vessels would call at the Consulate to request crew list visas, health certificates, and sometimes government assistance in settling labor disputes. Again, considerable documentation was required involving consular stamps and, yes, still more signatures.

Trinidad, BWI, 1944–46

When the consul assigned this work to me, he must have slyly thought that a woman vice consul would "tame" the generally rough and surly seamen. He was right. The sea captains seemed pleased to encounter an American woman after being at sea for a long time. Many of the ships came to Trinidad from as far as Lourenço Marques (now Maputo), Mozambique. I found it helped if I merely smiled, even flirted a wee bit with them, keeping it very low key.

When seamen were sick and had to be signed off their ships for treatment, it was often because they had contracted some venereal disease. As this proved a bit awkward, I worked out a sort of code with the captains to save us both embarrassment. I would simply ask if this was the "usual case requiring hospitalization." If the captain said "Yes," I would sign the seaman off and send him on his way to the U.S. naval base, which had agreed to treat them. It was wartime, and the government wanted its merchant ships kept on the move. When these seamen were discharged, they would return to the Consulate, and we would try through the local agents to find them other ships to sign on so they could return to the States.

Sometimes problems arose when seamen remained for any length of time "on the beach." They would steal sheets from the ships, and foodstuffs or other gear, which they would then sell locally, buy rum, get drunk, and usually end up in the local jail. After a time I would get them released and then help them find another ship back to the States. How many illegitimate children these sailors may have spawned in their cavorting on shore I will never know, nor did I want to.

One particularly friendly sea captain ran one of Alcoa's fleet of smaller vessels that sailed from Trinidad down to the rivers in then British Guiana to load up on bauxite. They would return to Port of Spain to transship the ore in larger vessels bound for the United States. This captain insisted I accompany him on his trips to see the "wonders of the jungle in BG." There, on the narrow rivers, the monkeys would leap from the trees onto the ships' decks. Naturally I wondered if that was all the sea captain wanted to show me. But in my best convent school manner, I declined with thanks but no thanks.

Shipping presented me with continuous problems. One day we received a message from a captain via a local agent urgently insisting that the "American consul remove a man in irons from a ship in the stream."

This meant the vessel was anchored offshore in the Gulf of Paria. Someone had to row out, get the man aboard the small dinghy, and bring him into Port of Spain for incarceration by the local authorities. The ship's captain refused to sail with the man on board. It was nighttime when I got the call. Surely my boss would not consider doing this, so I didn't even bother to call him.

What to do? I remembered a mysterious American guy, tall and thin, whose name I believe was Milton. He had some vague but unexplained connection with the Consulate, would float in, have a few words with the consul, and leave. He was clearly not on our payroll but was somehow mysteriously linked to our office. Neither he nor the consul ever discussed his business with me, but I suspected he was FBI with ties to local British intelligence. Throwing caution to the winds, I phoned Milton, knowing only that he lived "somewhere in the neighborhood." He immediately caught the drift of my dilemma and agreed to accompany me on the rowing expedition in the dark of night to pick up "the man in irons." He had enough gallantry and common sense to realize it was no job for a woman alone.

We called the shipping agent to radio the ship's captain we were coming and to prepare to assist us with the transfer. Out we rowed into the Gulf in the dark. As we came alongside the ship, the prisoner was led to the deck, climbed with obvious difficulty down the ladder, and stepped into our boat. I was very uneasy. My companion and I took turns at the oars but I almost preferred rowing to sitting there facing the handcuffed man, never knowing if he would fling those cuffs first around my neck and then Milton's.

The prisoner was obviously much smarter than that. Any struggle might have risked somebody losing their footing and falling overboard. Besides the seaman seemed quite comfortable sitting there like a Roman emperor being rowed by a woman galley slave, perhaps for the first and only time in his life. It certainly was a first for me and never to be repeated.

Free Rides Are Never Quite Free

Casting good judgment to the winds because I was anxious to return home for Christmas, I signed on as a "work-away" for a dollar a day to get a free ride on one of our merchant vessels returning to the United States. As if I hadn't had enough of the shipping business! And with all those troublesome seamen? Nonetheless, I accepted the offer of such a free ride on an Alcoa ship sailing from Trinidad to Mobile, Alabama.

I was the only woman on board a vessel that took more than a week to reach port, a very long week indeed. I was billeted below the water line, gratefully alone, in a cabin meant for eight, at the start of the passageway to the crew's quarters—not the greatest location. I had brought along a Siamese cat in a cage as a present to my family. The room assignment proved unworkable. The ventilation was so poor I had to leave my door open from time to time. That invited all sorts of comments from crew members as they passed my room to theirs.

When I explained the problem to the captain, he reassigned me to a room that the gunnery crew had used during the worst of World War II, located one deck up and across the hall from the so–called Slop Shop, where the crew bought cigarettes, toiletries, and supplies. While the traffic was less, I still received anonymous notes slipped under my door, but at least I had more privacy. Would I recommend such a voyage? Perhaps only for a girl who feels neglected. From that experience I learned that a single woman traveling alone on an all-male freighter leaves herself open to question regarding her motivation. Was I really innocently trying to save money, or was I looking for adventure and a good time? I was learning the hard way and would use better judgment in the future, I consoled myself.

Pan American Airways Plane Crash

Brief as was my Christmas vacation with family in Miami Beach, I returned to Trinidad refreshed and ready for work, even to my old shipping problems. But the familiar routine was abruptly broken with the tragic crash of a Pan American Airways Clipper plane (Flying Boat) in the Gulf of Paria. The Consulate was immediately notified of the crash by the British port authorities and told to stand by for details. They came soon enough. While there were only six or eight passengers on the flight, all were lost together with an American crew of three or four. This was the very same plane Charles Lindbergh had inaugurated for Pan Am with a historic flight around the world. Though considered virtually crashproof, it seems to have struck some hidden object in the waters of the Gulf.

The British authorities brought what salvageable personal items they found to my office to pass on to nearest of kin, some of whom had flown down from the States. The bodies and remains recovered were handed over to the local undertaker to be identified by Pam Am people. Fortunately, I was relieved of that grizzly task (although it was a duty I was unable to avoid at my next post, in Colombia, when a young American died and the embassy had to ship his body back to the States).

The Pan Am tragedy required paperwork and contact with the local undertaker, an East Indian by the name of Battoo. He was the blackest man I had ever seen. The sight of him in the black suit he always wore to the Consulate remains indelible in my mind. There was something haunting about him. Moreover, he insisted I review the photos of the crash and the remains of the victims. As ridiculous as it is to admit, because of my experience with Battoo, I had trouble throughout my life being comfortable when introduced to a very dark-skinned East Indian.

Life Could Be Beautiful

It was not all work and no play in Trinidad. Life could be beautiful. At the many parties at our own Consulate, Madam was at her very best playing the gracious hostess with her superb four- and even five-course dinners, which always had a Cordon Bleu touch.

And then there was Government House. I remember how intimidating my first dinner there was. Guests were met at the door by a liveried servant and escorted into one of the Great Halls, where they were announced. Cocktails were served on the enormous veranda overlooking the mansion's lush gardens, where the scent of night-blooming jasmine and other tropical flowers always hung heavily in the air. Dinner was served in yet another large and dazzling room. The long, heavy mahogany table was polished to an inky blackness. With neither vases nor baskets to hold them, flower blossoms without stems, often orchids, were scattered randomly about the table to appear as though floating on a pond of still, black water.

One evening Sir Bede and Lady Clifford had royalty as guests, Lord and Lady Athlone. We had been told beforehand that the event would require a curtsey. I spent days practicing so as not to pull the good lady toward me or to fall at her feet. I got quite a workout, as did my housekeeper. It is worth noting that the American consul and Madam were always exemplars of stately behavior on these occasions. And I learned much by just watching and imitating them and others. Madam always managed to get her husband away before he became too lugubrious and his speech even harder to follow.

Boat rides and fishing expeditions in the Gulf and luncheons on the small islands off Venezuela were hosted by the Army general and his wife, using his large and comfortable motor launch. The real showman at official entertainment was the Navy commodore billeted at the base. He had a fortresslike stone villa called the Castle, overhanging the Gulf waters. It had been built by a wealthy local businessman and was leased to the U.S. Navy as a residence. The commodore had enhanced it by installing a lovely orchid garden at the entrance and manning the Castle with what seemed like a squadron of Filipino servants. The food was always very good. Both the consul and I had membership in the Naval Officers Club further up on the base, which provided us an alternative for entertaining. It was quite convenient on weekends as it also had a small beach on a cove where one could swim or go boating. But it was not smart to venture too far by boat into the Caribbean because of trailing sharks.

The only problem with all this back and forth official entertainment with the British colonials, ranking local citizens, and visitors was the need for an appropriate wardrobe, as the standard set by the British colonials (never mind wartime and the tropics) called for long dresses for the women and formal attire with medals for the men. I had arrived with little in the way of formals other than a couple of old and tired prom dresses, which I sensed Madam did not feel were quite up to snuff. Because there were usually two or three evening functions a week, it was clear I needed to create something. Fortunately the local shops carried a surprisingly good stock of fabrics and the local dressmakers, while hardly expected to be up to French couturier standards, were quite acceptable. After all, the famous "frocks" of the British ladies were never a serious fashion challenge.

Trinidad, BWI, 1944–46

Did I have ANY personal life in this dance between the office and official entertainment? The correct answer is "hardly any"; yet I managed to enjoy myself, even to fall in love, I thought. Having carefully surveyed the local scene and eliminated a lot of the single Brits, whom I found "too oddly foreign" or too jaded for my tastes, I decided to focus on the U.S. Navy base. There I met an attractive Marine lieutenant at one of the weekly open air movies. We became quite good buddies for beach dates, dances, just "cruising," even horseback riding through bamboo plantations on horses borrowed from the nearby police barracks.

It wasn't long after several dances at the base and numerous beach outings that I found myself more than just attracted to the white starched uniform of "my Marine." It was wartime and there was a certain glamour about the U.S. base in addition to the tropical setting. The relationship had become rather serious just before the arrival of orders for my reassignment after eighteen months in Trinidad. It was hard to leave. We both took the day off and went to a wild and isolated beach on the north coast of the island. We simply enjoyed ourselves, rather than plan or even talk about our future.

Veronica, Housekeeper and Legend

The story of Trinidad would be incomplete without something on my domestic life after moving out of the residence and away from Madam and the Consul. I had found a suitable two-bedroom apartment a few blocks from the Consulate and off the Savannah on a street called Picton. A friend helped me locate a housekeeper named Veronica Valobra—a good, solid middle-aged woman with no professional experience other than taking care of an aged aunt and uncle.

Veronica was a sturdy woman, almost as tall as myself, with a dignified bearing. She could have been mimicking the British, but I rather thought her self-possession was natural, reflecting someone trying to conquer adversity. There was also a shyness about her. Would I kindly help her learn to cook "American style," teach her recipes, and be tolerant of her mistakes, she humbly asked. I promptly went out and bought her a Betty Crocker cookbook and told her to just follow directions. Although her pace was deliberate, she proved to be reliable and in time, a very good cook and housekeeper.

In Veronica I had found a prize of real value. She catered to my every need, kept an immaculate house, and watched over me like a mother hen. We developed a warm and close relationship though never expressed in words by either of us until many, many years later, when I realized how good she had been to me and how much I had meant to her, her daughter, and even her granddaughter.

When I thought Veronica was up to speed for having guests, I invited one of the jolly Irish Dominicans from my parish church down the street to lunch. The Dominicans remained refreshingly apart from my official life, yet keenly attuned to the local scene. Through them I had met the charming Irish archbishop, one Finbar Ryan. A true intellectual, he proved to be a wealth of information on the history, politics, and social conditions of the island—all good background for filling in political reports to Washington.

I had to be careful how I seated the priest at table in my little apartment, because directly across the street (I learned only after moving in) was a busy bordello, well patronized by sailors from the U.S. naval base. They would often ride up on their rented bicycles while on shore leave and announce their presence by loud shouts. The girls tended to advertise their business by hanging out the windows in full view of the street. So after carefully seating the priest with his back to the window overlooking the street, I prayed my neighbors' business would be slack that day. Fortunately, it was both quiet and uneventful. But I need not have worried that the priest might think I had chosen a bad neighborhood. I soon learned that there was not just a single red-light district in Port of Spain; business was pretty well scattered all over the town.

When I gave my first cocktail party in my new digs, I tried to mimic Madam's best form and style. I vaguely remembered watching my father make martinis, something about four parts gin to one part French dry vermouth. I mixed the two in a large pitcher and put it in the refrigerator. When guests came I plopped olives or twists in the glasses and poured. I had forgotten that mixing with a lot of ice was part of the recipe. Veronica had made a variety of canapes and was very helpful passing trays and generously pouring from the cool pitcher of martinis. Before long I noticed people becoming rather giddy and loud. It was when someone asked, "*How* did you make these martinis?" that I realized I was responsible for OD-ing my guests.

Veronica and I were both sad when I was transferred and had to leave Trinidad. I helped her find another job before I left. We corresponded off and on for the next five years or so. While I was assigned to Paris, I heard that Veronica's daughter, Ann, was taking ballet lessons and sent her some ballet slippers from France. Nearly twenty years after I had left Trinidad, Veronica wrote to me in Italy that she had married an Anglo-African widower, a tugboat captain who plied the waters of the Gulf of Paria. She seemed to be getting up in the world and happy. The captain had a house to which she could retire. I sent a wedding gift—a silver serving dish, which seemed appropriate.

Nearly forty years after I had left Trinidad, Ann phoned me from New York wanting to come down to see me in Washington. She arrived by train and stayed a few nights. She proceeded to tell me the story of her life, which included marrying a Chinese businessman and having a daughter, Elizabeth, whom she called Liz. Before that she had lived with a French businessman near the oil fields in the southern part of Trinidad. At the time she was a jeweler's agent, selling watches, bracelets, and whatever in the rural areas of Trinidad. She was proud about the Frenchman and bragged that his house was so large he had six toilets and many cases of champagne in the basement!

When Veronica's health declined, both Ann and Liz wrote urging me to return to Trinidad. They reported that Veronica talked of me often and wanted to see me. So after some forty-four years away from Trinidad, I awkwardly used the pretext of a brief excursion to the world-famous Asa Wright Bird Sanctuary on Trinidad's beautiful north coast mountain range. I flew down from Washington and stayed but a few days at the sanctuary, having seen more hummingbirds and oilbirds than one needs in a lifetime. I took a cab into Port of Spain, checked into a hotel, and called Veronica. She was overjoyed.

I found her in a nice little bungalow in a garden suburb on the north edge of Port of Spain, which had been left her by the deceased tugboat captain. She was confined to a wheelchair and having trouble taking her meals on a tray. So Ann and I went shopping and found something

Veronica really needed, a dining table and chairs. It was of tropical wood and made in Trinidad. Veronica was delighted with her gift, which I felt appropriate, given all the meals she had served me many years before.

Before I said goodbye to Veronica for the last time, she said something unforgettable. Indeed, it froze me in place and brought tears to my eyes. "I want you to know, Miz Jean, that ever since you left Trinidad forty-four years ago I have prayed for you every day of my life. I have never stopped praying for you." No wonder I made it through thirty-five years of life in the Foreign Service!

Here was a simple, uneducated, yet good and dignified woman whose life had been no picnic, who had worked far too long without pay for relatives, who was deeply disappointed many times in her life. Yet Veronica had found time in the midst of her own problems to pray for a foreign woman who had been roaming the world for decades, thousands of miles away, and—if the truth be known—thinking very little of Veronica. She explained that she could never forget me, because I had given her much more than her first paying job, suggesting that the job had given her not only self-confidence but, for the first time in her life, feelings of self-worth.

Less than five years later I received word that Veronica had died. Her lineage lives on in Trinidad: her daughter, Ann, whom I seldom hear from; and Liz, with her husband and two daughters. Some of the e-mails from Liz are nothing more than canned, round-robin jokes. But much of her mail contains thoughtful prayers, which I have come to understand as reflecting the virtues of love and concern inherited from her grandmother.

Farewell, Trinidad, Mon Amour

Before my second year in Trinidad was up, orders came from Washington assigning me to the U.S. Embassy in Bogotá, Colombia, preceded by language training of three months at the Foreign Service Institute at the Department of State.

Leaving Trinidad was hard. First posts are always like that. Foreign Service people invariably develop a special emotional attachment to their initial posting unless it is someplace like Devil's Island. Or Timbuktu. Trinidad had been idyllic in many respects. Everything was new and filled with excitement and adventure, and at the same time demanding—notably, the crash of the Pan Am flight in which Americans lost their lives; the death of a historic U.S. president, visits of British royalty to the island, and impressive parties by the British colonial governor, the U.S. Navy commodore, and the U.S. Army general. Topping all this glamour was my first, serious love affair. So how does a twenty-something neophyte in the Foreign Service cope with all this when official orders command you to leave it all behind?

To Marry or Not to Marry

Being a vice consul in Trinidad was my second job after college. Compared with the first, it had far more scope and responsibilities in and out of the office, given the nature of diplomatic life. It was my first experience living and working overseas, with the constant reminder that I was an official representative of the United States, always having to look and act the part.

Did I want to marry this dashing young Marine lieutenant and leave the Foreign Service? Regulations required that a woman, but not a man, resign if she married. Did I want to leave this interesting new work after only one short assignment at a very small out-of-the-way post, not even a capital? Was this a fair test of a promising career? Foreign Service life meant changing jobs, residences, and countries every two or three years. Did I really want such an unsettled life? Did I want to work in a highly competitive, male-dominated profession for the rest of my life?

More fundamentally, were my lieutenant and I sufficiently mature and experienced to know our minds and hearts and to commit to marriage just because I was leaving Trinidad? We delighted in our times together, but I wondered if our relationship was intellectually as deep as it was emotionally, and sufficient to stand up to the challenges of marriage and family. Would I be content playing second fiddle to a military man?

Although my transfer brought all these questions to light, I shrank from making decisions that might be premature. I cared deeply for the man, but one part of me was wildly racing to get away to find space and time, and perhaps answers. I knew I needed to be alone for a while for prayer and reflection.

Trinidad, BWI, 1944–46

After such a short experience at one post, and a consulate at that, my mind was conflicted. My reassignment was to an embassy in Latin America, where professional work and living would be wholly different. I wanted that kind of different experience. Without it, I would not be giving the Foreign Service a fair test. Yet I did not want to leave my Marine, a good and handsome man. I realized I was far too immature and inexperienced to make a sound decision at the time.

That was it. I needed more time. I did promise—and sincerely—to visit his widowed mother in Chicago en route to the family summer place in Wisconsin. He saw me off at the airport when I left by army plane from Waller Field. And although l did visit his mother, I never made a deal with her son, notwithstanding several urgent long-distance calls from Trinidad immediately following my return to the States.

Romance in the tropics can be almost overwhelming, But on careful reflection away from Trinidad, I feared that, despite our mutual attraction, there were too many differences for the long haul—differences in backgrounds, education, beliefs, outlook, hopes, and dreams. For better or worse, I am a person who tends to let her head rule her heart—not that it hasn't been broken a few times. I let it break, and painful as it was, knew it was for the best.

Trinidad, BWI, 1944–46

THREE

Bogotá, Colombia, 1947–48
(Third Secretary—Economic)

Departing Trinidad to Chase Hurricanes through the Clouds

I accepted a freebie military plane ride back from Trinidad to the United States aboard an Army hurricane reconnaissance plane. The flight would be mapping the winds from the extreme southeastern Caribbean up to the east coast of Florida, and it sounded like much more fun than returning by commercial airline. The Department of State granted my request for a brief leave in Florida to be with my family at Christmas.

Under a starry sky at the U.S. Army air base in Trinidad my Marine and I clung tightly to one another in a long and tender farewell embrace. We both seemed unsure of our futures and not yet ready to commit. Yet we each cared deeply and sincerely for one another.

I broke away, climbed aboard a waiting World War II bomber, and turned to wave, somewhat limply. I was drained of emotion. The doors shut and the plane rolled along the tarmac to lift up and away from Trinidad. I was confused and sad yet wiser, yes, far wiser and more experienced than when I arrived. Nonetheless, doubts filled my mind as I winged my way home in the cavernous cargo section of the old bomber.

Aside from the crew up front, I had the entire plane to myself and lots of time to reflect on my personal life and to wonder where it was headed.

Absent any passenger seats, the crew made me comfortable on an improvised lounge composed of a pile of old khaki padding and mats used to secure cargo. I felt a bit like the Queen of Sheba, atop a throne however inelegant, though my tearstained face suggested it might not be a happy kingdom.

We flew a complicated, zigzag course, gradually heading north by moving east and west, testing the winds over the waters of the blue-green Caribbean. Occasionally a crew member with a big grin and a cup of coffee would duck back from the front cabin to check on me. Was I OK? We had to shout to make ourselves heard. I would point out the window in a downward direction and simply mouth the word *beautiful* as the sun glistened on the white coral beaches and outcroppings in the sea below.

After a few hours of zigging and zagging, we made it to the British island of Antigua, where I was told we would refuel and overnight. I was put up temporarily at the home of a rather surprised but hospitable American consul and his wife. Early the next day I was picked up in a Jeep and taken to the airfield, where I was put back in my "private salon," the same old converted reconnaissance plane, to do the second leg of the "hurricane watch" journey into West Palm Beach, Florida.

Again I was checked on periodically, sometimes with a sandwich to go with the coffee. It was late afternoon when the pilot called me up front to ask if I wanted "to help land the plane in West Palm Beach." The copilot offered me his seat, and I had the excitement of pretending I was flying the plane to touchdown.

Later, when I told the story to my brother, a World War II B-26 pilot, he didn't believe me. It seems there were military rules against such behavior and my brother was a by-the-rules guy who drove his subordinates and family crazy. He failed to appreciate why rules had been broken by another pilot wanting to show off to a young woman. Brothers are always such killjoys!

It wasn't until many years later that my brother took his own turn at bravado, flying up to northern Wisconsin from Racine in a Civil Air Patrol trainer to our home town of Rhinelander just so he could show off. He flew me around the many lakes that dotted the landscape and over the old cottage where we grew up, swooping down over "our" lake. He laughed heartily as he pointed out a huge boulder some distance from the shore where he had perched me precariously one day while he went off to fish

Bogotá, Colombia, 1947–48

with the guy next door. Fearful that he might be up to more tricks—this time with a plane—I signaled it was time to go back and land.

But back to my return from Trinidad. After landing in the USA, I went immediately to a phone to surprise my mother with my return. Would she please come up and get me for the drive down to Miami Beach? Thus began a great family reunion. In those days no one telephoned overseas, so apart from U.S. military facilities (official business only) I was out of direct touch with the family while at the Consulate in Port of Spain, except for slow mail via the Army or Fleet Post Offices.

No Marine Landing, Just Lingering Love

Within a day after returning to the States I received an overseas call from Trinidad. It was my lieutenant. He had been thinking of me, even summoned up the courage to ask if I had I been thinking of him, and how did I like the idea of getting together—on a more permanent basis?

I was not prepared for his proposal. So I stalled with far too much idle chitchat, even some subterfuge. I told him I would be passing through Chicago en route to vacation in Wisconsin before going to Bogotá and would call on his mother in the Windy City. I had defused his question for the time being. He seemed willing to wait for a more definitive answer.

True to my word, I did call on his mother. However, not long after visiting Chicago and several rounds of golf with the family back in northern Wisconsin, I wrote a "Dear John" letter. I hated doing it, as I liked the lieutenant for his decency, sincerity, and goodness. When I closed my eyes I could still imagine I smelled his squeaky-clean, heavily starched white dress uniform when he would drop me off with a goodnight kiss or two at my apartment in Trinidad. But now, with my decision made, it was time to prepare for my next posting.

Se Habla Español in Bogotá

The Spanish language course preceding my assignment to Bogotá was given at the Foreign Service Institute. At the time it was located across the

Potomac River in Virginia, strangely enough in a converted underground parking garage in one of the many high-rise apartment buildings in Rosslyn. Our classrooms were small and dark, making for good concentration on the business at hand, if not threatening claustrophobia. Yet our vocabulary and accents seemed to improve from the forced concentration, deprived as we were of windows and sunlight. A select group of men and women native speakers took turns putting us through our paces in semi-militaristic fashion. I was the only woman in a class with eight male Foreign Service officers. This was to become a regular pattern throughout most of my career.

One woman studying a foreign language amid a bevy of males inevitably made for practical joking, sometimes in English, but also in newly learned Spanish colloquialisms. Memories of the Marine lieutenant in Trinidad started to fade from memory.

The men in my language class came to enjoy flirting in Spanish whenever our teacher was a woman. I had no such luck when Latin males were doing the instructing. They were generally too short and shy to approach a tall American, even in their Adler "elevator" heels. Besides I learned it was not part of Latin culture for the woman to make even the slightest form of advance. Maybe a sly wink or two. It set me wondering what life in Bogotá might be like for a single foreign woman.

Once the Spanish language course was completed, I flew to Panama via Miami. In Panama I was put up for the night in a rambling old white frame Victorian hotel, complete with broad verandah and cushioned wicker chairs. A sign somewhere attested that Teddy Roosevelt had stayed there when the Panama Canal was under construction. I remember feeling terribly lonely and far from home, as I was seated without partner in a vast dining room in that big barn of a hotel. It would not be my first time without a dining companion during a life in the Foreign Service.

Up and Away over the Andes

The next day I was whisked out of the hotel and on to the airport to catch a flight on Avianca, the Colombian subsidiary, I was reassured, of Pan American Airways. During the flight I kept looking down at lush green valleys separated by foaming brown rivers alongside jungles and rising mountains. I imagined it must be where the coffee was grown. This was long before Colombia turned to producing coca and before the infamous international drug trade.

My in-flight reveries vanished when suddenly, directly beneath the plane, green fields were rushing past. I realized we were flying, at 8,500 feet, within yards above the high Andean plateau on which the capital, Bogotá, is situated. Landings are fast at that altitude and in minutes the wheels were down and we were speeding toward the Bogotá airport terminal, rightly named El Techo (The Roof).

Embassy personnel met me at the airport and drove me into the city to the Embassy, where I reported in and was welcomed. I was told I would be temporarily billeted in the apartment of another woman officer, the consul, a tall Texan to whom I was soon introduced. Her housemate, a secretary in an oil company, was in the States on vacation. I could use her room until she returned; then I might—if I wished—share the Texan's double room until I could find my own place.

Although the apartment became tight with three of us, it was not uncomfortable. I especially appreciated the friendship in a new and strange place. The two women had found a good maid so that life was easy, with chores attended to and three meals a day provided. The walk to the Embassy was short but breathless until my lungs became accustomed to the altitude, after about six weeks. I was told that I would be playing tennis by the time my tour in Bogotá ended, and indeed I was.

I truly appreciated my initial housing arrangements and the companionship. Soon I was meeting friends of my housemates and integrating easily into their lives. That meant frequent weekend trips to *tierra caliente*, the warmer part of the country, which was rich in the rivers and lush valleys I had seen from the plane. My friends had made the acquaintance of a wealthy Colombian businessman who represented a large U.S. steel corporation. He owned an old and extraordinarily beautiful hacienda and cattle ranch along the Magdalena River, a major north-south artery.

While visiting there we shopped in historic, sixteenth-century villages for antiques and found some beautiful old *estribos* (stirrups) that were highly decorated with brass and copper fittings. They were said to have been used by the Spanish *conquistadores* while riding horseback as they explored the New World for gold, silver, and land to colonize. I was not at all convinced that the stirrups we found, handsome as they were, could have been 400 years old; I believed they were in fact very good copies and perhaps only 100 years old. Some said they were made in New England and shipped to Colombia with machetes and other tools and equipment needed to develop the country.

Another side benefit of coming to know many Colombians with coffee plantations and country estates in the "warm country" was the fact that they also produced orchids. It still took some getting used to when I saw my first large serving platter, yes platter, filled with cut orchids floating on a bed of water and nearly covering an entire coffee table. Equally impressive was the fact that the Texan's housemate, the oil company secretary, who was an attractive blonde with a saucy wiggle to her walk, received these massive bouquets of orchids almost every other week!

Much as I enjoyed my temporary quarters and the associations, I knew the search for my own place had to begin in earnest. But the pickings were scarce, and I wasn't at all sure after such a pleasant introduction to Bogotá that I wanted to live alone.

Silly to say, but the entire atmosphere of Bogotá was much more "foreign" than Trinidad. There were many differences—in people, ethnicity, and language, and Bogotá's far greater international sophistication. Eventually I met up with an English language teacher, a charming American girl from Oklahoma who was working at the U.S. Binational Institute and also looking for a place to live. She was going steady with a young American architect who was working on a USAID housing construction project. He had an architect roommate so we were soon a happy young foursome, enjoying outings and dinners plus some nightclubbing.

On one such evening when we were having a whale of a time at a local nightclub, I became so carried away with the music and atmosphere I took over at the microphone in front of the dance band and broke into the one Spanish song I had learned, "*Cantera Negra.*" It hardly brought the house down—I have little real talent for solos—but at least it was not booed, and I had fulfilled a girlish fantasy, which was a step up from the college choir. The atmosphere of that Saturday evening was so heady that we managed to dance the rest of the night away. As dawn approached, I asked my companion to drop me off at a neighborhood church for the

Bogotá, Colombia, 1947–48

6 a.m. mass! I am not sure I got much out of that church service before stumbling home and to bed in the early hours of the morning.

Before long the Oklahoman and I found a small duplex apartment four blocks up from the Embassy in the center of town. It seemed made for midgets, not lanky American women. It had a tiny kitchen and miniscule living room. A tight spiraling staircase led upstairs to two very small bedrooms and a bath. It would have to do, as we were exhausted hunting for quarters.

Party Anyone?

We should have been content with partying at the many local bars, clubs, and hotels, but I was insistent that my new housemate and I throw a thank-you party at our tiny apartment for all the good people who had helped us find it and the two fine guys who had been escorting us about town. Most important, I had imported a case of rum together with a few household effects from Trinidad, and we had to start using it.

When word of the party ("FIESTA!!") got out, those who were invited were greatly augmented by others who were not. We converted the tiny living room into a dance floor, rigged up the *toca-disco* (record player), for which people brought all their 78s, mostly of good Latin dance music. Upstairs, by pushing back the small bed and chair, I converted my bedroom into what I wrongheadedly declared would be "the gaming room"— cards and dice! These retrograde ideas were probably hangovers from fraternity party days at the University of Wisconsin, certainly not the lessons the consul's wife had so painstakingly taught me in Trinidad.

Admittedly, these entertainment ideas were a bit childish. When combined with the case of rum and limited food offerings, the setting proved a recipe for disaster. The riot police must have been asleep that night or we would have had a diplomatic incident on our hands. Surely the neighbors didn't sleep. It was well past 1 a.m. when we came to our senses, hid the remaining stock of rum, and announced that the party was over. But it wasn't until around 3 a.m. that we succeeded in pushing the last of the revelers out the front door, down the hall, and yes, even out into the street to bid them goodbye.

Bogotá, Colombia, 1947–48

That party in Bogotá was my first and last (believe me) experiment in trying to make new friends in a strange place. It might better be described as a misguided experiment in trying to get arrested for disturbing the peace. The neighbors in our apartment building shunned us, and some wives of embassy guests wouldn't speak to me for days.

I learned some important lessons the hard way: Once graduated from college, you leave collegiate ways behind, grow up, and follow local customs. Above all (so necessary in diplomacy), have an exit plan for any endeavor, be it personal or official, a social or a military campaign.

Official Duties among the Latins

Work? Ah yes, what were my official duties at the Embassy in Bogotá when I wasn't playing Perle Mesta on the cheap with a case of rum?

My assignment to the Economic Section meant working under the embassy's economic minister within a team of some five or six other officers, each with specialized duties. My chief responsibilities were financial reporting (Colombian Treasury, national budget, foreign and domestic banks) and the coffee industry, from production to marketing to shipping. There were various U.S. departments, especially Agriculture, which required firsthand reports. In those days international business reporting was rudimentary compared with advances of later years.

I remember my first "business call" on the Asociación Colombiana de los Cafeteros. I practiced quite some time before the mirror so I could rattle that name off flawlessly and get on with my first interview: "How is the coffee crop going?" "What is production this year compared with last? Prices?" And "Would there be any shipping problems to U.S. ports?"

After much careful preparation the day finally came for my first appointment with the *presidente* of the *asociación*. The man welcomed me in eloquent Spanish. Bogotá has long prided itself as "the Athens of Latin America," not only for the purity of its Spanish but for the eloquence and intelligence of its movers and shakers.

El Presidente, or "Mr. Coffee," was one of these. After welcoming me, he switched to perfect, unaccented English to wish me well in my new job. He did not in the least patronize me, even though I was probably the first woman who had ever made a business call on him. I sensed he must have daughters. We got on famously after that introductory meeting, and he was most helpful and obliging throughout my assignment.

Who Me? Cause a Riot?

I had to consult other prime sources and authorities, most notably the man in charge of International Transportation and Shipping at the Ministry of Foreign Affairs. Here things did not get off swimmingly in the least. The official spoke no English so I had to speak lean, technical Spanish. This man was obviously not particularly honored to have a call from a woman who was also a *gringa* (an American), slightly taller than himself, and with no apparent knowledge of maritime affairs. I sensed he was the type who was far more at ease with a woman on a dance floor than in an official business encounter. He motioned me to a chair and curtly asked my business.

Unfortunately, my business that day was not pleasant. I was there to deliver a formal U.S. diplomatic note of protest drafted in Washington. It charged the Colombian government with maritime infractions by its ships in U.S. waters. Its fleet, called *La Flota Gran Colombiana,* was one of the largest coffee shippers to the United States and the rest of the world and was a source of national pride.

Nothing or nobody in the State Department had prepared me for such a moment as the deliverer of bad diplomatic news. I had been told only to hand-deliver the note and wait for an answer. As I placed the note on his desk, I felt I had to animate the encounter because the official seemed so stiff. So I gratuitously chirped in my newly acquired Spanish: "My government is very unhappy with your government's actions," thus adding insult to injury.

The Foreign Ministry Desk officer, already visibly annoyed with this call from a woman, read the note quickly. Finished, he immediately stood and said, "You will hear from us." I also rose, hesitated a moment as if waiting for a soft conclusion (which was not forthcoming), and then promptly left his office. Obviously, there was some Spanish cultural nicety that I must have missed somewhere along the line. Or was the tension of the meeting

exacerbated because this official had never met up with a woman in professional life? Should I have asked my minister-rank embassy boss to pave
the way for me by calling his opposite number at the Ministry (with whom I
knew he was socially familiar and on a first-name basis)? Aside from the
critical nature of the note, I was sure something could have been done to
make the encounter easier.

It wasn't long after I returned to my office, perhaps two hours, when I
heard shouting in the street. I looked out to see a handful of student
demonstrators in front of the Embassy. Had that sneak of a low-level
munchkin at the Foreign Ministry called his radical buddies over at the
university to put on a show against the *gringos* who had insulted the pride
of Colombia?

Soon the streets in front of the Embassy were filled with several hundred hotheaded Latin students shouting and screaming denunciations
against the USA, holding up signs saying *Abajo* (down with) the USA and
others with *Viva* (long live) and hail to *la Flota Gran Colombiana*. If I recall
rightly, Colombia's merchant marine consisted then of no more than a
handful of poorly maintained, overage vessels, some of which the United
States probably had no business selling to them in the first place. It took
some well-placed calls from the political officer and on up to the ambassador himself before the police and units of the Army appeared and dispersed the protesters.

So much for delivering diplomatic notes. My colleagues at the Embassy
took fun in calling me the "riot maker" for weeks after that episode.

In due course the embassy received an official reply from the host government acknowledging the maritime infractions as charged and agreeing to submit to judgment regarding whatever indemnity was owed the
United States. It made we wonder if the United States, already regarded
as "the Colossus of the North" by most of the countries in Latin America,
might not have handled some of its international complaints with smaller,
less developed countries in a more informal, less confrontational manner.

Too often the United States was seen, and portrayed in the Latin press,
as a bully, brandishing a big stick, with Teddy Roosevelt the archetypal
model. Yet some of our leading "Old School" diplomats of those days believed firmly in educating smaller countries in the ways of "proper" diplomacy, while ignoring the inevitable backlash, especially in Latin America.

Bogotá, Colombia, 1947–48

Perhaps a softer, make-more-friends-and-allies kind of diplomacy would have been a more effective pedagogical device, if teaching was to be our diplomatic tool *du jour.*

On a Personal Note

To broaden "my economic beat" and range of contacts in Bogotá, I made the acquaintance of the head of an American accounting and consulting firm. He was mature and experienced. Eventually he and his wife became my close friends and confidantes. Not fully trusting my own judgment, especially in a foreign country out of sight of watchful parents, I found excuses for trotting a few admiring swains over to their house for "review" and judgment.

But the greatest service these dear American friends and longtime local residents rendered was more professional than personal. They shared their observations and wisdom on the local economy and provided a double-check against local government sources. This was especially helpful in the consulting we embassy officers were required to do with visiting American investors and in reporting to Washington.

Minor as some of my official achievements were in the bigger diplomatic scheme of things, I enjoyed some "firsts" during my assignment to Bogotá. One American businessman newly resident in Colombia was just getting started with an air transport business based on some old World War II surplus planes. He called at the Embassy seeking my personal and professional opinion on starting up a fresh-flower business between the two countries. This was in the late 1940s. I was flattered and told him I thought he was on to something lucrative, which indeed he was, as time has proven. Imported orchids, carnations, and roses have since become more commonplace on U.S. markets. He eventually became a very rich man, as he helped expand American flower tastes and availability, supplying them in the winter off-season to most of the United States.

Another imaginative entrepreneur called at the Embassy wanting my opinion on samples of newly developed and experimental instant coffee. I told him I thought he had a winner, and encouraged him into large-scale production. I have since regretted, in a way, not having gone into business with the man, or with the flower shipper, for that matter. But at the time I was committed to government service.

Comes the Revolution — *Bogotázo*

My most vivid memories of Bogotá unquestionably center on the famous and subsequently more infamous *Bogotázo*, the name given to the local political revolution. The death toll over the months and years that followed ran into the thousands and was to change Colombian life and history for decades.

It was not generally known at the time that Fidel Castro was in Colombia in the mid-1940s when the revolution broke out. Indeed he is credited with helping to plan some of the political strategy, which pitted the leftist-leaning Liberal Party against the traditional Conservative Party that had long been in power.

There had been no warnings of serious trouble or cautionary advice within the Embassy. Yet all hell broke loose on an otherwise ordinary day in April 1947.

Many of us officers regularly used embassy transportation—different vans to different areas of the city—to take us home and back to the Chancery during the lunch hour. On my return from lunch at my apartment, I walked to the bus stop a few blocks away on the corner of the main street, Carrera Septima. I noticed that the city had assumed an eerie silence. There was virtually no traffic and few pedestrians, only an occasional young man running down Septima toward the center of the city, shouting as he went, though it was not clear what he was saying. It seemed to be a warning of sorts. The embassy van finally pulled up but with few passengers on board.

The driver explained there had been an uprising in the center of the city; the Liberal Party leader, Jorge Eliécer Gaitán, had been shot, and his body was being dragged through the main streets! While we were headed directly for the center and the trouble, the driver nervously explained he would try to skirt the worst parts of the rioting. He was getting his instructions on the embassy radio link.

So we continued on through back streets, finally reaching the Embassy. We parked and hurried in, unknowingly unprepared for what was to become an all-night siege.

Marooned Overnight in the Embassy

We were immediately ordered to our individual offices and told to remain within the building, not use the elevator, and stay away from all windows. By then some American businessmen had taken refuge in the Embassy and seemed more confused than embassy personnel, but not for long. Somehow they found a store of liquor used for official entertaining, to which they freely helped themselves. That kept them busy and reasonably quiet, at least for awhile.

Soon bands of marauders formed in the streets. We learned from radio reports that the main jail had been broken into and more than 3,000 prisoners let loose. Convicts started breaking into storefronts and stealing whatever they could lay their hands on in the way of food and weapons. A large hardware store directly across the street from the Embassy soon became the center of attack for its stock of machetes, pickaxes, shovels, and even hoes and rakes.

Only a skeleton staff returned to the Embassy. The ambassador, Willard Beaulac, quickly assembled us and personally handed out assignments to deal with the emergency.

I was told to go down to the second floor of the building (the Embassy occupied the third and fourth floors) to the Avianca airline offices and inform whoever was in charge to communicate directly with the airport. The airport authorities were to detain the U.S. diplomatic courier just then about to land. Under no circumstances was he to bring the diplomatic pouch into town, a distance of some eight to ten miles. No embassy car would go for him, as it was doubtful it could even get through the blockades.

I made my way to the Avianca offices, feeling terribly important with my emergency assignment directly from the ambassador, also feeling just a bit frightened from what I had seen in the streets outside. As I opened the door of the Avianca office, I was greeted by two shouting male employees at loggerheads with one another, apparently just short of fisticuffs. They were having a political argument about the relative merits and foibles of the Liberal and Conservative political parties, each blaming the other for the general pandemonium in the capital city.

Suddenly the men stopped long enough to glower at me, curious as to just who I was and what I wanted. I identified myself and explained my mission, then asked, "Would they please call the airport now and stop the courier?" "Yes, yes," both assured me and then turned back to their political quarrel.

I stood my ground and explained that the ambassador of the United States had personally sent me on this mission and I could not return without clear-cut assurances that they had called the airport and delivered the message. "Would they kindly phone the airport in my presence?" I got their attention.

They tried calling but had trouble with the line. I said I would leave but return later to check on their progress. Again they agreed, but it was obvious the embassy's request was less important than the sorry state of their nation's politics.

I took the elevator back upstairs to look in on a second assignment I had been given—to help out as relief operator in the code room. There the clerks were sending and receiving cables nonstop with Washington, as our political officers and others kept feeding them reports of developments as heard over the radio and observed on the street. Our officers were also in nonstop phone contact with local officials and the press.

Within half an hour I returned to the Avianca offices to check on the status of the courier. The argument between the two employees continued in a lower key. In a moment I got their attention, and yes, they assured me, they had gotten through, and yes, the message had been delivered telling the courier to remain at the airport.

I reported to the ambassador, and then returned to my office to listen to the rising roar of the mobs outside. They continued to break into storefronts and steal as much as they could carry. Occasionally we dared to sneak looks out the window but it was becoming increasingly dangerous as the rioters started taking potshots at us and nicking the stone frames with gunfire around the windows. Slugs kept pinging around our windows, some going through the glass and lodging in the office ceilings. We tried to keep low and away from the windows, even crouching under our desks or seeking better protection in the Embassy hallways.

Bogotá, Colombia, 1947–48

At one point Ambassador Beaulac called a special meeting to review the situation of the U.S. delegation to the major inter-American conference meeting in Bogotá when the riots broke out. Next to the Colombian elections that had just occurred, the international conference being held in the Colombian Parliament building, was a major event for the entire hemisphere. But it had been completely disrupted by the rioters, who made it one of their primary targets.

As soon as we had advance warning of the planned attacks on the international conference, our security people took immediate steps to evacuate members of the U.S. delegation attending the afternoon sessions. These U.S. delegates were quickly moved from the conference site on the main Cathedral Square back to their temporary headquarters in the building across the street from the Embassy.

Their safety was still an issue facing the ambassador. Was our best judgment, he inquired of the assembled officers, that the delegation remain in their temporary offices or be moved—from across the street to the Embassy, which offered better physical and armed protection? If so, how best could this be accomplished without further endangering their lives in the midst of continued rioting in the streets? It was a tricky situation at best.

The chief of the U.S. delegation to that conference was no less than Secretary of State General George Catlett Marshall. Because his life had been threatened by the insurgent leaders, embassy security staff successfully moved him and a few top aides by fast car from the Parliament building to some safe houses in the suburbs. Indeed our security people had to keep moving him and his entourage for maximum security. Marshall's alternate and another notable, Norman Armour, had been relocated back to delegation headquarters across the street from the Embassy.

After hearing out his staff, Ambassador Beaulac decided that if there was a break in the shooting and looting in the streets, our defensive guard, with senior officers and local employees, would form a protective corridor in the street through which the delegates would run to the safety of our building. The plan was agreed and set in place. When a break in the street rioting occurred, the plan was implemented and it worked.

As the U.S. delegation joined our ranks, it made for an even larger number of anxious people crowded together with the refugee businessmen. They all kept inquiring if there would be food and if they would have to spend the night in the Embassy! As if any of us knew the answers! I suddenly remembered I had a camera in my desk. So whenever there was a lull in the rioting in the street or a halt in the gunfire, I would rush over to a window, click fast and return to my hiding place.

As it turned out there was no food; and while the supply of liquor held out, it didn't really help matters much. The businessmen who had fled to the Embassy continued to dip into the bottles to steady their nerves and relieve the tension. It soon became obvious that no one would be leaving the building that night.

At some point in the course of that terrible night I remembered that I had been given some powdered coffee samples by that businessman who was planning to start exporting to the United States. I found the jar in the back of a desk drawer. I also located a tea kettle and electric heating unit in the office of a secretary who liked her afternoon tea. Thus I was able to provide something of an improvised coffee break for the code room clerks, who had been working tirelessly to keep communications with Washington open.

As the local telephones continued to work, our political officers were able to maintain close contact with local police, army, and government officials on actions being taken to resist and contain the insurgent forces. Presumably the Colombian army didn't dare try to rescue our embassy contingent in the midst of the rioting until the situation became clearer and some of the intense initial fury was spent. We could see people being shot, killed, and hacked to death in the streets. Radio reports kept confirming this throughout the city.

The embassy got a real scare around midnight when we were told to prepare to evacuate because a paint store on the ground floor of our building had been set on fire. Our best informed judgment was that our chances in the street might possibly be better than being blown up with a chemical explosion in our building. However, just as we were preparing to evacuate, word came that the fires had somehow and miraculously been put out.

Added to this excitement the elevator bell began ringing nonstop. Although we were allowed to go between floors, we had been forbidden to go down to the ground floor, which had been blocked by a key switch. The elevator continued its insistent ringing. I was beginning to wonder if it might not be a short circuit.

Bogotá, Colombia, 1947–48

Without another thought I decided to investigate and summoned the elevator to my level. I entered and saw the call was coming from the ground floor. I turned the key in the panel and descended to the ground floor. As the door opened a man literally fell into the elevator, pushed in by a mob of shouting people behind him in our lobby. It was the American courier, dirty, sweating, and exhausted, the arm of his torn white shirt covered with blood where he had obviously been slashed by a machete. He was dragging the U.S. diplomatic pouch! I immediately reached for him, pulled him further into the elevator and slammed the door shut while I pushed the up button.

It was about four hours after I had first talked with the Avianca people, and the airport was a good eight to ten miles west of the city. As it turned out the heroic courier had *walked* most of the way into town! On the outskirts of the city he got some sort of ride downtown to a point near the Embassy.

I took him up to the top floor and asked one of the other embassy officers to clean and bandage his wound. Then I gave him some of my rare stash of coffee and a quick swig of the "representational" liquor, which was still making the rounds. It was the only comfort available. We still had no food. I made him as comfortable as possible on a couple of armchairs so he could rest. (Some years later I learned that the story of the brave diplomatic courier who had walked in from the airport through angry mobs to deliver the U.S. diplomatic pouch had become a classic in courier annals. His story became a critical part of every training session on "dangers to be faced" and how one man had overcome them.)

Twice during the night fires started up again on the ground floor below us. Again miraculously they were put out. For those of us who believed in a Supreme Being, a lot of prayers were said that night.

Just as dawn was breaking over the mountain range east of Bogotá, we were trying to get the kinks out of our backs and joints after what little sleep we had managed through the night of terror. We noticed there were no longer rioters in the streets and dispatched two of our political officers to survey the damage in our neighborhood.

The officers were gone less than a half hour when they returned after counting about thirty-five dead in the four to eight blocks surrounding our building. Another cable went off to Washington reporting on the situation and how embassy and delegation personnel had survived the night without casualties. No mention, of course, was made of those in our building who had nearly OD-ed from overindulging in the embassy's representational stock of liquor.

Army Troops to the Rescue

Our military attachés had worked assiduously through the night to arrange for Colombian government troops to rescue embassy personnel in accordance with host government responsibilities under treaty regulations. Sometime before 10 o'clock in the morning, armored personnel carriers and armored tanks moved into our street and parked in front of the Embassy.

We were assembled and instructed on evacuation procedures, which vehicles to board and where we were going. For fear there were still rioters and snipers lodged in office buildings in the city center, we were told we would make a very fast run through that section of town before fanning out onto the main arteries leading to the suburbs. There we would transfer to private vehicles that would take us back to our respective homes.

I was surprised, happy, and flattered with what I saw when the armored vehicles arrived. There among the troops, with his starched white shirtsleeves rolled up and looking very businesslike, was the oil company executive I had been dating—let's call him Trevor. It was a scene straight out of Hollywood, and in this scene the heroine cried as much from relief and excitement as from fatigue after the frightful night at the Embassy.

What we saw from the personnel carriers as we sped through the central square, where days before we had enjoyed ice cream sundaes at curbside tables, was terrifying. Cars had been upturned and burnt, dead bodies littered the streets, storefronts were burned out, and nearly every building had pockmarks where shells had landed. To the extent I was still thinking, I was glad to be alive.

As I recall, it was a warm American male shoulder and comforting hand that held me in control all the way out to our drop-off point. How "my hero" Trevor learned of the evacuation arrangements and responded so well I never knew. Yet this comforting boyfriend had driven his own car to the drop-off point. It was a dashing Studebaker of the time, front and

Bogotá, Colombia, 1947–48

rear ends almost identical. He offered to take me wherever I wanted to go. I opted for my own apartment about a mile from the Embassy and kept assuring him I would be fine, even though as it developed my housemate was not there. She was probably still at the school where she taught. I insisted I would be OK. So my rescuer left me to rest and recover, though I was sure he harbored doubts about my safety.

Scavenging for Food

But I wasn't OK. I found there was little food in the house. And it was a mistake to remain alone. But determined to make a go of things, I went out and walked down the block only to find our little corner grocery store had been sacked and burned. I saw a few cans of food among the ashes and tried to forage for them.

Suddenly I heard shouts and gunfire. Bullets whizzed over my head. Then came the frightening sound of hobnailed boots thudding in my direction. In gruff Spanish and at gunpoint, a helmeted Colombian soldier rudely ordered me out of the rubble, shouting something like "Who are you, a war scavenger?" At which point in my total exhaustion, I shouted back in English something like, "Hell no, just a hungry American in your 'blinkety blank' country!"

Then, totally out of control, I burst into tears. Though unintentional, the tears proved effective as a universally understood common language. The soldier dropped his menacing stance, asked where I lived, and escorted me around the corner and home. Mercifully, the phone was ringing.

Refuge with the Brits

It was my friend, the British consul calling from his little farmhouse by a tiny village just a few miles north of Bogotá. Would I come and stay with them? He apparently had been in phone contact with Trevor, whom he would send to pick me up. I quickly packed my bag and was ready when Trevor returned. It was only then that I realized I was experiencing some sort of nervous trauma, intermittently shaking and crying. It took me several days in the comfort of my British friends in the countryside with their good food, conversation, and fun-loving children running about, plus some sound sleep, to restore me to normal.

Bogotá, Colombia, 1947–48

Bogotá was never the same place after the fateful events of that April day in 1947. Personal safety and public security became a serious problem, with random shootings and assassinations. But, blessedly, I was soon to be transferred out of the country.

Not long after our frightful night at the Embassy, I was diagnosed locally with a type of leukemia and medically evacuated to the famous Gorgas Hospital in the Panama Canal Zone. Expressing doubts as to my true condition, the Gorgas doctors referred me back to the States.

Life among the Latins

Almost as a reward for my hair-raising experiences in Colombia, the department assigned me to Europe, which I had long wanted to see. But I did not take off for my new post at the Consulate General in Milan, Italy, until 1949, after medical assessment, temporary duty (TDY), and Italian language training in Washington, D.C.

What had I learned from my first experience at an embassy and my first assignment in Latin America? I found that Latins were indeed hot-tempered and hot-blooded. I also learned to expect the unexpected, like the day when, returning from the market in Bogotá with both arms loaded with parcels, I was pinched from behind, through a heavy topcoat at that. Yet I was able to turn and use my recently acquired language deterrent, "Aynano, tan peqeño, viayase," which could not have been more offensive to a Latin male. Translated, it means "Beat it, you little dwarf!" Hardly diplomatic, but neither was the pinch. I also learned to consult more with my many embassy colleagues before barging off to the Ministry of Foreign Affairs, as I had with the protest note on shipping.

And I learned that if a single housing accommodation was not available at a post, then group living (three such arrangements in Bogotá) could teach tolerance and understanding. At one point I shared housing with four others, including a divorced mother working as a secretary, plus two live-in servants. The mother was accompanied by her unruly and obviously lonely kid, a ten-year-old, who kept shouting at table in a heavy Texas accent: "I want my milk in my cow cup," referring to a painted mug she had brought from the States. Poor lonely child! Single women in the Foreign Service were one thing; single mothers quite another.

Additional tolerance and understanding were necessary in the case of yet another roommate in the same group house whose Latin boyfriend and pals would serenade her with guitars and song at two o'clock in the morning before yet another day at the office. The Latin serenading only stopped, and we all got some sleep, when the girl finally agreed to marry the suitor.

Postscript

This postscript is intended to clarify and interpret some of the events of my Bogotá assignment, which proved a critically transformative period in my life. A personal relationship helped me "come of age," though I was already a few years past twenty-one. Professionally, it pointed me firmly on a career path. This postscript details the transfer value of the lessons learned from the personal relationship for the practice of diplomacy. It also reflects on enduring friendships.

I started out dating a consulting architect with the U.S. Agency for International Development, but we were never serious about one another. He was from Oklahoma and claimed to have Native American blood. Whether Apache, Cheyenne, or another tribe was never clear; what mattered was that he had the fleet feet of an Indian tracker, which made him one heck of a good dancer. We spent many a Saturday night until the wee hours dancing to the lively beat of Latin rhythms at a local basement night spot. The relationship strengthened my self-confidence—a good thing, because it wasn't long before a petite, blonde American secretary was assigned to the USAID mission. She was obviously much lighter to whirl around the dance floor and certainly far better sized as arm candy. I grieved to lose such a fun-loving man, but we both moved on.

Not long thereafter I met up with "Trevor," who later rescued me from the U.S. Embassy the morning after the *Bogotázo*. He was tall, good-looking, and serious-minded, a junior executive with a U.S. oil company, and was more interested in me than in my dancing. Nor was he much interested in golf or tennis, yet he was quite gallant in rolling out his imported Studebaker to drive me to various sports clubs or wherever I wanted to go—to see friends or just sightseeing.

Trevor came from a distinguished New England family. Because he was not very observant nor verbal about it, he surprised me by also being

Bogotá, Colombia, 1947–48

Catholic, though it seemed to be in name only. In time I also learned that his father had some international business connections with Ambassador Ellsworth Bunker (was it Philippine sugar and shipping?) in addition to New Hampshire real estate. Overall, Trevor's background was impressive, including the family townhouse on Park Avenue in New York City. His résumé appealed to the snobbish instincts I was developing in my new and glamorous environment.

As time went on and our dating became steady, we were considered "an item." I even imagined myself ensconced in—or at least visiting—the stately, white-framed, rambling country home in New Hampshire, with its roaming flocks of sheep that conveniently kept the vast lawns mowed, I was told. These daydreams would be interrupted by some uneasiness, if not fear, that the family matriarch might not readily take to a Midwestern interloper with a "-ski" name breaking into her obviously upper-crust circle.

Since entering the Foreign Service and continuously meeting new people, I was often queried about my name and family origins, especially by foreigners, as in Trinidad when a visa applicant immediately launched into Polish in apparent hopes of making a favorable impression and expediting her case. The assumption of Polish background persisted, but the truth was that my origins were German and Irish. My paternal relatives in Wisconsin even spoke German, common in a state where many German immigrants settled and established a range of breweries and sausage and cheese factories. Both of my grandparents on the maternal side had emigrated from Dingle in County Kerry, bringing the Catholic faith with them.

I met Trevor through a professional colleague, H. F. C. Bartlett (or some such string of initials the British favor), the British consul. He went by the nickname of "Jimmy" and was one of those rare Brits who was also Roman Catholic, even claiming Stuart lineage. For years the family had an antiques and rare books shop in the square opposite Westminster Cathedral in London. While in the Royal Navy during World War II and stationed in Trinidad, Jimmy had met and married a woman of French colonial plantation heritage. Indeed, her family in Trinidad, had given me a letter of introduction to their daughter, Madeleine, Jimmy's wife.

Jimmy was very much his own man, a carefree and endearing soul with considerable personal charm. He was hardly a deeply committed

Bogotá, Colombia, 1947–48

career diplomat determined to make chief of mission at all costs. He always made me laugh with his irreverent references to "the Bolsheviks" in his Foreign Office. I hoped his betters never heard him, but they might have. He took early retirement not long after returning to England. His time in Bogotá was just a few years before the Burgess, MacLean, and Philby case surfaced, so Jimmy may have been on to something. Many years later we met up in Italy as he scoured the countryside for antiques for the family business.

While serving in Colombia, Jimmy and Madeleine, together with their vivacious ten- and twelve-year-old children, lived in the country a few miles north of Bogotá in a rustic old farmhouse, or *finca*. It was to the safety and comfort of their place that I had repaired for rest and recuperation after the *Bogotázo*. The Sunday luncheon parties at the Bartletts' *finca* were renowned for their conviviality and companionship, usually drawing a dozen or more thirsty and hungry members of the local diplomatic and business communities. Occasionally the event would be graced by the presence of His Excellency, the British ambassador, and his stately wife, who lent a continental air to the occasion.

There had been plenty of drums and flourishes and long dresses in my first assignment in the British Crown colony of Trinidad and Tobago. And though social life in Bogotá was not quite so ostentatious or demanding, there were frequent dinners and receptions at the ambassador's residence to which even the lowest-ranking officers were invited. All of this new living style made for rather heady stuff for a young woman, still in her twenties, from the north woods of Wisconsin.

The more informal Bartlett luncheons began with drinks in the garden and would often go on through most of the afternoon until sunset. Madeleine's French background showed up in her good cooking, but her charmingly erratic Trinidadian ways made me often wonder just when lunch would make it to the table. Despite little help and a rather primitive country kitchen, she did a surprisingly good job. She offset these culinary handicaps by enjoying rum punches with her guests, predating the style of the carefree Julia Childs. Her guests often joined her in the kitchen to chat her up during their breaks from various lawn games.

Guests also casually took walks down a dusty, country road to a nearby Spanish colonial village, sometimes to pick up additional supplies for

Madeleine's luncheon preparations, other times just for the exercise. The village consisted of a few ancient dwellings, randomly sited around a charming little central "plaza" and interspersed with some seedy-looking *tiendas,* or open shops. These were usually "guarded" by a few sleeping dogs. At the far end of the picturesque "plaza" was an old adobe church, white with red-tiled roof and two ancient bell towers. This otherwise tranquil scene was broken by the blare of Latin music from one of the shop radios. I sometimes wondered if the little church got equal time for solemn services or was merely a decorative leftover from the days of the *conquistadores.* I never saw the church open or in use.

Trevor and I liked to roam around the hills and woods abutting the Bartlett *finca* for some quiet time. Once we were discovered in a verdant cul-de-sac by the hyperkinetic and omnipresent Bartlett children. Later, whenever I saw them they would ask when we were getting married! Even to this day—many, many years later—the Bartlett "children" still communicate with me from England. After inquiring about my health, they invariably ask as to the whereabouts and welfare of Trevor, always referring to him by his surname, which has a slightly British ring to it.

Apart from our country outings, sightseeing, and visits with the Bartletts, Trevor and I spent many a pleasant Sunday evening playing bridge and having buffet supper in the downtown apartment he shared with another young American businessman. On one such occasion when Trevor drove me home, he had no sooner switched off the engine than he suddenly and aggressively grabbed me by the wrists in a lustful maneuver that both shocked and frightened me. It was neither loving nor caring. Indeed, I felt as though I were under attack from a complete stranger! I shouted "NO," abruptly pulled away, and freed myself. Then, having managed to open the car door, I bolted into my apartment building without another word, leaving Trevor to ponder his behavior.

Alone in my apartment I pondered what had provoked the man. Had I unconsciously become a tease in a quirky sort of way? I knew one thing for certain: I wanted no more *mano a mano* confrontations with someone who I thought genuinely cared for me, as I did for him. It seems I had a lot to learn about men and their passions.

It didn't take too long for me to realize what had really gone wrong. First, despite months of dating we had failed to communicate. We clearly enjoyed each other's company and showed it with deep but restrained affection. Yet we had failed to put our feelings into words, never discussing our basic beliefs, values, hopes, dreams, and desires. Second, the relationship had rested on far too many assumptions, and even these had never been put into words. Without some serious dialogue, the pantomime was going nowhere.

Third, and most important, it was clear that neither of us seemed to have the necessary skills—or was it just common sense—to examine, analyze, and assess the meaning and potential of our relationship. Without some conclusions, how could we ever advance to a common understanding?

And if I was the faith-rooted person I liked to think I was, why hadn't I prayed over the matter for guidance? Was I so questioning of the relationship as to fear God's negative response? To some extent I had been carried away by the romantic foreign environment and was acting mainly on my emotions, not using my head, not listening to my heart of hearts. There was that unspoken distance between us on the subject of values and religion, which figured in my shock at the time. I had spoken to him of my Catholic upbringing and convent school education, and I had assumed—among my long list of childish assumptions—that this was sufficient to indicate where I stood and how I might behave.

I didn't think it was necessary to make a formal declaration to the effect that I did not believe in premarital sex any more than I believed in abortion or capital punishment. I was too shy to say I believed in a God who created me, loved me, expected my love in return, and my love for my neighbor. I was keenly aware that I was answerable to my Creator for all my actions. I assumed that he understood all these things and, indeed, I would have been keenly uncomfortable making such declarations, just as surely as he would have been to hear them.

Trevor didn't realize how fortunate he had been that night. I had refrained from following the advice of an ancient nun in college who had warned "us girls" that if a man were to make an "untoward advance" (not further clarified) we were flatly to declare: "Unhand me, man, I am a temple of the Holy Ghost!" No kidding! Nonetheless, I might well have found some appropriate moment in our months of dating to clarify my basic beliefs and values for Trevor in my own words. The theology might be good, but such sermons hardly seem appropriate in the middle of a date.

Bogotá, Colombia, 1947–48

Further on my long list of misguided assumptions, I had thought that if Trevor really cared for me he would come right out and say so, thus providing the opening to go more deeply into the subject. I remained old-fashioned enough to believe that it is up to the man to initiate the proposal. That never happened. For two college graduates with responsible jobs and promising careers in international affairs, neither of us was behaving in an intelligent or mature manner. He may have been just as uncertain about his future and whether to advance or end the relationship as I was. Obviously, if neither of us had yet learned how to analyze and assess issues to reach sound conclusions, we were ill-prepared to apply the process to our admittedly different careers.

While the relationship with Trevor failed, at least it enabled me to grow up. I not only matured from the experience but—quite apart from the emotions—I gained intellectual insights applicable to my career in diplomacy. My first two assignments in the consular and commercial fields had been straightforward and rather elementary. But I knew from observing embassy colleagues in Bogotá that any future assignments would be more demanding. They would require analysis of complex political and economic situations and involve vital U.S. national interests abroad. They would call for mature problem-solving, crisis management, and sound policy recommendations to Washington. In addition, I told myself that I had better start drawing more heavily on my college course in logic if I was to advance in the Foreign Service. Forget about serious romantic relationships, because in those days regulations required me to resign if I married.

Not long after the episode that ended the affair, I was mercifully transferred from Bogotá back to Washington and eventually to Europe for the first time in my life, which had long been a dream. The wisdom and knowledge I took with me from Bogotá to future assignments could be summarized as follows:

Avoid all assumptions. Search widely for all the facts in any given situation, look for common interests, try to define goals, and then move step by step to find agreement on them. Define major differences; find ways of bridging or eliminating them through compromise or alternatives. Discuss issues in an orderly, progressive manner within a reasonable time frame. Employ subtlety, humor, and wit. Try to end any discussions or negotiations on reasonably good terms without giving offense or arousing hard feelings.

Still more lessons: Remember that successful marriages are not made, nor binding agreements or treaties reached, based mainly on mere assumptions and hopes. Frank and honest exchange of views is necessary. It is called negotiation. Making a deal in personal relations is seldom based solely on knowing glances, even embraces, except perhaps within the Mafia where issues (even life and death) can be settled by a mere gesture or glance. And while my Italian got good on my first European assignment, it never got that good!

The final lesson: If one claims to be religious, or just wants to imitate the Christians, Jews, or Muslims, each of whom likes to think they have a monopoly on communications with God, it is useful to say a prayer or two along the way for a good outcome to any discussion or negotiation. In difficult or doubtful situations, Christians sometimes pray to St. Jude, the patron saint of seemingly hopeless causes.

A few months after I left Bogotá, I learned that Trevor lost no time in meeting and marrying a Canadian girl, also introduced to him by Jimmy the Brit! She had been working in Bogotá as a secretary with a Canadian oil company, and they left for Venezuela on his next assignment. Over the many years he has written to me occasionally about his family, career, and travels, and I have responded in kind. At my age I will be darned if I'll seek a professional opinion as to the significance of this extended correspondence. I can say, though, that I found Trevor more eloquent at writing than he ever was in speaking. Even his penmanship was good!

FOUR

Milan, Italy, 1949–51 (Vice Consul)

Having left Bogotá some months short of a full tour because of health problems, I returned to Washington for a full medical checkup, rest, and recuperation. It took less time than I'd feared, and before long I received the long-dreamed-of assignment—Europe.

My new posting was to Milan, Italy's financial and commercial capital, which fit well with the training and professional experience I had gained in my first two posts, especially Colombia. Milan was landlocked—subject only to blinding fogs in the damp winter months—with no maritime problems or riot potential to cope with as in Bogotá! The closest water was Lake Como, one of several beautiful northern Italian lakes with any number of adjacent recreational opportunities of which I soon availed myself, from golf to skiing.

The Italian assignment required a language shift from Spanish to Italian, so I was detailed to training at the Foreign Service Institute in Washington before I could set sail for Europe and become conversational beyond the basics of classroom exchanges.

For the first time in my life I boarded an ocean liner, the SS *Saturnia*, an Italian merchant ship. My mother came up to New York from Florida to see me off on my Atlantic crossing, a first in the family, though a cousin had done "the big pond" to Ireland before I was born. My mother and I had a pleasant overnight at the Waldorf Astoria Hotel and some sightseeing before taxiing the next day over to the docks on New York's West Side.

The *Saturnia* was modest in size, accommodations hardly luxurious or even comfortable. Four women government employees bound for European assignments were crowded into one, closet-sized cabin with four bunk beds. Being tall, I was given one of the two uppers. Except for sleep I stayed far away from our tiny cabin as long as possible for fear of claustrophobia. We had to take turns changing clothes in the tight quarters.

There were clearly tradeoffs to this prisonlike, shipboard existence. My first taste of "real" Italian food came aboard the *Saturnia,* and it was addiction at first tasting. Nor had I ever before been offered wine for both lunch and dinner. I tried to restrict my wine consumption to one small glass in the evening, as I was prone to vertigo and never had been a good sailor. Since my introduction to *cucina Italiana,* I have seldom been without garlic, tomatoes, and basil in my home, growing the basil in my kitchen window or on the apartment balcony.

Another new experience offered on board the *Saturnia* was finding myself amid a heavy concentration of Italian males and learning to cope with the new cultural challenges they presented. I would not—I vowed—allow myself to be swept off my feet by the toothy smiles, affectionate glances, little pats, and soft words of endearment that never ceased. As a young American in her twenties, I probably should have been flattered. But being from the north woods of Wisconsin, it was not something with which I was really comfortable. I kept reminding myself that I had managed to hold my own in one Latin environment (Colombia) and could do it again—that is, unless and until something really touched my heart and mind and promised durability.

I learned something else aboard the SS *Saturnia.* Although I was only a low-ranking U.S. vice consul at the time, it was customary for any U.S. government official to be treated with deference by ships' captains at sea. Or at least it was in those days. I drew the captain's table and, somewhat out of character, did little talking. I just smiled and enjoyed the food, which must have intrigued my host.

On the second day at sea, as dinner was ending, the captain inquired if I would like to go up to his quarters for a *digestivo,* which when explained sounded quite harmless. But rather than take a chance, I quickly signaled to one of my cabin mates seated at the next table while simultaneously telling the captain that I knew one of my friends would also enjoy seeing his quarters. She was smiling sweetly at his side before he had time to answer. Rising to the occasion, he took both of us by the arm, gallantly escorted us out of the dining room, and confidently led the way up to the bridge deck and his quarters.

As we admired his spacious and well-kept digs (impressive compared to our crowded and poorly ventilated small cabin), the captain poured us drinks from a tall, narrow bottle containing an insipid-looking yellow liquid with a fancy label identifying it as Strega. "Do you know the meaning?" he inquired in his accented English. "Witch!" he said, grinning through his perfect Italian teeth and leering in my direction. Immediately defensive, I thought how dare he call me a name. Then I realized that "Strega" was Italian for "witch" and the name of the liqueur. Indeed the label carried a sketch of some old hag, All three of us enjoyed a hearty laugh.

As I was wondering if my throat would ever recover from the first scorching swallow of this witch's blowtorch, the captain was refilling our glasses. After handing them back to each of us, he slipped his arms around both our waists and alternately snuggled his chin against our cheeks. I edged sideways, as did my friend. As his hands began to wander, we both pulled away from his embrace and lunged for the door. Pushing hard, we were out on deck, squeaking out schoolgirl thank-yous as we fled. We breathed in the welcoming sea air, far more refreshing than Strega, I thought.

We spent the rest of the trip to Genoa avoiding the continuing advances of both master and crew. I avoided returning to the captain's table, which, while perhaps rude, made life easier. Nor did I ever touch Strega again—a real fire hazard if I ever encountered one. A few years later I learned that if you want to go in for syrupy, yellow, Italian after-dinner drinks, try Limoncello, not Strega. Though it lacks Strega's firepower, it still delivers a punch and is said to be preferred by Italian nuns!!

When I learned more about Italian after-dinner drinks, I tended to prefer one favored in Rome and offered by restaurant owners once the check is settled. It is Sambuca, a licorice-based drink usually served with a few coffee beans floating on top. They are for chewing, if you are so inclined. In Tuscany the natives like their own Vin Santo (literally, holy wine), fortified dregs from Chianti and not all that bad, strong and neat like cognac, and free from the sickening syrup of Strega.

While on my first Atlantic crossing on the *Saturnia,* I enjoyed a few dances on the rolling stern of the ship. My partner was a tall blond Nordic type, who appeared to be traveling with an older woman, though she was never introduced as either mother or other. It could have been a form of mutual self-protection, especially if he was, as rumor had it, gay and maintaining defenses. In addition to the occasional dance, which I thoroughly enjoyed, I spent most of the voyage walking the decks for exercise, vigorous exercise at that. I may well have been pegged as in training for the Olympics, but I needed the exercise to offset all that good Italian food.

Land Ho: Italy and Cultural Attractions

Docking in early morning Genoa presented a wonderful sight. The air was cool and there was the slightest mist rising around the hilly city and woods beyond. The sounds and noises of people and machines on the wharf were memorable. Italian longshoreman yelled at one another in a dialect that could hardly be understood by a beginner like me. The waiting relatives of the disembarking passengers were pressed deeply against the barricades trying to get a first glimpse of returning family. There were loud shouts back and forth from ship to shore. I quickly learned how much language and conversation, with never-ending gestures, mean to Italians. I loved it and have ever since. The Campari liquor people once published a dictionary of Italian gestures—good, bad, and slightly naughty—well worth reading to learn what all those shrugs and arm lifts mean.

The consulate had sent one of its trusty drivers to meet me at the port of Genoa and drive me up to Milan, a pleasant ride over the picturesque hills and valleys (before the age of superspeed autostradas and tunnel after tunnel). We rushed through Genoa without so much as a brief tourist stop to admire the architecture and monuments. That would have to come later.

So I was pleased when we made a brief luncheon stop at the Certosa of Pavia, a Carthusian monastery begun, I was told, in the mid-fourteenth century by Lord Visconti, one of the Sforza rulers of Milan, in fulfillment of a vow made by his wife. What an introduction to the history and art of

Italy! The Certosa mixes both Gothic and Renaissance design and is regarded as "one of the richest and most wonderful monuments of the world." Italians may be given to exaggeration, but the place was overstocked with white marble statuary—sculpture of emperors and mythological figures and hundreds of saints and martyrs.

Never had I seen anything like the beauties of the Certosa's architecture and decoration. I wondered how the monks who lived there hundreds of years before shut out these distractions to pray, or were they continually inspired by them? I had much to learn. So I said a prayer of thanksgiving for my new assignment and the opportunity to see the wonders of Italy.

As we came up onto the Po River Valley to Milan, I made out the unforgettable silhouette of the city and its towering cathedral (Duomo) on the skyline, with the Alps behind. It was a vision I wanted to retain forever.

Milan was a big and bustling city. It still bore signs of its early occupants and conquerors—the Romans, the Goths, the Spaniards, the French led by Napoleon, and, more recently, Hitler's legions followed by the liberating American troops of World War II. Over the centuries, Milan had seen it all, located as it was on the major trade routes to North, East, West, and Central Europe. No wonder its strategic location had made it a financial, commercial, and communications center.

Milan is not the typical, sunny Italian city most tourists seek. Instead, it is a rather forbidding city, with dark, soot-stained stone buildings, narrow, crowded streets, and a tight circular town plan with remnants of medieval fortifications. As I came to know the city and its people, I found the Milanese, people of obviously mixed ancestry from occupying forces, proud but united. When speaking of their city, they would often take a step back and draw themselves up to their full height (especially in talking with a tall American woman). Then in their quaint, French-influenced dialect, they would say something that sounded (in phonetics) like "Milano aye puh poo," meaning, "our town is the best—without comparison."

Temporary Housing

On arriving in Milan, I was taken to a hotel just three blocks from the cathedral, situated in a large square, the Piazza Missori—like the U.S. state of Missouri but with a distinctively different pronunciation (Me-SOAR-ree).

While the name sounded and reminded me of the States, the site was a long way from anything familiar to a green American who had arrived in Europe only hours earlier. Piazza Missori had been heavily bombed during an American air raid in August 1945, leaving a darkened crypt, half-standing walls, and a truncated remnant of the bell tower of a church that had once dominated the square.

Directly behind the ruin was a newly constructed Hilton hotel, the Cavalieri, meaning knights or horsemen. From the piazza one could clearly trace the swath of destruction the bombers had cut through the city, mercifully just out of range of the Piazza Duomo, with the famous and fabulous fourteenth-century cathedral that so distinguishes Milan.

The Cavalieri was the first completed part of a triangular-shaped development project by the famous Vatican-connected construction company, the Societa Immobiliari. This was the same company that ten years later, with the help of a distinguished Italian architect, built the Watergate complex in Washington, D.C., famous because of the political intrigue during the Nixon presidency. The other two sections of the Societa Immobiliari development on Piazza Missori—an office building and apartments—were still under construction when I arrived. Appreciating its central location, I immediately put myself on the waiting list for an apartment.

While temporarily lodged in the hotel I was awakened each morning before my alarm rang to the banging and grinding sounds of the construction crews. Located on a courtyard, my little twin-bedded room had its own early morning noises: the loud opening and closing of heavily cased windows, the grating of heavy-duty Venetian blinds, and shouts among the chamber maids, with the occasional shaking out from above of a rug or mop into the courtyard below.

My hotel housing situation became intolerable, and I wondered how I could endure the delay before the apartment side of the building was completed. The hotel room service of cafe latte and a hard roll did little to brighten my morning outlook even though I tried to perk things up at breakfast by adding a California navel orange, which I would buy from a street vendor the day before.

Once dressed and ready to face the world, I would stop at the hotel front desk to ask the clerk when he thought the apartment side of the Cavalieri complex would be completed. The Italians are great storytellers, very imaginative and probably at their most dramatic best when they haven't a clue what they are talking about, like the status of construction in their own building. Yet I persisted.

"*Fra poco, fra poco, signorina, bisogna spettare, ma non molto*" ("Within a short time, dear lady, you just have to wait a little"). This vague reply was always delivered with the broadest and most phony of smiles. The clerk was always dressed in his fine tailored livery, tails over striped pants and crossed gold hospitality keys on the jacket lapel. One could soak up just so much of that charming, false palaver about construction progress. He did stop saying "*Pazienza*" when he saw my eyes flash in annoyance.

Our exchange went on with deadening regularity until the day the builders put up a sign announcing the completion of the apartment complex. I wasted no time that day, extending my lunch hour to check out of the hotel and move into my new apartment. It was only an efficiency, but the outside exposure, air, and light were a great improvement. I now had a kitchen, a good-sized living room with an alcove and couch that converted into a bed at night, and my own maid, who cooked lunch for me.

The move was simple. In those days, after only two previous posts, I had acquired little baggage. It was only in Milan that I started to acquire things, as Foreign Service officers are wont to do in their many and varied travels. My first purchase was the obvious: a painting of that initial and indelible view of Milan, silhouetted against the sky of the Po Valley.

Perhaps feeling my oats as a Foreign Service officer in Europe for the first time, I "commissioned" this oil painting from a little artist who peddled his wares against a church wall across the street from the Consulate. Modest as was his place of business on the street, he seemed to have talent. But his first two attempts to capture the Po Valley focused too heavily on the crisscross pattern of the rice fields and drainage canals and looked more like a tick-tack-toe board game. On the third try he got it just right, with huge oak trees hanging over a small stream, along with some mulberry trees, where the caterpillars made cocoons that formed the basis of the Como silk industry. The final rendition of the painting was in delicate tones of blue, green, and earth. It became and remains the centerpiece of my living room.

From an antique shop I picked up two old heavily scrolled gilt mirrors. They completed the first round of the modest decoration scheme for my new apartment. Other small acquisitions were easy: flatware, hand-crafted Italian majolica dishes, and linens. I finally had my own home, and in Europe!

On the Job and Getting to Work

As I remained in the Cavalieri complex, I continued to enjoy the same daily walk from Piazza Missori to the American Consulate General some six blocks away. Not surprisingly, the bombed-out portion of the piazza remained an untouched eyesore throughout my stay in Milan. Italians are notoriously slow to start up and complete construction projects. Indeed, they themselves refer jokingly to anything under construction as San Pietro, a reference to the Vatican, which seemed always to have one part or another under heavy scaffolding while Holy Years, new Popes, canonizations, and millions of tourists came and went.

I continued to look forward to my daily walk to work in Milan, even in the darkest of winter days, as it never failed to offer adventure of one sort or another. I would pass along two blocks of arcades that fronted massive, Mussolini-style buildings of gray stone. Then the street opened up like a stage setting on the wonderful spectacle of the Duomo, the cathedral in the city's central piazza. It was invariably crowded with people crossing this way and that with no fixed pattern; others stood in small groups, deep in animated conversation and deal-making. Hundreds of pigeons either fluttered through the air or gorged themselves on scraps carelessly dropped by pedestrians.

Rome (I later learned) had its "wedding cake" in the Victor Emmanuel monument leading to the ancient Roman Forum; Milan's "wedding cake" was the Duomo. With its many eye-catching statues and spires and its massive splendor, it was by far more impressive than Rome's and merited all the unrestrained "oohs" and "ahs" the tourists gave it.

In my several daily walks across the broad expanse of the Duomo piazza, my feelings would alternate; one moment I was completely lost in the crowd; the next I was an active participant in the vibrant life of the city. Though I crossed the square four times a day I never tired of the experience or the complex feelings it aroused in me. The constantly shifting cast of characters and the rhythms were exciting. The Milanese are essentially business people, always busy and on the run to make a buck, or rather a lire. Make that *mille lire,* given the rate of exchange and the frenzy to build capital in those postwar years.

Lessons in Italian Culture

Once I had crossed the square in front of the cathedral, my mood changed as I faced a serious cultural challenge. Inside the galleria was a veritable reviewing stand of male observers sipping their morning espressos and cappuccinos at little bistro tables on the open terraces of the cafes.

This magnificent glassed-in arcade was comprised of two broad, intersecting pedestrian walks two city blocks in length. The galleria joined the Duomo piazza at one end to the La Scala piazza at the other. The male observers clearly found entertainment in critically eyeing the shape, dress, style, even "potential" of any woman who passed by. Unaccompanied women were prime targets of attention. And any foreigner, especially a tall American, was singled out for more audible comment.

I came to dread the experience. Occasionally I would skirt the galleria by taking the narrow streets on the outer sides of the galleria, but they were noisy and congested and I was often running late to work.

"Don't let it upset you," an Italian woman friend counseled. "It's when the men stop noticing and commenting that a woman should begin to worry; so hold your head high and try to strut a little as though you enjoyed it. Or just ignore it altogether."

The onlookers from the terrace bars in the galleria were less troublesome in the afternoons and evenings, when mixed couples were there to enjoy afternoon tea or an *aperitivo* and occupied with their own business or flirtations.

I found that one way of running the galleria gauntlet in the mornings was to fortify myself at the Motta or Alemagna bars at the edge of the Duomo piazza. The double cappuccino and croissant (*cornetto*) would provide me with the extra energy I needed to keep my head down and run a determined and undistracted course through the galleria to the American Consulate beyond.

Milan, Italy, 1949–51

I could never explain why it seemed easier to contend with in the United States, even be amused and enjoy the hoots and whistles of construction workers on a city street. You could grin and be on your way. Perhaps it was the difference between simple, redneck male appreciation and highly sophisticated, overcultured Italian male appraisal—something much harder to deal with, especially for Americans new to European manners.

Had I known when I was in Milan what I learned some fifty-five years later, I might have quit the U.S. government, made a deal with Motta or its competitor Alemagna, and beat Starbucks to the punch by starting up Italian coffee bars throughout the United States. What a missed career opportunity, to say nothing of the missed millions!

Instead, I kept plodding along as a vice consul in Milan but with little vice to show for either my own awkward efforts or the more artful advances of my pseudo-admirers or detractors in Milan's galleria.

Research and Consulting on Trade and Investment

What did I do in the way of work when I finally got out of the Galleria and passed the Scala piazza into the Via Case Rotte (Broken Houses), where the American Consulate was located on the second floor of a large bank building? My assignment consisted largely in receiving and advising Italians who had started up manufacturing businesses after World War II and wanted marketing information on exporting to the United States. Likewise, I received and advised visiting American businessmen interested in trade and investment in Italy. They were few and far between in those days.

An even greater volume of inquiries came daily through the international mail from firms in the United States wanting information on doing business in Italy. The Department of Commerce in Washington also sent official market survey requests. At the time few marketing journals or publications were available to business.

Most of the inquiries required research and consultation with local sources if we did not already have the data in our files or in our heads. Over time we developed a useful body of information and expertise. Because it was unusual for women to operate in the Italian business environment at that time, I frequently took one of my three able male assistants with me on calls to Italian corporate offices and manufacturing plants.

While we kept busy with commercial work, the bulk of activity at the Consulate General in Milan in the 1950s involved consular affairs. The consular section always worked at capacity delivering visa services to Italians, at times with people lined up in the hallway waiting their turn for visas to the United States. Consular staff also attended to U.S. citizens requiring passport and registration services.

We had a few other people at the Consulate handling U.S. library and cultural affairs. Others worked in a restricted area that we were neither to discuss nor visit because they were obviously engaged in intelligence work of sorts. Much of it may have been left over from World War II when the United States was in thick with the *Partigiani,* the partisans who served the Allies well, working secretively behind enemy lines close to the border with Switzerland. World War II had ended only a few years before my arrival in Milan, as attested by my occasional encounters with U.S. occupation currency still in circulation.

Milan Fair

Preparations for and attendance at the annual Milan Trade Fair, held in the spring, kept my little economic and commercial section busy. The United States usually took part, as did other countries, mounting a national pavilion to show off our place in world trade, especially our trade with Italy. Important U.S. firms also exhibited their products individually. In addition, the Milan Fair attracted increasing numbers of U.S. buyers and importers of Italian goods, who frequently sought out consulate staff for additional guidance and advice.

Washington sent an official U.S. delegation to the fair each year. The delegation would include the American ambassador, who came up from Embassy Rome with a few members of his staff. One had to arrange and endure far too much protocol and ceremony, but there was no easy way of escaping it.

It was in connection with the Milan Fair, I think, that the Italian Rose Society approached the U.S. ambassador's wife, saying they would like to name a new rose variety for her. She was enchanted and inclined toward accepting the honor, but wanted to know more about the rose's characteristics. The society informed her that the flower was a delicate shade of pink, a hearty early bloomer, and most important, did well in beds. The ambassador's wife was reported to have smiled and replied that the characteristics suited her well, and the society could move forward to name the rose for her.

Given the volume of economic and commercial inquiries we received at the American Consulate in Milan in those postwar years, we realized how dependent Italian business was on government sources for trade information. Although we often lacked concrete data on marketing opportunities in the States, we made our own best estimates and calculated guesses, at times even stretching our imaginations until we could verify our responses. As our Italian business visitors seldom questioned our opinions or returned to the Consulate to complain about trouble they might have encountered, we assumed that we were not too far off the mark.

Our Italian callers would often come bearing samples of their products, such as highly decorated ceramics, ball bearings(!), opera glasses, foodstuffs, and wearing apparel. Knitwear was especially popular. Things got a bit tricky when our visitors would inquire about differences in regional tastes and where they might best locate their distribution offices in the States, a country they knew to be large and diverse. It was on such delicate points as these that I would refrain from speculating and suggest the callers personally visit the United States, beginning with getting a visa and making the trip. Yet few of the start-up businesses at that time had the financial resources for such expenses.

Though it was possible for us in those early postwar days in Milan to get by on common sense and imagination, this would not at all suffice today. Not only have international commercial services developed in the meantime, but foreign manufacturers and exporters to the United States have become more sophisticated and professional. Most are well traveled and better able do their own research and marketing. Conversely, American firms have become better acquainted with European and other world markets and have less need to depend on government services.

Milan, Italy, 1949–51

Bitter Rice and Sculpture of Note

One of the more interesting trade inquiries received in Milan during my years there came from the U.S. Department of Agriculture seeking data on Italian rice production and exports. Was Italian rice competition for U.S. rice growers in the Carolinas or Louisiana, I wondered? One never asked; you simply answered all of Washington's varied inquiries, whether or not the motives behind them were clear.

It was about that time that the famous Italian actress Anna Magnani was playing in what became a movie classic, *Riso Amaro* (*Bitter Rice*). Besides making my way in downtown Milan to the Italian Rice Growers and Exporters Association for the requested data, I felt I had to see the real thing. I asked one of my staff to take me out to the rice fields in the Po Valley. Indeed, the local scene was just as Anna had portrayed it in the movies—barefooted (and nearly bare-busted) women in water up to their waists plodded through the sodden fields harvesting the rice. But hardly any were as gorgeous as Magnani.

Ah, Hollywood, or in this case, Cincecitta of Rome. These were poor, peasant women scratching out a living under the cruelest imaginable working conditions. Presumably modern technology has since transformed the system, and women have found less onerous modes of work.

Another rather routine part of my job at the Consulate in Milan involved preparation of documentation, called consular invoices (an authentication process), on certain shipments to the United States. It had been rather routine work up until the time I was visited by the representative of an artist named Giacometti living in Lugano, Switzerland, which was in our consular district. I found the attenuated cast bronze figures for which the sculptor was becoming famous to be rather weird, little knowing their eventual value. If I had, I would have asked for any flawed rejects from castings that might never have made it onto the international art market. What a souvenir that would have been!

But I was not very art savvy in those days and hardly saw the potential for something that seemed so grotesque and unreal. Yet Giacometti's sculptures were to become prized by the cognoscenti of the art world. His Swiss agent visited the consulate several times during that period, until the invoice practice was discontinued.

Milan, Italy, 1949–51

I continued to find the reporting requests from Washington excessive and unnecessary. I was visiting more factories and industrial plants than I could count. Among these were Pirelli tires and tubes and the San Giovanni steel works, both just north of Milan; shoe factories to the southwest; woolen mills to the northwest; and Olivetti and Fiat works on the road to Turin. Somehow no one in Washington seemed interested in Ferraris in those days, even though I secretly harbored some personal desires. But neither Ferrari nor Alfa Romeo nor other Italian automobiles of note were up to full commercial production so soon after the war.

On the other hand, the manufacturing of motor scooters had taken off and they were selling well. These auto substitutes were buzzing about the streets and threatening the lives of both drivers and pedestrians. Yet the majority of Milanese were walking in the city and taking trains between cities.

My "Bella Yella" Studebaker

Although I walked to work, I felt I needed a car not only for weekend recreation but for traveling about Italy and seeing the sights. So I eventually imported a rather handsome two-door Studebaker coupe, an exact copy of the car my old beau Trevor had in riot-stricken Bogotá. Mine was a brilliant canary yellow. So in a play on the two languages we called it the "Bella Yella." Soon after its arrival I became extremely popular, with people in and out of the Consulate begging to borrow it or ride with me, as cars were still scarce on the roads.

One of my first trips was to Rome for the Holy Year—a long weekend and a few days' leave. When I stopped for gas somewhere between Bologna and Florence, a group of nearly a dozen locals gathered around the car. A small child kept pulling at her mother's dress and repeating, "*Guarda, momma, una donna che guida*" ("Look, mom a woman driver!").

Back in Milan I met a young American student, an aspiring opera singer studying at La Scala. As he claimed to play golf, I was delighted to have him share the drive up to the Villa d'Este golf club at Lake Como and partner with me for a game. I soon learned that his singing was far better than his golf. But I could hardly knock an American escort. I was coming to realize that I was too tall, and perhaps too American, for the majority of Italians I met, except for the Visconti family, who were out of reach as aristocrats or spoken for. I had done little better than attract the local car import dealer, whose interests were more in driving my car than me; so our relationship was short-lived. Eventually I found that driving over weekends to the lakes or the Alps with American colleagues from the consulate—even if they were young women like myself—proved less problematic.

I made one very serious mistake regarding lending my car to friends. My Italian teacher, a serious, hard-working, and likeable Swiss-Italian woman, asked if her Swiss husband might borrow the car for a weekend run into Switzerland to see his family. Feeling the need to reciprocate her many kindnesses to me, I said yes.

Subsequently, I learned to my dismay from one of my ever-vigilant and protective Italian office assistants that the teacher's husband had abused the privilege. He had crossed the border into Switzerland safely enough. But on returning to Italy he was detained and questioned by the Italian police for "smuggling Swiss watches into Italy," which presumably he had. Usually the cars with CC (Consular Corps) or CD (Diplomatic Corps) tags—which mine was—were subject only to the most perfunctory of inspection by border police.

I never learned the full circumstances of his case, even how it finally turned out, though I suspect he was required to pay a fine. I also suspect the details were deliberately kept from me because my trusty Italian assistant, Alberto Morabia, who did all the negotiations, had sweet-talked the local authorities into a quiet settlement. Surely he and probably the Italian officials wanted to avoid involving me directly and the certain embarrassment that would have caused an American official as well as the consulate. After all, this was a time when Italy was deeply dependent on American aid for its postwar recovery.

I learned two lessons from this episode. Do not lend your private property, in this case, the Bella Yella. And when abroad, always remember that you are a U.S. government official and always in the public eye—a situation that can interfere with one's private life.

I had much earlier seen for myself how artful Morabia could be in dealing with the local authorities in time of crisis. One very foggy winter morning when I was driving to work, there was a sudden heavy thud against the car. A cyclist appeared sprawled across the hood of the car, looking me directly in the eye through the windshield. I was terrified that I had injured him.

Within seconds a huge crowd from the Duomo piazza surrounded my car, with everyone shouting and pointing at me: "*e la culpa de la signorina Americana*" ("the American lady is to blame"). As a policeman picked the poor soul off my car, I could see his raincoat was shredded and his bicycle awkwardly bent.

"Come immediately with me to the American Consulate," I said to the policeman and the injured cyclist. And surprisingly they did. Morabia quickly took over, promptly dismissed the policeman after forms were dully filled out, and negotiated a quick "no fault" settlement with the cyclist, a Pirelli employee en route to work, as it turned out. Morabia gave him cash on my behalf for a new raincoat and bicycle; then promptly had him checked out by a doctor—bruises but no serious injuries. This was one of the best and quickest diplomatic negotiations I had ever witnessed, with lessons learned from my Italian employee!

Morabia later told me that because he was Jewish he spent much of the war years hopping back and forth over the Swiss border to keep a few steps ahead of the Gestapo during the German invasion. He had obviously learned a lot of tricks during a trying time in his life. It was Morabia who had designs on buying the Bella Yella once I was transferred, and it was also he who suggested some remodeling to expand the car's interior.

The idea appealed to me, as the car was only a two-seater but with an excessively large deck of wasted space between the back of the front seats and the rear window. It was one of those 1950s Studebakers, about which people annoyingly joked that you couldn't tell the front from the back. So as only Italian artisans can do, they carved out a good portion of the deck and installed a small bench seat perfect for one adult or two children. It was beautifully done in beige leather and looked as if it had just come off the assembly line.

I agreed to sell it to Morabia on condition he take delivery in Paris. This allowed me to see more of the continent before departing Europe for Washington and my next assignment. I had three good friends who wanted to accompany me on a trip through Switzerland, Germany, Holland, and France. So we crowded into the Bella and made the trip with the three slimmest in the front seat. When we came to the castles on the Rhine, I took the jump seat in the back, where I curled up on pillows and enjoyed the view.

We dropped off my Italian secretary in Holland for her train ride back to Milan and another passenger in Brussels; the third accompanied me to Paris on the final leg before delivering the car. We rolled the Bella Yella right into Place Vendôme in the heart of the City of Light and treated ourselves to the comfort and elegance of a first-class hotel. I felt I could afford it, having sold the Bella. We further rewarded ourselves with some smooth French cognac, which had the desired anesthetic effect after the long, hard drive over the Alps and across Europe.

Export Controls against the Soviet Union

The story of my assignment to Milan would be incomplete without describing my work on export controls, which provided useful experience for further assignments. Washington requested us to run "end use" checks on U.S. exports of strategic materials to Italy. Those were the days of economic warfare against the Soviet Union.

The U.S. government had certain assurances in hand before authorizing outbound shipments, but it was never completely certain that the goods would actually arrive at the declared destinations. Our main objective was to prevent U.S. shipments to Europe from being diverted to the Communist Bloc. Seemed simple enough, but shipments could easily be rerouted at transfer points.

One day, Milan received a cable from Washington regarding some machine tools going to a new factory in a small town just west of Verona, near the foot of Lake Garda in north central Italy. The paperwork sent to us seemed perfectly in order, but we were asked to do an on-site inspection. I took one of my Italian assistants in a consular car with a driver for the two-hour trip to the factory of destination.

After a delicious lunch of Lake Garda trout and a bottle of local Valpolicella wine, we set out to the company in question to meet with the manager. Yes, they had ordered the equipment; they had all the relevant papers, and yes, this was how they intended to employ the machine tools and integrate them into their production line, for which they had orders, also shown to us. We were shown the new part of the factory where the imported equipment would be installed. It was a large new building with concrete floors and totally empty. It certainly looked to us like the future home of the machine tools from the United States. As everything seemed to be in order, we thanked the company officials, wished them well, and went on our way back to Milan to cable our clearance to Washington.

Not more than two weeks after our business trip to Verona, we were notified by Washington that after the machinery had cleared the port of Genoa, it had somehow been rerouted by train into Austria and onward to a destination in what was then Czechoslovakia!

The Italian firm was either in on the deal and had been paid off for playing the decoy, or it was an honest victim and may have been cheated out of a legitimate shipment by crooks along the way. Fortunately I was not blackballed for having been misled. It seems the rule of export control work was, "you win some; you lose some." But not everyone is fortunate enough to enjoy Valpolicella and Lake Garda trout along the way.

Encounters in Switzerland

My brother, who was with the U.S. Air Force in the States, notified me while I was still in Milan that he would be in Europe within weeks, leading a group of young American cadets from the U.S. Civil Air Patrol in glider training in Switzerland. I wanted to get up there to meet him, but I was a bit hesitant to undertake the drive over the Alps alone. Even though it was a day's drive from Milan to Geneva, I discarded the idea of taking the train because I knew the car would be useful in Switzerland.

So I asked Armando, one of the younger drivers at the Consulate, if he would help me with the drive and I would see that he got back to Milan by train. By then I would know the road and hoped one of the American secretaries might take the train up and accompany me back to Milan. Armando was delighted to help me drive, and off we went. It wasn't until we reached Geneva late that afternoon that I realized we would have to overnight, because my brother would not be arriving until the following morning. I hesitated to send Armando back on the night train.

We found a reasonably priced, old-fashioned inn on the outskirts of Geneva. As I had commissioned him for the job, I felt obliged to pay all expenses. When I explained this to him, he reacted as though he expected no less! Yet I was certain this was a totally new experience for him. As we were on different social and economic levels—he an Italian driver at the Consulate at a relatively low wage, and I an American official at a much higher salary—his reaction surprised me. Still, we went on to have a delightful dinner with excellent Swiss wine and then repaired to our respective rooms. Within a short time I heard a knock at my door. I opened it to find Armando, clearly expecting to be invited in. Shocked at his total misunderstanding of the trip and my intentions, I told him in no uncertain terms that he had better go back to his room or I would call the manager. He padded back on down the hall like a scolded child. I wondered if he had seen too many movies about rich American women and European gigolos. If so, he had it all wrong in my case.

I then realized that I had not been as observant or intuitive as usual. Back in Milan at work in the Consulate, Armando had not only smiled at me often but smiled with subtlety, which I had not taken the time to interpret. Nor had it ever occurred to me to want to date one of the consulate's drivers, unusually tall and good looking though he was. On reflection I wondered, yet again, about acquired snobbery in the Foreign Service.

Armando's appearance at my door that night in Geneva was absurd, and there was no point in discussing it then or later. When I saw him the next morning I only hoped he had slept well that night, though I didn't dare ask him. He was very quiet, even sad, and couldn't look me in the face. I fear I may have made him feel unworthy or inadequate, and I cringed at my lack of charity. He would simply have to get over it.

We quickly checked out of the hotel and left for the airport to greet my brother and his entourage of young American cadets. It was all too brief, as the Air Wing of the Swiss Army was waiting to load them all onto buses for the road trip to Gstaad, the training site. "See you later," my brother said airily as they drove off. I wondered if he was really happy to see me or had other plans for a vacation in Europe.

"Men," I muttered to myself as I took Armando to the railroad station. I gave him a sisterly hug before he boarded the train to Milan. He waved a limp goodbye from the coach window as the train moved out of the station. I hoped he would shake off any fantasies he might have had or feelings toward me.

Several years later when I returned to Milan and visited the Consulate, some of my old friends among the local employees eagerly asked if I had seen Armando. More important, it seemed, they asked if I had met his wife, who was also working there.

"You will be surprised," they all said, which made me curious. Then I met her—an English-speaker from New Zealand, tall, with dark hair, and to make the resemblance complete, her name was Jean! I realized then what a crush Armando may have had and how rejected he may have felt when I put him on the train back to Milan. Yet his New Zealander clearly made up for whatever loss he may have suffered. How often do we find carbon copies in life?

Beyond "Romance" to the Ski Slopes for Fun

Milan was fun in many ways. I had not skied since I was a child, but I gamely told my new Italian friends that I knew how. So I was invited to join them on a trip to St. Moritz—my first winter adventure in the snowy Alps.

The afternoon of our arrival we took the ski lift cabin (then a novelty) up to a dizzying 5,000 feet. My friends quickly and correctly pegged me as a neophyte with no downhill skiing experience. They suggested I try out the practice slope before taking off on the two-mile-plus run back to the village. I looked at the practice run, a short U on the side of the mountain and calculated that going down one side would provide sufficient momentum to carry me almost back up the other side to a point close to the start of the main downhill run. I tried it and managed not to fall. My friends were surprised and impressed and said, "Follow us." Off they went, zigging and zagging downhill in tight, controlled turns.

In Wisconsin when I was growing up and skied "our way," we never made downhill turns. Our method was all downhill, but short hills or U hills, like the practice run at St. Moritz I had just managed to navigate. Also, back in Wisconsin we skied Norwegian style, that is, off ski jumps. We would climb up on improvised scaffolding with skis slung on our backs, stand up on the top deck, attach skis with improvised bindings,

slide down the short artificial slope, jump, land, and if successful, continue on down the hill, "letting the cat run out." Toward the end of the run
we would make a brief telemark to stop. Then we would climb back up the
hill with skis on our backs or laboriously sidestep up, and do the run all
over again. There were no mechanical lifts or fancy turns on the run
down. In Wisconsin it was jumping for distance, not racing against a
clock as in the Alps. There was a world of difference. And it would take
me time to learn the difference, the essence of which was a succession of
controlled turns.

Not surprisingly, I was a mess trying to get down the mountain that
first time at St. Moritz without breaking a leg or running into another
skier. I would ski laterally, fall back against the slope to stop, get up, and
repeat the ugly performance all over again. I took a horrible spill at one
point, lost both skis and spent what seemed hours retrieving them and
putting them back on. Instead of controlled turns I was getting down the
mountain through a series of barely controlled falls. My friends had long
since gone off and left me to find my way down the mountain and back to
the hotel. And well they might have. Their presence would have embarrassed me even more.

I did not meet up with them until suppertime at the lodge, and only
after a long hard soak in a hot tub. They were polite enough not to discuss
my failings but gently suggested I enroll in a skiing class not far from the
hotel. Frankly, my body was too sore the next day. I had all I could do to
window-shop, have tea at the leading hotel, and get a good night's sleep
before we returned the next day to Milan.

The next venture to St. Moritz I went alone and stayed at an entirely
different hotel. It was alongside a baby ski slope with a T-bar lift, where I
spent much of the day eavesdropping on an instructor who was teaching
some children. I got enough of the hang of it to reduce the number of
pratfalls. I was still embarrassed, because the kids learned faster and were
better than I.

I noticed an attractive family also staying at the same hotel—a stunning young matron, nattily dressed, as were the many youngsters she had
in tow. It was my first introduction to European high society. The young
matron, I learned, was none other than Diane von Furstenberg, the fashion designer. I never knew whether all the kids were hers, as I never got

up the nerve to introduce myself, given my still ungainly performance on the slopes.

Until I became more proficient I vowed not to rejoin my consulate friends. On weekends I would go off on my own to places like Cortina d'Ampezzo or Sestriere, the resort the Fiat motor company had built in the lower Alps above Turin, where the 2005–6 Winter Olympics were held. On one such trip I drove to Turin, left the car and boarded a bus for the resort, expecting to arrive in time for dinner in the early evening.

As luck would have it we were within twenty miles of our destination when we found the road completely obliterated by a small avalanche. Fortunately we had missed seeing it come down. Those were the days before cell phones. We sat in the chilly bus, about twenty of us, until 4 a.m. the next morning when a snowplow arrived, dug us out, and freed the road to Sestriere. The people at the hotel must have alerted the local authorities when we failed to arrive as scheduled.

I survived that trip, I am convinced, only because I had in my hand luggage a small Christmas panettone, the sweet brioche type holiday bread filled with candied fruits, together with a small bottle of brandy. Sharing only with my seatmate, we got through the night. Since that experience, I have seldom traveled on skiing expeditions without a few provisions for such eventualities, especially brandy.

It was only after these repeated private training sessions that I felt qualified as a "dangerous intermediate" to rejoin my consulate friends on skiing outings. About that time I was "adopted" by a smart young Italian who was working in the visa section of the consulate. Attractive and well-dressed, she came from the upper crust, the daughter of an Italian admiral.

Would I join her and "a friend" going to Zermatt the next weekend? Her friend turned out to be an American businessman in the shoe machinery business in Milan—mature, handsome, and possessed of a high-powered Italian car, rare in those days. The two were reported to be excellent skiers. They also had other things going for them, but I didn't know that until after I had gone with them on the skiing weekend. I also learned after the fact that I was the "disguise," the chaperone. In Italy a threesome presumably made things look OK. I was such a slow learner in many things in those days.

Milan, Italy, 1949–51

Once at the ski resort for the two-day weekend, I saw a lot of the couple during the day and admired their expertise on the ski slopes. But after an elegant dinner in the evening they simply disappeared, and I was left to my own devices. Their après-ski activity was really none of my business, except that we had traveled together. After a few such weekends, friends at the Consulate began to chide me about being used as "cover" for an illicit liaison. Some cover, I thought, as the whole world seemed to know about it!

I never considered myself a prude, but being the third party made me uncomfortable. I knew I had to, and did, decline further invitations. Besides, I learned from the gossips at the Consulate that the man had an invalid wife attended by a nurse at home. Whatever the accepted protocol for playing third party in Italy, under the circumstances I wanted no part of it, though I regretted not having them as role models to study and imitate on the slopes.

Culture at La Scala and Beyond

Fun in Milan also meant going to La Scala Opera House, made relatively easy because one of our local consulate employees had "a family connection" (very Italian) with someone at the Scala. That season a group of us took a box and enjoyed ourselves. Milan the city and La Scala the world famous opera house were both hard pressed to recover after World War II bombings. But they finally managed to return to normal seasons of high-quality performances.

Perhaps the biggest thrill was being present at the Scala for opening night. It was obligatory in the orchestra section for the ladies to be dressed in all white formals, with the men in tails and white tie. We young Americans and some Italians in the upper tiers managed to sneak into our box with somewhat less than the ultra-high dress standards of the social elites. We also kept a very low profile during intermission but did a lot of observing.

One of our biggest thrills was attending Gian Carlo Menotti's premiere performance of *Il Console*. It was modern, innovative, and especially evocative, as we ourselves were engaged in the very same work that was being pilloried on the stage. Personally I preferred the old standards such as *La Bohème*, *Madame Butterfly*, *La Traviata*, and *Rigoletto*.

While my reasons were rather flimsy, if not trivial, I took a deep proprietary interest in La Scala. For one very brief month I house-sat the very fashionable apartment owned by the Toscanini family on the Corso Venezia across the street from the main park in Milan. The American renters were on vacation in the United States and the task allowed me a break from hotel living at the time. Unwittingly I left my mark on the Toscanini building. Distracted by pedestrians as I entered the narrow drive into the courtyard, I succeeded in bashing the left fender of the Bella Yella against one of the white marble pillars guarding the entrance.

Two of my most memorable experiences in Milan involved U.S. cultural exchange programs. The first was a visit by Louis Armstrong and his jazz band, one of a number of such ventures in U.S. goodwill and public diplomacy missions sent to Europe soon after World War II. The entire consulate contingent—about fifteen Americans and their families and our local staff, totaling around twenty-five—were granted courtesy passes. The performance hardly needed a supportive claque. Held at a downtown theater near the Duomo, it sold out to a wildly appreciative audience, which never slacked in its applause. I had no idea Italians liked jazz that much, but perhaps the dearth of entertainment during the war years amplified the warm reception. I never saw an audience more "gone mad." The more the crowd applauded the more Satchmo and his players laid it on hot and heavy.

For those like myself who had grown a bit homesick—notwithstanding the pleasures of life in Italy—the Armstrong jazz concert was an unimaginable treat and morale booster. A couple of our American secretaries were so carried away with this taste of Americana, they accepted dates from some members of the band who liked to party—and party hard—after the show.

Badly hung over and bedraggled the next day at the office, some of these staffers confessed to having learned the hard way the vast difference between partying among New York show biz people and simple partying "back home" in Po-Dunk, USA. This was still the early 1950s, but in retrospect, it seemed more like a foretaste of the 1960s.

On a slightly different entertainment level was the New York City Ballet, which also came on a goodwill mission to Milan under the same U.S.–

Italy cultural exchange program. The company performed at La Scala Opera House to a sold-out audience. In accordance with the demands of protocol, the American consul general, Joel Hudson, felt obliged to entertain the Italian officials and American tour sponsors who had arranged the performance. Included in his guest list was the Prima Ballerina of La Scala, a Signora de Santis (or something like that). Actually Emerita and "of a certain age," she was no longer performing but was still actively coaching the corps.

During the reception at the consul's residence, a number of us, including wives of some American businessmen in Milan, made small talk with the PB. Did La Scala offer ballet classes to nonprofessionals? we innocently inquired. She hesitated, uncertain if we or our children were the interested parties. We clarified that our interest was personal; we were looking for conditioning or fitness classes for ourselves. A bit put off by our honesty but, being a guest in the residence of the consul general and in a mellow mood with the champagne, the PB responded graciously. She invited us to meet at her studios in the upper reaches of La Scala where "I myself will 'teeech' you." We were overjoyed at the prospect.

The following week, we presented ourselves at her door on the appointed date. There were about eight of us, including some businessmen's wives and some consulate secretaries.

We had been told exactly what to wear—black leotards and a black tank top. That was easy for those of us who were skiers. We simply wore our underwear. But we left our ski boots at home and wore tennis shoes until we could find ballet slippers.

It wasn't long before the Prima Ballerina had serious reservations about our suitability and adaptability, but she felt constrained to keep her part of the bargain in a spirit of good Italian-American relations. Yet Madam PB did not suffer fools gladly, nor would she bend one iota from the strict discipline of her art, even though we were amateurs having a go at it. I feared our adventure might soon break up before we had advanced very far with it. We tried valiantly to master the basic steps and discipline. When we failed, we laughed at ourselves and one another, which of course was hardly acceptable to the PB, the perfectionist. However, even our clumsy efforts provided good exercise—good, hard exercise that left all of us pretty well tuckered out by noontime on Saturday.

Milan, Italy, 1949–51

So we would repair to the nearest pizzeria, where we indulged ourselves in a classic Margherita and a small beer. With that menu, of course, we undermined any benefit we might have derived from sweating off calories before the mirrors at La Scala's barre. Indeed, our mirror images improved little over the weeks we labored. We were losing dedication and purpose, and more important, the PB's patience was running thin. So by mutual consent we decided to draw the final curtain on those months of sorry performance, never to be repeated, more's the pity. However, there are few others in the U.S. Foreign Service or out who can claim to have "studied" ballet at La Scala in Milan.

I returned to my lackluster weekend golf game a few miles north of the city on the courses at Monza and Como. Or I would join a retired American business friend whom I had met in Bogotá. I helped him find and rent a villa on the Riviera for what he called his "sabbatical," to improve his piano playing. There we would hike through the olive groves along the coast west of Portofino. We would lunch in the tiny cove of San Fruttuoso beside an old, abandoned Benedictine abbey accessible only by water or mountain trail. It was much more peaceful and far less exhausting than trying to learn ballet steps.

Arrivederci Milano and Hello USA

My tour in Milan was cut short before my two years were up because word came from the States that my mother was ill and needed me home to help care for her. The Department of State was compassionate in assigning me back to Washington.

There were few immediate openings in the department where my experience and languages would be useful, so I was farmed out to the Italian Desk of the European Section of the International Trade Division of the Department of Commerce. Lesson learned: If the Department of State favors you one way (personal accommodation), you may be "penalized" or short-changed in another (insignificant assignment). But perhaps it was the best they could find for me at the time. Commerce was regarded in the bureaucracy as "backward" and no prize, just a lateral move and hardly a step forward or upward. *Pazienza,* as the Italians say.

Milan, Italy, 1949–51

In a way, the Italian Desk at Commerce was the obverse of the work I was doing in Milan, only less stimulating outside the Italian environment. I fielded direct requests for trade assistance from American businessmen, and while I was able to help them, based on my firsthand knowledge and experience in Italy, the work was dull and the environment downright depressing.

It would not be proper to appraise the intellectual and professional quality of my immediate associates in that office. However, all of them have since gone to God, and I seriously doubt that any of their progeny will ever read this.

I shared the office suite with three men. The one who covered Spain and Portugal was a man of some culture with a first-class mind and an interest in history and art, but he seemed to have given up on life. His only joy appeared to come from good wines and food.

The second of my office mates covered the Yugoslav desk. A former Yugoslav diplomat before defecting, he was a naturalized American citizen who had married a wealthy heiress he'd met at the Sorbonne in Paris. He loved tennis and would frequently take off for the courts on the west side of the Commerce building, just below the White House. Though he was a precisionist who did routine work exceedingly well, he totally lacked imagination or color.

Last was a squirrelly little man, a supernumerary of sorts, who tied up loose ends on a trade agreement and performed odd jobs for the front office. He rode in from Maryland to Washington on an Italian motor scooter he had bought in Switzerland while on an administrative job with the United Nations. He always arrived at the office in a state of dishevelment. When he wasn't out riding his scooter through Washington traffic, he was sound asleep at his desk. I took my chances one day when he offered me a ride on the scooter from Commerce to State, only four blocks away. Fortunately he stayed awake for the short trip, and I arrived windblown but exhilarated.

Also in this same, unforgettable little office of Southern European Affairs was a former Roman Catholic priest who had left the church to marry (uncommon in the early 1950s). He covered Italy at the Commerce Department, and I was to work in tandem with him covering the country until he retired in a few months. The gossipy woman in Central European files filled me in on the details of his checkered background, leading up to his departure from the clergy. Coming from a convent school background, I was shocked by my new colleague's background and uncomfortable in his presence, but I learned to adjust. He did speak excellent Italian, having been educated in Rome.

Weekly staff meetings of the European Division were a relief from the tedium and depression of the Italian Desk and helped lend some sense and coherence to the otherwise unimpressive operations of the regional office to which I was assigned. Actually, the overall leadership of the European Division, along with a few outstanding desk officers in key areas (Britain, Germany, France, and Benelux), did an impressive job of following economic and commercial development on the continent. This allowed me to have greater respect for the European unit as a whole while trying to mute my disdain for operations in my sad little quarter.

Eventually my complaints about the assignment and the uninspiring environment led to my reassignment, this time to Commerce's Export Control Division. The overall quality of personnel there was high, and I was pleased with the change. I learned I was to be groomed for a job in Paris with COCOM (acronym for Coordinating Committee). COCOM brought together a group of West European countries and the United States to collaborate in surveillance and control of strategic exports, to deny communist country access. It was a follow-up on my work in Milan.

The office in Washington was led by two highly intelligent and able government officials, Mishell George and Murray Rennert, who helped offset the unfavorable impressions from my initial assignment in Commerce. Our U.S. Mission to COCOM in Paris was led by another brilliant officer, Sidney Jacks, who came in often from the field.

After several months' training with George and Rennert, I was cleared for assignment to Paris. By then my mother seemed to be improving, and I was free again for overseas assignment.

FIVE

Paris, France, 1953–56
(Deputy Commercial Attaché)

I was assigned to Paris in 1953, when the U.S. government still used ocean liners to transfer Foreign Service personnel to their posts. We were encouraged to take American flag carriers but could also use foreign registry ships. Thus, I gained a head start on my French experience with a fantastic ocean voyage on the *Ile de France* from New York to Le Havre, followed by a pleasant train ride through Normandy to Paris.

About midway on my train trip through the French countryside, as we passed through the village of Lisieux, I saluted Sainte Thérèse with a prayer of thanks for her brief twenty-five-year life of memorable service and sacrifice. For her extraordinarily brilliant life of prayer and counsel to others she was made a Doctor of the Church.

I had spent several months training for my Paris assignment to the U.S. Mission to COCOM. Its offices were located on the rue du Faubourg St.-Honoré, close to the U.S. Embassy and just off the Place de la Concorde.

Upon checking in at the Embassy, I was stunned to learn that notwithstanding all my specialized training in Washington, my assignment had been pulled out from under me and I was shifted to a rather menial job on the commercial side of the embassy's Economic Section! It was, I learned, a classic case of "musical chairs" that sometimes occurs at large posts. One of the men in the Commercial Section saw an opportunity to slough off his dull job and grab my much more attractive assignment to COCOM. He felt he had done yeoman's service, and the system owed him something. He was on the ground, spoke fluent French, was a known quantity, and could and did obtain the necessary administrative support to switch jobs. His gambit never endeared him to me, though I tried to be as civil as I could.

My half-Irish heritage came into play as a result of this disappointment. From my mother I learned how much importance the Irish attach to signs and omens. Thus I suspected that my bad luck in losing a prized assignment and getting a punk one meant that something was not quite right about the Paris tour. And so it proved to the end. Paris turned out to be the most unhappy assignment of my entire Foreign Service career, bar none. I realized I had best be on my guard and stay alert, for the remainder of my stay in Paris.

I pondered whether I should formally protest the job switch to Washington, but I feared I might be branded as a complainer in the Foreign Service. As it turned out, the personnel people in Paris to whom I but murmured my timid concerns advised me to "stand back and realize that you are in Paris, and there are psychic advantages to any assignment here." And there were. So I dragged myself back to my desk and the dull routine I had inherited from that sneak who stole my job.

It suddenly dawned on me how important the nature and quality of my work and career had become to me after nearly ten years in the service and as I moved into my thirties. Not long after that (it was like discovering the first wrinkles on your face), an official notice came in from Washington confirming what had long been understood: that if a single woman officer married, she had to resign from the U.S. Foreign Service—not a single man, only a single woman! That gave me still more pause about this career I had chosen, initially as a war job to do my patriotic duty.

By then both the Marine lieutenant in Trinidad and the oil company executive in Bogotá were fast fading from memory. I only hoped they had found other interests. Moreover, I was beginning to doubt that marriage was in my future. To my dismay I was finding that Paris was really a man's town, maybe even that the Foreign Service was a man's province, at least as experienced in the 1940s and 1950s.

Paris, France, 1953–56

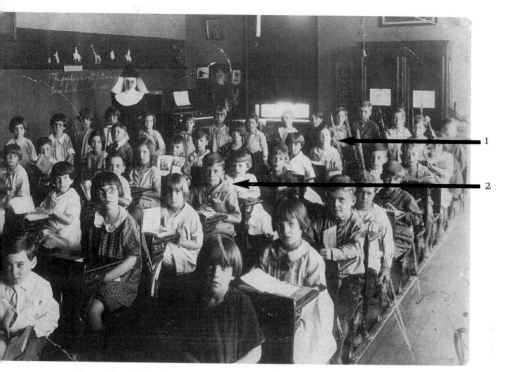

The author before being expelled from first grade. Arrow (1) indicates author; arrow (2) indicates Jimzie O'Melia, the basic cause of both students' expulsion. To left, the Franciscan nun who did the expelling.

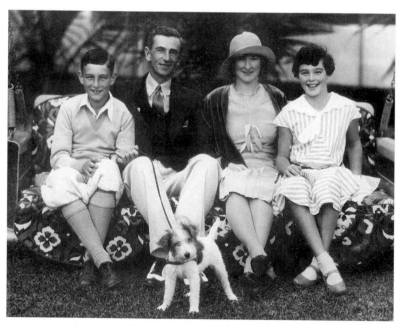

The Wilkowski family in the gardens of the Roney Plaza Hotel, Miami Beach, Florida, Easter Sunday, 1931. *L to R:* Ernie Wilkowski Jr., brother; Ernest W. Wilkowski Sr., father; Mae Dorgan Wilkowski, mother; Jean Mary Wilkowski, the author. In front: "Bugsie," the family's wire-haired fox terrier.

The author in 1947 enjoying the mountain view to the north of Bogotá, after Sunday lunch at the country home of the British consul and his wife and a hike through the foothills with her close friend "Trevor."

The author waving from her Renault Dauphine in a light moment off duty from GATT tariff negotiations as a member of the U.S. negotiating team, Geneva, Switzerland, 1961.

The 1962–63 Senior Seminar in Foreign Policy of the Foreign Service Institute, fifth graduating class, including officials from the Defense Department, Agriculture, Treasury, and Commerce. Front row only, *L to R:* Ray W. Bronez (Department of Defense); Wilkowski; Richard H. Hawkins (Foreign Service); Arthur J. Hazes (U.S. Agency for International Development); Harold Kaplan (U.S. Information Agency).

The Senior Seminar calls on President John F. Kennedy at the White House, June 1963.

Pen-and-ink sketch of Second Secretary of Embassy (Economic) Jean Wilkowski,
done by a member of a delegation from the Industrial College of the Armed Forces
visiting the U.S. Embassy in Rome in 1965 for country briefings led by Wilkowski.

The author after delivering the commencement speech in June 1966 at her alma mater, Saint Mary-of-the-Woods College, Indiana. *L to R*: Wilkowski; Monsignor Joseph G. Kempf, chaplain and professor; Mother Rose Angela, Superior, Sisters of Providence.

Pope Paul VI receiving First Secretary of Embassy Jean Wilkowski in a semi-private audience at the Vatican, November 1966, with attending Canadian cleric.

U.S. Embassy leadership, Tegucigalpa, Honduras, 1968, with Marine security detachment of five troops. *Center, L to R:* Deputy Chief of Mission (DCM) Jean Wilkowski; Ambassador Joseph J. (John) Jova; Administrative Officer Elmer Pittman.

Ambassador John Jova at head of table, with DCM Wilkowski, the country team, and officers of the Honduras-American Chamber of Commerce, Tegucigalpa, 1968.

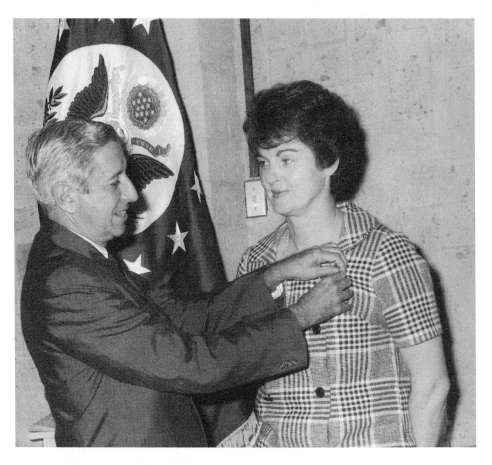

(above)
Ambassador John Jova pins the State Department's Meritorious Service Award on DCM Jean Wilkowski.

DCM Jean Wilkowski as mistress of ceremonies and club chanteuse at farewell party for departing ambassador John Jova and wife Pamela, Tegucigalpa, Honduras, early July 1969.

Chargé d'Affaires ad interim Jean Wilkowski at Toncontin airport in Tegucigalpa, Honduras, July 1969, welcoming General Robert W. Porter, Commanding Officer, USSOUTHCOM, Panama Canal Zone, on delivery of airlifted U.S. disaster relief supplies intended mainly for Salvadoran refugees held in Honduran custody during the so-called Soccer War.

In the shadow of cargo door of a U.S. Army plane from Panama, Chargé Wilkowski and local and church representatives inspect emergency relief supplies.

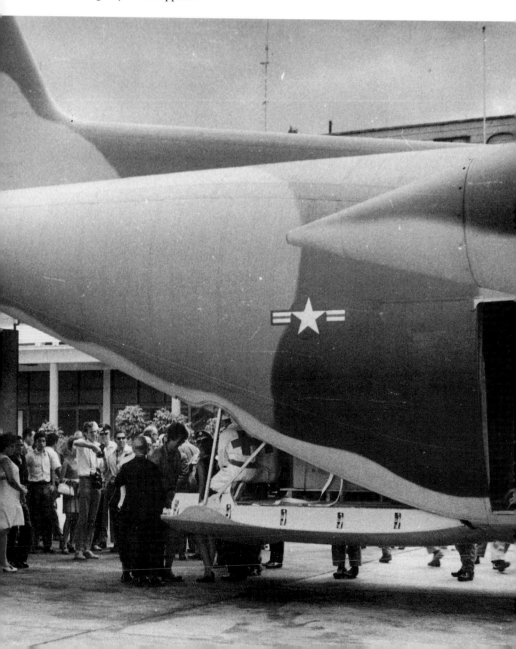

Wilkowski, head of the U.S. delegation to the Fifteenth Assembly of the Inter-American Commisson of Women, held in Bogotá, Colombia, in July 1970, signing the final set of twenty resolutions on behalf of her country.

(opposite - top)
At a reception at the Spanish Embassy in Tegucigalpa, Honduras, July 1969, Honduran President Oswaldo López Arellano listens to Chargé Wilkowski explaining a policy point regarding the U.S. position on the Salvador-Honduras War.

(opposite - bottom)
At a reception by the president of Honduras, the visiting guest of honor, President Anastasio ("Tachito") Somoza of Nicaragua, greets the U.S. Chargé appraisingly before engaging her in diplomatic discussion.

Author with friends
on the steps of the south wing
of her 350-year-old farmhouse
in Tuscany, Italy.

Minister for Economic Affairs Wilkowski at a meeting of European economic authorities hosted in 1972 by the Italian Government at the historic Villa Madama in Rome. Next to her is Ambassador Joseph Greenwald, chief of the U.S. Mission to the European Community in Brussels.

Wilkowski, Minister of Economic Affairs, U.S. Embassy Rome, 1972, being escorted through a machine tool factory in Naples that produced aircraft parts for a U.S. manufacturer.

U.S. Ambassador to Italy Graham Martin, left, accompanying First Secretary of Embassy Jean Wilkowski to Palazzo Malta in Rome in July 1972 to receive the Order of Malta's Cross of Merit with Star for humanitarian assistance during the Salvador-Honduras war. To right, Malta Minister Filippo Spada and Ambassador Armando Koch.

Settling In to a Very Routine Job

Rather than expend any further energy on protesting my assignment, I hunkered down and tried to learn my lowly job in Paris. Although it carried the dubious title of deputy commercial attaché, it did offer management training and experience. I supervised a group of about eight French employees who handled basic economic and commercial research and inquiries and routine French government contacts. The unit churned out World Trade Directory Reports, or WTDs, for the U.S. Department of Commerce and the American business community.

WTDs contained detailed commercial intelligence on (in this case French) firms interested in trade and investment opportunities with U.S. firms. They went somewhat beyond the limited credit reports obtainable from American and local banks. They required detailed research into local commercial publications and directories, often site visits to companies and plants, including interviews with business owners and managers. Our little unit also conducted local market surveys to assist U.S. firms interested in doing business in France.

Occasionally the job offered more surprises and satisfaction than I expected, especially when I was called upon to consult with important U.S. businessmen seeking embassy assistance. I remember meeting the U.S. president of the Levitt & Sons Company, which engaged in major housing developments in the United States. The CEO of Levitt believed the postwar climate of the Paris suburbs might offer investment opportunities. I helped him with site visits, assessment of building and investment possibilities, and some interpretation.

Officials from Disneyland also called at the Embassy to scout out possibilities for duplicating their California and Florida ventures and introducing Mickey Mouse to Europe. These explorations never reached a conclusion during my tenure, but they laid the ground for the company's future investment in France.

On another occasion I received the head of an American brassiere company (was it Lovable or Adorable?). He was interested in teaming up with a French company for the special cachet a French label and address would bring to marketing opportunities. Fortunately, the question of any modeling needs, and by whom, never arose during my official consulting on that case.

Paris, France, 1953–56

The title of deputy commercial attaché carried some advantages. For the first time in my career I had my own secretary to help me with all the commercial correspondence with U.S. and French firms. She was a talented, bilingual Russian émigrée named Madame Eva Dimetrieva, whose past was clouded in mystery. She had fled Russia with what she said were her own jewels—a rather extensive collection, it seemed. She claimed to have lived off the sale of her jewelry until she gained a foothold and steady job in Paris that could support her. She had a son whose name was Frenchified to something like Ditrie. She had put him through university and then helped find him an entry-level job with the Foreign Tourism Branch of the French government. It was never clear, though suggestions were strong from Madame herself, that her son resulted from some shadowy liaison with an American engineer who had been consulting in Russia in the 1920s. He may well have figured in facilitating her job at the American Embassy in Paris.

Madame Dimitrieva was herself a jewel—perhaps even a beauty in her youth. But at middle age when I knew her, she had become plump and plain in a rather drab East European sort of way. She had a lovely speaking voice, an attractive smile, and ingratiating manners, and she taught me a lot, from the mundane to the more sophisticated. In the former category I learned that it was always important—especially at lunch—to butter and eat a small piece of bread before starting to sip on a cool glass of white wine, which she never missed at noontime. I was not yet into wine at lunch, and only occasionally drank a glass at dinner.

Besides charming us all with her Slavic airs, Madame D tended to mother all the junior officers. This extended from correcting our clumsy mistakes in local protocol to hosting an incredible Russian brunch. Every two months or so, after she had saved up enough, she invited three or four us from the Embassy to her little apartment, which she shared with a woman friend in a rather grimy industrial suburb west of Paris. There we were treated to an eight-hour Russian feast beginning at Sunday noon. It was nonstop blinis and vodka interspersed with a wide assortment of cabbage and potato-based Russian specialties, which had obviously taken her many hours, if not days, to prepare.

The East European atmosphere was accentuated by two or three male "friends." Introduced as Russian Cossacks and garbed in native dress, they fiddled, sang, and played the accordion throughout the event, eating copiously between numbers. We American guests tried to help out in the festivities by always bringing several bottles of inexpensive, duty-free vodka and fancy chocolates and cookies from the Embassy commissary.

When my parents were visiting me from the States, I took my father to Madame D's for the Sunday affair. (My mother excused herself because of painful arthritis). When I returned with my father that evening, it was obvious he was feeling no pain, having enjoyed sipping vodka throughout the day. My mother put her foot down against further such outings— "Your father is not a well man." Yet it was clear to me that he had had the time of his life, totally free of any inhibitions.

Dinner at Versailles

During my stint in the Commercial Section, the U.S. Machine Tool Association chose Paris to hold their annual meeting and gala dinner (France was a good export market at the time). When they sought representation from the U.S. embassy, their invitation to the ambassador was passed down to my level.

I soon learned that the machine tool manufacturers' trade association was neither timid nor poor. They rented no less a venue than the Orangerie—a glass-enclosed greenhouse banked with large pots of blooming orange trees from which it took its name—that was an integral part of the Palace of Versailles. The evening was like a fairy tale come alive. Upon arrival at Versailles, the guests were invited to roam at leisure about the beautifully landscaped grounds of the ancient palace of Louis XIV to enjoy open-air cocktails at sunset. Strolling minstrels and sparkling garden fountains contributed to the tranquilizing atmosphere. Later, we were escorted into the greenhouse to elegantly decorated tables with spindly-legged gilt chairs the French favor for their gala events, most notably their fashion shows.

I had been invited to some of those Paris fashion shows, but I was never called upon to facilitate interest in French haute couture. Saks, Bonwit Teller, Bloomingdale's, and the other big name U.S. firms always sent their own buyers, and many had representatives permanently based in Paris. They moved and negotiated in their own rarified commercial orbit and never had need of guidance or assistance from the embassy, not that I would have been their best choice.

The setting at Versailles was glamorous enough for a fashion show, more so than for a machine tools promotion. After welcoming remarks by our hosts, out came waiters in Louis XVI–era attire, complete with powdered white wigs, ruffled blouses, and pale blue satin knee breeches. They marched into the Orangerie carrying huge silver salvers laden with food, course after course, all delicious, to say nothing of the varied assortment of wines, each of which begged for at least a sample sip.

Was I beginning to imagine I was Marie Antoinette, or Madam Pompadour? Well, up to a point, perhaps. And I suppose I was beginning to accept the "psychic value" of an assignment in Paris, which the embassy administrators had been hyping to offset my disappointment with the job switch. Perhaps I could do East-West trade work another time, I thought. Frankly, I don't remember driving back from Versailles to Paris or to my apartment, my evening with the machine tool people was so heady. But I know I must have. I was too low ranking to merit use of an official car and driver for such an evening on the town, or rather, at the palace.

However, I do recall eventually rising to the status calling for official cars in Paris, especially for calls at French government offices, for example when I had to go to the Ministry of Economic Affairs on the Quai Branley along the River Seine. I believe I went only once to the Quai d'Orsay, site of the Foreign Ministry. That beat was reserved almost exclusively for the embassy Political Section.

A Simply Dreadful and Awful Assignment

I went far more often on official business to the Ministry of Housing (*Logement*) for the dullest of my tasks, a basic report on French housing to which I was assigned. I never understood the purpose of the report and repeatedly questioned my boss regarding its need. Was it to be a general sociological and/or economic study? Or an investment opportunity? I spent many a sleepless night wondering if I would ever get a handle on French housing in general. And when I kept raising questions, my boss would simply say, "Just get it done!"

Paris, France, 1953–56

At the time there was the famous Abbé Pierre, who lived on the streets with the homeless and gained worldwide media attention. But try as I might, I was never able to discern why the U.S. government believed it needed a basic report on French housing in the mid-1950s. Could it have been the suburban development executive from Levitt who was thinking of investing in the outskirts of Paris? Was there a political threat from Abbé Pierre and the "Clochards," and were the facts important? The United States had no aid program that might be considering financial assistance to French housing. Washington was mute on the subject, and my boss seemed too timid to query headquarters. I was uncomfortable every time I called at the Ministry of Housing for research and information without being able to explain my mission, *sans raison d'être,* as the French would say. There wasn't even a comprehensive French report I could simply crib and have one of the embassy clerks translate for me.

Fortunately, my major source at the ministry proved friendly and accommodating, perhaps even flattered with the foreign attention, especially as I always made a point of asking about his wife and children, and even took him out to lunch one day, as a minor bribe for his help. Month after month I slogged on, trying to research and write something that might make sense to whomever in the U.S. government had requested the report. I was delighted that my source at the Housing Ministry did not inquire as to any conclusion I might reach in the finished product. He might well have found it full of bad translations and inaccurate interpretations, with even more questions than my own as to just what the U.S. government was up to.

Little did I dream that our ambassador, Amory Houghton, would take an interest in the stupid report. Houghton was a Republican political appointee from the corporate world (Corning Glass) and a large political campaign contributor. He returned his copy of my housing report to my boss, seriously questioning some obscure point. Called on the ambassadorial carpet to explain, I drew heavily on my Irish genes, which were given to blather if not blarney. I somehow managed to allay his petty concerns, even to distract his attention. After all, he came from the glass not the housing industry.

It was only some ten or twelve years later in Rome that I learned from a colleague how to handle such seemingly far-out and questionable requests for U.S. government reports on arcane subjects. Curiously enough, he was assigned not one but five such subjects while on temporary detail with Embassy Rome's Economic Section. He followed a simple formula: introduction and brief description of the problem; social, economic, political implications; significance to host country and region; significance to the United States; policy recommendations and conclusions. I don't believe that any one of his five reports ran more than six pages in length. How I wish I had met this man in Paris and saved myself a lot of grief. They say timing is everything in life.

Sadly, in the course of the several months it took me to finish the French housing report in Paris, I took ill, probably from the nervous strain of the effort. It was necessary to see the embassy doctor, who prescribed exercise, relaxation therapy, and massage. I suppose it could only happen in Paris but the treatment recommended by the embassy doctor came in the form of a Polish ex-cavalry officer who, while not young, was very fit indeed.

Appearing at my apartment door one evening with kit in hand to do his routine, I found his presence somewhat off-putting. In his quaint English, he announced: "First we do the exercise—arms up, arms down, arms to sides; then we do the rubbing." I took the latter to mean massage. After only a few rounds of perfectly discreet "rubbing" with only my shirt pulled up over my back, I decided I could do without his help. Truth be told, I did not feel completely comfortable alone in the apartment with him, old maid that I was becoming. Besides I could do much of his exercise routine on my own and substitute a hot shower on my back for the rubbing until I got back in physical and mental shape after finishing the housing report.

Looking for Joy on the Champs Elysées

With an assignment to Paris, one inevitably thinks of clothes. My mother went "all out" when she heard that "her little girl from Rhinelander, Wisconsin" would be assigned there. Nothing would do but that she take me up to New York and invest her hard-earned savings in a stunning but unnecessary fur coat—Persian baby lamb (broadtail) with mink collar and cuffs! The wives of fellow officers shot me a few looks, but it didn't seem to turn any French heads other than for the customary down-their-noses glance the French can be so good at when it concerns something obviously not *fait à Paris*. Had the working girl stepped a bit too far out of her class? Whatever, it certainly made one mother proud and happy that she was able to adorn her daughter in style for what was commonly regarded as the fashion capital of the world.

The personnel and administrative people at the Embassy (who had so readily assented to my assignment switch) never ceased reminding me of the "psychic" value of living in Paris. There was no denying that Paris is a stunning city, with world-class buildings, monuments, and boulevards. What compares with the Eiffel Tower, the Arc de Triomphe, and Notre Dame? These wonders notwithstanding, my work and life had become routine and dull. Opportunities seemed limited for single women of my age to fit in and make friends beyond visiting museums and churches. Paris in the post–World War II era seemed designed and operated more for a single man's pleasure and enjoyment. Forget about the single woman, especially a foreigner, unless you had some close link into Parisian society, which I did not.

There were exceptions, exceptional exceptions, in fact. The women of the Corps de Ballet at the Lido Club on the Champs Elysées and members of the oldest profession in the world who were ubiquitous in Paris never seemed to lack for companionship in the City of Light. But single, career women (there were no more than three of varying ages and interests in the Embassy at the time) were a unique and neglected, even a puzzling, phenomenon to the natives in the Paris of those days. Things became easier in the 1960s, it seems, when young adults started to move about more freely, first in the United States and then in Europe, followed by the expansion in tourism worldwide.

So what did single women "of a certain age" do in Paris back in the 1950s? The career types tended to stick to their narrow interests of history and art, while the many American secretaries at the Embassy paired or grouped together and moved easily about the city. Life for them seemed much pleasanter; they were younger, enthusiastic, and dated across national lines. They satisfied their interest in learning French with many young Frenchmen interested in learning English. More important, they wisely took their work less seriously than I did.

Paris, France, 1953–56

My efforts to produce a housing report soon reduced my outward appearance to a tight-faced grimace with glassy eyes. In contrast, while the many young American secretaries put in a full day at the typewriter (before computers), they learned a lot in Paris about makeup and hair styles. They also enjoyed greater work flexibility and personal vitality. Many enrolled in a popular course at the Sorbonne called French Civilization for Foreigners. The course offered such side advantages as time before and after classes for drinks and snacks in groups at sidewalk cafes along the Boulevard San Michel on the Left Bank.

Much of my free time after work or on weekends was spent in long walks in the Bois de Boulogne. Though not dangerous, these outings were a bit tricky as regards timing. One had to take care to stay near large, open areas and avoid late afternoons after dark when the Ladies of the Evening took over, with their hip-swinging marketing crawl, or just stood under lights in the most arresting of costumes. Yet the Bois was convenient for me, being located just a few blocks from my apartment in the 16th arrondissement. Was I flattered to be mistaken for one of the "girls" and be propositioned by appraising heads leaning out the windows of slow-moving cars? It was attention of a sort, but it was definitely not the sort I wanted. I learned to keep my eyes fixed straight ahead, walk fast, even stop abruptly and take an inordinate interest in passing wildlife, from chipmunks to poodles on leashes.

Making Friends in a Convent on the Left Bank

I took to using my free time as prudently as I could, intensifying my interest in museums and concerts, and in the many religious shrines in Paris, starting with the magnificent Notre Dame Cathedral. One weekend I made a pilgrimage to five Marian sites in the city, including the rather obscure church of Notre Dame des Victoires and a popular shrine called simply Rue de Bac on the Left Bank. I must have walked more than ten miles that weekend, returning to my apartment with sore feet and aching back, hoping that the pilgrimage may at least have served as reparation for past sins.

Totally disregarding Talleyrand's admonition (*"surtout pas trop de zèle"*), I became overzealous during that religious pilgrimage period. I was deeply struck by the crowds and aura surrounding the Marian shrine at Rue du Bac and kept going back to the place. It was located just off the Boulevard St. Germain on the Left Bank and right across the street from the landmark department store, Le Bon Marché. I went often to both places in my spare time: one for shopping for things I didn't need, the other for meditation.

Rue du Bac is the convent where Christ's mother Mary is supposed to have appeared to a religious order of the Daughters of Charity in the mid-nineteenth century. I found the place comforting and restful, even inspiring, in the midst of life's challenges. One of the French nuns guarding admittance at the gate suggested I meet *"L'américaine,"* a reference to an American nun stationed there. It turns out this was the world headquarters of the Daughters of Charity. Indeed, there were nuns there from every continent who served as country representatives to the French motherhouse, or headquarters.

Eventually I was introduced to Soeur Marie Basil (Sister Mary Basil), named for some strange reason for a fourth-century Eastern Church theologian. She was a mite of a woman, hardly five feet tall and nearly lost in the bulky blue wool habit of the order, modeled after French peasant attire in the Middle Ages. The Charities wore a distinctive headdress, before the 1960s, when Vatican II changed dress and customs. It was a heavily starched, white, winged bonnet, whose points extended beyond the nuns' shoulders. They looked as though they might take flight, which is why I often called them "airplane nuns." It was a pity they abandoned that eye-catching outfit.

Mary Basil and I soon became fast friends, incongruously paired as we were: I almost six feet tall and she at least two heads shorter and nearly swamped under her starched white *coiffe*. Whenever I arrived at the convent gate, the receptionist would loudly exclaim, *"Ah, La Grande Américaine"* or *"La Grande Amie."* It seems they had never before seen such a tall woman.

If I thought I was having cultural and work adjustment problems in France, it was minor compared to the problems of dear Sister Mary Basil. She seemed totally lost in a big blue sea of babbling religious, who filled the Rue du Bac headquarters, all speaking French in various accents. Next to Lourdes in southern France, it seemed, Rue du Bac was the other ultimate

Paris, France, 1953–56

destination of thousands of pilgrims from East and West. Mainly poor and travel-weary, the pilgrims would fill the inner courtyard between the massive convent gates and the chapel, waiting patiently to be admitted to the shrine.

Although such a show of patience and devotion would normally be edifying to most onlookers, I was occasionally distracted by the sheer grubbiness of the crowds. Most of these shabbily clothed pilgrims were poor East Europeans. Cramped together in the courtyard, they were a sorry and really smelly lot from their long journeys and infrequent bathing. Once into the chapel, these poor souls shoved their way up front to get as close as possible to the side altar of the chapel. They sought to touch (but could not) the blue velvet armchair on which Mary is supposed to have sat in 1830 when she spoke to Catherine de Laboure, entrusting to her the now famous Immaculate Conception medal. The Catholic Church honors Laboure as well as Louise de Marillac as saints who, together with St. Vincent de Paul, founded the Daughters of Charity, dedicating the Order to service of the poor.

Many of the nuns at Rue du Bac took turns at controlling the many waves of pilgrims, but Mary Basil was excused from such duty because of her diminutive size. She could easily have been lost in the crowds. Besides, she had a responsible position as U.S. representative to the Order's governing council, and she was doing it alone. Her work involved all formal communications on a variety of subjects between the U.S. Charity Order (which then embraced more than a thousand nuns) and the motherhouse in France, which exercised considerable control. She had frequent discussions and negotiations in French, followed by translations into English and preparation of documents for mailing to the United States. There was no e-mail in those days, nor was cable or telephone much used except in emergencies.

Mary Basil's French was grammatically perfect. But her spoken French was truly offputting, heavily accented as it was with Brooklynese and unmistakably marking her as American. I wondered if her work may not have borne a faint resemblance to how Benjamin Franklin conducted his diplomatic business as ambassador to the French Royal Court in 1785.

As time went on and my friendship with Mary Basil deepened, it became clear why we had become friends so readily. Not only were we foreigners who shared a common American background, but we were both something of innocents abroad, both suffering culture shock. Neither of us had integrated well into the alien society into which we had been thrust. Moreover, there were few among the host nationals with whom we worked to whom we could confidently complain about our problems. But together we could unwind and blow off steam in complete confidence and trust. Although my daily work was mainly with Americans and some French, Mary Basil's was the more difficult, being completely with Europeans, mainly French. Only occasionally did visitors come from the States with a letter of introduction to her.

Petit Déjeuner Fit for a Cardinal

One day Mary Basil asked that our visit be early in the morning right after Mass in the Shrine chapel. She ushered me somewhat furtively into one of the few small "private parlors"—no more than large closets—used for visiting priests and honored guests. She then excused herself for a moment and returned carrying a silver tray with what she must have believed was the equivalent of Ritz Hotel room service. She offered steaming *café au lait* in a silver pot with plump, flaky *croissants* resting on a white linen napkin and delicious berry jam. The service was fine china—perhaps Limoges, possibly a gift to the convent from some wealthy benefactor.

As I was never good at fasting under the old church rules, I made a quick grab for the light, flaky pastry, pushed a corner of it gracelessly into my mouth, and quickly washed it down with a big gulp of the coffee. Ahhhh, how satisfying. I doubted the convent had ever offered such an elegant *petit déjeuner* unless to a visiting bishop or cardinal. But to a single businesswoman, an American at that? *Jamais!* Surely my special breakfast was in sharp contrast to the ordinary peasant fare of the nunnery in keeping with the Order's mission to the poor. I felt nourished in heart, body, and soul.

Over the years I came to appreciate how much dear Mary Basil prayed for me and my entire family. Some more of that touted "psychic value" to living in Paris? I reflected on how difficult it must have been for her, the quaint little American abroad, to summon the courage and find the right moment to approach her rather stern French Mother Superior for the needed permission to "entertain." I didn't put it past her one bit to imply that I was some high-ranking official from the United States.

Later I was able to reciprocate some of her kindnesses with automobile drives away from the convent to the Bois du Boulogne (she loved the roses at the Bagatelle) and to the surrounding countryside. Then some months later, when she confided that she had to have serious surgery without benefit of family or countrymen, I tried to be at her side at a Paris hospital as much as I could. Fortunately she survived, but she had to return to Rue du Bac, which certainly did not have the kind of food and rest she needed for a speedy recovery. But I guess nuns living under such spartan conditions just toughen up and carry on. Many years later when I was back in the States I learned she had died relatively young from cancer. But she rose high in the leadership councils of her order, with frequent travel overseas.

In the greatest of confidence she once admitted she loathed the French convent food. It was starchy and unimaginative—potato-based soups and lots of bread, though with some lettuce, "more than Br'er Rabbit needed," she used to say. She claimed she never touched the wine that came with lunch and dinner, though the French and German nuns reportedly tossed it back habitually. Who knows, it might have helped them get through their days with whatever hardships they had to endure. I urged Mary Basil to try the occasional glass of red wine for medicinal purposes, but she refused. Occasionally I would smuggle some American food and goodies to her from the Embassy commissary. Her favorite was dried prunes to help with all the starch she was getting at the convent.

Housing and Renting Out Rooms

I was without a car in Paris for my first few months there, thus encouraging me to learn the subway system. After my first month in temporary quarters, I moved further out near Auteuil in the 16th arrondissement, said to be a "good" neighborhood. It was a block up from the Jasmine Metro stop and just off Avenue Mozart. Though the apartment was small, it was in a new building with a lovely view overlooking the Bois du Boulogne from the floor below the top, yet called a penthouse. I used to joke that I could watch the horse races at Auteuil—a bit of an exaggeration—

but at least I could see the top of the race track's grandstand, that is until a new high rise went up about a year later, blocking my view.

The apartment had two bedrooms if you included the maid's room in the eaves on the attic floor above me. I didn't need that extra room until I had guests, so I tried renting it out, because it had an independent entrance. Just how I found my tenant I do not recall; perhaps she was a friend of a French employee at the Embassy. She said she was the daughter of a banker in Le Havre and appeared to be a presentable young career woman who worked, she claimed, for the Singer Sewing Machine company. She was away all day. Everything seemed proper and in order for the first few weeks, until I started hearing suspicious noises right above my own bedroom. That maid's room was so tiny, holding only a bed, a small table, a chair and a sink, that the tenant and whoever was visiting her hardly had enough space to walk around the room.

Yet I noticed that one of the persons overhead was much heavier of foot than the other. So I made a tentative and not too charitable assumption. Then when I heard the bedsprings squeak riotously one evening I made another, but very firm assumption. The next morning without further ado I informed the tenant that she would have to leave at the end of the month, which was but a few days away. She did not question my sudden decision, though I felt like the prude I certainly had become. This was Paris in the 1950s, after all.

Never Buy a British Car in France

I soon tired of using the Metro not only because of its noise, but I thought the dust and grime unhealthful, to say nothing of the unsavory characters and beggars who loitered about the stations. I particularly disliked the suggestive graffiti on the walls of the underground. I realized yet again I was fast becoming a critical Old Maid—and in Paris, of all places!

I decided to change my lifestyle, lift my morale, and buy a car. At about the same time two fellows from the U.S. Embassy in London appeared at the Paris Embassy trying to sell theirs, a sporty little Hillman Minx. I failed to probe or even question why these chaps would bring a car from England to France to sell, whether it was a lemon, or whether servicing would present problems. Such questions never entered my head on seeing this little beauty—smart and snappy looking. I think it was called a cabriolet, in dove-grey with two doors, red leather upholstery, and a black roll-back top that could go all the way to the rear of the car or just half way which gave it an oh-so-rakish appearance. It was love at first sight whether it ran well or not.

Naturally I bought it. As it turned out, the little car was in the shop almost as much as it was on the road. It had real start-up problems and I had to figure it all out in French with the not-too-pleasant, know-it-all, gruff French mechanics, located some distance from the Embassy. Moreover, their shop was on a hill, which was always a challenge. There I was, a rather starchy American speaking passable French, arguing about spark plugs and carburetors on an English car with a pair of grease monkeys speaking French patois and loaded—I was convinced—not only with wine but off-color jokes and guffaws as they occasionally shot furtive glances in my direction. It's a wonder they ever got the little Hillman to move again, but miraculously they always did.

I dearly loved that car. It was all appearance but had a certain *je ne sais quoi* and looked so very right for Paris. I lived about a twenty-minute drive from the Embassy. I would sashay out of my apartment each morning, take the elevator down to the basement garage, and gun up the Hillman, always relieved when it made it from basement to street. If it was a nice day, I would roll the top partway back and drive along the Seine toward the Place de la Concorde and the Embassy.

It was easy driving in Paris in those days, with limited traffic throughout the city. Not too many people owned cars. I would pass the Eiffel Tower to the south and drive on down through the underpasses (yes, including the one where Princess Diana was later to lose her life), past the glorious Pont d'Alexandre, le Champs de Mars, and Napoleon's Tomb. Then a sharp turn to the left took me into the Place de la Concorde. I could always find a parking place there, an accommodation that would be unheard of today.

Daily Routine

My workday always began with a light breakfast in the Embassy commissary. I seldom cooked in Paris and kept only cheese and fruit in the refrigerator, with hardly any other provisions or staples in the apartment. Indeed, I wondered why anyone would cook with all those wonderful restaurants throughout the city in the days when meals were still affordable.

Yet I hated eating dinner alone. Lunch was no problem. The Embassy had a cafeteria that was always crowded and friendly, with shared tables. If one got bored with the cafeteria, a short walk a few blocks away would take me to an Embassy Annex on the rue de la Faisandrie that had a smaller but more Frenchified menu. And some fine little corner cafes and hole-in-the-wall bistros were within walking distance.

I tried to overcome my solitary splendor in Paris by seeking community. I started up a badminton group in a basement recreation room at a Protestant church on Quai Branley. It was hardly suitable, as the ceiling was a bit too low. But play we did, and it was sociable and enjoyable until the church decided it had other needs for the space. Or was it really because we resisted their entreaties to join their religious ranks? I then joined the local badminton league at the French Racing Club. After improving my game, I was emboldened to enter the French national championship at the Club. In my first match I drew a perky little maiden of no more than sixteen years of age from Le Havre. She slipped onto the court in a *de rigueur* white sports dress (with a small strand of pearls!). She whipped me mercilessly, knocking me out of the competition in the first round, bringing an abrupt end to any joy I was hoping for from badminton.

And then there was golf. I never joined a club, but I did drive out to the suburbs of Paris, first to a small public course along a tributary of the Seine at a place called Marly; then further west to a town called St. Germain en Laye. Their local club had been opened to the nearby SHAPE military headquarters. It took some pulling and hauling with the U.S. military to get on the course, only to find it hardly worth the effort, as my free hours never seemed to coincide with those of the American guys who played there. Or else they arrived with prearranged foursomes. So I went back to Marly and occasionally ran into some old duffer who was alone and would reluctantly accompany me for a few holes and then poop out— from fatigue, he said. Later I found another golf course some distance east of Paris. The drive was long and unattractive through the entire city and then some distance beyond into the countryside. Generally I played these courses alone, as embassy people who played were few and always seemed too busy with their families.

Another problem was that few European women played golf in those days; when they did it was usually as beginners with their husbands. The mostly French men who played golf were not about to invite a single woman, and a foreigner at that, much less an American woman who swung a club like a professional, even though I thought my game hardly extraordinary. Men could sometimes be uneasy about being overshadowed in sports by a woman. Besides, the French were just too proud to take a chance. And I was just too shy to invite myself to play with them.

I played the ritzy club of Saint-Cloud just west of Paris, but only once and then with a friend from the States. I found it not only difficult with its hills, but pricey and hardly the place to make friends or pick up games. It was almost British in its stuffiness.

After experimenting with solo weekends in the country, I met up with a group of Catholic legal students and faculty from the Sorbonne. We enjoyed wonderful family-style meals at the Paris apartment of a French widow patroness, somebody's aunt as I recall. We also had the occasional picnic in the Forest of Fontainebleu, a nice Sunday drive south of Paris.

In time I took a Sunday morning art class at the Louvre and have as a memento a magnificent book on all the world-class treasures housed there. In sum, and for some unfathomed reason, it was difficult for a foreigner my age to make friends in France in those days. It never occurred to me to see a psychiatrist, but that might have helped.

As for the embassy, there were only a few couples my age in the Economic Section or other offices that I came to know with any degree of closeness. All seemed preoccupied caring for wives and small children after work and on weekends. One memorable exception was a young couple in my neighborhood whose hobbies were canaries and horses. They let the birds fly freely about their apartment, a distraction to conversation to say nothing of the damage done to draperies. But they were a family of means who also bought and raced thoroughbred horses in Europe, often shipping them to the States. Friendly and kind as they were, it was a bit difficult trying to fit in with their lifestyle.

Another exception was a very dear family in the Embassy who seemed more foreign than American, consisting of a wife from Latin America and a husband who had spent his early years in Italy, where his father was an opera singer. He had various special assignments in the Economic Section, as well as being a part-time labor attaché. We shared an enormous office in a remote rear section of an upper floor next to the freight elevator, which said something about our rank and importance in the embassy hierarchy. Our shared office was distinguished by a massive old Oriental rug with several huge black ink spots in the center. When we weren't writing economic reports, we took turns playing Rorschach Test, trying to interpret the meaning of the ink stains. When it became clear that the embassy administrative people were not about to have the stains removed or get us a new rug, we stopped complaining about it. The rug was so ratty and old we concluded that it must have belonged to one of Benjamin Franklin's successors who had accidentally toppled his inkwell and quill pen while chasing his secretary around the office.

I really didn't mind sharing that barn of an office with that kind, loving father of three (or was it four?) girls, a compassionate and understanding person. He would help me plot ways to either dump the housing assignment (which made no sense to him either) or finish it in a grand flurry.

My colleague often invited me for Sunday dinner with his Latin American wife and their children in their home in the charming little suburb of Chatou, just west of Paris. It was always a nice drive out to see them and be included in their family. I don't remember if I ever reciprocated (aside from flowers and wine), given my penurious state in the lower ranks. Yet they were the kind of people who understood and simply felt I needed some social life, if not a family, so they more or less adopted me.

My Parents Visit Paris

Within a year of my arrival, my father and mother decided to visit their "children" in Europe—first, my brother, Ernie, and his family on Air Force duty in Wiesbaden, Germany, and then me in Paris. They sailed out of New York aboard the *Queen Mary*, landed in Le Havre, where I met them, and then went to Paris via the boat train. They stayed with me but a few days before taking a train to Germany for Christmas. After nearly six weeks, they returned to Paris totally exhausted, as they were getting on in years.

My brother, his wife, and four children (one just recently born there) were comfortably situated on the second floor of a large old German house. They had some domestic day help, but with two parents visiting it was a demanding household of eight. My mother and father readily took to helping out with the domestic chores but soon found they had become the virtual live-in butler, housekeeper, and baby sitters. It was too much of a strain at their age.

They returned to Paris seeking peace, quiet, and respite, so I tried to make few demands on them. But they soon told me to "cool it" with my overzealous plans for entertaining them on weekends. Over their nightly cocktails they would laugh aloud wondering, "Where do you think Jean is going to program us this weekend?" It became the family joke.

My parents wanted to do little beyond shopping at the neighborhood stores for the main essentials of bread, milk, fruit, vegetables, and meat. Loving the outdoors, they also wanted to enjoy the natural beauties of the woods and lakes in the nearby Bois. I soon discovered that, my father rather fancied the various propositions he was receiving from "the girls" on his daily walks. "Imagine, at my age!" he told my mother, somewhat vainly. He was hardly young and dashing but not at all shabby in his gray tweed wool topcoat and affected blue beret. He liked to visit the neighborhood wine shop on Avenue Mozart, carrying his tiny French dictionary. From reports on his wanderings he seemed to have no problems. But then I realized it was not difficult for him to point to a bottle of red wine or even say "encore" when his glass was empty. He made basic conversation by pointing to phrases in his little book, but he was at a loss to get the pronunciation right.

My mother had her own problems with the language. One day she was at wit's end, repeatedly asking directions to "Ave-A-New Moes-Art." After several tries the man trying to help her shouted a knowing "Ahh" and glibly, with emphasis, declared "*C'est ça, Madame, vous cherchez Avenue Mozart,*" smooth as silk and without pronouncing the final *t*. "That's what I kept saying," my mother shouted in English to the man. Dear, smart, outspoken Irish woman that my mother was, she never could have become a diplomat (those genes may explain why it took me so long to be recognized as one). Her red hair and Irish temper signaled little patience with the flights of fancy language, lofty airs, and superior manners of the French.

We had a truly glorious spring in Paris that year. So my father returned to his favorite hobby and first love—gardening. Undaunted by the small apartment's narrow terrace, he set to work building two large planters, filled them with soil and fertilizer, and then transplanted into them a variety of colorful plants. We had celebrated my parents' return from Germany with much champagne, leaving any number of empty bottles cluttering up the kitchen for disposal. My father ingeniously took them out on the terrace, piled them up in a pyramid in the corner, then collected rocks and bricks and soil whenever we went out and made a rock garden, albeit modest, on the very narrow terrace. With small potted plants artfully placed at various levels, it was a delightful creation and helped to brighten our lives.

The rock garden lacked only a waterfall but I drew the line there, fearing a leak and problems with the apartment below. Whenever my father murmured something about the idea, I would slowly shake my head, "Nooo." It was on one of these occasions that I heard him say to my mother, "You know, Mae, I don't think she will ever get married, do you?"

All Roads Lead to Rome

In the autumn we left terrace gardening in Paris to make a long promised trip to Rome. The parents might not have been physically up to it, but they could hardly refuse. The real test was for the Hillman Minx. We made it without incident through France and into the Valais of Switzerland, where historic signs reminded us that Napoleon had marched his troops over the Alps and on to Italy in the 1800s. But the Hillman failed miserably in rising to the task. We pressed the little car hard to climb the Alps over the Simplon Pass from Brig to Domodossola, but it balked about twenty-five miles out on the Alpine road, where it would whimper and come to a dead stop like some ornery donkey.

At least three times we rolled back down the hill to Brig until we finally admitted we had a serious problem. We turned ourselves over to Brig's best—and only—mechanic, who may never have worked on a British car before. After a couple of restless nights in a shabby hotel, the car was repaired and we again took off for Italy. By then my mother, who was never sick, had caught a bad cold. During the remainder of the trip, she succeeded in passing it on to my father, who was older and weaker.

Finally we made it to Italy, enjoying Milan and Florence en route to Rome, where we almost missed seeing the Pope. He was still in residence in his summer palace of Castelgandolfo high in the Alban Hills east of Rome. We left our hotel and drove the Hillman out from the Eternal City over the torturous Appian Way (rocky, but great atmosphere). We passed the ancient aqueducts on up to the Castelli Romani, another name for the Alban Hills. But the Hillman, which had behaved relatively well since the Alps, had other ideas. It coughed and whined to a stop about half a mile short of the Papal Palace. So we left the miserable little car, got out, and made the rest of the pilgrimage on foot.

We pushed our way into the courtyard of the palace with about 497 other people. It was a far cry from the grand ballroom of the Papal Palace overlooking Lake Albano, where I had been thrilled with my first papal visit five years previously. I was mildly disappointed because I wanted my parents to enjoy that same experience.

After we had waited some fifteen minutes crammed up against other pilgrims, His Holiness Pius XII appeared on a small balcony above us. In the press of the crowd I had become separated from both parents but they remained within sight. I noticed that my father was deeply moved and was brushing a few tears from his eyes. Then a fine mist fell. The Pope cut short his brief address, moved quickly to give us all the papal blessing, and retired behind one of the open doors along the balcony.

Quietly the audience moved out of the courtyard of the palace and into the piazza of the little village of Castelgandolfo. We three regrouped outside without a word, turned down the cobbled street alongside the palace, and silently returned to our car. Naturally, we had no trouble going downhill back to Rome. I dreaded the thought of facing the Alps again on our return to Paris.

Driving back I reflected on my father's deep emotion. I also noted that he had just caught a cold, or so I thought. I was to learn later that he was seriously ill. Little did I suspect that he had less than five months to live.

Across the Alps in Style

I was still young enough to care about fashion and shopping in those days and didn't miss the chance in revisiting Rome to pick up a few felt hats and some Baroque gilt endtables. This nest of tables was easily upended

in the back seat of the Hillman and the hats scrunched carefully in between the tables' legs, but it left my father with barely enough room in the
back seat. He remained very quiet throughout the drive, while my mother
and I alternated in the front as pilot and copilot. We took a different route
back to Paris, following the coastal road from Rome to Civitavecchia. There
we stopped to see the fortified harbor and sea walls built by Leonardo da
Vinci. We continued along the coast to La Spezia and over to Genoa before
driving on to Turin to take the ancient, historic Grand Saint Bernard Pass
back through Switzerland to France.

While my mother and I talked and joked along the way, I noted that my
father kept his silence, sometimes dozing in the backseat. Well, understandably so, cramped as he was with luggage, which he braced as we
rounded curve after curve on the Alpine road. I was shocked to see how
pale he had become since leaving Italy and wondered how much was due
to car sickness. I felt the sooner we got back to Paris so he could rest, the
better. My mother agreed. So we stepped up the pace and for once the
Hillman responded without balking. We had one more night in the French
countryside before reaching Paris. We stopped at a delightful little inn in
some remote village, where the excellent wine and food raised our combined spirits.

The next day we rose early, making it comfortably into Paris by noon.
But I knew something was not quite right with my father. So we put him
to bed and decreed extended bed rest. Within the week he was back on his
feet and into his walks to Avenue Mozart, his sign-language, and his drinking buddies at the local wine shop. He would sit there from about 10:30 in
the morning until noon and then happily return to the apartment for lunch
and a nap. My mother never accompanied him nor did he tell her about
the nature of his "conversations," just that the red wine was always good.

It was about this time during my parents' visit that I received orders
from Washington that I was temporarily assigned to Geneva, Switzerland,
as a member of the U.S. team engaged in multilateral tariff negotiations.
I received the news with mixed emotions. It was a welcome job change,
yet I felt my parents needed me near them. Neither spoke French. Still,
my mother felt I should go; they could manage, she insisted. Besides it
was a career opportunity for me beyond my humdrum commercial job at
the Embassy. I should go, she urged. Although I had serious doubts about

the adequate nature of their sign language capabilities for any length of time, my mother did drive, knew her way at least down to the Embassy and the commissary there, and some colleagues who could help in any emergency. She also knew her way by car to the English-speaking church near L'Etoile on the Champs Elysées.

Off to Geneva and Tariff Negotiations

So I accepted the Geneva assignment. Within the week an embassy car was at my apartment to take me to the train for Geneva. My father was impressed and insisted he accompany me to the station. I think he fancied the idea of being in a chauffeur-driven car; moreover he was curious—he had never been to the Gare de Lyon on the east side of town. As we said goodbye, I felt sad and began to cry. My father lent me his immaculate white handkerchief, which he always carried tucked into the breast pocket of his jacket. As things turned out for the worse in Paris, this was the first of about six handkerchiefs I requisitioned in coping with our family's problems.

That evening after I had settled back into my temporary quarters in Geneva, I called Paris to report my safe arrival. I was shocked to learn that my father had just returned to the apartment, having spent most of the day riding the subway around Paris—totally lost and unable to find his way back. He probably dismissed the embassy car, feeling he wasn't entitled to using it by himself; or he wanted to see Paris on his own. He had gone without eating or drinking. And that was not good considering those earlier signs of weakness on our Rome trip. My mother assured me things were under control; she could handle the situation. I should not be troubled but should go about my temporary work in Geneva.

So I settled into the wholly new and interesting work of tariff negotiations at GATT (the General Agreement on Tariffs and Trade), later renamed the World Trade Organization (WTO). I was assigned to a small, French-speaking team on the U.S. delegation to handle bilateral negotiations with the French and the European Coal and Steel Community. This was before the Common Market was formed.

I was also asked to be the chief negotiator with the Haitians, which while impressive on paper, involved dealing with two rather uncertain-

looking government officials from the Caribbean who had even less negotiating experience than I. But with guidance from GATT administrators,
we managed to settle a few problems on Haitian exports to the United
States (was it baseballs?) in exchange for a few concessions from them
on U.S. exports. This was my first diplomatic negotiation, though hardly
worthy of the label.

Our U.S. delegation was billeted quite comfortably in the new Hotel
du Rhône, alongside the river of the same name in the center of Geneva.
The U.S. Mission to the various UN organizations based in Geneva had
its offices in the same building, so we had convenient administrative support and communications. The only commute to work was the elevator.

The U.S. delegation consisted of not more than a dozen people, all
congenial and experienced government people on TDY (temporary duty).
They made excellent lunch and dinner companions and good company
for hiking trips to the mountains on the weekends. At last I was living in a
vibrant community—a welcome change from Paris. But my new and very
social life was short-lived.

Before long I received a phone call from Paris that my father was very
ill and needed hospitalization. I had to return to help my mother. Two colleagues from the delegation took me to the airport for the short evening
flight to Paris. When I reached Orly Airport that night, I was so fraught
with anxiety that I promptly got into a heated dispute with two *gendarmes*
who blocked my rush to the exit gates.

"Why was I in such a hurry?" No, I was not a criminal fleeing some
crime, I was on a medical emergency involving my father! That seemed to
make the "flics" even more suspicious to the point, I feared, of wondering
if the health emergency was my own, perhaps mental, as I kept shouting,
"*Mon père est malade, très, très malade.*" This may have been these French
policemen's first such encounter ever with a determined, apparently ob-
sessed American woman. Why, they must have wondered, was my obviously American father ill in Paris and not in the United States. After
several "*Mon Dieus,*" the gendarmes threw up their hands, allowing me to
storm on through the gates to the taxicab stand.

My father was indeed very ill, I learned upon my arrival at the apartment. We bundled him up, I called a cab, and we took him to the American
Hospital in Neuilly. It was hardly "an American hospital" in the full sense

of that phrase, but the embassy assured me it was the best and the closest. After the doctors examined my father, they gave a tentative diagnosis of "some sort of chest congestion." He was to remain there for a week of treatment, they insisted. I returned the next day to Geneva not the least certain how things would work out. My mother looked a bit weary but again assured me she could handle matters, indeed would double up on her arthritis medications and get some domestic help with the apartment.

The following weeks turned into a nightmare. While my father's condition at the hospital remained static and the diagnosis unchanged, with no prognosis, my mother's condition worsened. She admitted herself to the hospital, just down the hall from my father! Was it loneliness and concern for her husband or had worry aggravated her already acute arthritis to the point where she could not handle it alone?

I flew back to Paris a second time to help. Fortunately there were no difficult gendarmes at the airport, or perhaps the ones who had detained me earlier saw me coming and fled. I went immediately to the hospital and my mother's room. I thought she was as much worried about my father as she was suffering from acute arthritis. I myself was exhausted from the strain of it all and stretched out alongside her on the hospital bed. We talked in low tones for a long time. Alternately, I tried to comfort her and rest my own weary mind and body while storming Heaven for help and guidance. Eventually, I tried to get a few hours' sleep that night on the couch in my mother's room. Next morning I consulted the doctors about my father's condition. They confirmed the original diagnosis of congestion of the lungs, yet doubted it was pneumonia or a malignancy. They concluded he needed more time, rest, and care in the hospital.

They told me that my mother could return to the apartment within a day or two and they gave her some new medications. But did they really know? This was the mid-1950s and medicine still had much to learn. Normally the feisty Irishwoman, my mother did not, as she often did in medical consultations, say, "Guess again, Doctor!" So I stayed long enough to take her home to the apartment, and returned to Geneva.

I wasn't back at the negotiation long before I was called back to Paris yet a third time. My father's condition had worsened and he was put on oxygen. My mother was surprisingly strong and reconciled. We both understood my father was nearing his end. There was no weeping or gnashing of teeth. We simply tried to comfort one another. And then I began to send messages through the embassy to my brother so he might come to Paris.

A Death in the Family Overseas

Ernie was back in the United States from Germany on assignment at a Strategic Air Command base out in Montana. He kept trying but was unable to get a military flight to Europe. For two days I kept posting notes on the front door of my apartment and at the Embassy but to no avail. My brother never came. In less than 24 hours, as I watched over my father at the hospital, he slowly faded away and silently eased out of this life to the next. Despite our consent to an autopsy, for some unexplained reason, it was never done nor was any clear cause of death given!

What does a Foreign Service officer do when a parent dies while visiting overseas? The U.S. delegation in Geneva surely hadn't been getting full value out of me, but they had been magnificently understanding and helpful, as was Embassy Paris. One of my colleagues there, a single fellow in the Economic Section, immediately stepped in and took my brother's place. He stood valiantly by my mother and me during that week from the time the hospital released my father's body to the mortuary, on through the church arrangements at St. James in Neuilly, the funeral, and burial at the cemetery in Neuilly at the west end of Paris.

The burial at the cemetery was especially touching. As four unknown French pallbearers carried the casket from the hearse through the black wrought iron cemetery gates, a pair of yellow butterflies escorted the coffin, followed it to the grave site, and briefly hovered over it before vanishing. For a man who dearly loved all of nature, especially winged life and flowers, it was a haunting yet fitting farewell to my father. Since then I never see yellow butterflies that I do not think of him. I reflected that my father would not be the first American to be buried in France. He was in the company of many American heroes, indeed thousands of them resting in American battlefields from World Wars I and II.

I had no regrets about my father's burial in France, but my brother certainly did. Perhaps it was guilt that he could not get a flight over to be with us. Several years later he insisted that I have our father's remains returned to the States! "You can do it," he urged. "That's your work, you know all about it. I don't." Well frankly, neither did I. I was an economic not a consular officer, but I inquired. With the help of superb consular services in Paris, I made all the necessary arrangements through correspondence, so my father's remains could be returned to the United States for burial in his native Wisconsin.

Within days of the funeral in Paris I swept up my mother and took her with me back to Geneva. I exchanged my hotel room for a temporary apartment that could better accommodate the two of us. I used a bicycle to commute to the mission and left the weary Hillman for my mother. By then we thought of it less as a Minx and more of a jinx. But it still got us to a variety of excellent restaurants and good food in the evenings. My mother seemed to be on a sleeping jag, managing a bit of breakfast and lunch in the apartment but otherwise spending entire days in bed, wrapped in my old green plaid winter coat. It must have been her comfort blanket.

Au Revoir, Belle Europe

Within the month, my TDY in Geneva ended and we returned to Paris to wind up my assignment there and pack for our return by ship to the States and a different tour of duty. We flew to Madrid, before taking the boat train to Algeciras to board an American Export Lines ship bound for New York. While in Madrid, a strange thing happened. Like most Americans we resented having to wait until 10 p.m. to have our evening meal. We looked for alternatives and with the help of the desk clerk at the hotel found a restaurant in an old part of town—a cave, or wine cellar. We taxied there at about 8 p.m., still rather late for us, and were alone in the restaurant until a man and woman, obviously Europeans, came in. They were seated on a banquette directly opposite us with a large dance floor between us. We were the only people in the restaurant throughout the meal.

The woman kept staring at us and speaking in a low voice to her husband. I caught enough of her words to identify them as German, which I whispered to my mother. The woman's staring continued. Then rather abruptly, this very tall woman got up from her table, strode across the dance floor to our table, and without so much as an introduction bluntly inquired in heavily accented English, "You are Jean Mary Wilkowski, no?" I was stunned. The woman was a former German exchange student by the maiden name of Anna Maria Seegar who was in my college class in Indiana twelve years earlier, in the 1940s. She had played goalie on our college hockey team.

What a strange reunion in a basement restaurant in Madrid! She introduced her husband and I introduced my mother. We learned they too were going to Granada the next day to see the El Grecos. But we declined their invitation to join them in their chauffeur-driven Mercedes (he was an official with the manufacturer, it seemed). I feared it might be too much of a strain on my mother in her bereavement; moreover, we were already booked with American Express. We did see them briefly again in Granada before final goodbyes, perhaps never to meet again in our lifetime.

Paris on Reflection

It may appear that my assignment to Paris held far more low points than high points, but that would not be completely accurate. Although it may have been short on interesting work (with the exception of the brief detail to tariff negotiations in Geneva), it was long on new opportunities for personal as well as spiritual growth, working through career and personal disappointments, caring for loved ones, and coping with mortality.

Of particular value was my uplifting and prayerful relationship with a new friend and confidante, Sister Mary Basil, a beautiful woman religious who taught me patience and endurance both by example and humor. My faith certainly deepened and was enriched in Paris, as I searched hard for purpose and meaning in life without falling into existential hopelessness and despair à la Jean-Paul Sartre, whose nihilistic ideas were the French rage at the time (*"l'enfer, c'est les autres"*).

Some memorable good experiences stand out. I made a weekend retreat to a convent a half-day's drive south of Paris. By accident I met there a university professor from England, Hilda Graef, a Jew who had escaped Hitler's Germany for Great Britain, where she became a naturalized citizen. At the time we met she had sought the peace and quiet of the French countryside to work on the page proofs of a book she had written—among the first—on the German-Jewish convert to Catholicism, Edith Stein, who was later to be declared a saint and a doctor of the Roman Catholic Church. In the three short days at the convent, when I probably should have been praying more about my own problems, I learned a great deal both about Stein and the author. Graef's life bore striking similarities to Stein's. Both had suffered persecution under Nazism—Stein, even death. Both were converts from Judaism to Catholicism.

Not long after escaping to England, Graef had been caught in one of the many German air raids that devastated London during the height of World War II. Miraculously, she escaped death. Dazed from the bombs and destruction, she wandered aimlessly through the rubble and smoke of central London until she found herself before the rectory of the Jesuit church on Farm Street near the fashionable Connaught Hotel, not far from the U.S. Embassy on Grosvenor Square. She knocked at the rectory door seeking shelter and material assistance. Quite incidentally she also found spiritual help, and it changed her life. She became a convert and went on to become a professor at Cambridge University and to pursue a writing career.

Compared with Graef's extraordinarily brave escape from Germany and the air raid, my own personal and professional problems seemed miniscule, if not childish. The clear lessons I learned that unusual weekend in the quiet French countryside were "chin up" and "count your blessings." Some fifty years later while in Europe, I learned more about Edith Stein. As a declared saint she had become "a hot item" among young seminarians studying at the pontifical universities in Rome. Many were fascinated by her theology and martyrdom.

There was yet another French countryside experience that offered equally strong lessons in faith, endurance, and trust. It happened on a pilgrimage to Chartres. I had made many a weekend trip to Chartres as a tourist alone and guiding visitors from the States. But an opportunity was offered to see and feel it from an Old World faith perspective. A small congregation of English-speaking Catholics in Paris to which I belonged included embassy people and others from private life and the business world. Among them was the Catholic wife of then-struggling journalist Art Buchwald, who was later to become the well-known newspaper columnist and humorist.

Paris, France, 1953–56

Our English-speaking parish had been invited by the Catholic Students Club at the Sorbonne to join them on their annual pilgrimage to Chartres. It involved a hike of some forty miles over back roads from Paris to the famous Chartres cathedral, with an overnight "camping" stop on the grounds of an eighteenth-century chateau. On medical advice (I was still recovering from the burdens of the infamous housing assignment), I had to forgo the walk and the sleep under the stars. So I drove the Hillman halfway and met up with the group the next morning at the chateau. The second half of the trip on foot proved a sufficient test of physical strength, but it enabled me to capture the essence and savor the experience of true pilgrimage in Europe.

The idea for the long march began in 1917 when Charles Péguy, the writer and a teacher at the Sorbonne, experienced the death of his child. He took some university students to Chartres to pray to the Blessed Virgin Mary for the gift of this child and the repose of her soul in heaven. It became a tradition. Each year all of the various schools and faculties of the University of Paris would deck themselves out in costumes to identify their branch or school. The Beaux Arts group always took first prize for their imaginative and colorful, if not bizarre, costuming.

We were a rather prosaic-looking group of mostly Americans in simple hiking clothes, which the organizers positioned right behind a group of Vietnamese students and before the Beaux Arts group. It was a hot day and a hard march. It happened to be the day just after the historic fall of Diem Bien Phu in Vietnam in 1954. The frail Vietnamese students had probably slept little the night before after hearing the news from their homeland. Several were literally staggering along the eighteen-mile walk. Many were crying for the loss of their countrymen in the war with the French.

Often the Asian students were so exhausted they would fall back through our numbers into the ranks of the Beaux Arts students. With extraordinary fellowship and flair, the French students literally picked them up and carried them around our ranks back to their rightful position in line. It was at once a pathetic, often amusing, scene, yet filled with deep human kindness. Given the Beaux Arts group's outlandish costuming, the scene reminded me of an old movie I had seen of a marauding band of Huns—many with poles and staffs—carrying off their dead victims.

Paris, France, 1953–56

Somehow the various tribes from the Sorbonne managed to make it to the cathedral, much the worse for wear, but with no casualties, so we all thanked God. Altogether we must have numbered close to 1,000. We jammed into the enormous cathedral leaving hardly a free place to stand. As if by magic at communion time, a troop of Boy Scouts joined ranks with a number of priests carrying host-filled chalices. Together they fanned out to various prearranged stations to distribute the Eucharist throughout the Cathedral. The scouts appeared to be carrying scrolls until two of them would stop and unfurl long white linen altar cloths with a flourish to hold for the priests to administer the sacrament. It was an impressive sight to behold.

With the liturgy over, the pilgrims were invited to remain if they wished—and our band of Americans did—to assemble in circles on the cobblestones in front of the cathedral. We were instructed to take what remaining food we had in our knapsacks, place it in the center of the circle, and share our evening supper with others.

We were to return to Paris by whatever means we could find! With some others, I managed to catch an interurban train to the chateau where I had parked the Hillman. I collected a few riders and drove back to Paris. There was little need or energy for conversation on our return.

The Chartres experience was transformative—a genuine sharing in some of the hardships as well as the joys of life. Few experiences in my life ever made such an indelible and lasting impression. After Chartres my work at the Embassy took on new meaning and energy. With what I was convinced was heaven-sent grace, I managed to finish the dreaded housing report and submit it to Washington.

Over the intervening years people have frequently asked me, "Didn't you just LOVE Paris?" My reply is usually a harsh, emphatic "NO!" which tends to cut off further inquiry. By the looks on their faces I have come to assume that those who thus inquire believe it must have been some unhappy love affair that cannot be discussed, or that my experiences were such that discretion dictates they probe no further. It has only been in reflecting fully on the Paris experience in this review of my years there that I have been able to understand in any balanced way that there were many pluses as well as minuses, and much learning came out of that period in my life. Paris helped me to grow and gain perspective as well as maturity

Paris, France, 1953–56

of vision; perhaps it was a coming of age for me after my youthful flings in Trinidad and Bogotá.

I cannot help but recall a saying from childhood: "I would not have missed the experience for all the tea in China." Just what one would do with such a quantity of tea was never explained.

Paris, France, 1953–56

SIX

Santiago, Chile, 1957–59 (Second Secretary)

From New York to Valparaiso

As is often the case in Foreign Service rotations, which take account of language and area experience, I was transferred from Europe back to Latin America—from Paris, France, to Santiago, Chile—just as I had been earlier from Bogotá, Colombia, to Milan, Italy. Given my Spanish language proficiency, I had no need for further training at the Foreign Service Institute. Following area briefings at the Department of State, I headed for Chile.

It was a long and lazy sea voyage for my mother and me on Grace Line's SS *Santa Rosa* from New York to Valparaiso, the major port on the western side of this string bean–shaped country. On docking, we found the port scene not too dissimilar from seaports we had known in France and Italy, although much smaller. It was obviously a resort area for the people of Santiago, with beaches and gambling casinos, according to our shipmates. Ranged along the hillsides were small houses and modest low-rise apartment buildings. It had its commercial fishermen as well, and their tiny homes and grungy apartment buildings could be seen beyond the warehouses and commercial buildings.

I was pleased that my mother had stood the journey so well. Perhaps it was the excitement of the trip and the newness of everything. She and my father had made their first long ocean voyage on the *Queen Elizabeth* from New York to Le Havre, France, when I was stationed at the Embassy in Paris. She had loved it then, and she loved the thirteen-day ocean voyage to Chile as well, including passage through the Panama Canal. Why wouldn't she, with no domestic chores, fine meals served three times a day, and shipboard entertainment?

But not long after our arrival in Chile, loneliness, the vast distance between us and the United States, and the poor communications of those days made us both question the wisdom of her residing with me at a Foreign Service post, at least one as distant as Chile. She came to realize that she had to return, even though she had lured an old Wisconsin friend down to Chile for a month to keep her company. Perhaps it was the strain of being alone in a foreign country during the entire day while I worked at the Embassy, total unfamiliarity with a foreign language, and no friends to turn to, even though embassy families were kind in many ways. But having to rely on them and on American missionaries was awkward for her. She became increasingly conscious that she had no real role to play. In the end her painful arthritis got her down, and we were both forced to acknowledge that she might be better off back in the States, this even before our first year was out. In the meantime we had some amusing and curious experiences, together with some painful ones.

Hotel Living and House Hunting

On arrival, we were put up in a hotel a few blocks from the Chancery. The meals were quite acceptable, but we soon grew tired of the monotony. Occasionally I did a delicatessen supper in our hotel rooms. We stayed there about a month but it was a trying time for my mother.

Her "job" was to hunt for appropriate housing, following leads given us by the embassy administrative office. My personal car had not yet arrived from the States. So it fell to my mother to take taxis out in search of housing. Before long, the "local plague"—fleas—in the rattling old taxis got the better of her, to say nothing of her struggles to give proper directions in the few words—the very few words—of Spanish she knew, like "sí" and "no" and "alt! aquí!" after pointing to the address on a typewritten note from the embassy.

Santiago, Chile, 1957–59

One evening when I returned from the Embassy, I found her in the hotel room crying and very sad. Her tender, white Irish skin was a mass of flea bites. "Count them," she ordered. "Just count them." I found she had roughly ninety flea bites all over her arms and legs and visible parts of her body. She whimpered, "And I didn't even find a suitable place for us to live." My heart went out to her, and I realized it was sheer torture for her to continue with this kind of living. So I begged off work temporarily, borrowed an embassy car, with strong justification, and we set out looking together.

It wasn't easy, but mercifully it wasn't too long either. We found a nice little bungalow about twenty minutes by car due north of the Chancery, near the Escuela Militar (Military Academy) a few blocks off the main drag, Avenida Apoquindo. The house had a nice entry, fair-sized living room and fireplace, a charming little dining room, two bedrooms, two baths, and a maid's room; also a small walled garden and some very poor and very noisy Chilean neighbors on the other side of the wall. The house was unfurnished except for a few basics. The owner, a local politico, had just been named Chilean consul general in Barcelona. He was still around for the negotiations before departing with wife and brat-like son of about eight years of age. He was taking the dining room table, no doubt in expectation of much entertaining at his new post.

I didn't mind too much, as I rather enjoyed the prospect of shopping in a strange land. But it was not that easy, as there were few stores selling ready-made furniture in those days. Most everything had to be made to order. But that was even more fascinating, as I enjoyed going to a *taller* (workshop), in this case for woodworking, picking out a Duncan Fyfe table and chairs from a magazine, and waiting nearly a month for them to be completed. In addition, I had brought from Italy a handsome Renaissance-style glass-paneled chandelier framed in gilt metal, which I had bought in Venice and could hang elegantly over the table.

Unhappiness of Dependent Mothers

We added some bits and pieces from my shipment of household effects and soon had a fairly livable space. But again my mother was home alone all day, and her arthritis was getting progressively worse, perhaps from the stress. Coincidentally, another woman officer—someone I had known as a fellow vice consul in Italy (she in Florence, I in Milan)—had her mother with her in Santiago. They had taken an apartment acquired by the U.S. Agency for International Development about a mile away from us. But if we thought the two mothers would hit it off and keep each other company, we were sadly mistaken.

Both were once redheaded Irishwomen, accustomed to their own ways and friends. Try as all four of us did, the two "mothers abroad" were really not compatible. They had dissimilar backgrounds and experience, even though both were good God-fearing, churchgoing women. But being of a certain age, each seemed to think she had all the answers on most any subject and neither left much room for any sort of accommodation, despite being thousands of miles from the familiar and comfortable. Perhaps because both were fiercely independent, each may have feared that any degree of intimacy or closeness would cause them to admit their keen discomfort at having reached a stage in life where they were totally dependent on their working daughters. They were also smart enough to realize this was an untenable situation. So they kept their distance, their feathers intact. What they also seemed to have in common were culture shock and instant resentment about the differences in local folkways and customs.

I came home one day to find my mother in a real snit over her discovery that the noisy, low-income neighbors beyond our common red brick wall were illegally drawing on our electrical power supply through wires they had thrown up over our lines! This enabled them to have their radios (the days before TV) going full blast, with shrill Latino music and booming announcers, all in a language my mother did not understand. These living conditions were hardly designed to ease her arthritic pains. Increasingly, she took to her bed and spent entire days lamenting her fate, saying her prayers and dreaming of release—a quick flight back to the States to friends and relatives.

House Afire

The high point of our stay in the little bungalow came one night when I tried to distract my mother by playing the new *toca-disco*, or record-playing console, I had shipped from the States. We had some nice classical music going, a lovely fire in the fireplace, and some quite good Chilean white wine on ice to distract my mother from her arthritic pains, alien status, and the general "foreignness" of her surroundings.

Suddenly, we were distracted by a strange roaring sound like a nearby fire, but we had only a very controlled fire in the fireplace. What could it be? Ah, the *toca-disco* must be defective and the sound system had gone bad. So I turned it off. Still the roar, and it was getting louder. Then came a series of hurried knocks on our front door. I looked out and saw a crowd gathering in front of our house. As I stepped into the twilight, the gathered neighbors were engaged in animated discussion and pointing nervously to our roof. The chimney was on fire! Call the *bomberos* (firemen), they kept shouting at me. "Hurry or your house [not mine really] will burn down."

So I made a quick phone call, only to have my Gringo Spanish questioned. They wanted to be dead sure of the address. Never mind, I shouted I will meet the truck where our street crosses Avenida Apoquindo and lead them in. OK? And we both hung up. I quickly explained the situation to my mother, grabbed the car keys, and raced outside again, pushing my way through the crowd, with many of them shouting, "You are crazy. The fire truck will run you down and split your car in half. It is dangerous. Stay here! They will see the flames and follow them here."

"No way," I yelled out the car window as I backed up madly, swung the wheel, and roared down the street. When I reached Apoquindo, I turned the car around in the middle of the street so that it was pointed in the direction of the house. I waited what seemed an hour and then finally heard the siren in the distance, perhaps a mile away. Firemen hung from the rig, swinging their arms and signaling me to get out of the way. Maybe my neighbors were right, I feared, as they rolled up alongside me. I leaned out and shouted something like *"Sígame"* (follow me). Too bad I lacked a sign for the occasion—like those Jeeps that lead planes off the landing strips at airports. I was even more surprised when the fire truck followed me.

When we got to the house, a covey of men in heavy fireproof gear and helmets immediately jumped down from the rig, pulled their long hoses, hitched them up to the street hydrants, and started spraying away at our chimney. The lead man, hatchet in hand, pushed our front door open and ran into my harassed mother. Suddenly recovered from her arthritic pain, she shouted in English, "What do you think you are doing?" as water flowed in the windows and in and out of the fireplace.

Santiago, Chile, 1957–59

"Mother," I offered, "he's Chilean and speaks Spanish."

"I don't care what he speaks. He's ruining our house," she yelled back.

At this point Mr. Chilean Fireman stopped dead in his tracks and, in perfect English, said, "Madam . . ."

"Don't you Madam me," my mother shot back. "What took you so long—nearly 45 minutes since my daughter called you, and I could have died of smoke inhalation and the house burned down?"

"But it didn't burn," the firemen responded.

"No," she asserted, her voice rising, "because I went about sprinkling holy water all over the house and furniture."

Finally the Chilean got a word in edgewise. "Madam," he began again in even more perfect Oxford English, "I wish you to know a few things. First, we have a volunteer fire department in Chile. I am a doctor and my colleagues here are doctors and lawyers and other professional men. We are doing our duty. It takes time to gather up the volunteers from their homes to do their civic duty. So you understand," he continued without a break in his steady, cold-as-steel delivery, "we are all volunteers. Second, it is obvious you are a foreigner and do not speak Spanish. Be that as it may, if you do not like it in this country and you have complaints, you should leave. Now I must go about my work." Not to be outdone, my dear Irish mother shook her mop of fiery red hair from side to side and shouted, "I will!" I knew then and there she had her foot on the ramp to the first plane leaving Chile for the United States.

Well, the dear Chilean volunteer firemen thoroughly flooded our home, ruining rugs and *toca-disco,* leaving my mother in tears to repair to her relatively dry room, and the maid and me to try to restore some semblance of order to the mess left by the firemen. As they were leaving, the head man who had taken on my mother and her flacon of holy water approached me, saluted, wished me well, and departed. The crowd of neighbors was still there, almost sorry, it seemed that the show was over.

House Hunting Yet Again

It wasn't long after this experience that I got word that the Chilean consul general would be returning to reclaim his house—what was left of it after the chimney fire. It seems his eight-year-old cried nearly every day he was in Barcelona—he was inconsolable, missed his friends, and insisted the family return. I managed to get the house in the best possible order before turning it back to him.

Curiously enough, he and his wife were fascinated with the Venetian chandelier over the new dining room table and begged me to sell it to them. Presumably they had little time to bring home souvenirs from their short-lived European assignment. After the trouble he had caused me—mainly by not telling me that the contractors for his bungalow had left the flammable wood molding planks in the chimney when they built the fireplace—I thought I should refuse. Moreover, he had cut short our year's lease by six months. Although I liked the chandelier a great deal myself, I decided he could have it—but at a price. I said I might let it go for $300, never revealing that that was about five times my purchase price. He agreed so readily I felt I should have raised the asking price by eight- or ninefold!

Luckily we found another place to live, a small apartment in the center of the city, about a 15–20 minutes' walk from the Embassy. It overlooked a park and had a superb view of the in-town mountain, Montserrat, on which was perched an imposing statue of the Virgin Mary—the Madonna, a prominent city landmark frequented by the devout on Sundays.

As the social life connected with my embassy duties became more active, the apartment proved terribly small. I was frequently converting one of the two bedrooms, my mother's, into a dining room. The maid conveniently lived away from the apartment, which helped on the space question. My incorrigible mother had chosen that very period to invite her friend from Wisconsin down for a month, and we had to put her up on the living room couch! When business guests came for lunch, it was like backstage at the theater, with major rearrangement of props, to say nothing of the busy little kitchen where the inevitable *lomito* (roast tenderloin of beef) was being cooked up. I had to send my mother and her friend off to a nearby park or church or restaurant to free the tiny apartment. Often I would just take the business guest to a hotel or restaurant to avoid the major furniture reshuffle, but not before hearing the inevitable joke bluntly put to me by herself, "Where are you going to park your mother?"

Santiago, Chile, 1957–59

Embassy Organization, Work, and Miscellany

During my tour in Chile, a minister counselor headed the embassy's Economic Section, to which I was assigned. He was not an old-line Foreign Service officer but someone who had been moved over from the U.S. Agency for International Development's growing in-country assistance program. He was an experienced and competent economist but unfortunately not completely at ease among FSOs with broader diplomatic and international experience. His Economic Section staff was relatively large, with about eight officers and four secretaries. There were three attachés: a commercial attaché, together with an assistant, handled bilateral trade issues; an agricultural attaché mainly promoted U.S. exports of corn and soybeans; and a minerals attaché followed developments in Chile's important copper-mining industry, with its heavy U.S. investments and exports. Two general economic officers and one financial officer, me, completed the section's staff.

My "beat" included the Ministry of Finance, Ministry of Economic Planning, Treasury Department, Central Bank, and local and foreign banks. Occasionally I engaged in close liaison with an important American consulting firm, Klein Saks, which had been commissioned by the Chilean government to advise on the country's general economic and financial policies and relations with the International Monetary Fund and the World Bank.

One noteworthy, albeit amusing experience of my work in Chile involved contacts with some leftwing economists at the Central Bank, whom I often visited for background and statistical data for required reports to Washington. I found these economists intriguing. They were not only flashy dressers with expensive clothes, but one even sported a huge diamond ring. It was hardly something one expected from an acknowledged Communist, supposedly committed to helping the poor and downtrodden masses while in the employ of the Chilean government.

During one of our meetings they told me how much they admired Fidel Castro of Cuba. When Castro first came to public attention, announcing his revolutionary plan to overthrow the corrupt Batista government and help the poor of his country, he drew an initially favorable response, even a promise of assistance, from the United States government. Unfortunately,

I was inadequately prepared at the time to spell out U.S. policy intentions toward Cuba for either the short or long term. But Washington agencies using my reports were intrigued with my left-wing sources at the bank and asked me to develop detailed biographic information on them, which I did. I was surprised to receive a minor commendation for this small effort.

Little did I realize at the time that at least two of these Central Bank sources were so deeply committed to Castro's cause that they would leave within months for Cuba. Later I learned that they had joined a close circle of foreign economic advisors to Fidel Castro. The time was early in Castro's campaign, as he was moving out from the Sierra Madre and on to Havana in his overthrow of the Batista government.

Another memorable experience occurred when I had completed some background studies reporting on Chilean thinking concerning a $40 million U.S. government loan to Chile. That week a *Time* magazine reporter skewed the facts on the loan payment conditions. But I refrained from writing a letter to the editor. Some things are best left to Washington.

One day when others in the section were either out to lunch or on leave, it fell to me to receive a caller who turned out to be the wine producer Underragga, whose name I quickly recognized from the squat little green bottles of white wine I had been enjoying locally. Seems that neither the agricultural attaché nor the commercial attaché was in the office at the time.

Señor Underraga came bearing a basket of fresh green grapes to inquire if such fresh produce had a chance along with his wines on the New York market. I tasted one, washed free, I hoped, of sulfate spray and dirt. It was one of the juiciest, most refreshing grapes I could remember eating. Utterly delicious! It was midwinter up north but summertime in the southern hemisphere. Underraga intended to fly up to the States the following week with a large shipment, which he would hand-cull himself at the port of entry prior to testing the market. The rest of the story of off-season fruit shipments from Chile to the United States is history. For nearly fifty years now, Americans have been enjoying not only Chilean grapes but blueberries and raspberries we had thought could only be grown on a commercial scale in New England and other northern states during the summer months.

Santiago, Chile, 1957–59

Had I not been so deeply committed to government service, which I had entered in a spirit of patriotism during World War II, here was yet another opportunity to break away and move into the private sector, with its more lucrative employment. I was prepared to go anywhere in the world the State Department chose to send me and to undertake life and work in a different land, culture, and language; but I seemed to lack the nerve and confidence to break away from government service.

Reflections on Women in Latin America

It was probably in Chile that I became reconciled to the fact that as a woman in the Foreign Service, I was something of a novelty abroad, most especially in Latin America, where men still ran everything and women mostly stayed at home. Although not guarded by window grills nor as cloistered as in Colombia and other parts of Latin America at that time, Chilean women were still quite sheltered and protected, albeit relatively sophisticated and cosmopolitan because of immigration from Europe and travel.

In my introductory and subsequent business calls I was always graciously, often quite gallantly, received by my principal contacts, from ministers, heads of budget, and bank presidents on down, but they were all men. There were no women in government on which to call. Not until fifty years later did a Chilean woman run for high political office, even the presidency, and well ahead of the United States!

Recognizing the stark social differences of my era in Latin America, I had no choice but to respect them and accommodate myself to them. I had to work hard in this all-male environment always to appear knowledgeable, well informed, timely, and relevant. Inasmuch as I was generally seeking information, my attitude was naturally deferential. That seemed to suit my male contacts, and I had little difficulty in carrying out my assignments for Washington. Moreover, my local contacts in Latin America usually realized it was in their own country's self-interest to maintain close relations with the "Colossus of the North," regardless of the sex of the representative, and not to "kill the messenger." Chile, Colombia, and other Latin American countries at the time were essentially developing

Santiago, Chile, 1957–59

countries in great need of foreign assistance, loans, and trade to help them grow in an emerging world economy.

Embassy Leadership

When I arrived in Santiago, our chief of mission was Ambassador Cecil B. Lyon, a distinguished and accomplished career diplomat. He was soon replaced by a political appointee, Walter Howe, a tall, impressive patrician from New England who seemed more like a John Barrymore diplomatic-presence-in-residence than a political analyst or keen observer of the local scene. He was extremely well served, professionally and administratively, by his No. 2, William Kreig, a career diplomat who was able and appropriately accommodating to his superior. While inclined to aloofness, Ambassador Howe could be personable and friendly, almost fatherly to junior officers. He hosted quite elegant dinners, luncheons, and receptions for a selection of locals and often visiting dignitaries, the invitees usually based on recommendations from the various embassy sections. In addition, the ambassador's very able local protocol staff always applied a master touch to every final guest list. The ambassador lived in a beautiful old stone mansion near the center of town that had been built as a monument to one of the first silver-mining barons in the country. It was the sort of medium-sized diplomatic residence one sees in Washington along Massachusetts Avenue or in the Kalorama area. I understand the residence in Santiago has since been torn down, as U.S. diplomatic relations with Chile expanded in the 1960s and 1970s. A new residence was erected in a fancy new section on the northern outskirts of the city.

The Chancery in my day was in the heart of downtown Santiago across the street from the leading Intercontinental Hotel and almost diagonally across from the main square, site of the Presidential Palace. Both square and palace would be prominently featured in television news coverage in later days, when the Socialist president Salvador Allende was under attack and Chile made front-page headlines and nightly newscasts in the United States. Things were far calmer in my day when President Jorge Alessandri held office.

Most of my business calls were in offices surrounding the Presidential Palace square, where I parked my car when driving into work at the

Chancery. My car is worth noting for the attention it drew in Chile. It was but a modest four-door Chevrolet sedan with fins, so popular at the time, which I had shipped from the United States. Little did I know beforehand that I had made a very bad choice. The car was black and white and identical in make and color to the Chilean government police squad cars, also imported from the States. The main difference was that my car lacked sirens and flashing lights and the word *Carbineros* identifying it as police, making it all the more curious, along with the woman driver in civvies. I immediately became the butt of many jokes from my embassy colleagues. Locals who noticed me driving about town probably thought the police had gone coed in plainclothes. It could have been taken as a sign of the times, for it was only a few years before my arrival that women had gotten the vote in Chile. Nonetheless, my black and white "police" car gave me a certain respect on the road, causing a few heads to turn even without the police markings, a few jaws to slacken and some mouths to open, although I hardly stopped traffic.

Gifts and Regulations

Foreign Service regulations prohibit embassy employees from accepting gifts of any kind for services rendered, be it economic or commercial assistance, passport and other services to American citizens, or visas to foreigners visiting or emigrating to the United States. Foreign Service officers are reasonably well compensated by their government and have no need for outside remuneration. However, the niceties of Latin culture occasionally prompted flowers in gratitude, a small gift, or product samples with the hope we would test them and give a favorable opinion as to their stateside marketing potential. Generally, most offerings were of negligible value and could hardly be refused without giving offense. I had heard it was not beyond some visa applicants in desperate straits to offer bribes, yet that was one sure way of getting an immediate denial from the reviewing officer.

In general, gifts from host country nationals were not much of a problem, in my personal experience. But then it was not as if anyone ever offered me a yacht, a sports car, a seaside villa, or other valuables, except in Chile (and later in Rome). In Santiago I was offered a weekend at a luxurious country estate, which I accepted primarily because my mother was included.

"Friends" of the Embassy

The business of diplomacy is mainly about facts and figures related to bilateral relations, the people involved in them, finding common interests, and seeking understanding and agreement. Person-to-person contacts are thus important, but mixed up in the process are people whose interest is less government-to-government and more personal. They seek to know embassy personnel for their own reasons, sometimes personal and self-seeking. These can be people who like to have an ace-in-the-hole in emergencies, who have escaped from one bad situation and want to line up people or institutions potentially helpful to them in times of trouble. It is amazing how many of these kinds of people hover about embassies seeking to ingratiate themselves, from Latin America to Africa (but few in Europe, I found).

One such contact was a refugee, a doctor who had fled Nazi Germany and installed himself quite successfully in Chilean society. He was rather low key, not prominent yet extremely well connected. He had to be, for his specialty was performing abortions for considerable fees among many of the *alta sociedad,* the prominent and well-to-do. I made his acquaintance when he called at the Embassy seeking information on U.S. farming practices on a day the agricultural attaché was out of the office.

He appealed to my most vulnerable point when he mentioned his "farm" about three hours' drive from Santiago and invited me to bring my mother down for a weekend. I knew she would be thrilled for the change and thought it would be good for me to get away from work. So I accepted.

I drove my "squad car" out of Santiago, heading south through the beautiful countryside to what we learned on arrival was less a Chilean ranch than a European country estate, literally transported into the heart of rich agricultural land south of Santiago. We were treated royally. The house was like a mini-chateau and elegantly decorated. All male servants were in white jackets and dark trousers; the maids wore black dresses, white aprons, and headpieces that mimicked French maids to a tee.

Santiago, Chile, 1957–59

Madam, the doctor's wife, was resplendent in the latest Parisian fashions, and we "dressed" for dinner. Neither my mother's wardrobe nor mine quite measured up to the occasion. We felt like poor relations. My mother, almost too energetically, made the mistake of admiring a bejeweled blue sweater that Madam wore. Immediately Madam withdrew to her room, took the sweater off, and gave it to my mother! I immediately felt we had been taken captive.

The next morning while my mother and the doyenne toured the "chateau" and made small talk, the doctor took me off to the stables, where we mounted horses and toured the "farm," which was in fact an enormous ranch. He recalled that in our talk at the Embassy we had gotten onto my experience (it was only a summer job) at the Agricultural Extension Service of the University of Wisconsin. In his eyes, or perhaps just to ingratiate himself, I was something of an expert and would I pass judgment on the way he had set up a large piggery. He claimed to have followed precisely some advice contained in an Ag Extension Service booklet from the University of Iowa, where hog-raising was big. I was deeply impressed with the concrete flooring and stalls, the fancy automatic feeding and cleaning systems, the modern equipment and overall efficiency of the place out there in the wilds of Chile.

After leaving the pigs, he showed me—almost dismissively, with a wave of the hand—where his farm workers lived. I could not help expressing the first thing that popped into my head, namely, that the pigs seemed to live better than the workers. It was hardly my greatest diplomatic moment, but the contrast was shocking.

As if to offset my unveiled criticism, the doctor assured me that he took good care of his workers, even trying to get them politically involved in local issues. "Indeed?" I asked. He explained that during the last elections he had insisted they go to the polls. He had made it easy (none had transport) by rounding them up and trucking them to the polls. I did not have the gall—though I was tempted—to ask how he had primed them to vote. Surely for his preferred candidates and probably not for social issues like better housing.

My mother, on the other hand, was having a ball. She was her own person, not a dependent. She was enjoying the hospitality of our hostess, who revealed that she had trained at the Cordon Bleu in Paris and was

Santiago, Chile, 1957–59

thus equipped to pass on to her kitchen help all the niceties of food preparation and service that made dining in this Chilean backwoods an experience straight out of the Tour d'Argent on Paris's Left Bank. *Incroyable,* as the French would say. Not only did our hostess cater to my mother's every whim, she organized a bridge game, a near passion of my mother's, who would have gladly paid for the game, had it been suggested.

For my part I couldn't get away fast enough, especially after the episode at the piggery. I hated our host's blatant efforts to curry favor with a foreign diplomat. I had no idea what his ultimate goals were. The next day, after profuse thank-yous, we took our leave, and I never saw the couple again. Presumably they continued to live happily ever after on his ill-gotten gains from an illicit medical practice in a country that, at least on the surface, was then regarded as conservative and Catholic.

R & R in Argentina, and Playing Golf

Despite the hardships of service in those early days at such distant posts as Chile, including the responsibilities of caring for my newly widowed mother, there were leave times for rest and recreation. One of these was an Easter weekend trip with my mother over the majestic, snow-capped Andes Mountains to see Buenos Aires and a bit of the Uruguayan coast. We gorged on renowned Pampas steaks and superb red wines and shopped 'til we dropped for Argentina's famed leather goods and woolens.

On another weekend I took my mother directly north to a small junction town in a long north-south valley, where the road turns sharply east and up toward the mountains and the ski resort of Portillo, on the border with Argentina. There we visited a convent of French nuns who did first-class embroidery work. I commissioned a set of place mats and napkins for eight. The design was Cluny lace on ecru linen and took nearly a year to complete. The work was so delicate I kept the set more as a collector's item than as a working table setting. I do remember using it once for some official luncheon but then stored it away.

Halfway through my Chilean tour of duty, my mother returned home on a Pan American Airways sleeper, an innovation in those days. After that, I was freer to use my weekends to resume golfing at the Prince of Wales

Club (Principe de Galles), just below the snow-capped Andes mountains. Embassy staff enjoyed some sort of diplomatic rate that made it easier to use. Besides, the restaurant had a good kitchen. I always enjoyed their sandwich special, called *churrasco,* thin slices of quickly grilled steak between luscious slices of ripe avocado on thin toast—a great combination. When I later served in Africa, I cooked these for my guests on an open grill in the garden before showing an American movie, usually at Sunday night suppers.

My golf was hardly memorable. Despite my Sam Snead clubs, sent down by mail order from the States, I developed a wicked slice that was hard to shake. However, one day, after checking the fairway, I teed off on the 10th hole, a dogleg. One player ahead of me was just rounding the bend in the dogleg after hitting his second shot. All clear, I thought. Wrong. Instead of my usual slice, the ball took off straight and low like a jet plane. As it rose and soared I imagined the trajectory arching and coming down just where that player was walking. Sure enough, it got him flat in the back and he dropped! I was shocked and said to the caddy, "Go to him and explain." I had never driven that far. It must have been the *churrasco* that gave me the extra strength.

The caddy argued, "You go; you hit him," whereupon the man got up and with firm stride quickly covered the 225 yards between us. When he got nearer I could see his shock at recognizing a woman (we had just started to wear slacks on the golf course in those days). I recognized him as a Japanese diplomat. He was so furious I feared he was going to hit me with his fist or club, diplomacy be damned. Instead he stopped just short of range, and in that strange manner the Japanese have of speaking English, said, "Dohn you evah do dot agahn." I tried to explain that I had never had such a long drive before, thought him out of range, and so on. But he had already turned hurriedly back toward his ball on the fairway, undiplomatic incident closed.

I seemed to have less trouble on the ski slopes high in the Andes, but I never came even close to competitive or professional levels. Dangerous intermediate probably best described my class, despite my having taken lessons in Italy ten years earlier. I tried Farellones, about an hour and a half by car due east from Santiago and visible from the Galles golf club. But the high wind would often blow much of the snow off the slopes,

Santiago, Chile, 1957–59

baring rocks and pebbles. It could be difficult at times, but it afforded a lovely view of Santiago and the countryside beyond.

Portillo on the Argentine border was different. It took four hours by car and more by train when the roads were closed. I went up for a long weekend with a friend who had come down from New York on business. We stayed at the lodge and lo and behold it was the time Robert Kennedy and his family had flown down for skiing in July. I probably spent as much time watching the Kennedy family glide gracefully over the slopes as I did skiing myself. Besides, I found skiing high in the Andes less satisfying than skiing in the Alps. South America offered far fewer conveniences for recreation than Europe, the runs were shorter, and the terrain was much more rugged.

Chile End-of-Tour Review

In summing up my assignment to Chile, the fourth in less than eight years in the Foreign Service following Trinidad, Colombia, and Milan, I realized what a growth experience it was, with greater work responsibility and the need to observe and keep broadly informed on a variety of subjects—in sum, the most intellectually stimulating of my early years in diplomacy.

The Chilean political, economic, and social scene was clearly in ferment in the late 1950s, but in retrospect it was hardly as tumultuous or engaging for the United States as it became in the 1960s and 1970s during the presidencies of Salvador Allende and Augusto Pinochet. Nevertheless, when I served there, it was a time of stage-setting, if not central casting, for Chile's later social transformation. Unfortunately, that change came with a heavy toll of human pain, suffering, and death. Though hardly as grim or tragically manipulated as later years in Chile, the late 1950s had their own special excitement.

Many academics from around Latin America and Europe came to Chile to study the political and social frictions developing between traditional conservatives and the ideological left. The wealthy, landed class was coming under increasing criticism from both Christian Democrats and Marxists, who competed ideologically on issues of social responsibility, political participation, and the "right" theories for organizing and managing society. These developments were acknowledged in Embassy Santiago's political reporting, although our submissions at the time seemed rather routine and unimaginative. In hindsight, I think they lacked a prophet's foresight, which was within reach had the embassy made use of all the valuable assets available to it.

The U.S. Information Service (USIS), for example, does many good things in the arts, education, information, and grant programs through its officers at embassies overseas; but political and social reporting is not part of its mandate. Yet in Santiago the embassy had as its USIS chief Hewson A. Ryan, a man of great intelligence and an extraordinary scholar in cultural and social matters. He had a Ph.D. from the leading university in Madrid, coupled with a talent for knowing and understanding people on all rungs of the social ladder. Ryan's deep knowledge of the local political and social scene and his wealth of contacts with local opinion leaders and scholars might have been drawn on more heavily by the embassy's responsible political officers. Embassy Santiago's political reporting was good and met basic Washington requirements, but it could have been outstanding, at a time of social ferment, had it benefited more from Ryan's views and wisdom. At the time Chile was beginning to transform itself from the old "feudalism" of a Latin aristocracy into a modern society. Ryan eventually rose to the top of USIA's (United States Information Agency) career service, was "loaned" to the State Department as a deputy assistant secretary in the American Republics Division, and later became ambassador to Honduras. Subsequently he retired to teach at Tufts University in Boston. Few in the Foreign Service impressed me with their professionalism more than Ryan did.

To its credit, Embassy Santiago did benefit from the observations and research of at least one outside scholar, a noteworthy Belgian sociologist and Jesuit priest named Roger Vekeman. Later he became "notorious" for his alleged connections with the CIA and USAID, which, it was widely reported, were supposed to be financing him, though this was never publicly proven.

I first met Vekeman in 1958 through a bright young officer in our USAID mission, married and with a very small child. I was delighted to be a frequent dinner guest with Vekeman at their home. I learned a lot from listening to the priest tell of his ongoing sociological research in

Chile, where he had been in residence for several years before I met him. Subsequently, I had Vekeman to some small luncheons at my apartment with a few key local contacts in and out of government. The resulting exchange of views provided me with excellent background on what was really going on in Chile in the seesaw involving Christian Democrats, Socialists, and Marxists.

These conversations also introduced me to an emerging social theory known as "liberation theology" that was to sweep Latin America and give the Vatican heartburn out of concern that it was "too Marxist-based." Rome eventually denounced the theory and banned many works by its leading scholars.

I still remember Chile fondly, not just for its stupendous natural beauty and landscapes, but for its well-educated and interesting people of mixed nationalities and the many embassy friends I made and kept. Given my work responsibilities and with a dependent mother, any kind of a personal relationship in Chile was problematic at best. But helping fill the vacuum were several embassy officers with and without families who could not have been more understanding, inclusive, and kind in their hospitality.

I also made friends among a number of foreign missionaries in Chile, some of whom served as chaplains for the diplomatic community's regular Sunday mass. Some of us at the Embassy also volunteered to help the American and foreign missionaries in their work among the poor living in the *callampas,* or shanty towns, clustered on the edge of the city on the road leading to Santiago's airport. The Irish missionaries were especially good fun because they loved singing and dancing at informal potluck suppers. We also came to know the Holy Cross Fathers, who had come from South Bend, Indiana, to staff the boys' high school (Notre Dame) they had established in Santiago. These contacts with missionaries in Chile set something of a precedent, prompting me to check in with missionary folks in two other developing countries to which I was later assigned, Honduras and Zambia.

Santiago, Chile, 1957–59

SEVEN

Interim Assignments: GATT Tariff Negotiations,
1960–61; Senior Seminar, 1962–63;
Diplomat in Residence in California, 1976–77

Geneva: GATT Tariff Negotiations

Personnel assignments are never easy in the Foreign Service, either for the administrators making the decisions and issuing the orders or for the assigned officers, with their questions and doubts as to where and how they will be spending the next three to four years of their lives. The process does have some virtues: personnel panels making the recommendations involve some Foreign Service officers (FSOs), though only on decisions related to officers below their own grade. Such decisions are professional and far from capricious. They can even be compassionate and are usually soundly based on assignees' proven capabilities, professional experience, and career potential.

Nevertheless, jokes persist within the Service that assignments are made by using roulette wheels or randomly throwing darts at target boards, or that administrators look to see what preferences officers may have expressed and then make assignments directly contrary to the stated preference, like Djibouti for Paris. Further speculation arises because FSOs' preference statements are—or used to be—requested on April 1 of every year.

All joking aside, Foreign Service assignments are more often than not made for sound, administrative reasons, most especially because it is a job for which the assignee is especially well qualified and has the necessary language capability. Timing can be critical. Sometimes the good-match job is not always open when the candidate is ready for assignment and vice versa. Occasionally an available officer may have to be put into a holding pattern, like an aircraft circling for hours before it can be cleared to land. Temporary or special duty assignments (TDY) can and sometimes do provide a solution as well as a wider experience for the officer.

I found myself in such a position in 1960 following my assignment in Chile, when I could not have been more anxious for a change to easier, less stressful living accommodations. My language capabilities at the time were in Spanish, French, and Italian, and as some in-house jokers used to say, "ay leetle eengleesh." When the "perfect" bilateral country assignment was not found, Personnel thought that a multilateral TDY might be appropriate—one that could build on my past economic and commercial experience.

The European Common Market, officially the European Economic Community (EEC), had been formed in 1958 with its first six member states—France, Germany, Belgium, Italy, Luxembourg and The Netherlands. By 1960 it was a going concern and sought adherence to the rules and regulations governing international trade. It applied for accession to the General Agreement on Tariffs and Trade (GATT) in Geneva with the intention of engaging in the next round of tariff negotiations. This session was scheduled for 1961 in Geneva and was called the Dillon Round, in honor of the U.S. under secretary of state, Douglas Dillon, who had proposed it. The State Department was thus looking for economic and commercial officers to staff the U.S. Delegation to the Dillon Round.

One might suppose that when the personnel people in the department punched in "GATT tariff negotiations" and "European language capabilities," the name "Wilkowski" among others might have popped out of the assignment machine. This data would have reflected my TDY assignment in 1956 from Embassy Paris to the GATT in Geneva for negotiations with the European Coal and Steel Community (ECSC), the institutional foundation on which the EEC was built. In what seems to have been a good fit, I received another TDY assignment to GATT, this time for the Dillon

Round. I quickly learned that before any of us could take off for Geneva, considerable preparatory work—months of it, in fact—had to be done in Washington.

Along with three others I was selected to be on the team that would negotiate with the newly formed EEC. I knew something about GATT, but the EEC as a composite of six countries was another and very new kettle of fish. For the United States to be negotiating with the EEC was considered a historic event. The terrain was virginal, unploughed, and not easy, either for the EEC or its negotiating partners. The scenario would unfold as we moved forward.

The four of us on the so-called EEC team faced a unique task, but we were confident we had the necessary technical expertise. Two of us came from State: our team leader, Herman Walker Jr., a Foreign Service Reserve officer, had been a senior economic officer at Embassy Paris and a former academic. I was named his deputy. Our teammates were Robert Sarich, a former Yugoslav diplomat and naturalized American, from the French Desk at Commerce, and William Hart, a talented professional from the U.S. Tariff Commission.

Once assembled, we looked and felt somewhat like a pickup baseball team with no bats or balls and in search of a sandlot, even an opposing team. We were assigned space in State's Office of European Affairs, commonly referred to as EUR. This office enjoyed a fabled reputation for always being at the center of major diplomatic events and was thus considered a must-have assignment for up-and-coming Foreign Service officers, especially those in the political cone.

Inevitably our little team ran into some minor ego problems, as well as some real space problems trying to get settled into EUR. Staffers there were so busy moving from one country crisis to another, they had little time or patience for TDY assignees in their midst. I had absolutely no experience in bureaucratic infighting among the administrative types at State and was of little help there. Even worse, we were engaged in economic work, always considered inferior to political work in those days. The EUR attitude toward us was somewhat akin to that old, negative British view toward "anyone in trade."

Walker and I were assigned to share an already small office, which until then was the sole domain of a busy, budding, young diplomatic luminary, Samuel Lewis. (Years later Lewis became ambassador to Israel under Presidents Carter and Reagan). Far from being a prima donna, Walker was a notably practical man and thus chose to find himself more suitable and hospitable quarters with some old economic cronies not too far away in Main State. He left me to cope with the EUR permanent stakeholders and to fetch my own coffee, as no one else offered.

Walker was a tall, somewhat gangly man, sort of a "country boy" in appearance and manner, not especially handsome. But looks can be deceptive. He had natural charm and a winning smile and could project authority and gravitas when the occasion warranted. He was also slow to anger when provoked—in brief, a natural diplomat. I watched and learned how to stake out ground and employ tactics with care and discretion. Most surprising of all, Walker was sophisticated and knowledgeable in the fine arts. His French was perfect with only the slightest hint of a southern drawl.

Because of the obvious space limitations at State, the other two members of our negotiating foursome stayed in their own home offices at Commerce and the Tariff Commission. We quickly learned to do most of our business by telephone, courier service, and the occasional group meeting whenever we could find a free conference room.

We were taken aback at the outset of our preparations to learn that the EEC in Brussels had yet to establish and publish its first unified tariff schedule, which would serve as a negotiating base. We thus had to improvise in preparing our brief. We began by working from the old tariff schedules of the six individual member states. We did some averaging and made some reasonable assumptions as to what the tariff levels might be once the EEC agreed on a unified schedule. We then tried to assess the negotiability of projected 10–15 percent tariff reductions in both the U.S. and the imagined EEC schedules. We drew on historical trade patterns between the individual European countries and the United States, and then made more assumptions on future trade levels by value and volume so as to develop working hypotheses. After a few months of this highly technical but provisional preparatory work, including heavy-duty education and training from the EEC and GATT experts at State, we packed up our tentative negotiating brief and flew off to Geneva together with the rest of the U.S. delegation. While our team would work exclusively with the EEC, the rest of the U.S. delegation would be negotiating with other countries, including such major trading partners as Japan and the United Kingdom.

Our negotiations with the EEC had hardly begun when notice came from Washington that Spain belatedly sought GATT accession and would FSO Wilkowski assume this additional negotiating responsibility? Thrilled to be named a team leader, even if I was to do the job alone, I rolled up my sleeves. With help from the Spanish-speaking wife of a member of our delegation, I prepared an opening statement, a portion of which I wanted to give in Spanish. I hoped it would put them at ease and dispel any shock or discomfort upon encountering a woman negotiator. After all, it was still 1961.

I also turned to U.S. Embassy Madrid for all the background information they might provide. The response was disturbing: the Spaniards had recently and unilaterally raised all their tariffs by 25 percent, and then had the temerity to come to Geneva offering to negotiate them down by 15 percent! After I went through the motions of my ceremonious opening statement, I lost no time in the business session by bluntly asking the Spaniards what they thought they were doing playing games with the United States. The session was brief and inconclusive. I heard nothing further from them for a fortnight.

During that time, whenever the chief of the U.S. delegation would ask me how things were going, I would point to a Picasso print I had picked up at a local shop showing Don Quixote and Sancho Panza on their horses at a standstill—"my status report." During that halt in negotiations with the Spaniards, the delegation received a cable from Washington from none other than Under Secretary of State for Economic Affairs George Ball. Ball pointedly wanted to know "why the U.S. negotiator (unnamed) was being so 'tough' on the Spaniards" when it was important politically that they become members of GATT.

In a carefully crafted reply and with help from my wise boss, Herman Walker, and added support from Embassy Madrid, we gracefully eased out of that awkward situation. The Spaniards never returned to the Dillon Round, but I understand they reapplied some years later and were admitted, under what conditions I never learned. So ended my brief stint as a team leader. I soon returned quite happily to my EEC team as deputy.

By then our team had settled comfortably into U.S. delegation offices in Geneva, thoroughly enjoying the location close to United Nations head-quarters and directly overlooking Lac Leman, its famous *jet d'eau*, and the French Alps. In contrast to Washington, our space was commodious, with three adjoining offices and an appropriate room for Walker to meet with the ranking head of the EEC delegation from Brussels. An unanticipated dividend was the respect with which other members of the U.S. delega-tion regarded our team of four, because of the importance and glamour of the EEC as a new economic and political entity on the international scene, making history in seeking GATT accession and trade negotiations. It also had something to do with the reputation and popularity of Walker among his fellow professionals. By then he had become "Herman" to his small team, the rest of the U.S. delegation, and his opposite number on the EEC delegation. Our entire delegation numbered about thirty; the EEC had about the same number, as it too was negotiating with others.

Capable, conscientious team leader that he was, Herman quickly demonstrated that he was not all work and no play. His Paris experience, first as a student and later as a professional economist, had given him surprising qualities of finish and sophistication behind his "country-boy" manners of dress and speech. Herman knew good food and wines and loved music, ballet, and opera, rarely missing a performance in Geneva. To balance it off, he loved the outdoors and was always teaming up with any other delegate willing and able to spend weekends or even just a day on long hikes in the nearby French and Swiss Alps.

We single "girls" on the delegation, both officers and secretaries, were soon taking turns as Herman's date for supper, evening entertainment, or mountain hikes. I proved especially handy, having acquired a small but quite adequate French Renault sedan into which four could squeeze for the short trip to the mountains. I soon developed a shamefully girlish crush on Herman, which I could justify only by telling myself "life begins at forty!" This made no sense at all, of course. Herman was married (whether happily or not I never knew) to a rather high-ranking U.S. gov-ernment employee in Washington and had a college-age son who occa-sionally visited him in Geneva on school holidays.

Indeed, I remember the son accompanying us one Sunday afternoon on a long hike into the Jura Mountains north of Geneva. We stopped about midway on the trail to have a picnic lunch of local cheese, sausage, hard-crusted bread, and a bottle of wine we had carried up in our backpacks. After that we stretched out to rest on the grassy slope along the trail to listen to the breeze through the fir trees and gaze at the drifting clouds overhead. As I recall, during the return trek from that excursion I noticed that my cheap hiking boots (which had served for après-ski in Chile) were split right across the soles from excessive wear and tear on rough Alpine trails. I managed to drive back to Geneva over the narrow, switchback country roads without getting tangled up on the brakes or accelerator. That would have been disastrous. Herman was asleep in the back and his son of little help as copilot—though very good as a chaperone.

My private time with Herman was hardly exclusive. I knew that the next weekend he would probably be out and about with someone else from the delegation, but I enjoyed my time while it lasted. It was my first experience with a brilliant man whom I believed I liked as much or more for his intelligence and sophistication as for his looks and personality. Alas, he was married, and that was a major impediment I was not prepared to even try to overcome. Moreover, by then I had learned to pray over such matters—fervently.

Following our year together in Geneva, I did not meet up with Herman again until thirty years later. I had retired from government and was a corporate director living in Washington. He had returned to academe and was visiting D.C. from a state university in New York, where he was teaching political science. He was divorced from his first wife and married to a woman teaching French at the same university. We met for lunch, and I was shocked when I saw him. He had aged considerably over the intervening years and almost shuffled when he walked. Yet he still had that same charm—the smile and soft, laid-back, attractive manner. I realized then what a sensible, good, and kind man he also was—sophisticated and experienced enough to save me from my foolish, midlife crush, reining me in and helping to keep me on the straight and narrow path he somehow knew I was destined to follow.

Senior Seminar

Soon after reporting back to the Department of State in Washington, I was informed that reassignment to Europe was not in the cards. I was to attend the 1962–63 Senior Seminar in Foreign Policy at the Foreign Service Institute (FSI). The course was often referred to as "the breeding ground for future ambassadors" and a time for mid- to senior-grade officers to pause and reflect. Selection was considered an honor. Instead of an appropriate location at some country estate in Virginia or fancy townhouse on the heights of Georgetown, the seminar was located at FSI, then still housed in that vast windowless garage of a condominium in Rosslyn, Virginia.

Being more the handmaiden than the lady-of-the-house type, I had never aspired to ambassadorial heights in the Foreign Service. Besides, the few women officers were vastly outnumbered by men; there were no high-ranking women role models at the time. It was not that I lacked ambition, but I was so imbued with the basic culture and tradition of the service that I readily accepted whatever assignment I received and wherever I was sent, always hoping I would be up to the job and like the location. Though that may sound ever so Pollyanna-like, ambassadorship was a subject I neither entertained nor had it ever been raised directly with me until much later in my career. This contrasts with the attitude of young people in the twenty-first century, who continually ask me, "How can I become an ambassador?" as if it were merely a matter of knocking on the right door.

When I dutifully presented myself to the coordinator of the Senior Seminar, Andrew V. Corry, I was a bit put off on two counts. Not unlike my first trainer in Old State, who demanded a quotation from Shakespeare for the smallest infraction of the rules, the coordinator was yet another older, scholarly, Phi Beta Kappa type who enjoyed twirling his gold key in public (I think the practice finally went out of style in the late twentieth century). Corry was later named ambassador to Sierra Leone and thereafter ambassador to Ceylon.

Far more daunting, I was to be the only woman in a class of twenty-five, a small sea of males. Most of them seemed clearly aspiring to diplomatic heights, the exceptions being a few students "on loan" from the armed services and other U.S. government agencies. This latter group had been temporarily assigned to State for purposes of "cross-fertilization" in government, just as some of our Foreign Service officers were occasionally assigned to the Navy and Army War Colleges.

The most keenly aspiring "ambassadors" in the seminar were easily identifiable—always cozying up to the speakers, usually first to raise their hands for questions or to extend a point by drawing on their own personal experiences. I found their gamesmanship highly amusing.

Some of my classmates stood out without even trying. Martin Herz was one of these, always serious and brainy to the point of intimidating some of his classmates. Eleven years after the seminar, Herz finally made it to chief of mission as ambassador to Bulgaria. His amusingly self-denigrating book on that assignment, *Two Hundred Fifteen Days in the Life of an American Ambassador*, aimed, he said, "to show people what it is like to be an American ambassador in a place that is unimportant."

Another standout in the seminar but an entirely different type was Jack Lydman, a classy, delightful, and witty man who also made it to the top as ambassador to Malaysia. And then there was Philander Priestly Claxton Jr., a State Department lawyer—with a Tennessee-gentleman name like that, a distinguished head of gray-white hair, and a sonorous voice, who could forget him?

I had known some other classmates before, even as good friends, such as the soft-spoken, modest, and very able E. Allen Fidel, who had been in Rome when I was in Milan and later in Trieste, and Robert Lyle Brown, a true friend, whom I had known from the very beginning in junior officer training. These good friends helped ease my way among "the boys." They were considerate, even protective, especially against the practical jokers who enjoyed taunting a single woman in a class with twenty-four men.

On the day we made our formal courtesy call at the White House, it wasn't my classmates who tried to maneuver me into a spot near the president; it was President John F. Kennedy himself. In a commanding voice as we entered the cabinet room, he said, "Aha, you have a lady in your class. Have her come up here and stand next to me." And that was the lineup when the photo was taken. I can't remember a single word President Kennedy said to me at the time but it must have been charming, in keeping with his well-publicized reputation with the ladies.

So what was the Senior Seminar all about besides making the rounds of the U.S. bureaucracy from the top down and all around the town? It was certainly broad-gauge and comprehensive, intended as a re-Americanization program so that we might better represent our country abroad. But our training at or near senior level was also regarded as a respite—perhaps even a reward—from the rigors of life overseas. Many of us had served at so-called hardship posts, even enduring risks to our health and safety.

Much of our nine months of "study" was spent in the lecture room, where I had my first face-to-face contact with Henry Kissinger. At the time he was a sort of high-powered consultant to the State Department some years before he became its secretary—and years before I pestered him from Africa to the point of being called his "nemesis."

Among the many other distinguished speakers were officials from the Bureau of the Budget, Treasury Department, Agriculture, and on up to and through members of Congress. We were meant to know all these powerful people and their work, and be able to engage them in free and easy discussion and debate. Some of them either had or would come to our posts overseas. I don't recall a single notable woman in or out of government who lectured to us. This was, after all, the 1960s.

Besides hearing from government insiders, we were also treated to lectures from distinguished academics and business people. We were also frequently challenged intellectually by our fellow students, with Martin Herz often in the lead, closely followed by Phil Claxton, and, in his contrastingly modest yet confident way, Hugh Appling.

Other challenges were thrown out by our own erudite seminar coordinator. Without giving us advance warning or time for research, Corry would order us to take turns standing before the class and responding to whatever controversial issues or current political events he could think up. I vividly remember being asked what I thought of a two-China policy, never having been there or done that. My reply was rather lame until those of my classmates who were Asian specialists and far more knowledgeable gracefully came to my rescue and helped me save face, in classic Oriental fashion. Ah, there was indeed chivalry among my male classmates.

The nine months' "work" at the seminar was hardly work at all, though before we "graduated" we were required to "do a paper" on a subject and site (foreign or domestic) of our own choosing. To simplify matters, I chose to do something already familiar to me—multilateral diplomacy, specifically the GATT tariff negotiations, which I hoped would not get me into too much trouble. I enjoyed a ten-day study trip back to Switzerland to gather the required data. (Later, while I was serving in Honduras, a Senior Seminar student visited the post to do some sociological research on a small enclave of Christian Arabs who had emigrated to Central America to go into business, many becoming quite wealthy landowners.)

The Senior Seminar was generous in offering group travel for a variety of purposes and destinations, but generally to expand our knowledge and understanding of domestic and world affairs. One such trip was to NORAD in the mountains of the West to learn something about U.S. military defense capabilities against any perceived nuclear attack. On an extension of that trip we visited the U.S. Air Force Academy in Colorado, where I encountered a bizarre situation. After a few lectures our Air Force guide took us to the main dining room for lunch. Awkwardly, he drew me aside to explain that women were not allowed in the mess hall! I demanded a better explanation from him. By then the group including our coordinator had made its way well into the cavernous hall. Never mind, my guide insisted, we have made other arrangements for you.

Wondering what I had to lose, I stood my ground, then sweetly inquired if it was true that President and Mrs. Kennedy would be visiting the Academy within the month. The guide confirmed this. What then are you going to do with Jackie Kennedy? He was unable to answer. Instead he abruptly took me by the arm and escorted me down a flight of stairs to the basement under the hall and through a number of storage areas, coming out at an open space set up as a staff dining room. This is where you will have lunch, the guide said, pulling out a chair for me at a linoleum-covered table holding open cartons of milk and cellophane-wrapped stacks of bread with the ends torn off. Soon I was joined by a friendly group of kitchen staff in their work uniforms. We had a pleasant lunch, but I was unable to judge whether it was either up to or below Air Force Academy officer standards.

Later I told our coordinator that I thought the treatment was totally out of order and hardly acceptable, but what could I do. I was hungry. As far as I know, a formal protest was never made nor any sort of formal apology ever offered by the Air Force Academy. Many years later when the Academy got into so much trouble over disciplinary problems, my reaction was "Serves them right!" I had no pity whatsoever for any organization that to my eyes seemed so poorly informed and managed, so graceless and out of touch.

Not long after our seminar group returned from Colorado, we made an interesting trip to Puerto Rico. During our few days' visit we were shown the university, met the president, discussed with him the island and its people's education, and learned something about the local government from the local politicians. We were even treated to a minor ocean voyage coupled with a U.S. Marine–style amphibious landing on the bombing-range island of Vieques, wet boots and all. We prayed there would be no test shooting while we were there "storming" the beach.

Those of our classmates "on loan" from the military services (there were Army, Navy, Air Force, and Marine Corps officers among us) helped enrich the landing experience with mini-lectures on the side. This was in return for the interpreting we State officers did during some of our more formal lectures back at FSI, when the "diplobabble" from guest speakers and political scientists became too thick. Thus, the cross-fertilization and unique learning experience within the seminar continued apace.

The seminar's generally informal and relaxed atmosphere was probably never more evident than when the group visited Cape Canaveral in Florida. En route from Fort Bragg in North Carolina, our bus stopped overnight at a small-town motel. For some reason I was last out of the bus and the motel clerk looked up from his desk to ask, "How come you're the only woman with this group of men?"

"Oh, I'm the singer in the band," I promptly replied, which seemed to satisfy the clerk. Some of my classmates had overheard, but made no comment, storing the information for later use. At the reception in our honor at Cape Canaveral, the wife of the commanding officer sent a messenger over to the table where I was seated to say she had heard I was an accomplished singer and would I be so kind as to join the military band and sing a few songs for the occasion!

That practical joke wasn't half as bad as the night when we arrived in a fair-sized town somewhere else in the South after a long day's bus ride. All twenty-five of us congregated in the lobby of the hotel waiting for our room assignments. As if on signal, one of my classmates shouted, "Who's going to sleep with Jean tonight?" The others quickly joined in with their shouted bids. So much for brotherly love and camaraderie in a mixed group, where the lone woman is badly outnumbered.

I managed to have the last laugh on at least two of my classmates when we revisited Colorado, this time to visit a molybdenum mine high in the mountains east of Vail in a town called Leadville, at an altitude of around 7,000 feet above sea level. I had known from my days in Bogotá, Colombia, and visits to Mexico City how risky alcohol can be at that altitude. Nevertheless, the "boys" had their usual rounds of predinner martinis at the hotel before moving on up another 1,000 feet to the mining company's administrative offices and guest dining room. There was yet another round of cocktails before dinner. The main menu offered the best and biggest lobsters and steaks that could be found in Denver, Colorado. Some of Denver's most distinguished leaders accepted the invitation to meet with the country's "future ambassadors." By the time the second round of wine had been served on top of the cocktails, both the submariner Navy captain and the Air Force colonel (who shall remain nameless) had passed out flat on their backs and had to be taken to the nearest clinic. It was a rare case of the State Department outsmarting the Pentagon, and it couldn't have happened to two nicer guys, sick as they were.

Despite all the interesting travel and the effortless "job" of listening to lecture after lecture, I did not really enjoy the nine tedious months of the Senior Seminar, and I said so to my closest friends and classmates. They were appalled and could not understand, as they were thoroughly enjoying themselves, free from professional responsibilities and domestic chores, especially the demands and problems of their children, whom they nevertheless dearly loved. My problem was not with the lighthearted joking and occasional hazing, nor even being the only woman among twenty-four happily married men. Rather it was my unsuppressible feelings of guilt. Guilt? Yes, because I enjoyed work and the sense of accomplishment and fulfillment it gave me. I liked to create and produce things—to collect information, conduct interviews, brief people, write reports, make recommendations. I did not like the feeling of being an unproductive sponge and taking a paycheck for what was essentially an intellectual vacation not of my own choosing. Nor was I convinced that the elaborate and expensive program for acquiring greater knowledge of country, government, and policies was critical to improving the conduct of U.S. diplomacy at high levels.

I did not make an issue of the subject, but I was surprised to discover that I was virtually alone in my views and that there was such a difference between male and female opinions of the Senior Seminar. Quite frankly, I was glad when it was over and I could get back to work and take my own vacations and make my own retreats wherever and with whomever I wanted. Yes, there is a difference between Venus and Mars.

Diplomat in Residence in California, 1976–77

Besides the Senior Seminar, an "off-track" assignment well past the mid-point of my career, I received one final special assignment—as a visiting college professor.

Following nearly four years in Africa, I was given orders to Occidental College ("Oxy") in California as a Diplomat in Residence, under the Department of State's domestic assignment, or "re-Americanization" program as I dubbed it. Hoping to broaden my "home" experience, I drove at a leisurely pace across the country in the new Alfa Romeo to which I treated myself.

As I hit the freeway on the outskirts of Los Angeles, I was unsettled by the rush and confusion of the traffic. What had happened to my nerve? I had slugged it out quite successfully with the best of the eighteen-wheelers en route to the West Coast. Perhaps it was cross-country fatigue coupled with a growing excitement over the new assignment. I pulled off at a rest stop to calm down, sipped slowly on some bottled water, reconsulted the map, then drove slowly and cautiously on to the Oxy turnoff.

As soon as I arrived on campus, I reported in to the college president, Richard C. Gilman, who had personally arranged for my assignment. I found him warm, friendly, and welcoming. But I also sensed he intended to exercise considerable control over my assignment. Having a Foreign Service officer on campus was his own idea, and it was clear he wanted to manage my housing, academic schedule, and speaking engagements. Having been an in-charge type of person myself, I feared it might be a hard adjustment. But I decided to go with the flow. Over time this attitude proved the right one.

I found Occidental College pleasantly sited on the western fringes of L.A. in a small, surprisingly modest, almost rural village called Eagle Rock, just between the Ventura and Foothill Freeways, with Pasadena to the east and Burbank to the northwest. The campus was close to the Rose Bowl (not that I ever went to a football game there) and to an excellent golf club just off the Foothill Freeway. As a VIP visitor at Oxy, the club kindly extended me an honorary membership, providing easy escape and diversion. There I spent many a pleasant late afternoon chasing golf balls and watching with delight as rabbits scampered in and out of the woods and hills bordering the course. Although I had too little time to make golfing friends and arrange games, I found the club useful for my type of quick, nine-hole golf and for entertaining guests at dinner.

In the Public Eye

I was surprised that the arrival of a woman ambassador in cosmopolitan Los Angeles was considered such a newsworthy event. In no time, a reporter from the *Los Angeles Times* came to interview me. A full-page article with photo on the front page of the Society section followed.

As I was just back from Africa, the African-American mayor of Los Angeles, Tom Bradley, with obvious support from the local pro-African lobby, treated me to a formal reception at City Hall, where I was given the keys to the city! This royal treatment was far and beyond what I dared expect from such a sophisticated city as Los Angeles. But I suppose it had its political purposes, so I went along.

The attention might also have reflected the subtle community influence and public relations savvy of Oxy's president more than whatever substance or background I was bringing to the college. Yet people seemed curious about a seasoned career woman ambassador who had come into L.A.'s midst in the mid-1970s.

Following the *Times* article, a variety of civic and women's clubs extended speaking invitations to me. Lo and behold one of these affairs was attended by none other than Shirley Temple Black, a hometown girl with strong political connections and some diplomatic experience of her own. President Gerald Ford had appointed her America's second woman ambassador to Africa, following my historic first. She had been posted to Ghana in 1974 while I was still in Zambia. So we had something in common to talk about.

Not surprisingly, my own fifteen minutes of fame on the L.A. scene, coupled with the special attention shown me by Oxy's president, did little to endear me to the rank and file of Oxy's faculty. They kept their distance, regarding me with some skepticism, perhaps doubting that I had anything significant to offer their classes as a guest lecturer.

Notwithstanding the faculty's cool attitude, I was becoming something of a cult figure among the students, especially the women students. They frequently stopped me on campus to chat or engage informally in Q and A, or popped in unannounced at my campus office. Perhaps because of this student interest and curiosity, the faculty gradually came down from their ivory towers to invite me to address their classes. But having had only limited formal teaching experience in my background and certainly no time between Africa and Oxy to prepare a credible course syllabus, I agreed with President Gilman, my mentor, that I should make myself available only for informal lectures throughout the college.

Appearances Off Campus

Certainly the extramural speaking invitations that started coming in from organizations up and down the state of California helped to thaw the atmosphere with the Oxy faculty. As the year progressed, I received speaking invitations from such diverse institutions as Vanderbilt University in Nashville, Tennessee; Rotary One in Chicago; the University of Nebraska at Lincoln; and an international relations group in Phoenix, Arizona.

The Nebraska experience had its downside. The airline lost my luggage, and I was forced to quickly find an appropriate dress in order to fulfill the engagement. Given my size, to say nothing of the shortness of time, I was lucky to find a pale blue, tubular knit thing, which was to become a wardrobe staple as well as a reminder of the baggage foul-up.

Nashville was another memorable experience. As I was leaving the hotel and heading toward a large black limousine waiting curbside, apparently to take me to Vanderbilt, I heard a rush of people behind me. I turned to look into the faces of a burly pair of visibly armed bodyguards flanked by others escorting a hurried celebrity toward the same limo—not a country singer, as one might have expected in Nashville, but none other than Israel's minister of defense, Menachem Begin, whose limo I was trying to commandeer! It was at that moment that the hotel bellboy rushed up and told me the university had just called to say I was to take a taxi. I later learned that Begin was in town for an academic meeting on military affairs.

The Ambassador's Seminar

Soon after my first excursions off the Oxy campus and out of state, President Gilman called me in for a private consultation. He was aware that I had brought with me to California a Honduran couple who had served me well in Rome and Africa as houseman and cook/maid. He was impressed. He explained that he had recently obtained a Ford Foundation grant for a faculty enrichment program and wanted me to use it and to engage my household help for a very special seminar!

I was to pretend that the house the college had assigned me to live in was an ambassador's residence in some far off country and to entertain at a series of formal dinners in typical embassy style. Gilmore had selected eight faculty members as the core seminar group. I was to choose some international affairs subject and work it into a series of seminar meetings-cum-dinner parties. His imagination and his confidence surprised me.

As it turned out, the project was not as goofy or staged as it sounded when the president proposed it. As to the subject, I decided to stick with the immediate and familiar—southern Africa—and to organize the eight weekly sessions around the eight faculty members, assigning each to one of the eight countries or blocs in southern Africa: Zaire, Zambia, Zimbabwe, Angola, Namibia, Mozambique, South Africa, and the BLS countries (Botswana, Lesotho, and Swaziland). I assigned myself the general subject of U.S. foreign policy toward Africa, with special emphasis on policy toward the southern Africa region.

We opened the evening sessions with cocktails, during which I made brief introductory remarks. During dinner individual faculty members, one per week, introduced their assigned country and related problems, reflecting their personal research. After dinner over coffee in the living room, the faculty members and I would continue our presentations, leaving a good hour for questions and answers before ending the session.

After two months we concluded it had been a worthwhile project both educationally and socially. The faculty seemed to enjoy the food and service as well as acquiring knowledge of a heretofore unexplored area. The stiffness between Oxy faculty and the visiting diplomatic lecturer started to wane; indeed the warm atmosphere from our little seminar extended throughout much of the campus, and I started getting more smiles and hellos as I walked from house to office. What a clever man, that Oxy president.

My seminar graduates told me how much more intelligible the news reports of poverty and disease in Africa had become, as well as the continuing turmoil in southern Africa in the late 1970s. I was pleased and so was President Gilman. It may have been an oversight that I neglected to invite him and his wife to join us for at least one of our soirées. Yet he rendered a solid report to the Ford Foundation of a successful faculty enrichment program, with only a minimum of grant funds expended on food and drink.

Hollywood at Eagle Rock

My year at Oxy always possessed an aura of Hollywood: the school's location on the east side of Los Angeles; its close proximity to the many studios in Celluloid City; the frequent use of Oxy's campus as a movie set; its reputable film-making courses; and, not least, the mindset of its administrators, faculty, and students. This aura permeated the Oxy atmosphere, like fog rolling in off the Pacific.

Unconsciously, I had become a part of this atmosphere, with my uniformed Honduran couple in residence and my Alfa Romeo in the garage. The wild coyotes fit right in, coming down hungry from the woods of the San Bernardino mountain behind my house and howling for food at my back door.

Oxy's president had the background and capability to be a film studio director and he showed his *savoir faire* in always treating me like a movie star. The students called my place Ambassador House and seldom missed an opportunity to stop by to hear "war stories" about life in the Foreign Service, or to hitch a ride in the Alfa Romeo. Indeed it was these students' begging to hear, "What life was like in the Foreign Service" who first suggested the idea of a book on the subject.

President Gilman was pleased with the publicity that my assignment as a diplomat-in-residence brought to the campus, even though the college boasted its own appeal as "the Harvard of the West." For my part, I was pleased to be an advocate for U.S. foreign policy, seeking West Coast political support for the State Department and advertising the U.S. Foreign Service as a career opportunity, already far from unknown among Oxy graduates. An impressive number had pursued successful diplomatic careers, and a few had become ambassadors.

Her Excellency and His Magnificence

On one occasion when President Gilman and I appeared together on a speaking platform, an amusing interplay ensued. The presenter introduced me as was often the case as "Her Excellency," while Gilman came off with just his simple title as president of Occidental College. After he took his place at the lectern, he paused a moment before launching into his prepared remarks to declare that he had to admit he felt overshadowed by the contrast in introductions, one simple, the other elaborate.

I immediately rose from my place, went over to the lectern, and stood beside him. I thought there was indeed need for elaboration, I said, and proposed that henceforth the Oxy president be introduced as "His Magnificence." Given the prevailing Hollywood atmosphere, Gilman immediately warmed to the appellation, and "His Magnificence" was repeated whenever we shared a platform thereafter. I was reminded of Henry Kissinger, who used to say, "I do not stand on ceremony, just call me Excellency."

Prominent among Oxy's benefactors was a Hollywood screenwriter, Elizabeth Pickett Chevalier, the wealthy widow of Stuart Chevalier, a former businessman and political figure who had once been on a U.S. delegation to the United Nations. Once was enough, it seems, for her to have been bitten by the diplomatic bug, and she was instrumental in setting up a special curriculum to honor her late husband, which she fancifully called Diplomacy and World Affairs. The courses were located in the Political Science Department and managed by a faculty member who, to my great surprise, was a retired CIA operative who was quietly recruiting graduates for clandestine government service!

When he invited me "to join forces" with his office, I felt uncomfortable and politely declined. I found an excellent excuse. The space offered was a tiny cubicle, or closet, at the building's entrance, which had been used by the former janitor! Aside from seeing it as a put-down, I felt the close association would be totally inappropriate. A separate, independent location, not tied in any way to the CIA, would enable me to be most effective in helping educate students on U.S. foreign policy and interest graduates in careers in the U.S. Foreign Service.

So I held out for more comfortable space befitting a visiting U.S. ambassador. My benefactor, President Gilman, fully agreed and accommodated me, but only at considerable expense and labor to Oxy. I was given a large, well-appointed private room in the college library, which had been dedicated to a famous alumnus. It needed some remodeling, but in a sensitive manner so as not to offend his family. Oxy literally went through the wall to install a telephone with a private tie-line to Washington.

The students who stopped by for a chat loved the arrangement. I could put them directly in touch with a country desk officer and other State Department offices, where they got firsthand help on their term papers from the specialists and experts. Moreover, one of the librarian's secretaries was assigned to assist me.

All in all, it was a successful year. The supervisor who came out from Washington noted that my hundred or so lectures on and off campus during the year had set something of a program record. I was not necessarily aiming for volume, just responding to requests. I did not admit to him that the bulk of the talks were reruns, just like television.

There was a big surprise at the end of my year at Oxy. "His Magnificence" showed his gratitude for my efforts with a classic Hollywood ending. At the graduation ceremonies the college awarded me an honorary doctoral degree. I found myself in excellent company, as the college also awarded an honorary doctorate to the chairman of its board of trustees, none other than Warren Christopher, who later became under secretary and secretary of state.

By then I was familiar with Christopher, who practiced law in L.A. and chaired the Los Angeles chapter of the Council on Foreign Relations, where I had lectured. Moreover, I had been a guest at some of the periodic meetings of the Oxy Board of Trustees. Occidental College well merits its reputation as the Harvard of the West. It is an excellent liberal arts college with class, manners, and distinguished alumni. I am grateful for the many kindnesses and courtesies extended to me during my year as a diplomat in residence there.

Leaving Oxy was not easy. I had to help the Hondurans, Alicia and Agostine Narvaez, return to Central America and to prepare my own return to Washington. The Hondurans faced some minor problems with transportation. They had flown into Los Angeles but wanted to buy a car and return by land. The only hitch was that neither had a license or knew how to drive! Buying the car—a used Honda camper—was easy. The license was another matter. Agostine tried but failed several times to pass the California driving test. The couple finally had a cousin come up from Honduras to the States to handle the overland drive through Central America and back home.

I tried to be helpful by going to the local AAA to get them the most direct routing through central and eastern Mexico. Within the week after they departed I received a postcard from the world famous resort of Acapulco on Mexico's west coast, far off the AAA itinerary! Written in Spanish, it was the equivalent of "Having a wonderful time, wish you were here."

I was happy that the year as well as their return to Honduras had gone well for Alicia and Agostine. It helped to balance the unpleasantness of their arrival by air at the busy, humongous airport known as LAX. Something was wrong with their documentation and the purpose of their stay with me was misinterpreted. They were detained overnight by immigration authorities and held incommunicado. Their explanation—"to be with an American ambassador here in L.A."—did sound a little incredible!

It was fortunate that the *Los Angeles Times* story of my assignment to Occidental had been in the newspaper that very week so, with clipping in hand, I was able to spring the Hondurans from captivity, but only after managing to get an appointment with the top immigration official in L.A. and engaging in a lot of diplomatic sweet talk.

Having done the Ford seminar for Occidental and a number of lectures on and off campus, it was time for me to leave the Hollywood scene and return to Washington for my next "on-track" assignment.

Eight

Rome, Italy, 1963–66 (Second Secretary), 1969–72
(Commercial Counselor; Minister/Counselor for
Economic Affairs)

After departing from chronological order to recount three interim or "off-track" assignments, I now turn to my two nonconsecutive postings in Rome. The first followed the 1961–62 Senior Seminar, the second my years in Honduras, 1966–69, which are detailed in chapter 9.

On Becoming a Holy Roman of Sorts

Because I learned to speak Italian in Milan in the early 1950s, it seemed only logical for the Department of State to make the most of its investment in human resources and assign me back to the only fully Italian-speaking country in the world—Italy. Memories of my two tours in Rome tend to blend together, although my living arrangements were quite different in each case, as were my official responsibilities.

When first assigned to Rome, 1963–66, I was a second secretary of embassy and deputy to the minister/counselor for economic and commercial affairs. Upon returning for my second tour, 1969–72, I was for a short time the commercial counselor and later moved into the slot of minister/counselor for economic affairs with responsibility for a staff of around thirty, including such attachés as treasury, commercial, agricultural, maritime, and air.

Thus I moved up in rank from being chargé d'affaires at the Embassy in Tegucigalpa, Honduras, a Class 4 post (the lowest), to Rome, a Class 1 post. In Rome I became No. 3 after the ambassador and his deputy. At the time I felt I had soared into the diplomatic stratosphere from my starting point as a vice consul in the West Indies.

It was not all that easy in the 1960s being new and a woman in a leadership assignment, that of chief of the Economic Section. My staff meetings were composed entirely of men, including a few misogynists, most notably the agricultural attaché. Formerly an agricultural specialist in the Dutch foreign service, he had moved laterally into our Foreign Agricultural Service. I never thought he was fully adjusted but felt it was not my job to undertake his rehabilitation as well. In time the economic team got over being led by a woman, and we managed to work reasonably well together, most especially when the agricultural attaché was on leave. Besides, I had a wonderfully supportive ambassador in Graham Martin on my more responsible second tour. He showed me great respect and seemed to depend on me a lot for assessing the Italian economic situation, especially at his staff meetings.

Bombing and Security Concerns

Only once was I called upon to "take charge" of Embassy Rome, which while short-lived was a heady experience at the time. The deputy chief of mission (DCM) was on brief leave while the ambassador was away on business in Northern Italy. That day a local terrorist with some grievances against the United States chose to bomb the Embassy! He lobbed a small but powerful pipe bomb into the entrance courtyard of the stately Palazzo Margherita, where the U.S. Embassy was and still is housed on the fashionable Via Veneto. Despite its smallness, the bomb caused a stir with its deafening sound and cloud of smoke. Happily it caused only minor structural damage. It hit the stone wall next to the interior driveway and grand entrance used exclusively by the ambassador and his visitors.

What does the stand-in for a day do? Fortunately, the embassy staff in Rome was large, well organized, and trained for emergencies. They didn't even call on me for instructions! The security and administrative staff together with the U.S. Marine Guards and the local police immediately took over, neutralized the scene, restored calm, and began a search for the perpetrators. So much for briefly "being in charge" at a Class 1 post, certainly less fulfilling than being Queen for a Day on TV.

Yet this minor bombing was a warning to Embassy Rome to tighten up on security. Indeed, over the years since then and following on Embassy bombings in Africa and the World Trade Center in New York, the security at U.S. posts abroad has been progressively tightened.

During my time in Rome in the 1960s, it seemed that almost anyone could saunter into the Embassy. For visiting Americans, it was little more than a hand wave or two of hello toward the Marine Guards. Italians and other visitors usually had to state their business in full before going on to whatever offices they were visiting. After the minor bombing incident when I was "in charge," the approaches to the Embassy in Rome were given an entirely new and more secure look.

Out front on the street the local policemen (*carabinieri*) added more men both in uniform and plain clothes; and the Italian military (obliged to protect us under treaty convention) brought in a couple of armored vehicles, which they parked before the main entrance. Later a small guardhouse was built at the Iron Gate perimeter as an initial checkpoint. A second checkpoint just beyond the Embassy's main entrance door in the Palazzo Margherita was set up and manned by local security guards and U.S. Marines. They used a room formerly occupied by a small part of my Economic Section, the U.S. Commercial Library, which previously had been open to all visitors without question. The final security touch was installation of airport-style screening gates for people, as well as conveyor belts with X-ray screens for parcels and luggage.

More recently security has become even tighter. I learned the hard way in 2003, when I last visited Rome. All visitors were required to show photo ID and be escorted to Embassy offices, by prearrangement. Being a retired U.S. ambassador with a valid U.S. diplomatic passport cut no ice whatsoever. I was denied entry because I had made no prior arrangements and no one was expecting me. As a matter of fact, I had no serious mission. Truth be known, my real "mission" was personal, though I did not divulge it to the guards, I simply wanted entry to the Embassy commissary in the basement, which I had usually entered quite freely to buy duty-free liquor or toiletries as gifts for local hosts and friends, something I had done many times in the past when security was not so high. But times had changed, and rightly so.

This "out-you-go" experience was topped only once, some months later. Back in the United States, I suffered a similar humiliation when I was literally "tossed out" of the State Department! I had taken a friend to hear a prominent speaker at the department's Open Forum. Entry had been no problem. But following the talk we wandered over to the department's cafeteria for lunch. While pushing food trays on the racks of the cafeteria line we were approached by a guard, who told us to leave the building immediately as we were "off limits" as lecture attendees. There was no way to persuade the guards otherwise, despite holding a valid U.S. diplomatic passport, past years of service, present hunger, white hair and limping on a cane. So this is how present-day security regulations rudely restrain—even embarrass—a retiree. How soon we are forgotten!

Bella Roma—Its Attractions and Curiosities

My memory of Rome and life there in the late 1960s and early 1970s is one of great delight and peace with work and life in general, except for the hectic and noisy traffic of motor scooters, pedestrians, and zooming cars. Not too long into my first assignment I learned the intricacies of the city plan. It was not really a plan in the modern sense but rather an accretion of centuries of living, building, destruction, and rebuilding, in addition to letting many of the centuries-old ruins just lie in state, forcing people and autos to move through and around the ancient ruins, almost to become a part of them.

I found that the most effective and defensive way of getting around Rome is to learn to drive "a la Romana"—just like the Romans—fast, confidently, even aggressively, if occasion demands. This includes going up on sidewalks (where they exist) but always carefully and respectfully, avoiding all shapes and forms of pedestrians. Finding a space and parking becomes a creative art form. I also found that driving a car in Rome was far more sporting, even more graceful, than in Paris, where people rather coldly and dismissively explain, "To drive is to aim. And then pedestrians simply flee or dodge."

Rome, Italy, 1963–66, 1969–72

This is but one of the many differences between French and Italian cultures. I have never doubted that the Italians have the most fun, even though the French like to pride themselves on being the most expert on food and intimate relations. I always thought the French lived their lives far too analytically, missing a lot of the joyous abandon of the Italians' *dolce vita*.

I am reminded of an aphorism, attributed to Helen Keller, that life is not worth living unless lived as an adventure. That certainly epitomizes the right spirit for living in Italy, as well as for driving a car in Rome. For me life in *Bella Roma* was nothing short of thrilling, and educational to boot. I recall encountering only two rather weird experiences—threatening but minor in retrospect.

One occurred in the peaceful and rather bucolic setting of the Borghese Gardens, in the very heart of Rome and midway between the Embassy and where I lived. I would often walk to and from my residence to the Embassy by way of the gardens, which paralleled the Via Pinciana leading into the Via Veneto. As all tourists soon learn, the Borghese Gardens are an oasis of umbrella pines, acres of woods, gardens, lakes, and sculpture. From the Promenade atop the Pincio Hill one can see the orange tile roofs and many different church spires over the entire city of Rome, including the cupola of St. Peters at the Vatican. At sunset the place is bathed in a golden glow and one is enveloped in a symphony of bells from the many churches throughout the city.

One late afternoon after work as I wandered back home through the gardens it struck me to detour around a little grotto by a tiny waterfall. As I came out of the thicket into a small opening, I was startled by a rather untidy and shabbily dressed man, who might have been making the place his home. He stood there looking at me while boldly exposing himself to all and sundry, but I was the only one in sight! I screamed and ran as fast as I could up the hill and out of the Gardens to my apartment, which was just across the street from the Borghese Museum. No one heard or responded to my outburst, nor did I see anyone in my flight out of the Gardens, but I did report it to Embassy Security. Later when I told the story to a friend, she asked "How did you handle *that?*" My reply: "I didn't!"

The pathetic "man in the park" could have been a homeless foreigner, possibly even a refugee from Eastern Europe, of which there were many in Italy. I have no understanding of the rationale and psychology of such behavior as the man's in the park. But it is certainly uncommon in Italy. Rome is more noted for its pickpockets on buses and trains, especially across the Tiber in Trastevere, and for its male and female prostitutes, who have well-known beats, or "marketing" areas. On cold nights the ladies of the evening often stand behind illuminating fires on the Via di Puerta san Sebastiano, alongside the Baths of Caracalla.

The other disturbing incident in Rome involved a near miss from a stray bullet. One quiet Sunday afternoon while reading the newspaper and seated on a couch in my glass-enclosed terrace, I suddenly heard a "ping" and the soft sound of breaking glass just above my left ear. I turned and saw a small sunburst of shattered glass radiating from a tiny hole in the window! I ducked down on the floor and crawled into the living room, then went immediately to the phone to call the Embassy, only to realize that the Security Office was closed on Sundays. Next day the security officer got to work on the trail. After careful investigation he learned that the fourteen-year-old son of the publisher of the Rome newspaper *La Repubblica,* who lived next door beyond an open lot, was trying out his new .22 rifle. The father was ever so sorry and was there anything he could do in the way of reparations? I suggested he impress upon his son that it was not open season on American neighbors, nor was the heart of Rome the appropriate place for a firing range!

Housing and Family

During my first tour in Italy I had the good fortune of finding an apartment near the Dutch Embassy on a quiet street just north of the Zoological Gardens. It was a penthouse with sliding glass doors giving onto wide terraces awash in luxurious color from potted azaleas and other flowering plants. Umbrella pines bordering the apartment building reached up to the open terraces and provided a delightful background of greenery. It was like a little oasis in the heart of Rome.

The apartment came with a few problems, however. When I first moved in I was disturbed by the occasional obscene telephone call in unaccented English. It was before the days of caller-ID so it was hard to know who the offender might be. I assumed it could be a male prankster connected with the Embassy who knew my phone number and address. Again, I felt obliged to report the disturbance to Embassy Security. In time the calls stopped.

Then there were the infernal nightly roars of the lions at the nearby zoo, which seemed to come with the heat of the summer months. Was it possible these lions were the descendants of those beasts who feasted on the early Christian martyrs in the Colosseum? Probably not, I mused; more likely they were recent imports from Africa.

The third drawback was my open-ended lease, whereby the owner, a single mother, could reclaim and reoccupy the apartment on short notice. As it turned out the woman's adolescent daughter persuaded her mother to move back just short of two years into my occupancy. While preparing to leave, I discovered I had done some minor damage to a valuable family portrait in moving it to storage in the cellar. The canvas was so old and priceless it had to pass scrutiny by the Italian Superintendent of Fine Arts before being turned over to the proper restorer. Suddenly the rent was not as big a bargain as I had originally thought. I turned to the embassy's administrative section for help in finding me one of a number of official apartments as soon as one became available.

The government apartment to which I was assigned turned out to be on the top floor (another *attico*) of a four-story former "safe house," which had been transferred to the embassy from an undercover U.S. government agency. Three other embassy families were already in residence there. The building was located on the outskirts of Rome, just off the famous Via Flaminia leading north toward Florence. It was a twenty-minute drive to the Embassy that required crossing the Tiber River over the ancient Ponte Milvio, renowned for the battle between Constantine and Maxentius. Beyond and up a hill ran the Via Cortina d'Ampezzo, which overlooked all of Rome if you were in a tall enough building to see it. My apartment was off the short street called Val di Sole. It was literally "nowhere," and hardly the place to bring my invalid mother, who had rejoined me and again become my dependent living overseas, some five years after Chile. She assured me not to worry. "It would work out."

Unfortunately, it did not work out, as her health had been failing. So I prepared as best I could for the inevitable. We were in the apartment for about a year when my mother took seriously ill and had to be hospitalized twice at the Salvator Mundi Hospital, on the Janiculum Hill far across town. She died there within an hour of her second visit. Embassy personnel, from administrative to consular, were superb in their attention, compassion, and support during this distressing time.

The funeral Mass was held at the historic Santa Susanna Church, operated by the Paulist Fathers in Rome. Christians have worshipped there since the fourth century. It has a rather plain seventeenth-century Baroque façade. Inside the church are four huge frescoes by Baldassare Croce depicting the life of Susanna, an obscure Roman saint martyred there, as well as a better-known Old Testament Susanna, who was spotted bathing in her husband's garden by two lecherous old judges.

In a quirky sort of way, while still mourning, I thought of some analogies to affirm why Santa Susanna Church was so fitting for my mother's funeral. She loved history, especially ancient history. Her intense pain from arthritis, especially in the dampness of Rome, and her isolation from friends and native tongue were a sort of minor martyrdom for another good Christian woman. I remembered that when my mother's arthritis became unbearable she would spend hours soaking in a tub of hot water covered by a bed sheet so that when she rang the emergency bell in the bath, the concierge (*portiere*) in our apartment building could come in and lift her out of the tub but in much more modesty than the Old Testament Susanna had had in her bath.

Regrettably my mother never lived that year to play hostess at her beloved St. Patrick's Day Irish coffees. So determined was she in planning for the event it was as though she were trying to banish ominous feelings about her limited future. She had always been a prescient woman, almost psychic. Her going back to God left my apartment a lonely place.

"Equal under the Law"

In my grieving I became sleepless, restless, and irritable. Small wonder that I took to resenting deeply my next door neighbor's barking dogs and decided to do something about the nuisance. I tried dropping well-aimed bags of water from the small terrace off my bedroom, even bricks, but to no avail. The dogs continued barking. So I decided to call on my neighbors. Before doing so I checked with one of my colleagues, who told me the lady of the house in question was the mistress of a prominent Italian government official, no less than the minister of the interior, the well-known Mario Scelba. He had made a reputation for himself in the way he maintained law and order in Italy after World War II. He was known best for the way he broke up huge Communist rallies in the central piazzas of the larger Italian cities like Milan and Rome. He would send in the *Celeri,* four policemen in a Jeep, who would drive directly into the center of the crowd. They would then start accelerating in gradually widening circles until they had effectively dispersed the crowd.

Undaunted by the report of the neighbor lady's political connections, I dressed up a bit one Saturday so as not to look too American casual. I walked up the road from our apartment and down the neighbor's private driveway. I was greeted by an iron fence with posted name plate and buzzer on an iron gate. Behind and surrounding the house was a walkway that resembled a small moat. I rang the buzzer and a uniformed maid soon appeared at the main door, which was recessed into the house about ten yards from the main gate. I was asked to identify myself, which I did, before being invited to enter.

I passed through the door into a wide hallway. For a moment I thought I was suffering from double vision. On the wall at the end of the hallway hung a huge life-size portrait of an attractive, dark-haired, small-boned woman (obviously Sicilian, as was Scelba) with three small children standing beside her. Below the portrait was the real-life original of the painting, although the woman seemed to be sheltering her children more protectively than in the portrait. I looked back and forth from real life to the painting before I suddenly collected my wits and launched into my best Italian, introducing myself and apologizing for any inconvenience. After the lady of the house returned the courtesies, I lodged my complaint about her dogs and the disturbance they were creating.

Madam was totally at a loss to understand my complaint. "Everyone, but everyone leaves their dogs outside in Italy." I replied that "no one but no one leaves their dogs outside to disturb their neighbors in the United States," adding that I worked at the U.S. Embassy, needed my rest, etc., etc. I pleaded for Madam to keep her dogs inside. But it seemed a losing battle because dogs were not kept inside in Italy, etc., etc. Finally I thanked the woman, took my leave, and decided, rather foolishly in retrospect, to take the matter to the local police.

So up I went along Via Cortina d'Ampezzo to Monte Mario and the nearest police station, not far from the well-known Cavaliere Hilton Hotel. The captain in charge received me promptly. I was concerned about just how I could gracefully complain against the mistress of his top boss! Without using names I explained my problem was most delicate. We were talking about "a very close acquaintance of a very important person." Immediately the captain replied that rank and titles were of no concern. "In Italy," he asserted, "everyone is equal under the law." Well, OK, so I plunged ahead, explained the problem—still not using names—and gained his assurance he would "immediately look into it."

That was Saturday. Early on Monday morning at the Embassy I was called down to the political officer's office and summarily asked what I thought I was doing complaining about "the close companion" of the minister of the interior. It seems Scelba was so enraged with Madam's report of my visit that he promptly called the American ambassador to say that one of his employees—me—was totally out of order and that I was to cease and desist complaining about neighbors and take life as I found it in Italy. So much for "equality under the law"; I went out and bought ear plugs.

More Housing—In a Prince's Palace

On my second tour in Rome I started out living in an apartment hotel for the first month while searching for something suitable for a commercial counselor required to do official entertaining. It took me well over a month of hard searching until I found a small apartment just two blocks from the Embassy. It was in the ancient palazzo of the Principe (Prince) Boncompagni e Ludovisi, whose illustrious double-barreled family name was attached to the street between the U.S. Embassy and the Excelsior Hotel on the Via Veneto.

The palazzo and its location were quite extraordinary, occupying an entire city block. It was perched atop a huge mound of earth and braced on all four sides by a brick wall about two stories high. There was a gatehouse on the north side across from the Eden Hotel on Via Boncompagni e Lu-dovisi. I usually drove up to the gates in my German-made, two-door Ford Capri. I loved the rather rich sound the tires made as they rattled up over the stones on the U-shaped driveway, through the lush garden of palms and flowers to the palazzo. I had my own private entrance on the east side, with a tiny elevator in which two people could barely stand, pressed closely together. I called it the "matrimonial lift."

The apartment was surprisingly modest—two small public rooms, one bedroom and bath, a kitchen, and maid's quarters. It was the setting and view over the city of Rome that made it elegant. Both the sitting room and dining room were small but I could still entertain a few couples at a time. I had a Yugoslav *tutto fare,* a maid, who was an excellent cook, having worked before for embassy people. She was highly temperamental but well worth the strain. Our most serious confrontation occurred when I invited my deputy, who had been a Yugoslav diplomat before he became naturalized and married to an American heiress. His background was Serbian and the maid's Croatian. She refused to cook for him. Somehow we managed to overcome the difference and enjoyed an excellent meal. No one was poisoned.

My landlord, the prince, lived alone in solitary splendor on the other side of the palace. Once when I made my periodic call to pay the rent, he told me that he took his meals in different rooms (of which there must have been at least thirty) to help break the monotony of single life. I smiled, thanked him for his suggestion, wondered why he did not think me worthy of sharing his table, and returned to my tiny apartment.

Before long I was elevated from commercial counselor to minister for economic and commercial affairs and assigned an entire floor of an old palazzo across from the Borghese Gardens for my living quarters. The embassy had acquired it right after World War II and made it into four apartments for its senior officers: DCM, economic minister, political coun-selor, and consul general. My quarters held an enormous living room, which had been the palazzo's ballroom, and a library. A large dining room had a marble-top table that seated fourteen, with gilt and gray chairs, ser-vants' quarters, and four bedrooms. An open terrace and a large, glassed-in sunroom completed the layout. I used it a lot for entertaining visiting notables, Congressman (later Secretary of Defense) Donald Rumsfeld

Rome, Italy, 1963–66, 1969–72

being one among many ranking U.S. government visitors, Italian officials, and business people from the banking and financial world.

A concierge/caretaker/guard and his family lived in a corner apartment on the ground floor and basement. We parked our cars in the driveway alongside the palazzo under two rather inelegant green plastic sheds, improvised in a quaint Roman way.

Official Duties

On rainy days I would drive to the Embassy, where we had reserved parking on the south side of the Palazzo. My work was interesting and stimulating. Chiefs of sections had their own regular meetings plus weekly staff meetings with the ambassador. We each reported on relevant daily news and contacts with host government officials and important visitors, both local and American.

My official "beat" was to protect and promote U.S. economic and commercial trade and investment interests in Italy, and to oversee, manage, and direct the commercial work of six constituent posts in Palermo, Naples, Florence, Genoa, Turin, and Milan. One day it might be intercessory calls and discussions at the Italian Foreign Office, perhaps trying to gain support for votes at the United Nations on a variety of economic issues. Or, I would be hosting a U.S. manufacturer of large commercial aircraft who was either selling to the Italian government or working out subcontracting deals for Italian manufacture of components. Washington once requested me to visit and report on a firm near Naples that did first-class work stamping out parts of the aluminum fuselage of aircraft for assembly in the United States. A much more difficult assignment involved representation "at a high level" at the Ministry of Foreign Affairs to urge the Government of Italy to make payment on a long overdue, significant financial claim against it by the electronics firm Raytheon. Awkward as our official intervention was, it proved successful.

On another occasion I was asked to speak at a business luncheon of the U.S.-Italian Chamber of Commerce in Naples, hosted by the mayor of Naples. In closing the meeting he expressed his gratitude by making a gift to me of a new device, a quite large and hissing espresso coffee machine. Missing yet another opportunity, I could have gone into business back in the States before Starbucks! Our DCM didn't believe that U.S. rules and regulations prohibited acceptance of coffeemakers, Italian or otherwise. So I brought it back to the States but never managed to get it working properly.

Other out-of-town matters involved attendance at the Milan Trade Fair, described earlier (as vice consul in Milan). Frequently I was called to consult on import-export matters or problems of subsidiaries of U.S. firms. A large part of my work had to do with multilateral issues between the United States and the European Community. Although EC headquarters were in Brussels, many questions had to be dealt with on a country-by-country basis as well as multilaterally in Brussels.

Two of the more noted questions that took up considerable office time concerned U.S. exports of live and frozen poultry, which soon became the story of the "chicken wars," and U.S. exports of oranges. Questions could revolve around U.S. subsidies and pricing or matters of sanitation and whether exports to Italy were in full compliance with its laws.

Seasonal U.S. exports of citrus, specifically California oranges, which the Italians often complained were competing unfairly with Sicilian production, proved another difficult issue. Growers in California were anxious not to lose any part of the good market they had developed in Europe and wanted to protect it at all costs. Conflicts were often resolved by negotiating fixed calendar periods during which U.S. exports could enter Italy—not before nor after specific dates. Naturally disputes arose over suspected or real infringements of these agreed-upon schedules. All such issues had to be brought to the attention of appropriate officials in the Ministry of Foreign Affairs and sometimes in other ministries as well, such as Trade and Commerce and Agriculture. Embassy officials could often be kept busy just navigating their way through the local bureaucracies in their countries of assignment, to say nothing of interpreting whatever turf battles and policy shifts might be in play among them.

Perhaps the two most noteworthy commercial negotiations during my time in Rome concerned aviation and shoes. The former involved American flag carriers (mainly TWA and Pan Am at that time) flying into Italy compared with Italian flag carriers (mainly Alitalia) flying into the United States. The frequency and destinations of this two-directional traffic needed some sort of balance or fairness in landing and takeoff rights. Considerable research was required—as in most trade negotiations—to ensure a sound statistical basis with respect to historic flight patterns, past vs. present volumes of trade, and realistic future projections. For example, would U.S. flights to Milan and Rome fourteen times a week be a fair trade-off for Italian flights of equal number to New York and Detroit? Not only were executives of commercial companies involved behind the direct negotiations but also the responsible officials of both governments who regulated and controlled the aviation industry. The responsible embassy officer was usually the designated U.S. spokesperson or negotiator. Both countries subsidized their respective aviation industries—another variable factor which, to the extent possible, had to be weighted into the equation in striking a fair trade balance. The negotiations tended to be brisk and straightforward, because the trade was serving a fast-growing business in both cargo and passenger lines.

Unfortunately, free plane rides were not offered to those of us leading the negotiations, at least not on the U.S. side. As discussed earlier, government regulations prohibited the acceptance of such gifts. Back in those days, however, there were the small psychic compensations of always being treated like a *principessa* or a *contessa* by staff at the hospitality lounges of Rome's Fiumicino (later Leonardo da Vinci) Airport—small beer, but offering a real high in the feel-good department.

Whereas aviation negotiations could offer something quite clear in balancing advantages for both sides, negotiations with Italy on shoes were a bit stickier, certainly more sensitive. We in the United States were pressed hard by a declining domestic shoe industry, especially in the Northeast, which was encountering a host of problems, notably in style, pricing, and rising labor costs. American industry insisted the U.S. government negotiate controls on Italian exports that were flooding the country in the early 1960s, when I was first stationed in Rome. Our objectives were not easy to negotiate. For we were asking another country in effect to take on some of our basic economic problems and either reduce their exports "voluntarily" or face quotas on exports to the United States. When the supplying country realizes that it stands to lose a significant amount of market share if it does not cooperate, it is often disposed—however reluctantly—to limit some of its exports.

U.S. Secretary of Commerce Alexander Trowbridge came to Rome to impress the Italians with the importance of the problem and help make the deal more palatable with "voluntary" restraints. It was not long after this negotiation with the Italians that the problem arose again, with still lower-priced exports to the United States from Spain and Brazil. Today the problem persists with even cheaper imports from China. While the American consumer may benefit, some U.S. domestic industries suffer and fail unless they diversify, sell out, or team up with companies abroad—making globalization either profitable or costly for U.S. business.

While I was working on the shoe problem, I identified a number of small producers in Tuscany. More important, I learned that they made large sizes—my own being embarrassingly queen-size. Having grown to nearly six feet tall, I was blessed with a significant foundation of two solid feet. I had always tried to hide them in shoes too small, as it had been difficult to find large sizes when I was growing up. Mail-order shoes were not always the perfect fit or solution. The opportunity to have shoes made to order in Italy—and at wholesale prices—was a surprise and joy beyond belief.

Getting Hooked on Tuscany

Trips to these shoe companies enabled me to enjoy the ravishing beauties of the Tuscan countryside, long before contemporary writers discovered it and began writing books "under the Tuscan sun or sky." I learned that one of our embassy military attachés and his wife had bought an old farmhouse overlooking the Arno River, between Arezzo and Florence, and were restoring it and reviving an old vineyard. It sounded idyllic, and I longed for such an experience. Visiting them for lunch one day, I saw what fun they were having with restoration, negotiating with the natives for carpentry, masonry, and plumbing, and just tending a vineyard. I got the bug.

It wasn't long before I engaged their realtor and spent weekends going from one old abandoned wreck to another, thoroughly charmed by the beauties of the Arno Valley, with its memories of saints and sinners. Even Napoleon and his armies had trekked their way north and south on the main route between Florence and Rome.

Rome, Italy, 1963–66, 1969–72

Soon I "invested," with a distant silent partner, in a 350-year-old farmhouse with eighteen rooms, including oxen stalls on the ground floor, and three outbuildings that seemed to offer "possibilities" as a farmer's house, vat room, and winery. Its small vineyard needed expansion to be economic, and the Italian government was subsidizing expansion. I was in way over my head but never took the time to calculate potential losses or turn back. Instead, I plunged boldly ahead, starting with the *sine qua non* of finding a farmer who could tend the place and try to make something of it.

I sought further assistance from the realtor, even though I strongly suspected he was feathering his nest off foolish foreigners turning Tuscany into their summer playground. But at the same time I was learning colloquial Italian, and fast. The realtor arranged for me to meet with a farm laborer in the dead of night at a remote property off some donkey trail deep in Tuscany. The realtor drove me onto the grounds of the place, led me to the door of a ramshackle old granary, and stayed in the car. My interlocutors and I sat at a long rustic table in the center on a few ancient chairs. The place was dark, illuminated only by the small flame of a kerosene lantern, which cast eerie shadows about on assorted bags and bales of farm produce.

My attention became riveted on the pathetic little group facing me across the table. There was the short grimy farmhand in dirty, ill-fitting work clothes. He stood and awkwardly gave me his leathery hand and a toothy half-smile. His young but weary-looking wife did the same. And then he nodded toward the two sad-eyed little girls and said their names. They were shabbily dressed, both under ten years of age, I guessed. It made me feel like a representative of some welfare agency come to help this poor family out of whatever misery they were in. Or was I here to "steal" this family away from their present work and home? More the latter, I presumed with the realtor wanting no direct part in the negotiation.

I was immediately filled with compassion at the thought of possibly offering them a better life. And so I hastened to conclude a deal without the foggiest notion of whether he was a good and reliable farmer or what in the world I—a single woman and foreigner facing an imminent transfer from Italy—was doing taking on the responsibility for four human beings as an absentee landlord. Yet I recited my lines as the realtor had coached me, and the farmer nodded. Then I shook hands with him and his entire family on the deal. He would start work the very next day—presumably after his escape with his family from his present miserable surroundings.

Almost immediately I set to work to make the little caretaker's house alongside the old farmhouse habitable, patching up broken walls, setting tiles in the floors, and installing a bathroom and kitchen. We also had problems with the old well and water supply, which may certainly have been the reason the place had been abandoned. The farmer and his family needed water and the "enterprise" needed water as well if we were to do any serious cultivation.

My madness in acquiring a 350-year-old farmhouse in Tuscany and engaging a farmer/caretaker started a whole new cycle and experience in my life. I may have done it subconsciously to take my mind off my mother's death; certainly I had no experience in property management, much less knowledge of winemaking. But I was euphoric being in the midst of Tuscany and a part of that historic and idyllic land. Then came the rather painful "bloodletting" of cash for a new wine press, new stainless steel vats, bottles, capping machines, and the rest. But the press and the other equipment in the old cave under the farmer's house alongside the road would serve us well. And the location was good on the one-lane road off the main highway between Rome and Florence.

We eventually got our production up to more than 2,000 liters of wine a year and sold the bulk of it to the local cooperative as certifiable Chianti. I did not count on all the drinking by the farmer and his many friends, including the realtor. But since the venture was undertaken more as a game than an economic venture, I relaxed and played Marie Antoinette, who had also tried to run a farm outside Versailles, but with unlimited funds and farmhands. I also managed to live a silly dream. I filled a huge, raffia-encased demijohn with our Chianti, strapped it to the top of my little car, and drove triumphantly back to Rome, looking ever so much like the true landed Italian with the fruits of her own harvest.

There was much work with restoration of the farmhouse (never fully completed) and many frustrations with local suppliers and artisans, yet there was an entertaining side to this venture in Tuscany, though at the time I did not see the potential of writing it all up as Peter Mayle did many years later in Provence.

Rome, Italy, 1963–66, 1969–72

Embassy friends and others from our Consulate in Florence would gladly come to the farm on Sundays for a typical country outing. I would serve a Campari and bruschetta to all guests on arrival. They could sip their drinks on the steps or terrace of the farmhouse or walk with drinks in hand around the grounds, through the small olive grove, wheat fields, or down the hill to the vineyard in the valley; or they could stroll the half-mile or so across the foothills to a nearby village, as if called by its occasionally ringing church bells.

At lunchtime Mirella, the farmer's wife, would pull out from the huge outdoor oven—part of the supporting foundation of the farmhouse— whatever she had roasted for the occasion, sometimes chickens, other times a veal or pork roast, seldom beef. She would bring this up the stairs to the main oak-beamed room, where we were all seated around a long refectory table, just finishing our pasta with the superb rabbit sauce she herself had made. We usually had salad with the roast, lots of wine from *nostra produccione,* as we local farmers called our own product. For dessert we usually had mixed fruit, liberally sprinkled with cognac, lemon juice, and sugar, unless I had found an impressively decorated cake from the bakery in the village nearby. Espresso coffee helped take the edge off any excesses from the cocktails or the "wash" at dinner. Life could be beautiful. Mirella was there to do the dishes and clean up while we all drove slowly back to Rome. We let the racing nuts on the Autostrada—Italy's north-south superhighway—roar past us in their Alfas and Ferraris with throttles wide open. Other delights were the frequent sightseeing and shopping trips to Florence, just a half hour away on the Autostrada, and excursions west to Siena or east on the lower ridge of the mountains, or just exploring on back roads around Arezzo.

Before long I came to realize that complete restoration of the farmhouse was beyond my needs or my means. I installed two complete bathrooms, one at each end of the huge barn-like building; I kept the very attractive main room in the center pretty much intact, with its large beamed ceiling and huge, walk-in fireplace. It became less a sitting room than a dining room. A small basic kitchen was rehabilitated. On the south side, which was somewhat warmer, I redid three rooms as bedrooms, decorating a fourth as a sitting room and installing a small fireplace. The room looked out to the west over the Arno Valley to the Chianti Hills beyond. By then the many British who had also bought and redecorated farmhouses were beginning to call the area Chianti-shire. I had bought some rustic furniture on a skiing trip to Cortina d'Ampezzo in the Tyrolean section of northeastern Italy on the border with Austria. It fit in very well. Later I found a junk shop in the village of Montevarchi in the Arno Valley and bought an antique couch with graceful curved arms and knocked off the back to make a sort of chaise. It has been reupholstered at least four times and now graces the center of my Washington apartment, making it approachable from either side.

My greatest challenge in being an absentee landlord of a less than economic enterprise in Tuscany came when I was posted to Honduras. The farmer wired me to say that he would quit unless I bought him a tractor. What to do? I was thousands of miles away with job responsibilities. Yet I managed to take leave, persuade an Italian-speaking friend, the wife of an embassy officer, to accompany me and help steady my nerves, and flew back to Italy. In less than two weeks I managed with the help of the always available (at a price) realtor to find a secondhand tractor for sale. We rented a car and went up into the hills on one very cold winter day. The owner of the tractor turned out to be the mayor of the village, not a farmer. He had bought and used the tractor largely for status to impress his villagers, parading it through the town on special occasions like saints' days! It was in great shape. I bought it and thus retained my farmer, Giuseppe.

I used my visit back to Italy and the farm to lay down the law to him. I had to assume that he probably wanted to rent out the tractor as much as to use it on my property—a very Italian way of doing things. I told him we would continue to lose money unless he branched out a bit. Forget the uneconomical activities of tending the olive trees and growing wheat and corn, and raising his own smelly pigs, and concentrate instead on the wine—cultivating it, that is, not drinking up all the profits. I told him to give serious thought to a chicken farm, something the expatriates in our neighborhood seemed to be making money on. At that time, the Germans were also flocking into Tuscany, buying up old farms, and raising chickens commercially with the most modern assembly line techniques. They were selling in quantity to restaurants in Florence and Arezzo.

The farmer had a ready answer for me. It would be too much work, and we did not have enough water from our tired old well. Then, in typical

190

Italian fashion (they are loath to admit shortcomings or inabilities, even to give proper road directions!), he claimed he had all he could do to keep his five or ten odd pigs and make prosciutto and salami on the side. And didn't I enjoy the samples he had given me? Of course. End of discussion. He was certainly right on the water, so I did not press too hard for profits, asking only that he try to break even and no more losses, please. We struck an uneasy peace. I returned to Honduras thousands of miles away.

The spring following the tractor episode the farmer rudely informed me by letter that he had to leave by the end of the summer for family reasons, the full story not disclosed. So when my leave time came round, I returned to Italy on summer vacation and found to my surprise that the farmer had another job already lined up (probably on the realtor's recommendation). He was soon to be installed in a beautiful, fairly modern two-story stone house some thirty miles away, across the valley on the west side of the Arno River. It was property recently bought by some Germans who were setting up the most modern chicken production facilities. My farmer had already been assigned a uniform, cap, and muckraking boots! The chicken farm was organized in typical German fashion—everything well ordered and highly regimented. If the chickens could have worn uniforms, the owner would have arranged that too. And they had water!

Faced with a fait accompli, I realized I had to cut my losses as soon as possible and sell the farm after playing at it for six years. The deal I cut with the farmer was to split the remaining livestock and wine. But that was never to be. If I hadn't realized it before, it was soon crystal clear that an absentee landlord is a sitting duck for a resident farmer—I could never dignify him with the title manager. The local real estate agent who had sold me the property, promising on his dead mother's memory to protect my interests, was, I continued to assume, in close cahoots with the farmer, guiding him in his dealings with me so that they both benefited, even profited, especially when it came to selling the wine to the local cooperative.

Though the farmer had left his little house and the winemaking cave in fair condition, the livestock, meat products, and wine had disappeared, though my furnishings and other personal property were left intact. I spent a day or two foolishly driving about the countryside in search of farmer Giuseppe and the purloined prosciutto and salami, but neither he nor the

Rome, Italy, 1963–66, 1969–72

livestock could be traced. Giuseppe had left his wife and little girls to put me off the scent. The neighbors and the realtor were keeping mum on the subject, probably bought off with bottles of my wine and secretly praying "Yankee Go Home." I knew when I was beaten and finally gave up on the third day of my fruitless search.

Had it all been worthwhile? It was indeed a wonderful learning experience, and I had certainly improved my Italian speaking ability, arguing and fighting with farmers and vendors. One fine weekend I had slyly brought my elderly Italian language teacher up from Rome to see the sights in Florence, enjoy an excellent, wine-filled lunch, and visit the farm. When I took the language proficiency exam some weeks later, she gave me a grade of 4 (5 being bilingual). We both knew it was a bit exaggerated, yet very Italian. As my tutor had enjoyed her outing in Tuscany, she perhaps gave me extra points for "manhandling" the natives, though seldom out-maneuvering them.

Pettiness from Important Visitors

U.S. embassies the world over are regularly called upon by the State Department to receive and extend hospitality to important visitors from the States (so-called VIPs), who come in all sizes, shapes, and forms but mainly from the U.S. Congress (CODELs). One such was the former governor of Texas, John Connally, who will be remembered for his proximity to President John F. Kennedy when he was assassinated in Dallas. For reasons long since forgotten, Connally arrived at Ciampino Airport, close to the center of Rome near the Appian Way, and used mainly for government and VIP visitors.

In prior phone conversations, there had been some differences between the ambassador, Graham Martin, and the governor over the visit's goals, appointments, and scheduling. It seems the ambassador was fed up with the prima donna manner Connally had adopted. Precisely what had gone wrong during the telephone exchanges regarding plans for the visit was never clear other than that the two men had become deeply antagonistic. Ambassador Martin decided that while he would extend appropriate hospitality, he would be darned if he would go out to the airport to welcome the governor. Instead he dipped down a couple of ranks and sent me as his emissary. Surely Ambassador Martin had assumed that assigning me as VIP greeter—a woman and not his deputy—would hardly be especially appreciated by a man of Connally's nature.

I had been instructed to use the ambassador's limousine and chauffeur and extend all courtesies in receiving the governor and accompanying him back to Rome. The governor arrived with a sizable entourage. An embassy-hired bus was to bring the rest of the party into the city. When the plane touched down just at dusk on the appointed day, I walked over to the ramp, introduced myself, and greeted the governor in my most gracious manner, explaining the ambassador's absence and that I was there to escort him back to town in the limo.

"Where is the ambassador?" Connally growled. I feigned some "previous commitment with the Italian government" for the ambassador's inability to be at the airport. Connally immediately shot back, "Unable or unwilling?" That I do not know, I replied. So we walked in dead silence over to the waiting limo. Obviously piqued at the slight and possibly annoyed that the ambassador had sent a woman to meet him (it was still the 1960s), Connally shoved me away from the limo, motioned to the bus, and said, "You go back there, with my staff." So I rode back into town in the bus, hoping he was enjoying his solitary splendor and fat ego in the limo. Later, during the reception in his honor at the ambassador's residence, I kept my distance, and the governor did not once look my way. Lesson learned: pettiness does not make for true greatness.

Off Hours—Holy Water Golf Course

When I had a free weekend and wasn't tending the farm in Tuscany and haranguing the farmer, I enjoyed playing tourist and driving around Rome. These jaunts among the city's ancient and dazzling sights, museums, and galleries, as well as brief excursions to the Castelli Romani or Alban Hills to the east of Rome, freed me from always feeling "official," with government responsibilities. Besides, I knew that my Roman assignment would not last forever, nor would I be lucky enough to enjoy a third one.

Rome, Italy, 1963–66, 1969–72

I also played golf, strange as that may seem, given the endless attractions in a city like Rome. But the setting was idyllic—a golf course just a few miles east of Rome, roughly in the area between the lines of the old Roman aqueduct and the Appian Way. The club was called Aqua Sancta, meaning Holy Water. When I told friends back home the name of the course, they just rolled their eyes and said, "You've got to be kidding!" And to make the fable complete, that particular golf course was frequented quite often by the princes of the Catholic Church—hardly ever the Europeans, mainly the Americans. They took great delight in striding along sunken fairways that had once been catacombs and putting on greens that might have been the site of Nero's or Claudius's fields, pastures, or vineyards.

The American churchmen came to the course fairly well disguised in their sports outfits. When I would catch up with their twosomes or threesomes (seldom foursomes, curiously enough), they would either let you go through, or if in a sociable mood, ask you to join them. Cardinal Krol from Philadelphia was a frequent player. Once when I met up with an archbishop who introduced himself as Benincasa, I quipped, "Oh, you must be related to St. Catherine of Siena." "Yes I am," he replied nonchalantly, although four centuries separated them! I found it rather hard to concentrate on my game after that encounter.

A Notorious American Prelate

I also played golf at a place just north of Rome called Olgiata, a newer, more U.S.-type course built around beautiful homesteads or villas but minus the historic aqueducts, catacombs, and Roman ruins that surrounded the Holy Water Club. It was at Olgiata that I met up with the notorious American archbishop, Paul Marcinkus, who was in charge of the Vatican Bank. From Cicero, Illinois, he was tall, strong, and a former high school baseball player who sounded like it. This archbishop could really hit the hide off a golf ball. Knowing him over a span of several years and perhaps because we were both midwesterners, I found him to be a warm, personable, and generous individual, not at all a distant and cold churchman. He was especially concerned about the poor in Africa, where he had served briefly at the Nunciatura in Uganda. Despite his somewhat gruff exterior, I came to appreciate him as a genuinely good and kind person. I feared he might have an incredibly poor talent for picking business associates and trusting them far too much. I wondered if things might not have gone better for him had he been a Harvard Business School graduate in addition to having a degree in theology. He retired to Sun City, Arizona, and I never saw him after Rome or heard his side of the Vatican bank scandal story. He has since gone to God.

Certainly every American in Rome and many foreigners as well as Romans knew or heard of "the American archbishop in charge of the Vatican Bank." Somewhat out of curiosity and because of the easy entrée it afforded to Vatican City, I set up an account at the Vatican Bank, which would prove useful on my next assignment to Africa. Because of our shared midwestern background and interest in golf, I found the archbishop easily approachable and helpful with some of my official duties with the Vatican. He gave me the opportunity to test and sort out some of the problems I ran into as I was shutting down the PL-480 Food for Peace U.S. grant program, which meant ultimately denying the Vatican some of its political levers of influence in Italy.

Archbishop Marcinkus was a frequent guest at Ambassador Martin's receptions. He was extremely popular with the expatriate American community. Indeed some of the "Mafiosi" (a nonpejorative label sometimes applied to the well-meaning Italo-Americans among the expatriate community) banded together and bought the archbishop an old villa on the outskirts east of Rome.

Over the years the area had degenerated from residential into a messy industrial site. The villa was located close by the Autostrada and smack in the middle of a building contractor's work site with heavy machinery and equipment all around. No family in their right minds would have wanted to live there, but it was useful for the American prelate's private entertainment purposes. It may well have reminded him of parts of Cicero.

The site was well hidden and isolated, with no construction work going on over the weekends, thus ideal for the prelate and his friends in the American community to use for their Sunday picnics and outings. It afforded the American archbishop a strong link to home and probably a welcome escape from the Vatican.

Rome, Italy, 1963–66, 1969–72

Difficult Dealings with the Vatican

It was inevitable that I would have some professional connections with the Vatican, given one small aspect of my embassy work—closing down the PL-480 food relief program. Begun immediately after World War II, the program had dragged on for twenty years for both humanitarian and Cold War–related reasons. Few beneficiaries wanted to lose out on American largess. It had originally been administered by a large USAID mission but had gradually been reduced to a small Italian staff of some five or six clerical people, including, supposedly, a relative of a certain Cardinal Ugolini, whose name was always spoken in hushed terms. I assumed that the relative could hardly be the first to go in the reduction in force that I was about to administer, or I would soon hear about it from "on high" across the Tiber. (Years later, I learned that this particular cardinal was the famous contemporary of St. Francis of Assisi!)

But my orders were clear: begin immediately to reduce the total value of U.S. PL-480 food assistance (mostly wheat but some corn, cheese, and margarine) to zero. From an initial grant totaling $350 million, disbursed annually in decreasing amounts, $60 million remained, which I was ordered to phase out in three years.

The program was only a tiny part of my work yet something of a big nuisance. Hardly a month passed that I didn't receive notices that shipments of food assistance from the United States had gone astray. The operators of a small pleasure craft in the port of Bari, for example, had been able to buy American flour from the local black market. It was obviously from the PL-480 program, as the sacks were clearly marked "Gift of the People of the United States" in bold blue letters on the sack. Or a call would come in reporting that a priest in some obscure Italian village had sold the U.S. gift flour to buy shoes for the children's First Communion ceremony! I had only to walk down the Via Veneto to a local pastry shop that sold the most delicious small pizzas ever, sneak a look into a back hallway, and there see sacks of our flour with U.S. gift markings that had somehow found their way on to the black market and into the Via Veneto shop.

When I complained to the Vatican's supervisory office, manned by an American monsignor (on the make to becoming bishop of Brooklyn), he would blandly cite statistics and what he claimed were U.S. government tolerance levels of "unavoidable losses" from 5 to 10 percent. He asked why I was always so exercised about reported losses. My standard reply was to urge greater vigilance and control, complaining that the losses were something the American taxpayer would not appreciate. It became a dramatic skit that we would play and replay. Presumably this monsignor felt I should share in his pain that the U.S. grant food program was gradually being phased out, because the net effect, he argued, was that the church in Italy and the closely aligned Christian Democratic Party were losing valuable political leverage to the leftists. I argued that serving the poor, *not politics*, was the reason for the program and it was phasing out.

One day the monsignor phoned me to say there was a command performance at the Vatican of some bishops and a cardinal at which I was to appear. (Was I to be measured for a noose around my neck?) Reluctantly, I appeared as "invited" to the kangaroo court. I went to one of those Mussolini-style buildings along the Via della Conciliazione leading to the Bernini piazza of St. Peter's Basilica, and then upstairs to an enormous conference room. I was given a place with my back to the door and seated in a circle of high-backed chairs arranged in a large oval. Strangely enough there was no conference table, making all the participants rather exposed. I immediately saw it as an awkward situation, probably intentional. There I was, the only woman in the assembly, dressed in a suit with a skirt to my knees, while all the prelates were in black. A few assorted bishops and one cardinal offered some color in cassocks or skirts down to their ankles! Forget the diplomatic training course; this seemed more like the Spanish Inquisition.

The monsignor led off, then took a question or two. The bulk of the interrogation was directed at me and reducible to such main essentials as: "Why was the U.S. government cutting out this program when the needs of the poor continued so great? Was I informing my government? Was I urging it not to phase out this program? Did not my conscience and faith inform me of the great human needs in Italy?

As calmly as I could, I asserted that the U.S. government had provided a great deal of humanitarian assistance to all the people of Europe in the post–World War II period. The war had ended nearly twenty-five years ago, and times were changing. Italy in particular had benefited greatly; besides, there had been no open-ended U.S. commitment to continue such assistance indefinitely. Moreover, U.S. assistance had been clearly targeted to help economic recovery so that Europeans might begin to help themselves. And wasn't the "economic miracle" in Italy proof that these objectives were being achieved?

I could almost sense hearing the Italian equivalent of "bold hussy" (*troppo coraggiosa*) in the heavy breathing of my clerical audience. So I thought it time to stand and take my leave, as gracefully as I could under the strained circumstances. The monsignor had obviously set me up with this theatrically staged meeting at the Vatican as a means of easing his own pressured position and shifting some of the criticism for the closure of the U.S. food aid program, of which the Vatican and Italy had been the beneficiary for well over twenty years.

When I was about to take leave of Rome, and perhaps to offset any negative impressions from the Vatican "inquisition" over the PL-480 drawdown, the monsignor arranged a beautiful farewell luncheon in the reception rooms of the Vatican warehouses, where U.S. relief supplies had been stored before distribution. To take even more of the sting out of that Kangaroo Court at the Vatican, he presented me with three magnificent gold medallions bearing the images of recent Popes—a handsome gift indeed, this after a graceful and laudatory little speech about my work at the Embassy.

Generally Foreign Service officers and U.S. Government officials are prohibited from accepting gifts of any value. So I hurried back to DCM Francis Meloy at the Embassy to ask, "What do you think?" He took a careful look, shook his head, and judged the gold to be "fake."

What do you mean?" I insisted. "See this certificate attesting they are real gold, of lower carat, to be sure, but gold."

"I don't think so," he insisted, "so you can keep them." And so I did. Years later at a dinner party in New York for the monsignor, he asked me, "By the way, did you ever sell your gold papal medals?" I was shocked with his query, especially when he added, "I sold mine, and I can tell you they're worth about $3,000 to $4,000!"

(A footnote on Frank Meloy, our fine, middle-aged DCM, who very soon thereafter became ambassador in Beirut, Lebanon. Before he could become fully involved in delicate peace negotiations there, he was gunned down in June 1972 by alleged terrorists at a checkpoint. His body was rolled up in an Oriental carpet and later found by the roadside.)

Rome, Italy, 1963–66, 1969–72

Silenced by the Pope

While my mother was still alive and able, I took her to a Good Friday cere-mony at the church of Saint Paul Outside the Walls over which Pope John XXIII was to preside. My mother had a strange fascination with that church. On her first visit she wanted her picture taken in the courtyard by the statue of Saint Paul. She stood right under his outstretched arm hold-ing a sword over her head—another of her forebodings in Rome?

At that particular Good Friday ceremony, we were up near the altar with a throng of hundreds pressed tightly against a temporary wooden barricade to allow good Pope John XXIII to pass with his courtly en-tourage. As we stood in the front row to receive his blessing as he passed, I heard some muted shouts of "Viva il Papa" in the background. Caught in the spirit of the ceremony, I repeated "Viva il Papa" at the top of my lungs. The Pope looked directly at me with piercing eyes and in a loud voice said, "*Silencio.*" I was shocked into silence, realizing that he wanted no exultation on one of the most solemn days of the Church, Good Friday, and didn't I have the sense, foreigner that I was, to respect the solemnity of the occasion?

Having been silenced by the Pope himself, I have tended ever since to spend Good Friday between utter silence and whispers.

In Somma (To Conclude)

There is something about Italy; the people, their mannerisms, their cus-toms, and food that is very special (*unico,* as the Italians say). Nothing quite like the Italian experience can be found anywhere else in the world. It can be subtle, satirical, and almost always exquisitely humorous. As for the wonderful Italian foods and wines, they almost defy description and can only be appreciated for their beauty and deliciousness if one takes the time and leisure to enjoy them to the fullest and in good company. A book I recently discovered in English, entitled *Sprezzatura,* confirms this. Hard to translate, it means that uniquely Italian style of excellence in whatever art, profession, or human endeavor in which the Italians are engaged and deals with their special way of enjoying life to the fullest.

Rome, Italy, 1963–66, 1969–72

People invariably ask me, "What country or assignment did you enjoy the most?" The answer has to be Italy, where I enjoyed three assignments—Milan once in the 1950s and Rome twice, once in the 1960s and again in the early 1970s, for a total of nearly eight wonderful years of total immersion. The country offers not only rich history and rich geography but deep humanity and beauty—in art, music, and landscapes beyond compare, from seashore to mountains and hillside vineyards, far more sustenance for soul and body than any one human being can absorb in a lifetime. I owe Italy a deep sense of gratitude for enriching my life and never taking anything too seriously, for there is always *domani*—tomorrow.

The Romans say, "*Roma c'e voule una vita*," meaning it takes a lifetime to see it all. The same and more could be said for the entire Italian peninsula—the work of thousands of years and millions of lives that made it the treasure it is for the entire world. I must confess to having become an Italophile after eight glorious years there. *Tante grazie*.

Rome, Italy, 1963–66, 1969–72

NINE

Tegucigalpa, Honduras, 1966–69
(Deputy Chief of Mission; Chargé d'Affaires a.i.)

Sensitivity Training for Leadership

As my first assignment to Rome in the mid-1960s ended abruptly with the death of my mother, who had been my in-residence dependent for ten years, the Department of State was at its sympathetic best with my next assignment. I was transferred to a different continent, a different language, and a leadership responsibility that became a turning point in my career—deputy chief of mission (DCM) to Embassy Tegucigalpa in Honduras.

I thus became the first woman assigned as deputy ambassador to a Latin American post. I spoke Spanish, had geographic familiarity from previous assignments to Colombia and Chile, and had gained some leadership experience as commercial counselor at Embassy Rome. Also in my favor was the year in the Senior Seminar in Foreign Policy in Arlington, Virginia.

The State Department seemed to think that my preparation for Honduras should also include "sensitivity training" with a group of midlevel peers. Again I was the only woman in an otherwise all-male group of twenty-five. A curious course, its location at Garmisch-Partenkirchen in Germany was even more curious, apparently chosen because of easy accessibility for participants selected from around Europe and the Middle East. I came up from Rome, still grieving deeply only weeks after my mother's death—not the best circumstances for "sensitivity" training.

With superb mountain scenery as backdrop, we sat for a week through trainer-led modules on leadership, group dynamics, and behavioral problems, then took turns sitting on what was called "the hot seat." This meant being the center of attention while colleagues fired challenging questions on whatever subject they could get away with of a personal or official nature. It was vitally important to keep one's cool.

Once on "the hot seat" I was thrown a curve: "What makes YOU think YOU will make a good DCM in Honduras?" Even though my colleagues were generally of minister-counselor rank and came from heading sections in the largest embassies in Europe, none had yet been named No. 2 in an embassy. Perhaps none would have given a second thought to a small post in Central America. But it was the title that caught their attention and the chance it represented to stand in for an ambassador as chargé d'affaires ad interim, whether for a day or possibly months.

I resented the pettiness, perhaps even jealousy, behind the question. But I hid my feelings, realizing it was only a game of sorts. In the mid-1960s, the Feminist Revolution hadn't yet taken hold. Many men were still having trouble adjusting to the possibility that women might be their equal, or even be leaders like men. I refused to be assertive on the subject and was silent on the revolutionary feminists, who seemed at times to focus almost exclusively on gender and to ignore quality of performance, experience, and compatibility as critical factors in achieving their goals. I believed there was a different way, based on natural complementarity and not rocking the boat.

It was clear that men had primacy of place in jobs and leadership in those days, but women were increasingly getting into professions like the male strongholds of law and medicine, as well as business. Women were generally tolerated, even liked, if they were "humble" enough, didn't push too hard, or get too far out ahead of the men.

When that rude question was thrown at me during the course at Garmisch, it appeared to go beyond theoretical testing to convey real doubts about my leadership ability. I drew a deep breath, then replied in such a soft, measured voice I hardly recognized it: "I did not ask for the job. The

Department of State assigned me to it and seems to have confidence in my ability to discharge it; so I will try to do the best I can, based on my background and experience."

Although the question deeply offended me, it was probably legitimate within the bounds of what the course was trying to achieve, and I was determined not to break into tears. Unfortunately, the man before me had wept when mercilessly set up by his classmates. While on the hot seat he left himself wide open by "running at the mouth" with some foolish admissions about his domestic life. He said he expected his wife to be waiting for him after work with a cool drink and his slippers! The questions that followed were heartless. As he stumbled about with answers, his self-confidence faded and he broke down.

Following the session I sat next to the trainer at lunch. I told him I thought it was nothing short of jealousy that prompted the question I got regarding my competency to be a DCM. "Then why didn't you go right back at those men and speak your true feelings of resentment? Being frank and open, able to deal with adversity, and remain self-confident are among the objectives of this course." I mumbled something to the effect that we were all supposed to be diplomats with training and experience, able to act in well-mannered, cordial ways, rather than being blatantly assertive and controversial, or at worst, riding roughshod over others. I thought there was a point beyond which one should not go in the interests of civility and decency.

While not saying so to the moderator, I was beginning to have serious doubts about the risks and efficacy of this so-called sensitivity training, especially if it drew in some emotionally unstable people. I understood the methodology of the course was "borrowed" from the corporate sector, where it had proven an effective training technique for upper management. But wasn't it risky?

Some years later I learned just how dangerous the course could be for certain people. Several trainees had completely broken down, just as the man before me in Germany had. Also making the rounds was the story of one State Department official who, under the strain of the course, had been pressed to reveal personal things about his life and later committed suicide! A few other trainees had even been hospitalized. Eventually, the Department of State discontinued the course. So much for trying to teach

Foreign Service officers how to be "more sensitive" managers. Frankly, I thought one learned on the job from kind and considerate colleagues and mentors.

One thing the course taught me was to be extremely cautious in delving too deeply into the personal motivations and behavior of employees, but instead referring questionable cases to the professionals in the medical and personnel fields. While personnel oversight was a good part of my new responsibilities (fortunately, I encountered only a few genuine oddballs), my basic challenge as DCM in Tegucigalpa was to know, understand, and support my boss, the ambassador, and be able to stand in for him should the need arise. I also had to learn about the country and the Central American region in general and the nature of our bilateral relations and country program objectives.

Wheels Down in the Mountains

My arrival in the Honduran capital in 1966 was a near disaster. I had flown out of Miami on an American carrier, then changed in Guatemala to TACA, a local company that was flying a British Aircraft Corporation (BAC) 111 on its maiden commercial voyage into Tegucigalpa. The city acquired its name from the Mayan Indian word for the silver hills that surrounded it, which the Spaniards had mined in the sixteenth century. Teguse is high in the mountains at nearly 4,000 feet. Honduras is bordered by El Salvador and Guatemala to the north and west and by Nicaragua to the south. It was the poorest country in Central America.

No one had warned me that at that elevation the landing would be fast; nor had they noted that the landing strip had been built for propeller planes, not jets. The runway began at the very base of a minor mountain range and ended at a small, narrow canyon. It required the pilot to fly in wing-over-wing, level off abruptly, and immediately drop his wheels on the landing strip, while braking heavily before reaching the canyon side. No wonder the Honduran military had sought aviation training from the United States! Even the president of the republic, an army general, had taken flight training in Arizona. Nor did I know—perhaps just as well—that a few planes, and prop jobs at that, hadn't quite made it on landing and ended up going over the cliff into the canyon at the end of the runway.

During the BAC III's racy approach down the mountainside all the food trays suddenly flew out of their moorings in the galley and clattered end over end through the aisle with a frightening noise. I wondered if the plane were coming apart at the seams. As we rolled to a stop and turned at the short runway's very edge, there was a deathly hush among the white-faced passengers. Then the captain's voice came over the loudspeaker with a humble "sorry about that." Perhaps because it was the jet's maiden voyage and we were still alive, all was forgiven.

As we taxied back to the terminal, I could see a lineup of about ten men and women, all sparkling in their Sunday best, some of the men in uniform. Aha, a dignitary, I thought. But no, they looked American and guess what? It was my new boss and his wife and the whole Country Team to welcome me! Ambassador Jova broke away from the group and came out to the steps leading down from the plane. "Welcome to Honduras," then quickly, "Are you all right? That was some frightening landing." I told him that the ground under my feet never felt better. Then he led me over to introduce me to the lineup of senior officers and wives. Each commented on the "scary landing" and inquired as to my well-being.

Appreciative as I was of the courtesies extended, I was relieved when the formal ceremony ended and I was driven off to my new home, where I could stretch out and rest from the trip. It was a lovely house in the hills overlooking the capital, with bluish mountains in the haze beyond the city. I was quickly introduced to a domestic staff of three: a cook, a maid/housekeeper, and a gardener, in addition to the driver and car that had brought me in from the airport. The bed welcomed me. After twenty years in the Foreign Service, it seemed as though I had arrived—and in high style. Forget the flying lunch trays on landing. I could take it.

Trying not to let the job and accompanying honors go to my head, I soon settled into my new home and office, met my secretary—a wonderful older woman who had been in Honduras for years, seemed to know the ropes well, and obviously had not the slightest feelings about working for another woman. Indeed, she tended to mother and protect me without overdoing it. I must have looked very naïve in those days. I considered myself fortunate indeed.

Tegucigalpa, Honduras, 1966–69

My New Ambassador—A Wonderful Man

My new ambassador, Joseph J. Jova, had shown courage and innovation in choosing me to be the first woman DCM in an embassy in Latin America, "land of machismo." I was deeply in the ambassador's debt and soon forgot all the chauvinists I had met during the sensitivity training course in Germany and elsewhere. Whenever he introduced me, Jova delighted in telling people that the history of the world showed how men and women working closely together, indeed very closely, had created truly beautiful things (big smile!).

Psychologically speaking, I often wondered if his decision to choose a woman as his deputy could have been to offset some problems he encountered with the previous DCM, whose wife had been the real problem. She reportedly stuck her nose constantly into her husband's DCM business. If this was a factor in the ambassador's thinking, his choice of a woman DCM was a clever ploy to excuse him from appearing prejudiced against women. But more than likely, given the man he was, fairness probably governed the decision far more. He had been chief of personnel in the Department of State, where he had certainly noticed that women were not getting a fair share of the leadership positions. He obviously thought the times were right to break the male monopoly and make history at the same time. He was that kind of person.

I quickly learned in "Teguse" (as we came to call the capital of Honduras) that it was important for ranking officers to have a good, healthy relationship with the ambassador's wife. My first lesson came the hard way—at a reception at the ambassador's residence. I suddenly realized I was being "just too helpful," with my suggestions to the domestic staff, especially when someone needed a drink or a canapé. Just one look and a word from Mrs. Jova cured me from further encroachment on her territory. It was her house and she, not anyone from her husband's staff, would manage the reception, thank you very much. She was too nice a person to be that blunt in saying so, but her look was right on. If guests didn't get a second drink or an hors d'oeuvre quickly enough, I learned to just smile and keep the conversation going. No frantic signals to the ambassador's domestic staff. I had my job and the hostess had hers, and she clearly considered any assistance from embassy staff a reproach.

Tegucigalpa, Honduras, 1966–69

I was learning that my work as second to the ambassador put me in the position of both filter and buffer regarding anyone on the embassy staff who "simply had to see the ambassador." This meant staying in close and daily contact with the heads of embassy sections—political economic, consular, administrative, public affairs, military, and USAID, as well as the country Peace Corps director. It also meant learning how to sift the important from the trivial and when not to stand in the way of access to the ambassador.

All in all, we had nearly three hundred Americans at our embassy in Honduras, our core diplomatic ranks having been swelled by USAID, Military Assistance, and Peace Corps personnel. The secretarial and clerical staff of U.S. and host country nationals numbered only around thirty. We also had a U.S. Marine security detachment of some seven noncoms. The consulate in San Pedro Sula, near the north coast, had a staff of eight, of which four were Americans.

The ambassador—or the chargé (me) in his absence—held weekly staff meetings at which all heads of section reported on developments in their areas. We tabled and discussed issues. We carefully reviewed Washington's cables and instructions, and we made decisions on courses of action, including recommendations to Washington. The ambassador frequently asked "country team" members about a given topic to ensure that he heard all views before devising an appropriate action plan. For example, when a major international paper company made plain its intent to undertake a massive investment in a pulp and paper mill on the north coast, the department asked the embassy to assist. The ambassador encouraged all section chiefs to present their views on the political, developmental, environmental, social, and cultural implications of such a massive effort, and in time, the embassy was able to fine-tune a helpful assistance strategy.

My highly competent deputy and chief of the Economic Section, Albert Zucca, reminded me of one very touchy economic issue that the country team labored over—the imposition by the State Department of "voluntary import quotas" on Honduran exports to the United States of various grades of beef (not unlike the case of shoes in Italy). This highly protectionist measure adversely affected agricultural and business interests not only in Honduras but also in other Central American countries, even beneficiaries of U.S. development assistance. The embassy's country team discussed the problem in its broadest political and economic implications and devised ways to make the new policy palatable to the Honduran government and industry, using appropriate political suasion, public relations measures, and alternative assistance strategies.

Our bilateral economic relations, normally cordial, became strained. Not surprisingly, the Honduran military had certain links with the business sector, even high up in government. In earlier days, while still in the lower ranks of the armed services before he became president, Oswaldo López Arellano had been personally involved in the cattle industry, both as a rancher and shipper of beef products by air to the United States. Eventually, we were able to mitigate the worst effects of the restrictive measures by bringing various embassy elements, including political and military, to bear in a tightly coordinated manner.

Banana Republic of Honduras

Honduras was a friendly "banana republic" ruled by a benevolent military dictator. American corporations such as Standard Fruit Company (now Dole) and United Fruit had considerable investments in Honduran agriculture. The majority of numerous small mining interests (lead, silver, gold, and zinc) were also American. Shrimping, fishing, and tourism in the Bay Islands off the north coast were just coming into the economy in the 1960s, and the considerable potential for exploiting large tropical forest reserves frequently brought prospective American logging investors calling at the Embassy for advice.

The country had an interesting colony of "Turcos," Christian Arabs for the most part, who had emigrated from Lebanon and elsewhere in the Middle East. Along with a few Chinese, they had literally taken over much of the mercantile trade, especially in textiles but also branching out into real estate. A small colony of Cuban exiles concentrated on the legal profession and some agriculture. One family had developed rice and tobacco plantations and was turning out first-class cigars for export. Surprisingly, a number of mainland Chinese had gotten a toehold in the country, especially in the import-export business, some through legal immigration, others more casually through a corrupt sale of passports until the authorities stopped it.

Welcoming Nelson Rockefeller

My first challenging assignment in Honduras came with the two-day visit of New York Governor Nelson Rockefeller on a survey trip of Latin America. Honduras was his first stop and we needed to make a good impression. I was designated control officer, which meant being in charge of all arrangements for the visit. I assembled a small team of key embassy officers and developed an overall plan, from welcoming ceremonies to housing the VIP and his delegation to country briefings, receptions, and calls, starting with the president of the republic.

To facilitate communications between the visiting party of some ten people (including bodyguards) and my control staff, we set up a network of walkie-talkies borrowed from the U.S. military in Panama. With the "over and out" gobbledygook of those early days before earpieces and microphones, the system was rather primitive. It seemed we were constantly saying, "Would you repeat?" because of weak signals.

Wives were also engaged in helping to make all arrangements as smooth as possible. I remember one wife who was appalled with the furnishings in the one and only hotel deemed suitable for the Rockefeller party. She rushed back to her home, swept the bedspread off her own bed and exchanged it for the one in Rockefeller's room. She also exchanged a few pictures on the wall. Wives have long been the unsung heroines of embassy life, volunteering and stepping into emergencies with great panache and getting necessary things done.

The VIP delegation was in Honduras not more than a few hours when an armed troublemaker zeroed in on the Rockefeller party, took aim, and fired. Fortunately, the shot went wide of its mark and only took a chip out of an adjacent building. However, when the mass of demonstrators against Rockefeller (read, the USA) rioted in front of the cathedral on the central plaza, a policeman accidentally fired his rifle into the crowd, killing a student. Although Rockefeller had been scheduled to leave Honduras the next day after further meetings, including one at the Central Bank, we hurriedly canceled these when demonstrators again assembled with the clear intent of marching on the bank. Embassy Tegucigalpa doubled its own security for the remaining hours of the Rockefeller visit.

We had little choice but to rush Rockefeller out of the city to the airport for departure ahead of schedule. It was with some embarrassment that we bade him a hasty farewell and a more peaceful onward journey. The shots fired in Tegucigalpa were heard round the continent, and security at other posts on his itinerary was strengthened. The political leftists and anti-U.S. forces who staged the demonstrations must have hoped they could discourage the mission from continuing beyond Honduras. But Honduras turned out to be the only blotch on Rockefeller's goodwill tour through Latin America.

Almost simultaneously with the aborted attack, I came down with a blood clot in one leg and was hospitalized. My deputy control officer, Al Zucca, took over and did a superb job. Confined to a hospital bed, I was deeply frustrated. I heard all communications on my walkie-talkie but was unable to take any action or offer much useful advice.

Instead, my communications unit proved a source of some embarrassment. Left open by mistake at my hospital bedside, the walkie-talkie broadcast all the most intimate details of a conversation with my doctor on my physical condition. When told of this blooper, I decided to keep my hands and ears totally out of the visit and leave everything to my deputy. Learning when to step back and delegate was an important management lesson, hard as it was to accept.

Rockefeller was a man known for his kindness and gentility. When he heard of my hospitalization, he promptly sent two of his aides over with a large spray of orchids and a sweet get-well card. What a charmer! I realized that his reputation as a lady pleaser was well deserved.

We all relaxed when the Rockefeller plane took off, but we had not heard the last of this visit-gone-wrong. Honorable man that he was, keenly attuned to the political significance of unfavorable publicity, the governor had his people cable us to offer compensation of $5,000 (this was 1969) to the mother of the student who had lost his life during the demonstrations. The embassy's country team debated vigorously about the propriety of the U.S. government's getting in the middle of an offer to a poor Honduran family, which might interpret the offer as "blood money" and putting a price on life. We called Rockefeller's office in New York to express gratitude for the governor's kindness but reservations as to how such an offer might be interpreted in the Latin American context. But the Rockefeller people insisted we make the offer.

Zucca flew up to Puerto Castillo in the north to the mother's humble shack and presented her with a check in her name. She coldly refused the money, and we reported this back to the Rockefeller people. Both they and we learned a hard lesson about the sensitivities of the "poor but humble" people of Central America. To the victim's mother, her son's life was priceless.

President Lyndon Johnson in Honduras

Not long after the Rockefeller visit, Washington announced that President Lyndon Johnson would be coming to Honduras following the summit of Central American leaders in Guatemala. In a grand gesture so typical of the Texan president, Johnson invited each of the assembled presidents onto his plane for rides back to their capitals. One by one he dropped off the El Salvadoran, Honduran, Nicaraguan, Costa Rican, and Panamanian presidents.

Because the Teguse airport was too small to take the presidential aircraft, the drop-off and courtesy visit to the country had to be made at the much larger airport in the flatlands of San Pedro Sula on the north coast. The visit was to last no more than two hours, with formalities, speeches, and—at Johnson's personal request—a special show of paintings by Honduras's well-known artists. Because all of these artists were located in the capital, the embassy was required to negotiate temporary loan of their works and safe-packing and transport of the canvases and artists by air to San Pedro—no small task. Once delivered, we set up a makeshift gallery in the terminal building. This placed a demand on embassy services I had not envisioned; but I learned from Girl Scouting days to "be prepared" for most anything in diplomatic life.

Concurrently, the embassy was required to invite and then arrange with a local airline to bundle up the entire local diplomatic corps from their perches in Teguse and transport them to San Pedro as well so that

President Johnson would receive proper homage. The appropriate Honduran officials and military managed to get themselves there by military aircraft. After all, it was their president who was returning as well as our president who was arriving, if only for a brief visit.

It was fortunate that we had an American consulate in San Pedro headed by an able consul, Darwin Swett, who was well up to the task of handling all the ground logistics. The Honduran airport and local authorities proved most cooperative, and before too many hours we had two large waiting rooms in the terminal sectioned off, one for the ceremonies, one for the command art show, with easels set up and guards in place.

President Johnson cut his usual larger-than-life figure, tall, heavyset, and domineering. The official greetings and speeches over, he moved briskly with authority through the rows of paintings, saying, "I'll take this, that, this . . ." and so on, until he must have acquired ten or fifteen paintings. He kept repeating himself, "This will look good at the ranch." Aides trailing behind him kept handing out dollar bills, while others took possession of the canvases. Awestruck artists and VIPs looked on in amazement. It appeared to me as though Johnson was buying the stuff more by color than artistic merit. Mine not to reason why. The president showed none of the exhibitionism often seen in art galleries: moments for general ogling, stepping back, putting hand to jaw, tilting head, or any of the familiar gestures that usually go with buying a painting. No, it was more like Johnson was cutting sugar cane with one quick thrust of his arm after another as he walked the rows of easels.

Time was soon up. After a series of quick goodbyes and waves, a kiss thrown here and there, Johnson was out to the plane and off to deliver the last of his presidential guests. Johnson gave the impression of a man always in a hurry, doing business wholesale—never retail.

Civil Demonstrations

Soon after the high-profile visits of Rockefeller and Johnson, trouble struck Honduras in the form of anti-American demonstrations on the street outside the Embassy. University students marched on the Chancery carrying the Stars and Stripes upside down or tarred—no feathers. A few of their best hurlers would step out of the ranks and throw rocks at our building. Honduras was proving to be hardly the quiet, simple country of O. Henry's *Cabbages and Kings*.

On one such occasion the street demonstrators managed to wreak considerable damage on the Chancery's large glass windows. Flying glass nearly scalped a local employee, who received a severe head wound that bled profusely. I tried to get the local hospital down the street to send an ambulance but instead got a frightened voice informing me they wanted to go nowhere near the American Embassy during the demonstrations.

I recalled that President López Arellano had once told me, "If ever you have serious problems, just call me." So I called the Presidential Palace and said I had urgent need to speak with the president. He came on the line, and I explained the situation—"One of *your* citizens . . . injured at the Embassy . . . can't get him to hospital." He said he would immediately send his personal car. In no time a Mercedes-Benz appeared at our gates and whisked the local employee off to the hospital for treatment.

Another time, while I was chargé, demonstrators tried to scale the steep embankments fronting the Chancery. Three narrow garden levels led up to a high wall surrounding our building. As we warily watched the demonstrators, the Marine sergeant rushed up to my office and asked, "What are your orders, ma'am?"

Orders? I had no idea that commanding troops was part of my job description. "Orders?" I mumbled, biding time for inspiration.

"Yes, ma'am, what do you want us to do?"

Still temporizing, "Are those tear gas canisters on your belt?"

"Yes, ma'am."

I heard my rather automatic voice saying, "Well, I don't think you ought to use them until they start to breach the top wall. Is that understood?"

"Yes, ma'am"—whereupon I slumped back into my chair to contemplate my next military order without a clue as to how it would play out.

Perhaps the sight of our Marines in battle gear at the top embankment was enough to deter the aggressive university students. When next I peeked out the side of my office window, I saw that the "invaders" had scrolled out obscenities on our walls and were beginning to climb back down to rejoin the larger mob still shouting and hurling stones from the street.

Tegucigalpa, Honduras, 1966–69

Some of the anti-U.S. demonstrations we experienced in Honduras in the 1960s related to U.S. involvement in Vietnam, more specifically to what I personally thought was a rather high-handed U.S. diplomatic effort to engage the Hondurans as token allies in direct support of the U.S. war effort in Vietnam.

On their own initiative, without seeking Embassy Honduras counsel, the Washington power centers had provided a U.S. aircraft to the Hondurans, repainted and mocked it up with Honduran colors and flag, and "invited" the Hondurans to fly materiel assistance to Vietnam. Nonetheless, the scheme fitted in well with our ongoing training exercises of the Honduran Air Force. The Hondurans had never had such a long flight over water! I had misgivings about the phoniness of the mission, but I was too timid and too new in my job to raise objections. Nor did anyone else on the Country Team, including Ambassador Jova, who must have received some heavy arm-twisting from Washington.

The Honduran mission to Vietnam came off with far less local criticism of the sham than I had anticipated, except for continuing student demonstrations. In addition to providing the aircraft for the mission, the United States had supplied a few relief pilots and airmen to accompany the flight. The whole thing was so thinly disguised I wondered whom we thought we were fooling. For the Hondurans it was clearly a once-in-a-lifetime adventure, as well as a symbolic acknowledgment of and gratitude for substantial U.S. economic development assistance to Honduras.

One can always find nationals abroad who, for a price, are willing to get deeply in bed with Uncle Sam, especially if it is not understood as a permanent affair. There is a certain desire to please and return favors, also to feel close to the strong and powerful. It is risky to speculate on all the psychological factors at play in such international deals, minor as they may be and certainly as this flight to Vietnam was. No wonder these Latin American university students demonstrated when they learned their country was playing a game to curry favor with the Colossus of the North.

Once on another occasion when the ambassador was away and I was again the chargé d'affaires, I had reason to consult on matters of state (!) with the "President of the Republic and Generalissimo of the Armed Forces," Oswaldo López Arellano, a somewhat monosyllabic type, of limited education and words, who ruled mainly through a tough-minded civilian *eminence grise,* Ricardo Zuñiga. The meeting with *el presidente/ generalissimo* occurred at a formal reception at the Spanish Embassy. I thought my attire appropriate for making a favorable impression, garbed as I was in a formal black velvet evening dress, plus white leather opera-length gloves. Someone snapped a picture of this encounter. We were seated at a small table, which was good. Otherwise, had we been standing I would have towered about two feet over the president's head—not good.

What was bad, indeed very bad, was my posture. I was leaning toward the president with an outstretched, gloved hand with the most menacing of gestures. *El presidente/generalissimo* was in civvies, not his best dress uniform and hardly looked the part. Rather, he looked positively defensive if not threatened by this far-too-serious-looking young lady who had obviously been carried away by her temporary role as acting ambassador. Whatever I was advocating at the time was hardly worth the fierce intensity written on my face.

In retrospect, if the photo ever had any circulation, I may well have set back the cause of women diplomats in Latin America by long years rather than advancing it. Clearly I was a slow learner. The *presidente/ generalissimo* might have been far more receptive to my arguments at the time had I taken a page or two from the manners of Clare Boothe Luce or Pamela Harriman, dignified, stately, and yet ever-appealing to men.

Fortunately, no one ever showed the picture of my "attack" on the Central American president to my boss when he returned. But the experience and the photo served to remind me of what St. Francis of Assisi once said, "You can catch more flies with an ounce of honey than a barrel of vinegar." The lesson: Lightness in diplomacy is certainly more desirable— if the occasion permits—than heavy-handedness. But then beginners tend to be rigid, unsure of themselves, and even a bit frightened, if the truth be told.

Soccer War: El Salvador versus Honduras

The biggest thing that happened during my assignment in Central America was the miniwar in 1969 between Honduras and El Salvador. The United States was automatically involved because of our military assistance programs in both countries. It is hard to believe that the war arose mainly out of bruised national feelings over football matches between two mini-states, but it did, as the straw that broke the camel's back in a rivalry built up over years. Called the "Soccer War," it caused a lot of damage and human suffering.

Causes of the War

It seemed inconceivable that two countries that together were no larger that the state of Wisconsin or Georgia would go to war over a soccer game. But it wasn't just one game; it was actually two. The first between the two national teams had been played in Tegucigalpa. The Salvadorans won, but they returned home feeling they had been badly treated by their hosts and remained embittered. These bad feelings seemed to spread to the entire Salvadoran nation, proud Latins that they were.

When the return match was played in El Salvador some weeks later, the Hondurans took offense that their national anthem was played in jazz rhythms. And they were even more offended when—once again the losers—they were roughed up as they left the stadium. Later, on the road back to Honduras, their buses and cars were attacked by gangs throwing bags of urine and feces at them. Fistfights ensued whenever the Hondurans stopped en route back to their country.

There seemed to be too much bedlam and animosity for truth and accuracy in reporting; moreover, radio reports in both countries were contradictory and misleading. To the best of my recollection and that of Zucca, there was never a formal declaration of war, not even a published statement by the Government of El Salvador or its Military Command announcing and justifying Salvador's invasion of Honduras. There was considerable focus and publicity in the Salvadoran media—especially inflammatory radio accounts—of Honduran "abuse and mistreatment of Salvadorans in Honduras." For their part, the Hondurans focused on the "misbehavior and illegality of Salvadoran squatters" to explain why Honduras had incarcerated them. In fact, Honduran jails were full when the war began.

Little thought or analysis was given in either country to the root causes of the tensions dividing the two Central American neighbors that led to

Tegucigalpa, Honduras, 1966–69

the explosive, armed invasion by Salvador across its border with Honduras. The Salvadoran army's troop movements and artillery attacks occurred mainly along and parallel to the Pan American Highway in the south. Salvadoran forces also conducted rudimentary aerial bombardment of Tegucigalpa to the north and Choluteca to the east.

A critical factor behind this armed invasion was that Salvador's population had been bursting at the seams for many years, outstripping its natural resources. These pressures impelled many of its citizens to migrate north and east into Honduran territory in search of land and jobs. Honduras has five times the land area of Salvador with a million fewer people and little or no border control to impede this migration. Entire families moved freely across the border from Salvador into Honduras, even as far as the isolated plains (*llanos*) in the northeastern part of the country, and on into the open Aguan Valley below the Caribbean Sea.

Another cause of tension between the neighboring countries was Honduras's aggressive implementation of its agrarian reform program, begun in the mid-1960s and accelerated in mid-1969 under the energetic ideologue, Rigoberto Sandoval. The program was intended to survey and title land parcels and remove foreign squatters (largely Salvadorans), forcibly if necessary.

Understandably, this flood of more than 300,000 Salvadoran squatters caused resentment and friction between the natives and newcomers, leading to kidnappings, rape, murder, and other brutalities, mostly by Honduran civilians. The Honduran authorities did little to control or stop the violence, except for jailing the most flagrant offenders among the Salvadorans. These detentions provoked massive repatriation of Salvadorans to their homeland, increased demographic pressures there, especially in the poor rural areas—the natural base for the Salvadoran military—and only intensified the hatred and desire for revenge.

The soccer games between the two countries competing to qualify for the World Cup in July 1969 provided a separate but highly visible occasion for further confrontation. Each of the three games brought public violence in its wake. Exaggerated and distorted radio reports of the events helped inflame passions, until they reached the tipping point for the Salvadoran military, inciting their leaders to take matters into their own hands and invade Honduras in force.

The actual shooting at the border on the Pacific side of the country started up on July 14, Bastille Day, when we diplomats with host government officials were sipping celebratory champagne at the French Embassy. The party quickly broke up when Salvadoran planes started dropping bombs over the city, the first sortie causing more alarm than personal or property damage. Almost simultaneously, Salvadoran troops charged eighteen miles across the border into Honduran territory. Most of the damage was done there, near the border, from random shootings and wanton attacks on innocent peasants who were terrorized, some even killed, by columns of advancing armed soldiers. From the mountainous heights of Tegucigalpa we could look into the night sky and see the flashing lights of the heavy mortars and artillery on the border, though the sound was too distant to hear.

It was a trying time for me as chargé d'affaires—Ambassador Jova had just been transferred from post, leaving me in command of the U.S. embassy. I faced difficult and urgent decisions and also had to make important policy recommendations to Washington. But I had the support and comfort of a highly professional and able Country Team, all wanting to be a part of the action. I let them know I needed each and every one of them to help me, especially my newly conscripted deputy, Al Zucca, the economic officer. We worked well together in the emergency, and I was proud and grateful for their support.

Unfortunately a nasty rumor arose to the effect that the ambassador had anticipated the attack, departed the country before it occurred, and left a woman in charge of Honduran relations with the United States! This was grossly unfair, as nothing could be further from the truth. There was never a more chivalrous, responsible leader than that particular ambassador. But we had to make do without him during the war.

Just as Honduras went on high alert and the government decreed a curfew, I quickly assembled the Country Team to appraise and clarify the nature of the political and military situation. We intensified contact between key embassy officers and our opposite numbers in the host government, reported our findings and analysis to Washington and to our colleagues in neighboring San Salvador, which had launched the attack, and to the U.S. Southern Military Command in Panama.

Tegucigalpa, Honduras, 1966–69

The U.S. Embassy in El Salvador was doing more or less the same things as we were with their local contacts. But it wasn't long before Washington was receiving conflicting reports as to what was happening in the field and which side bore greater responsibility for the hostilities. Both countries were long-term recipients of U.S. military assistance and both were pleading to Washington for more weapons and material to defend themselves. The situation was becoming more than awkward. At one point the Honduran prime minister, Ricardo Zuñiga, screamed at me on the phone about the "planes flying overhead . . . and you MUST help us!" I could offer him little comfort or support.

Almost immediately after the first shot was heard, Washington declared a moratorium on all military assistance and a strict policy of evenhandedness. As instructed, we informed our host countries at the highest level that they were to implement an immediate cease-fire, withdraw all troops to their own borders, and cease all air attacks.

We in Honduras were somewhat annoyed that Washington failed to recognize that the only troops that had crossed borders were the Salvadorans. They had met little or no resistance, as the Hondurans seemed helpless to push them back beyond their borders. The Honduran air force had, however, sprung into immediate action and was flying some quite successful bombing and strafing missions into Salvadoran territory. It was hardly a secret that these actions were a source of pride to the U.S. trainers based in Teguse!

While temporarily out of a job with the military assistance moratorium, our U.S. trainers were closely monitoring the activities of the Honduran Air Force and Army. What more they might be doing I hesitated to think. I deliberately refrained from offering any direct instructions, leaving these delicate matters to the Defense and State Departments in Washington to sort out with the Defense trainers on the ground.

To the Presidential Palace with Machetes

Soon after hostilities began I was awakened from a sound sleep at 2 a.m. by a call from the Presidential Palace. It was none other than "OLA" as we called him, General and President Oswaldo López Arellano, himself with his gruff voice. "I want to see you immediately here at the Palace."

I quickly dressed, raced out the front door to my waiting car, and roused my driver, who was asleep behind the wheel on 24-hour duty. I explained my mission. "At this hour?" he queried in disbelief. So down the hill we went, sweeping up my deputy, Al Zucca, whom I had alerted by phone. As we attempted to cross a bridge, we were stopped by a roadblock manned by vigilantes armed with machetes. Between swigs of "guaro" (slang for the popular local alcoholic drink, *aguardiente*) they claimed they were ready (but were they able?) "to kill Salvadoran 'spies.'"

"No traffic past here," one of them shouted out.

"I'm going to see the president at his request."

"Well, well, well, that is a likely story," at which the vigilantes exchanged suggestive laughs and poked one another in the ribs, knowing the general's reputation and taste for the ladies. "No one gets beyond this point."

"Well I intend to, so you had better get out of our way, as I am going through. If you don't believe me, you can stop waving those machetes and get in the car and accompany me to the Palace."

What inspired that wild invitation I do not know. Yet two of them accepted, and together we drove on to our destination. We were escorted upstairs to the general's office, where we found him deep in phone conversation. He waved us to chairs by his desk. By hand signals and stage whispers he explained he was talking with his ambassador in Washington, who had been at the State Department for much of that afternoon. Given our evenhanded policy, he had been flatly turned down on the Honduran request for more arms to defend themselves. He told his ambassador to wait a minute while he asked me had I not described the local situation to Washington so that they understood Honduras was under attack and needed to defend itself, repeating his country's pleas for arms and ammunition. "Have you told them we have been *invaded* on land and are being bombed from the air?"

"I most assuredly have, and there is no change nor will there be a change in our policy of strict neutrality; you must negotiate a cease-fire and withdraw your forces, meaning your air force."

His repeated assertions and my responses were beginning to sound like a Greek chorus. I could say absolutely nothing beyond reiterating my official instructions: "U.S. policy is neutral and *evenhanded*—no arms to Salvador; no arms to Honduras. Sorry." After nearly an hour of this futile, rather ridiculous exchange, I stood, followed by Zucca. We excused ourselves, departed, and returned through the dark streets to our residences in the hopes of getting some sleep in what was left of the night.

The very next night, Zucca phoned me from the Embassy to say the Marine Guard had summoned him down, because a delegation of ranking Honduran officials at our closed gates were demanding entry and a meeting with me. The group included Prime Minister Ricardo Zuñiga, Minister of Economy Manuel Acosta Bonilla, Central Bank President Roberto Ramirez, and another cabinet official. Would I come down and receive them? Reluctantly, I dressed and made my way down to the Embassy in the dark. By then the vigilantes at the bridge recognized the car, the flags on the fenders, and the driver. They drunkenly waved me through.

I was somewhat irritated to find Zucca had given the visitors entry. I was even more annoyed to have to meet with them in our conference room only to hear them repeat the same unreasonable pleas I had heard from the president the night before. The only new touch, it seemed, was their colorful insistence that "even without U.S. arms, the Hondurans will defend themselves to the death, with machetes and bare hands, if necessary."

Tempted to reply "Well, then go to it, boys," I reminded them instead that I had met with President López the night before, heard the same pleas, and could only reiterate what I had told the president, based on firm and irrevocable instructions from Washington: U.S. policy was no arms, no ammunition, "*nada*," and this applied equally to Honduras and Salvador, both military assistance clients of the United States. It took no longer than a few minutes before I said, "Goodnight, gentlemen," stood, and left the Embassy, once again to try to get some sleep.

Enter the Organization of American States

Soon other actors became involved, obviously at the behest of the State Department in Washington. We were advised that the Organization of American States (OAS) was immediately sending two observer/negotiators, who would be based at U.S. Embassy Honduras.

We interpreted the choice of location for the OAS observers as tacit acknowledgment that El Salvador was the primary offender and Honduras the victim in the Soccer War. This despite mumblings from El Salvador that it had "gone to the rescue" of its oppressed citizens in Honduras "who needed protection." These assertions ignored the fact that these

Tegucigalpa, Honduras, 1966–69

Salvadorans had fled their country for lack of land and a livelihood and were squatting illegally in Honduras.

Washington asked U.S. Embassy Tegucigalpa to provide all administrative support for the OAS representatives, from necessary housing to important communications and transportation needs. The OAS had authorized its representatives to negotiate and enforce a cease-fire and a withdrawal of all troops.

Meanwhile our work at Embassy Tegucigalpa was clear and constant. We delved deeply into the causes and effects of the war, recorded all provocative events leading up to the attack, kept in close touch with the host government, and reported all developments to Washington. For a week it was 24/7 duty, as they say today.

The War and Its Consequences

The entire country of Honduras seemed to be in a state of mass frenzy. The misleading radio accounts of both the soccer games and the armed invasion undoubtedly incited listeners in Honduras. The Salvadoran squatters became like sitting ducks before mobs of angry Hondurans. Many Salvadorans were killed or injured, others arrested and jailed. It was thus understandable, but also alarming, that the military was able to round up an estimated 50,000 Salvadoran men, women, and children and, with all prisons and jails full, herd them into the sports stadiums of both major cities, Teguse and San Pedro Sula. The Honduran authorities explained the action as taken to "protect" the lives and safety of the Salvadorans and prevent further violence and bloodshed. By then an estimated 2,000 people had lost their lives from the armed invasion, the attacks on squatters in the rural areas, and general violence.

I sent Zucca to the stadium in Teguse to check on the situation there. He managed to enter and, out of range of the guards, talk with some of the detainees. Although he saw no signs of mistreatment or abuse, there was neglect as well as serious need for food, shelter, water, and sanitation among the thousands cooped up there.

Back at the Embassy I called yet another country team meeting to assess the overall situation and consider what action might be taken by the U.S. government. Our experienced military and USAID members provided excellent advice on dealing with such emergencies. We wasted little time in concluding there was urgent need for an immediate, large-scale relief mission. But first we had to make our intentions known to the host government and obtain their clearance, then seek Washington's approval of our recommended actions while urgently petitioning the U.S. Southern Military Command (USSOUTHCOM) in Panama for the necessary emergency relief supplies. As chargé d'affaires ad interim, I promptly registered my country's concerns with the Honduran government, insisting that international justice and human rights called for immediate correction of this callous treatment. Receiving no assurances in reply, I informed the Honduran government that the United States could not stand idly by under the circumstances and would immediately order up relief supplies from our military bases in the Panama Canal Zone. Furthermore, under international law we would expect no Honduran objections or problems when our planes landed in Tegucigalpa.

This brilliant, quick thinking did not spring magically out of my own head. For the most part I was running on nerves and little sleep, but I knew something had to be done for these poor, imprisoned people. Both my USAID director, Bob Minges, and military attaché, Col. Stephen Pagano, were well informed on international laws and our capabilities and limitations in emergency situations, and they gave me unerring guidance.

With all signals "Go," it took less than twenty-four hours for US-SOUTHCOM to stock and fly in one of those huge cargo planes (an early C-17 Globemaster). Miraculously, it found its way over the close mountain tops and landed without mishap on Teguse's tight airstrip. No sooner had it rolled up to the terminal than it let down its enormous cargo hatch in the rear and began discharging relief supplies to the waiting trucks we had ordered up.

I had invited the wife of the president, Doña Gloria López Arellano, the Catholic archbishop, the head of the local Red Cross, the dean of the Diplomatic Corps, and others to be present for the dramatic landing and cargo transfer. At that moment, Doña Gloria squealed, "Ees ours."

Rather sternly I replied, "No, Doña Gloria. These relief supplies are for the 50,000 or so Salvadorans you have incarcerated in your stadiums!" Not my most diplomatic moment, but necessary, I thought.

Tegucigalpa, Honduras, 1966–69

Cooler heads among my embassy staff who overheard the brief exchange reminded me that there were also urgent relief needs among Honduran peasant victims along the invasion route on the southern border. Apart from the dead, many had been wounded, were in shock, suffering from nerves, or had lost their dwellings and were without food. In brief, the relief supplies must be shared among affected Hondurans and Salvadorans, even though the latter were far more numerous.

Much later, Zucca recalled for me that during that long hectic week of war between the two countries, some Salvadoran vice consuls had run from their neighboring embassy to ours seeking asylum, because their lives had been threatened. We realized we could take no more than one of them and only for a limited time. Indeed, we had to hide him from our local employees, whose hatred was so intense against all Salvadorans we knew they would not hesitate to attack him if he were found on our premises. Under cloak of darkness a few days later, we were able to spirit him out of our building to another safe haven.

Soon after the invasion began, at moments when we in the Embassy felt it safe enough to venture forth, we had sent a few embassy officers out to observe firsthand what was happening within and about the capital area. Meanwhile, we were receiving good reports from our consulate in San Pedro Sula on the vast rural areas surrounding that city in the north. We also received an informative firsthand report from an American missionary bishop stationed in the northeast around Olanchito, where many Salvadorans had settled. He was a Catholic Dominican priest from the States whom everyone referred to by his first name, as Bishop Nick. He had flown into Tegucigalpa to report on his diocese to the local archbishop and visit the U.S. embassy.

The most moving, but pathetically amusing, part of his account concerned the Salvadoran madam of a local bordello, which had catered to a large battalion of Honduran soldiers stationed in the area. Some of the soldiers had gone after her Salvadoran women at gunpoint, more to menace them, it seems, than to injure or kill them. Nonetheless, the madam, who genuinely feared for her life at the hands of her enraged clientele, had fled to the bishop's house seeking refuge for herself and some of her girls. The bishop had put them up overnight and arranged the next morning for their return back to El Salvador. Somehow commercial flights had resumed service after only a brief interruption. Money seemed to have been no problem.

Another story coming out of the war was more sad than amusing. It concerned another American missionary—a Jesuit based in San Pedro Sula who had been helping the immigrant Salvadorans find work and shelter. Because of his help, he had been jailed and thrown into a cell with Salvadoran land squatters and prostitutes. When freed, he immediately called at the U.S. Consulate there, and the matter was promptly taken up with the local authorities. We included the story in our annual report to Washington on Honduran human rights abuses. It would not be the only time Honduras would be involved in human rights abuses. There was something about the military culture and authoritarianism of this underdeveloped country that had become deeply imbued in its society.

The wholesale manner in which the Honduran military authorities had rounded up all identifiable Salvadorans—some 50,000 in all, including small children and babies, as Zucca had personally seen—was perhaps the most flagrant human rights abuse during the war. Not long after the U.S. relief delivery described earlier, certainly less than a week, the Hondurans released the hostages incarcerated in the stadium, leaving them to find their way back to Salvador. It was one way of dealing with the influx of illegal land and job seekers. But in the north around San Pedro Sula, where they had been useful in the corn and rice fields and on the banana plantations, their absence was felt.

The war was never a serious threat to the capital city of Tegucigalpa. There were only the occasional buzzing of aircraft and rather pathetic attempts by the Salvadoran Air Force to drop bombs. Their planes had no bomb bays and their improvisations can best be described as quaint. As the Salvadoran cargo planes would fly low over the city, we could see the soldiers inside the open doors as they strained to roll the bombs and literally kick them out of the plane. So much for precision bombing. Naturally they fell wide of any intended target.

During that crazy week of war between Honduras and El Salvador, I received a tense phone call from one of our Peace Corps volunteers. No formal address or hello, just, "I hear you are in charge, and I want to know what you are going to do. A bomb just fell on my house and narrowly missed the baby in her crib. What are you going to do?"

Tegucigalpa, Honduras, 1966–69

"Did the bomb explode?" I asked.

"No."

"Then count your blessings," I said, "and move out into the open with the baby when you see or hear a plane coming." Then I hung up.

As soon as it seemed safe to do so after the first bombing attack on Teguse by the Salvadoran Air Force, I asked a few officers to check on the known Americans living in the capital city to ascertain if they were all OK or needed help in any way. We found one family where a bomb had fallen just outside their living room, leaving a small crater of about two meters deep. It seemed to have exploded skyward, fortunately doing no damage to building or residents. The family declined our offer to move them, contending that "lightning never strikes twice in the same place."

When reports came in that important oil storage facilities in El Salvador had been completely demolished in efficient bombing missions by the Honduran Air Force (HAF), our country team could not help but note somewhat wryly that our U.S. training mission to the HAF might have done a far better job than their opposite numbers in San Salvador. Sometimes pride of mission can become a form of clientitis—a "disease" in the Foreign Service in which Americans overseas develop a severe case of sympathy and defensiveness for the country to which they are assigned, sometimes swallowing uncritically everything the host government tells them about the local situation. I sensed a certain rivalry developing between the U.S. embassies in the two warring countries.

Among the many copies of messages from Washington during the hostilities, we received a brief direct cable from our embassy in San Salvador. The ambassador there, William Bowdler, suggested that he needed a fuller picture of the strategic situation and believed some personal surveillance in Honduras by his own political officer as well as with Honduran officials would be helpful. Would we please meet and consult with his embassy officer, who would be arriving that very morning in Tegucigalpa?

I could not help but feel that Bowdler—able officer that he was—might not only be pulling rank, but perhaps also sex! Did men know best in time of war, at least in those times? It was obvious that our ambassador in El Salvador had little confidence in what U.S. Embassy Tegucigalpa under the leadership of a woman chargé d'affaires was reporting to Washington and copying to El Salvador. I took offense at the implication, for I had the greatest of confidence and respect for the professionalism of our country team—all men of talent and experience in political, economic, consular, military, and USAID affairs. Hadn't we pulled off that relief mission from Panama? Had Washington complained or corrected? Had the OAS chosen to send its observers to San Salvador? No, it had sent them to Tegucigalpa!

And so ensued something of a war within a war—a minor but unpleasant tension between U.S. Embassy San Salvador and U.S. Embassy Tegucigalpa in the midst of what was already a rather silly though tragic "Soccer War" in the heart of Central America. Each U.S. embassy believed the other guilty of clientitis. Offended by the implied insult to the veracity of our reporting, I refused to meet with the uninvited U.S. political officer from San Salvador. I told my political officer to receive him, attend to his needs, stay with him, consult freely both within our embassy and with the host government, and, finally, to put him on the next plane back to San Salvador—all of which he did. I heard nothing further on the subject.

Inequality in the Service

However, it wasn't long after this incident that Ambassador Bowdler and I were both recalled to Washington to give full and detailed briefings to officials in the State Department, Pentagon, and other interested agencies. Once assembled in a large conference room in the upper reaches of the State Department, the chairman turned to Bowdler and began, "Well, Mr. Ambassador, would you like to tell us what's going on down there in your territory?"

Bowdler talked at length as to the who, what, when, and where of the miniwar, which had by then been brought to a cease-fire, pending withdrawal of troops to their respective borders. There was one minor fly in the ointment. A Peace Corps volunteer from Honduras had been captured by Salvadoran troops and was in a military prison there, despite repeated orders from me to the director of the Corps to keep his volunteers away from the border. Mercifully, the ambassador did not belabor the incident. Nor did he make a point of questioning U.S. Embassy Honduras's reporting or discussing our differences in the assessments we sent to Washington.

Tegucigalpa, Honduras, 1966–69

After his comments and some discussion around the table, the meeting seemed to be coming to a close.

Almost as an afterthought the chairman turned to me and asked, "Oh, is there anything you might *add* to the presentation, Miss Wilkowski?"— no title, no recognition that I had been in charge of Embassy Tegucigalpa or in any way might be a near-equal U.S. representative in the disturbed area, albeit from a different location, with a different optic, and only a chargé, not an ambassador. So much for women in the Foreign Service in the mid-1960s! Certainly the men present in that conference room in Washington had witnessed inequality. As men were a preponderant majority in the Foreign Service and in government, when would *they* do something about it, as dear Ambassador John Jova had? I always felt that, with time, women would exhibit sufficient dedication to their tasks and quality of performance to overcome the occasional unfairness and injustice within the system. But it called for a lot of time and a lot of patience. My personal strategy for dealing with the problem as subtly as I could was once questioned by a middle-grade feminist leader within the Foreign Service who challenged me, "Lady, you never would have gotten to where you are today if it wasn't for our movement." I didn't agree that the issues were that clear-cut nor that her movement had directly affected my promotions.

But back to the story of the Washington meeting on the miniwar in Central America. I was admittedly nervous and hardly capable of a smile when the chairman turned to me and asked if I had anything "to add." Again, I was the only woman in a roomful of men, not for the first time in my life. I could handle it.

I drew a deep breath and made a summary presentation of developments as viewed from the Honduran side, based on what I thought had been solid, neutral, and yes, excellent reporting from Tegucigalpa by a highly competent embassy staff of military and civilian officers. Our reporting also covered the role of the OAS observers we were hosting in their efforts to bring about a cease-fire and troop withdrawal.

I emphasized strongly that both countries were seriously at fault, for historical economic and social reasons. Most recently the Salvadorans were the more culpable for being the most provocative, first with vicious civilian attacks following the soccer game in their country, and then for

Jean M. Wilkowski takes the oath of office as U.S. Ambassador to Zambia at the Department of State, Washington, D.C., in July 1972. *L to R*: Protocol officer (unidentified), nephew Frederick Wilkowski holding the Bible, and veteran diplomat Ambassador U. Alexis Johnson looking on.

Following her oath of office at the Department of State, Washington, D.C., the new U.S. Ambassador to Zambia talks with the Zambian Ambassador to the United States, G. Unia Mwila, and Ambassador U. Alexis Johnson.

In appreciation for hospitality during his concert visit to Zambia in 1973, Duke Ellington presented Ambassador Wilkowski with his photograph, signed "Yo Ho. Most Beautiful Essence of Excellenci, Thanx and good luck, Duke Ellington."

(opposite)
Ambassador Wilkowski with Coretta Scott King in a hurried moment during her visit in 1975 to Lusaka, Zambia, before meeting President Kaunda; in back and between them, U.S. Representative Andrew Young.

U.S. President Gerald Ford receives Zambian President Kenneth Kaunda in the Oval Office of the White House, April 19, 1975. On left, Zambian Foreign Minister Rupiah Banda, Zambian Ambassador to the U.S. Siteke Mwale, and Mark Chona, Special Assistant to President Kaunda; to right includes Secretary Kissinger and Ambassador Wilkowski.

U.S. Secretary of State Henry Kissinger delivering his new foreign policy statement on southern Africa at the State House, Lusaka, Zambia, in April 1976, as guest of President Kenneth Kaunda. Ambassador Wilkowski looks on. Others, *L to R:* Secret Service agent and State Department Press Officer Robert Funseth.

Kissinger talks with Zambian Foreign Minister Rupiah Banda outside the State House.

Zambian president Kenneth Kaunda officially receives U.S. Secretary of State Henry Kissinger and Assistant Secretary of State William Schaufele, accompanied by Ambassador Wilkowski, at the State House, Lusaka, Zambia, in April 1976.

Ambassador Wilkowski presents a book on U.S. history to President Kenneth
Kaunda during her farewell visit, before departing from Zambia in 1976.

On special assignment as Diplomat in Residence at Occidental College
in Los Angeles, California, the author points to a figure in a State Department
exhibit on women in diplomacy. Looking on is "Oxy" student Lorrie Foster.

Special U.S. mission to the People's Republic of China (PRC), June 1979, in preparation for the United Nations Conference on Science and Technology for Development. Photo taken before the Ministry of Foreign Affairs with various Ministry staff. Front row, *L to R:* the author; U.S. Ambassador to PRC Leonard Woodcock; Father Theodore M. Hesburgh, C.S.C, president of the University of Notre Dame; unidentified PRC official hosting U.S. delegation; James Grant, President, Overseas Development Council; Julie Perkins, spouse of Professor Dwight Perkins of Harvard University (standing tall behind her).

Welcoming meeting of U.S. mission at the Chinese Ministry of Science and Technology. *L to R:* the author, Leonard Woodcock, Father Hesburgh, and unidentified translators and official of the Ministry.

Pope John Paul II at a reception including members of the Order of Malta at the Vatican Embassy, Washington, D.C., October 1979.

On her retirement from the U.S. Foreign Service in 1980, the author is presented with her ambassadorial flag by Secretary of State Cyrus G. Vance in the Benjamin Franklin Room of the State Department, Washington, D.C.

As CPC corporate executive and traveling board member, author visits an overseas plant and meets factory technicians in Durban, South Africa.

Ambassador Jean Wilkowski, extreme right top row, one of fifteen selected by President Theodore M. Hesburgh for the degree of Doctor of Laws *honoris causa* at the University of Notre Dame's 142nd Commencement Ceremonies, June 1987. Among the honorees are Rosalynn Carter, Coretta Scott King, Joan Kroc, David Rockefeller, and Derek Bok.

State

UNITED STATES DEPARTMENT OF STATE   JUNE 1995

Honored on Foreign Service Day

The author holding the Foreign Service Cup, with Ambassador Morton
Abramowitz holding the Director General's Cup, on Foreign Service Day, May 5,
1995, when she was honored for "fifty years of service to the Nation in govern-
mental and private capacities."

The author in Havana, Cuba, January 1999, visiting with Cuban children and single mothers in a CARITAS-related asssistance program inaugurated by Cuban Cardinal Jaime Ortega.

allowing their troops to cross the border deep into Honduras for artillery and aerial bombardments of civilian populations. Granted, the Hondurans had not been blameless; they responded with several air attacks and incarcerated thousands of Salvadoran nationals who were illegal immigrants in Honduras. Both countries had engaged in high-pitched, misleading, and scurrilous radio commentary, adding to the panic and confusion.

When I finished my brief presentation, the chairman, hardly disguising his surprise, thanked and commended me. Those around the table seemed to go out of their way, rather unctuously querying me to elaborate on some points. I ended up grateful for a fair hearing and a good discussion.

Back to Normal Diplomatic Life

Apart from the week of war, life in Tegucigalpa was pleasant and interesting. Our relations with the host government ran smoothly, with no major bilateral problems. We had the usual run of visitors, mainly from Washington, some from the Southern Command of the U.S. Army in Panama. There were lots of embassy dinners and receptions—ours and other countries'—where one got to know the diplomatic corps, influential local business people, and government officials. Despite my awkward official encounter with him in the middle of the night as chargé, the president himself was friendly and hospitable to me at the lavish dinners and receptions at his country villa just outside of town.

One of the more memorable evenings was a reception López Arellano gave for his *compadre*, the president of Nicaragua, the famous, or infamous, Anastasio "Tachito" Somoza, and his American-born wife, Hope. Our U.S. military attaché had been Somoza's classmate at West Point. Unfortunately the day of Somoza's arrival, when I was chargé but bedridden with some minor blood sugar problem, I was unable to be part of the airport arrival ceremonies and had to ask Al Zucca to replace me. So we were at the third level of U.S. representation for the event. Tachito being Tachito, and always expecting tribute from the Americans, he not only noticed the absence of the U.S. ambassador but asked why his deputy had not appeared. He was obviously offended.

Tegucigalpa, Honduras, 1966–69

When this was reported to me by phone, I dragged myself out of bed to go to the reception. As soon as he entered, the Nicaraguan president spotted me and waved. Minutes later he had his aide escort me over to where he was "enthroned"—at a small table with two chairs on a low balcony at the edge of the enormous ballroom. We were literally on stage to the entire gathering, just as he wanted. He did most of the talking, as I recall. And it really didn't matter what I thought or had to say; indeed I was unable to say much at all. The important thing was that Somoza, the military dictator, be seen lecturing (which indeed he was) the acting American ambassador. Male chauvinist and downright bully were among his other less endearing qualities. How did his wife stand him, I wondered?

As soon as I could break away, I scurried home and back to bed. Some years later when the Communists took over his country, Somoza fled to Argentina only to be followed and assassinated there by his old enemies.

Oops, I Made a Mistake

There can be flagrant gaffes in any job, but if one is lucky they may go unobserved and unreported to the supervisor and not make it into one's efficiency report. The snatching back of a wrongly issued visa was my first big boo-boo, dating back to my first post in Trinidad. I made another one while chargé in Honduras.

Washington informed me quite confidentially while I was chargé that I was to seek the requisite host country approval for the person chosen to be the nominee as the new U.S. ambassador, a black man with fine academic and diplomatic credentials who shall remain nameless. I was in a hurry to get off to an official luncheon so I called in the chief administrative officer (AO), who also handled the archives and regulations. I told him to research the previous request as a guide to the proper wording of a formal diplomatic note, which I would then present to the minister of foreign affairs to solicit the host government's *agrément*, or approval, of the new nominee.

Apparently my hasty instructions to the officer were just that—too hasty and badly misunderstood. He was to have had the completed document ready for me to sign and deliver in the afternoon. When I returned after lunch, I found he had not only located the proper format and precedent but had it typed up, signed it himself (instead of having it signed by the acting chief of mission), and hand-carried it to the foreign minister! I had never known him to think or act that fast in the past! It may have been because he had never had the opportunity to do official business at that level.

When I realized the breach of etiquette, I phoned the foreign minister to seek an immediate appointment, rushed over, explained a mistake had been made, and apologized. The foreign minister, a proud old-timer, had been piqued by the call from the AO and said he had not acted on the request nor did he intend to. He pulled it out of his desk to show me where he had stuffed it and where it would remain. Nor did he want me to correct the mistake. The interview was over.

Later in the day I heard via the official grapevine that President López himself had somehow heard of the intended assignment (a leak in Washington? in Honduras?) and declared to a friend, "I don't want any GDN here in Honduras." The country had a sizable black population on the north coast and Bay Islands, descendants of former slaves, but the government remained lily-white, composed mainly of Spanish descendants or Mestizos, mixtures of Spanish explorers and Mayan Indians.

I was furious with the AO's misunderstanding but equally displeased with my own carelessness and haste. How would I explain what had really happened to Washington? Ignoring our own stumblebum actions, I decided simply to report to Washington that the host government had chosen not to act on the request and so informed me, leaving it at that. Had we given them a perfect excuse to refuse the candidate? I certainly hoped not but feared we may have. *Mea culpa, mea maxima culpa.*

Time to Lighten Up

Life in Honduras was not all official or stressful. There were play moments on the tennis court and golf course. I may have spent just a little more time than necessary trying to ride horseback well because Ambassador Jova was such an old pro. He loved the sport and liked company. So nothing would do but that I buy a horse and stable it with a group of other foreigners at a place not far from my home. My horse, being all white, was called Paloma (Dove). He had seen better years. But it was the "in" thing to team up with a few riders and head for the hills on weekends.

On one of our weekly junkets, the ambassador and I decided we would try for an entirely different kind of ride, not following any old trails but blazing our own path on the south face of a wooded mountain range to the north of the capital city. We had both been invited to a Sunday luncheon on one of the summits and felt an hour was adequate to climb the hill and arrive on time. The uncharted route became hard on both horses and riders. We brushed through thick foliage and kept doing switchbacks to reach the top of the hills. Finally, we came to a road that ran along the summit to the friend's home. As I dismounted in great relief I felt something "airy" about my riding breeches. A quick look revealed I had split the crotch with the vigorous climb up the hill. What a way to arrive at a Sunday luncheon!

I quickly snatched the scarf from around my neck and held it strategically in front as we greeted our hostess. When the ambassador moved away, I explained my predicament to the hostess, asking if I might borrow a pair of her husbands' slacks. Certainly hers would not have fit me. My dear hostess rose to the occasion, ushered me into a bedroom, and found me a pair of her husband's slacks—hardly appropriate to the occasion, but I got by.

Honduras offered little in the way of formal entertainment such as theater and concerts, so we took to making our own, like the farewell party, or *despedida*, for Ambassador Jova. We took over the auditorium of a local school and set it up like a nightclub, with tables, low lights, and a floor show. With neither voice nor singing experience other than in the back row of my college choir, I pretended to be the chanteuse of the club.

I borrowed a wig from the local hairdresser, who piled it into a beehive on my head and did an over-the-top make-up job on my face. Then I pulled out a tight-fitting orange and black tubular shift from the giveaway box, found a bar stool, and did my best to keep time with the local orchestra, which mercifully drowned out my higher and scratchier notes. It was fun, and no one seemed to recognize me, which made it even more fun.

Honduras was many things for me. It proved a marvelous training ground under a kind, patient, and able teacher. Ambassador Jova was a consummate diplomat from whom I learned a great deal, as I also did from his wife, Pamela. He taught mostly by example, not by lecturing or hectoring. Thanks to his guidance I came to believe that I might actually have management and leadership skills. Working with him also gave me the confidence I needed to head up a diplomatic mission. I learned I could run an embassy in time of crisis. Without the Honduras experience, I never would have become minister-counselor in Rome, ambassador to Zambia, and principal U.S. spokesperson for science and technology with ambassadorial rank at the United Nations.

Tegucigalpa, Honduras, 1966–69

TEN

Lusaka, Zambia, 1972–76
(U.S. Ambassador, Chief of Mission)

Late one afternoon, about an hour before closing, during my second posting to Rome, the phone on my desk rang. "Washington calling," the embassy operator said. Then, "Is that you, Jean? This is Cleo Noel in Washington. How would you like to go to Zambia?"

"What as?" I immediately asked, without thinking.

"Well, as ambassador, of course," Cleo replied. I had known Cleo Noel socially from years before and assumed he must be on detail to Personnel in the State Department.

I hesitated, then rather lamely said, "That is certainly something to think about. Thank you. May I get back to you, Cleo?" I don't believe I even said "Wow!" or "Are you kidding?" Cleo's startling and totally unexpected news hit me as an enormous surprise. I was dumbstruck. My totally inappropriate response was almost as bad as saying I would have to ask my mother! Indeed, I was accustomed to doing just that on important matters, as my mother had been living with me as a dependent until her untimely death in Rome ten years earlier. Old thought patterns tend to die hard. Imagine, being offered an ambassadorship and not immediately accepting it—after twenty-eight years in the Foreign Service and at fifty-two years of age! Talk about naïve, or was I just frightened of the future? Probably both.

After putting down the phone with Washington, I immediately called my ambassador, Graham Martin, a floor below me in Embassy Rome. He had proven to be a good and supportive friend. Breathlessly I rushed into his office to tell him Washington had just phoned to offer me an ambassadorship, and what did he think, and what could he advise me to do? Should I accept? Words seemed to spill out all over the place.

He got the drift immediately and asked me to sit down, but refrained from saying, "Cool it!" Rather, he deliberately shook his head in wonder and said, "I think you can do anything you set your mind to!" He said the Personnel people back in Washington had already asked for his advice on nominating me and he had immediately endorsed the proposal. I suddenly came to my senses, thanked him, quickly backed out of his office, and rushed back to my own to call Washington to accept.

On Meeting Real Africans

It wasn't long before my nomination to Zambia was announced. Within days the Zambian ambassador to Italy phoned and asked to meet with me. He proposed a farewell dinner before I left Rome. He suggested the Grand Hotel, one of my favorites, located not far from the U.S. Embassy in the center of the city. He explained it would involve most of his small embassy staff and any friends whom I cared to invite. Life was assuming a new dimension.

The evening proved both incongruous and delightful. There we were, gathered under the Venetian glass chandeliers of the Grand Hotel's ornately decorated Belle Époque reception room. The Zambian women were clad in their brightly colored national dress, the chitenga, wrapped tightly around their rather full figures, with perky matching headdresses. They were drinking beer out of the bottle—beer being the Zambian national drink, as I soon learned (but more of that later).

These lovely Zambian ladies kept drinking beer as if there were no tomorrow and really enjoying themselves. Though a native of Wisconsin and literally weaned on beer, I was still not up to the challenge. But then like most diplomats I had become accustomed to sipping slowly on a light Scotch at official functions. I had much to learn from the new African culture. (Later on the ground in Zambia my learning progressed. Beer was almost always drunk out of the bottle. Empties were simply dropped to the floor where they joined up with well-chewed and slippery chicken bones, presenting a minor environmental hazard.)

And happy! Zambians could be solemn-countenanced and stiff at first meeting, but at a party they behaved joyously and never seemed to stop giggling or talking. They spoke in rather deliberate, cadenced English, sparked with a sort of cackling laugh. A bit difficult to understand at first, it slowed down the pace of conversation but made for easier understanding. I learned that English is a second language to most Zambians, who normally speak among themselves in one of about seventy different tribal languages, of which about five predominate. Later I learned a few simple phrases in one of the tongues common around Lusaka, only to find that Zambia's president, Kenneth Kaunda, strongly disapproved the use of tribal dialects in public. He believed the practice fostered sectarianism, preferring English as a unifying force for the nation's politics, especially in his one-party state. Later, in discussions at the working level of the Zambian government, I found the slower pace of Zambian English useful for thinking over proposals before responding. In contrast, President Kaunda, his foreign minister, and their close aides were far more sophisticated. They traveled considerably and were excellent speakers in conversation and in public.

From the time of my first encounter with Zambians at the Grand Hotel in Rome, I was struck by their innate sense of humility and courtesy; between their self-conscious giggles, the Zambian women kept congratulating me on my new assignment. They were clearly flattered that my government had chosen their country for America's first woman ambassador to Africa. Women in Zambia were not conspicuous in public life in the 1970s. Their main role—carrying considerable work and responsibility— was as matriarchs of large and extended families. They were generally homebodies, very caring and loving people. On one occasion the foreign minister told me there were twenty-five people, including his family but mainly relatives from the bush, staying in his home that particular week.

Washington Consultations

During my introduction to Zambian people at the delightful ambassadorial reception in Rome, I explained that before I could move to their country from Europe I had to return to Washington for training and orientation. As matters developed, several months elapsed between my departure from Rome and my arrival in Zambia.

Back in Washington, when I reported in to the Department of State for the requisite briefings, I was informed that a very knowledgeable Africanist, Harvey Nelson, would be my deputy chief of mission (DCM). Thank heavens! I needed experienced close support. Nelson was a fine young man with previous postings in Europe, the Congo, and South Africa and on the southern Africa desk at State. I liked him immediately; he was intelligent, easy-going, and not the least uncomfortable with the prospect of a woman boss. Rather, he seemed quite at ease with strong women, having a highly intelligent and capable wife, as well as three children of high school age. We agreed I should arrive at post first for the transition from the departing chargé d'affaires. My DCM and his family would follow later.

While I was in Washington I had a most interesting meeting with the previous U.S. ambassador to Zambia, Oliver L. Troxel Jr., for some background briefing. He appeared to be an unusually relaxed sort of person. (At least he showed no strain from his service in Africa, I thought.) He did not confide the details of what I came to assume was perhaps too long an assignment in a remote and perhaps monotonous post. He promptly set out to acquaint me with the history and folkways of a strikingly different land and people by taking me out to dinner in Georgetown. After our meal he insisted we barhop for a few beers! It wasn't long before I realized I was not all that steady walking down M Street toward my temporary quarters in Foggy Bottom near the Department of State. And my stomach was feeling just a bit queasy. Nevertheless, my predecessor escorted me safely back to my digs without serious embarrassment.

When I met up with Troxel the next day at the Department of State, he was not the least apologetic about his role in my wilted state the night before, explaining that he had deliberately set out to test my capacity, given the fact that beer drinking was Zambia's favorite sport and national pastime. I told him I had some inkling of that from the send-off party given me in Rome. Frankly I was not too pleased with the prospect, having managed without incident to get safely beyond the heavy beer drinking days during my high school summers in Wisconsin. I determined then and there that my male staff in Zambia would have to do the barhopping and beer drinking, even though, as Troxel explained, it was where all the good political gossip was to be collected. I told him that I would just have to trust my staff to keep me current on news from the local bar scene. Having failed to pass my predecessor's beer test, I fear he may have doubted the wisdom of sending a woman to Zambia, at least one with limited drinking capacity—a result of my incurring hepatitis while assigned to Chile.

During my Washington briefings I was prepped on Zambian history, politics, and economics by experts on the Country Desk in the Division of African Affairs; also by a fine scholar/consultant from Harvard, Dr. Robert Rotberg, who had spent much time in the region. He knew many people there and insisted I meet them all, especially South African whites in the mining business in Zambia. He claimed they had an inside track on the important official players and the workings of the Zambian government. His counsel and advice proved invaluable, not only professionally but also in providing the basis for some enduring professional and personal friendships.

Scrutiny before the U.S. Congress

But the two main events of my time in Washington related to preparations for my confirmation hearings before the Senate Foreign Relations Committee, chaired by Senator William Fulbright (D) of Arkansas. I hardly knew what to expect, but my coaches in the department kept saying, "You'll do fine; just be straightforward and honest in your answers."

I went up to Capitol Hill with a group of five other ambassadorial candidates—all about to be "crowned" for one post or another. One of the candidates, Beverly Carter, destined for Tanzania, immediately preceded me before the committee. He was a tall, handsome, articulate, well-dressed African American—a real "hunk"—former football player, and no slouch on the golf course. When I followed Carter to the stand, Senator Fulbright began with a thundering question, "What in the world is the Department of State doing sending you to Africa? It says here that you speak four languages including English and have served in Europe and Latin America." His question was far from rhetorical. He stared down at me, clearly expecting an answer. There was a moment of silence; then I blurted out a rather lame *non sequitur:* "Beats me, Senator. Maybe it's because I'm almost as tall as Bev Carter!"

Fortunately the senator took no offense at my inane response, having satisfied himself by voicing his disapproval of the bureaucracy's assignment process. He proceeded with the usual set of questions about my education, diplomatic background, Zambia, and ideas on our foreign policy in Africa, then thanked me for my appearance. The other committee members threw out a few softballs as to how I might enhance our diplomatic relations with Zambia, noting that Lusaka was an important political listening post in the midst of the liberation struggles of southern Africa. Then the committee moved on to the next nominee.

Fulbright's question prompted me to ponder the rationale behind my assignment to Africa. What indeed was the Department of State to do with a career woman who had worked her way up through the ranks, headed up some trade negotiations in Geneva, temporarily led a U.S. embassy in Central America during a mini-war, and served as minister-counselor and No. 3 at a major U.S. embassy in Europe? Perhaps the department reasoned that the Latin Americans were probably not ready for a woman chief of mission from their big neighbor to the North. With still distinctly "macho" societies in the 1970s, could they be expected to take a woman ambassador seriously? The Latins had few if any women of that rank. It could embarrass them, as well as me, for that matter.

The department may also have reasoned along the obvious lines—that many of the European countries, especially the larger ones, were traditionally reserved for U.S. political appointees or far more experienced diplomatic professionals than I was at the time. Other European countries were too small or did not offer the kind of experience the department wanted me to have at that stage of my career, leading to the possible conclusion: why not experiment by sending the first woman U.S. ambassador to Africa? It seems one Jean W. was never a person to refuse a dare or even—as a very young girl—a double dare, when at that time it was little more than climbing a tree or playing on her brother's football team.

Senator Fulbright seemed averse to belaboring the question, preferring instead to get on with the hearings. I certainly didn't want to try second-guessing the Department of State in public. So the senator's pointed question went unanswered in public, leaving me to ponder in private. Several days later I learned from the Zambia Desk at the Department of State that I had passed the Senate's scrutiny. Thus with the required "advice and consent of the Senate," I was entitled to my marching orders, the official document to the effect that the President of the United States has nominated one JW as his personal representative to the Republic of Zambia.

Swearing-In

What followed next was the official swearing-in ceremony in the formal diplomatic reception rooms on the State Department's elegant eighth floor, beautifully decorated with colonial antiques and historical artifacts. The adjoining broad terrace overlooks the Mall, the Lincoln Memorial, and the Potomac River. I could invite whomever I wanted for the reception to follow but the cost would be borne by me! On the advice of the caterer, I went for modest hors d'oeuvres and flutes of champagne containing a strawberry. I invited friends and family and Zambia's ambassador to Washington. As is customary, the ceremony was presided over by the chief of protocol and a ranking department official, in my case Ambassador U. Alexis Johnson, a veteran diplomat and kindly elder statesman.

Traditionally one's spouse holds the Bible for the swearing in. Being single I called upon my twelve-year-old nephew, who came in with his mother from Montana for the occasion. That entailed not only getting him the proper attire—a nice jacket and slacks with new shoes—but a proper rig for myself as well. I had intended to wear a trim pale blue raw silk suit that I had tailor-made in Paris, but it proved a bit too snug and rigid looking. So at the very last minute I pulled out a black and white animal-print silk dress with black patent leather belt—not all that inappropriate, I thought for the implied symbolism of white woman going to black Africa.

High Fashion for the African Jungle

Obviously women worry more about clothes than men, or at least they used to in my day. Before I left Rome I prepared my African wardrobe with great care. Rome had been my third assignment to Italy. Everyone knows it is a fashion-setting country, tending to influence its admirers and those

Lusaka, Zambia, 1972–76

who have the good fortune to live there. I had become far more fashion conscious than I needed to be for a bush post in Africa. But once appointed an ambassador, I became blinded with my own self-importance. Some call it "ambassadoritis." It can manifest itself in many different ways.

Before I left Rome I had two special outfits made—the dress I would wear presenting credentials to the president of Zambia and a tropical wool safari suit with jacket, skirt, and slacks for whatever occasion. The latter was exquisitely made in a fine lightweight beige wool by the famous Italian tailor Brioni, who was just starting to do women's clothing in the early 1970s.

The so-called credentials dress had an unusual origin, though I had no thought of whom I was going to impress other than myself. One Sunday afternoon in Rome with little to do, I stopped by a theater and tried to buy a ticket to the matinee. All sold out! A man standing nearby overheard, said he had an extra ticket, and offered it to me. I tried to buy it but no, with typical Roman gallantry, it was his pleasure. Then he gave me the ticket and his business card. It was none other than Tiziani, one of Rome's foremost fashion designers at the time. A sign, I thought. So I called his atelier and made an appointment within the week. We went over bolts of fabric. He suggested and I agreed on a beautiful white silk material printed with red strawberries. Over the course of a couple of fittings, he worked it up into an appropriate afternoon dress with a soft red leather belt and a handsome red linen vest with large revers. Handsome and yet rather low key. It would work. At the price, what wouldn't?

I later heard that in Zambia, most any kind of dress passed muster. But that was not wholly true. While it was indeed bush country, there was an active and somewhat sophisticated diplomatic corps that kept itself busy entertaining one another, so I made good use of the couturier dress beyond the credentials ceremony. Indeed, it helped satisfy my newly acquired feelings of self-importance, as well as serving appropriately for my serious new role.

Wheels Up for Zambia

With Washington briefings and preparations for my first ambassadorial post completed, the day finally arrived for my departure by plane for

Zambia, with rest stops in Rome and Nairobi, Kenya. My arrival in Lusaka, Zambia's capital, was inauspicious. My plane was met by the embassy's chargé d'affaires, Art Tinken, a pleasant, easy-going man, knowledgeable in things African. He had planned my entry carefully, knowing I was a greenhorn to the region and the job.

It was just turning dark when we set out from the airport over the asphalt highway leading into Lusaka. No jungle, no animals, just a lot of high grass, some umbrella-like trees, few buildings or houses, and occasionally a few lean and poorly clad people walking slowly and peacefully along the highway. Just before we reached the city limits the driver cut off onto a dirt road. Soon we were passing through a typical native village, dimly lit from kerosene lamps and a light bulb or two in the modest shacks along the road. Sagging roofs of straw thatch or corrugated metal covered the humble dwellings. The smoke and smell of charcoal fires wafted into the car. Then I heard a low steady drum beat, somewhat muted but still unsettling as it cut through the evening air. This was Africa all right. I was to hear this haunting sound often on very still nights, as my residence was not too many miles away from this village and sound travels far on the high African plateau.

We soon found ourselves in a quite modern, well-lit residential section of Lusaka. Eventually we reached the gates of a circular driveway, the entry to my official residence, I was told. Hanging rather limply from a high metal pole was the American flag. Would I be expected to hold daily ceremonies, I wondered? Hardly, I reassured myself. Beside the gates, standing like an emaciated copy of a Giacometti statue, was a bedraggled sentry holding a gun. Loaded? I hoped not. I was told he was part of my security detachment and would regularly patrol the perimeter of the property. It hardly gave me a feeling of security.

At the precise moment I got out of the car, a loud clap of thunder and flashes of lightning sent the sentry loping off to seek shelter in a shed behind the house. Thunder and lightning struck again as I entered the front door, where I was greeted by a waiting staff. There were two male gardeners in khaki and bare feet; two male house servants in white jackets, black pants, and shoes; and a male cook all in white. To a man they were grinning nervously, showing their very white teeth against the blackest faces I had ever seen. It was an awkward moment for them and for me. I

Lusaka, Zambia, 1972–76

tried not to reflect their obvious discomfort over the scene of five short black men welcoming one very tall, foreign white woman. It was a first for all of us, so I determined we would all just have to get used to this new form of domesticity. While I couldn't help but wonder about the future of such an interesting household, I refrained from saying so aloud to Tinken. Specifically, how was I to deal with washing my personal items and dealing with other such personal matters and needs? Apparently no ladies-in-waiting went with the job.

Tinken explained that my first meal in Africa would be at home alone. He thought it would be more restful after the trip. Or was it because he felt he'd had enough for one night? As he was leaving he lowered his voice and without so much as a snicker whispered, "The staff all think you're a lady witch doctor because your arrival was greeted with thunder and lightning. Good luck," he added, as he walked out to his car. I was sure I would need it.

I somehow managed to sleep, surrounded by the many uncertainties, including being alone in the house. The servants all went to their own homes at night, with the exception of that sentry. I couldn't help wonder whether his gun was loaded or not.

Saul Mutemba, R.I.P.

I spent a little time the next morning getting to know my driver, Saul. I believe his last name was Mutemba, but we never used it. Strange as it may seem, Saul was to become my best and closest friend in Zambia, even though I was sure he was also on the payroll of the host government to report any curious or deviant behavior on my part. He would certainly be obliged to report on my comings and goings, perhaps even my thoughts and opinions. Indeed, it wasn't long into my assignment before I was talking to myself in the back seat of that new Ford LTD sedan the government had assigned me.

Each morning when I awakened and looked out my second-story window over the vast savannah and brilliant blue sky, at an altitude of around 4,000 feet, I could see the faithful Saul waiting for me below in his always-clean navy blue uniform and visored cap, usually leaning against the car in the driveway below. Over the nearly four years of my assignment in Africa I don't recall ever spending so much time with any one person, except as a child with my family growing up. Saul was my constant companion morning, noon, and night as he took me to the Chancery, to official calls and business, back to the Residence for lunch, and then again to the Chancery, back home for dinner or to dress if there was an official engagement in the evening, and then on to a reception and back to the Residence.

As I came to know Saul, we seemed to talk about everything under the sun. He was a chatterbox, almost like the Town Crier. He had news about everything. I hardly had to read the local paper, which was not especially informative to begin with. Saul covered most of its contents of any importance on the way into the Embassy. How he was so well informed and had so many opinions I did not know, just born wise I guess. Yet his manners were rather childlike. He would laugh and giggle at the slightest things, bending over and shaking with joy, especially when offered even the smallest of gifts.

Saul was also bald as an eagle. To cover his embarrassment, on weekends when he was out of uniform, he wore old golf hats and begged me for used ones. When he was wearing his uniform, he would frequently tell me his cap was worn out and needed replacing. I think he probably sold the old ones. Seeming to have no hobbies or cronies, he would hang around either the Residence or the Chancery when off duty. He told me he was married and one day he brought round a woman whom he introduced as his wife. He was hoping for some used women's clothes, which he had earlier asked for and received. From then on I kept the supply coming, which he assured me his wife enjoyed.

He used to tell me about the shebeens, roadhouses or watering spots hidden away out in the bush where the blacks could enjoy themselves freely, drinking and dancing. Presumably these forms of entertainment grew up during colonial days and persisted, affording a sort of secret retreat from strict segregation in the early days when Zambia was still Northern Rhodesia under the British. I later learned that "shebeen" was probably a native corruption of the word "shebang," which the British and Irish colonials used to designate most anything.

On a whim I once asked Saul to take me out to a shebeen, and one evening we were free to take off and explore. It turned out to be miles west

Lusaka, Zambia, 1972–76

of the city and deep in the bush—a sort of open-air thatched roof dance hall supported by rough-hewn wood pillars. Beneath the roof was a circular concrete platform on which crude wooden tables and chairs were set up and beer was served, mostly to groups of men. I was the only white person in the place. In the corner stood some musicians scratching out rather tinny music that was hardly danceable. Nevertheless, I took a brief turn around the floor with Saul, who, while he showed some rhythm, constantly laughed and giggled like an idiot child. He was beside himself with glee. We left soon thereafter, as I came to my senses, knowing I did not need that much local color. Moreover, the experience could hardly do anything to advance my diplomatic career. Surprisingly, the story never got around, which proved Saul capable of keeping some things to himself. However, the "intelligence" on the event was no doubt passed by security officials to someone in President Kaunda's close circle, who may have surmised that the new lady ambassador was either off her rocker or actually researching local entertainment.

I only hope my own colleagues never got wind of my unusual outing with the chauffeur. Despite being "in charge" of the embassy in Lusaka, I had enough trouble with one staffer from "another agency," the details of whose work I was never privy to; moreover, much to my annoyance, he occasionally made it clear that I had no authority over him, his work, or his staff of two. In Washington, when briefed "upriver" at Langley, I had made the point that I wanted "no cowboys" on my staff, which was company slang for those "other agency" officers inclined to ride off on questionable projects of their own, always keeping the ambassador in the dark.

Many years after I had left Zambia, I learned that Saul was among the first to contract and die from AIDS. When I was in Africa, AIDS had not assumed the epidemic proportions it acquired in later years. Indeed it was hardly ever talked about at that time. I was told by an American nurse stationed at the Zambian Teaching Hospital that one of the British doctors there had some sort of informal and unofficial relationship with the National Institutes of Health in the United States. Indeed, some of the first experimental specimens of the HIV-AIDS virus had been taken by this doctor from homeless street people in Lusaka and mailed to NIH for basic research.

Lusaka, Zambia, 1972–76

Presentation of Credentials

Soon after an ambassador arrives at post and before "going public," making official rounds and calling on diplomatic colleagues, one has to be officially acknowledged by the host government in a ceremony known as "presentation of credentials." It took some time after my arrival in Zambia, twenty-eight days to be exact, before the host government decided to grant me an appointment to present my credentials. There was a clear political message in this delay. The Chinese ambassador had arrived but a day or so earlier than I, yet within two days he was invited to present his credentials. After all, the Chinese were spending millions of dollars in aid to build a railroad from the Indian Ocean into the mining area of northern Zambia to benefit the country's copper exports. The United States had no aid program with Zambia in those days. But the delay had broader meaning.

As I tapped my toe waiting for the call to present credentials, there were clear hints from the Zambian Foreign Ministry that Vietnam was the bone of contention. President Kaunda was greatly displeased with the United States for being at war in Vietnam. The delay in receiving me would be only the first of a number of instances during my assignment that Kaunda would use to criticize the United States on this issue. I could do little but wait it out until Zambian displeasure had been fully expressed and, they hoped, understood by the United States. Nothing personal, it seemed. After nearly a month a formal note was delivered inviting me to present credentials to President Kenneth Kaunda at State House. At last I could put on my new Italian dress for the occasion.

Harvey Nelson, my deputy, accompanied me to State House in high style, with American and ambassadorial flags flying on the fenders of the official car. We were met at the door by the president's secretary and special assistant Mark Chona, who ushered us into a small reception room for a short and simple ceremony. President Kaunda stood behind a plain table in the middle of the room attired in his trademark short-sleeved khaki-colored safari suit. I was in my expensive Italian couturier dress of strawberries. We made a charming, mixed race couple in the heart of Africa.

After brief words of welcome, Kaunda invited me to speak. I read from a rather formal note prepared in Washington to the effect that "the President of the United States reposing special trust and confidence in my integrity, prudence and ability had nominated me and with the advice and consent of the Senate appointed me Ambassador Extraordinary and Plenipotentiary of the United States of America to the Republic of Zambia, authorized me to do and perform all such matters and things as to said place or office, to hold and exercise during the pleasure of the President of the United States for the time being." My very formal statement was signed by President Richard Nixon and cosigned by the acting secretary of state. It was dated June 27, 1972, "in the year of our Lord" and the "one hundred and ninety-sixth year of the independence of the United States of America." I wondered what the Zambians might be thinking regarding my declared claims to "personal integrity, prudence and ability."

President Kaunda then replied graciously. He made special note of how pleased he and his country were that the United States had chosen Zambia out of all of Africa to send its first woman ambassador. He hoped I would enjoy my life and work in the country and assured me that he and his government would do everything possible to deepen and extend the good relations between our two nations. Being first in Africa was important to me, as later I would be chagrined when people asked, "Oh, you followed Shirley Temple Black, no?" No, I would assert, I was BST, before Shirley Temple, who served as ambassador to Ghana. The formalities concluded, I had thus been anointed, accepted, and charged to go about my official duties, instead of lurking in my residence as I had for the past month, waiting for the "all clear" to transact my diplomatic business.

Being a teetotaler, Kaunda offered us some orange juice and cookies after the credentials ceremony. As we were sipping and chatting, a covey of tame peacocks took over the front garden of State House with their piercing screams, which made the event even more memorable. After thanking our host, we left for my official residence where I had some champagne chilling in the refrigerator for Nelson, myself, and other embassy officers. We popped open the bottle and for a second time and on our own turf toasted ourselves and our mission in Zambia.

Diplomatic Colleagues ("Dips")

Immediately after presenting credentials I made the customary round of calls on fellow diplomats and ranking government officials, starting with the dean of the Diplomatic Corps, a bachelor Dutchman. Dutch interests in Zambia were far less than those of the United States, but the man's usefulness was twofold: he had been in the country for many years and knew many people and much history. Both of us being single, we came to be paired often at formal dinner parties, so chatting with him became easy. Being stolid and without spirited or agile movements, however, he was hardly a candidate as a dancing partner. That role came to be reserved for my far more nimble, gregarious, and colorful colleague, the Nigerian High Commissioner, also single, who loved dancing to "High Life" music, which he claimed gave birth to American jazz. (The title "High Commissioner" is used instead of "Ambassador" among the members of the British Commonwealth.)

My British colleague was another matter. He prided himself on being "an old Africa Hand," meaning an ex-colonial. I found him something of a know-it-all old fuddy-duddy. He was too smug about Britain's once having "owned the place"; but he did know where all the bodies were buried. He kept telling me that the best solution to any problem in Africa was merely to bring the concerned parties together and thrash it out "under some big old African shade tree!" Oddly enough, he pointed to the one in his front yard. I smiled and rolled my eyes at that piece of advice.

For leisurely discussions and sorting out problems I preferred a gin and tonic on the back terrace overlooking my well-manicured lawn, well-tended gardens, and swimming pool with changing "hut." The latter was a replica of a round, whitewashed, thatch-roofed African hut, or *rondavaal*, which I had had built to add local color. It stood there amid modern housing to remind me of where I was—on the vast continent of Africa, which had a way of casting spells on people, reminding them of the origins of the human race.

But to return to my British diplomatic colleague, I found him far more useful when he explained things bureaucratic, for example, how the Brits had managed to include "security guards" in their staff complement when the Americans had none. I had learned that Lusaka was one of the few U.S. Embassies in the world without the benefit of a U.S. Marine Guard detachment. With armed guerillas from neighboring countries at large in the capital city of Lusaka, I believed we had a strong argument for security protection. So I made it a priority objective of my new mission to get the

Department of State to arrange with the Department of Defense for a security proposal we could present to the Zambians. Eventually, a security agreement was negotiated between the United States and Zambia, though the protective Marine guards did not arrive on the ground until after I had left the country.

Following my call on the Brit, I felt my next most important call should be on the High Commissioner of Tanzania. I chose him because of the strong personal and political ties between his president, Julius Nyerere, and President Kaunda and for this diplomat's likely insights into the liberation struggle in the region. I was not disappointed. I found him extremely helpful, as was Harvey Nelson, my own very knowledgeable and capable DCM.

I asked my Tanzanian colleague if he thought life and work would be difficult for a woman diplomat in Africa, given the tribal tradition of male dominance and because women were few and far between in public life. He didn't hesitate to answer. He recognized that I was something of a pioneer not only for my own country, but in international diplomacy generally and certainly in Africa. He explained that women held a unique position in African culture. They are the centerpiece of the extended family in society, not only for their creative and nurturing role but, very importantly (and he stressed this), "Africans trust women; in fact, African men trust women even more than they trust their own fellow men. So you have a great advantage," he assured me. He told me to go about my work in confidence. He added, "You will find President Kaunda is a great gentleman, and he will make it easy for you to work with him." This was comforting, and true, and I never forgot my Tanzanian colleague's advice and guidance.

My courtesy calls on the other diplomats in Zambia were formal if not perfunctory, except for the Italians. They eventually became dear personal friends. Because I had spent eight years on assignments in Italy, we had much in common. Moreover, staying in close touch with them afforded me the opportunity of keeping up on my Italian language fluency.

My memories of the French ambassador were pleasant enough from our first formal exchange of visits. It was only later that he and I had our differences. We were both in the Diplomatic Gallery of the National Parliament one day when President Kaunda—as he was wont to do in expressing his socialist/humanist philosophy—spoke ill of the United States for its continued presence in Vietnam ("a social injustice . . . the killing of innocents . . . wanton destruction in poor countries, etc."). It was classic Kaunda, with tears and ever-ready white handkerchief for waving or weeping. His performance was designed to appeal primarily to United Party faithful, as it did. The members of Parliament shouted their approval with "hear-hears" and foot stomping.

I remained calmly in my seat even though many eyes were leveled in my direction. I refused to rise to the political bait, assured that with Kaunda it was showtime for the Party and nothing personal, just another worn-out message for my government. The French ambassador, however, took offense, given his country's background in Indochina. He passed me a note declaring that he was walking out in protest and urged that I join him. Given the setting, I thought it pointless to show public disapproval of Kaunda's remarks. As the French ambassador rose and left his seat, he signaled me to join him. I shook my head, "No." I think I was more offended at his trying to dictate to me than I was at Kaunda's canned and wearisome remarks, which had become old hat since my arrival in Zambia. Besides, I was sure the French had even fewer interests and less at stake than we did in the region, marginal as ours were at the time.

The Russian diplomats had a small, very ordinary-looking chancery yet kept busy behind the scenes. Their offices were equipped with one-way mirrored glass so they could see who was coming near while an outsider approaching could see only his reflection. The Americans and the Soviets were not on friendly terms in those Cold War days, so we had little to chat about beyond the weather and some generalities on life in Zambia. I hardly expected the Russian ambassador to tell me about the financial and military support his country was giving the freedom fighters in neighboring countries.

Special Case of the Chinese

The Chinese Embassy was different. Their chancery was enormous, with a reportedly huge staff to support their railway assistance program. It was understandable that the ambassador preferred to receive me at his residence. I enjoyed a cup of excellent tea, admired the Chinese wall hangings, but found the ambassador almost as taciturn and inscrutable as the Russian. Trying to enliven the meeting, I made the offhand and rather frivolous suggestion that we consider a game of ping pong, which it will be remembered was a gambit used to thaw relations with the Chinese elsewhere. I received little more than an Oriental stare in return. So much for levity with the Maoists.

The Chinese enjoyed a privileged status with the Zambians as a result of their enormous aid project of building the railroad from Dar es Salaam in Tanzania to Ndola in the copper belt of northern Zambia. Another time, during a Parliamentary session after President Kaunda had again criticized the United States for the war in Vietnam, he commended the Chinese for their assistance efforts, saying, "Had it been any other country working in Zambia, the nation would have been left with 'half-breeds' along the line of rail. But not with the Chinese," he concluded.

The Chinese made themselves incredibly inconspicuous in the northern area, as they moved earth, laid rail, and built bridges over the rivers in highly disciplined fashion. In addition, they built and moved their own housing and even planted gardens for growing their own food as they advanced along the rail line. The major objective of the rail link was to provide Zambia with improved access to the Indian Ocean for its copper exports to the rest of the world. But there was a serious economic problem in that the value and tonnage of Zambia's exports would far exceed anticipated imports, with little expectation of a reasonable balance of trade. Yet construction of the potential White Elephant continued. Earlier warnings on economic viability had been issued by no less a statesman and U.S. railroad tycoon than Averell Harriman, who had visited Zambia some years before my time. As an alternative to an uneconomic railroad Harriman had recommended that the existing East-West Highway, called "the Hell Road" by truckers because of its lack of maintenance, be widened, improved, and maintained. But the generosity and low cost of Chinese aid was irresistible to the Zambians.

When the railroad project was completed a few years later, the diplomatic corps were invited up to the main rail junction at Ndola to witness the first engine and cars as they steamed into the station. Old animosities were forgotten. Congratulations were exchanged, drinks were poured, and everyone present seemed to be in the jolliest of moods, including all the government dignitaries who came from Beijing for the occasion. About ten years later when I visited China with a U.S. government delegation on science and technology, I was dumbfounded when one of the officials approached me to say, "I remember you. You were in Zambia when last I saw you. It was for the opening of the Chinese railroad."

And Still More Dips

The Nigerian high commissioner was a standout in the diplomatic corps, with his elegant native costumes in a variety of bright colors, accented with gold and silver threads and complete with matching, braided cap, which he never seemed to be without. He said he had a wife in Lagos and had been head of the country's most prestigious foreign policy research institute there. But as he spent much of his time singing or humming lively tunes, no one ever stopped to question him or to discuss either point. Nonetheless, he was an amusing and charming emissary. I had to assume his main business in Zambia probably involved promoting exports of fuel oil from Nigeria.

The Romanian ambassador, a somewhat clownish figure who lived near me, was quite sociable both as a tennis player and in hosting lavish dinner parties, where he enjoyed serving some quite respectable wines from his country. He was memorable not only for his bulky white figure on the tennis courts but for his off-putting admonition to tennis partners (of which I was one): "Take no prisoners!"

Israel, Japan, India, and a few other Asian countries also followed their national interests on the Zambian scene, especially trade and regional political-military developments. Many of them were importers of Zambian copper, some fellow travelers in the Non-Aligned Movement. Others, like India, enjoyed special status because of Kaunda's strong admiration for the political and philosophical views of Mahatma Gandhi. Besides, the Indians had a large national presence in Zambia, a remnant of colonial days when Indians had been brought in as cheap labor for economic development. The Swedish ambassador and his wife were a friendly and popular couple, often on safari in their Land Rover, checking on their various small aid projects throughout the country.

Lusaka, Zambia, 1972–76

Zambian-U.S. Relations

Zambia is often touted as "the real Africa," but visions of fabulous game parks and Victoria Falls near Livingstone on the Zambezi River obscure the genuine reality of a very, very poor country with gross domestic product of no more than $1 per person a day. Its overdependence on copper mining, low rate of agricultural growth, undeveloped tourist potential, and economic investment needs have long stood in the way of achieving a needed growth rate of 7–8 percent just to pull the country out of poverty.

Zambia's importance to the United States during my tour in the 1970s might best have been described in political rather than economic terms. It would have been inconceivable for the United States *not* to have recognized countries in Africa like Ghana and Zambia that began throwing off the colonialism of European governments and declaring their independence in the 1950s and 1960s. Having fought for its own independence in the late eighteenth century, the United States became—and remains—a vigorous and faithful advocate of independence and democracy throughout the world. It was inevitable that the United States would welcome and embrace Zambia when that nation declared independence in 1963. I was there in 1973 to celebrate its tenth anniversary, and it was still a very new and needy country.

The U.S. government may well have been surprised to discover that Zambia held a few thousand American missionaries whose interests it had to promote and protect. But it was quick to realize that Zambian votes at the United Nations on major issues of importance to the United States were worth cultivating. U.S. interests were only modestly involved in the country's economic mainstay of copper, and these were vastly overshadowed by predominant South African and British investments.

During my tour in Zambia, copper prices went into a serious downward spiral from which they have never fully recovered in the intervening years. It was also during the 1970s that Zambia sought to offset foreign exchange losses from copper by borrowing heavily from private U.S. banks and international organizations, whose representatives were steady visitors to the country. As a result, by the early part of the twenty-first century Zambia had become one of the most heavily indebted developing countries seeking relief and forgiveness.

Lusaka, Zambia, 1972–76

It has been said that because of its vast reaches of arable land (only about 14 percent of which is cultivated), Zambia could be the breadbasket of southern Africa. But even now, thirty years after my tour there, agriculture accounts for only 15 percent of GDP. Its main products, some of which are exported, continue to be maize (corn), soybeans, cotton, sugar, sunflower seed, wheat, sorghum, and tobacco. Floriculture, with exports mainly to Europe, was just beginning to take off during my years there.

Given the socialist bent of the Kaunda government and historic ties to the United Kingdom, there was little interest either on the part of Zambia or the United States to consider economic assistance arrangements like those in other poor countries. Nor for that matter were the Zambians interested at that time in any connection with the U.S. Peace Corps, which was occasionally challenged by minor government officials and the press as being a front for undercover political activities. Moreover, the United States took the view that Zambia had sufficient resources, from copper and agricultural development, to meet its own needs.

The closest we came to helping the Zambians with their agricultural problems during my time there was to mount, at the embassy's initiative, a commercial farmers' mission to the United States to observe modern growing and marketing techniques. It was only moderately useful, given the state's heavy role in agriculture. However, during the last few months of my tour in Zambia, after bad weather and serious crop failures in maize production, the Zambians only reluctantly approached us for PL-480 surplus food aid. My tour had ended before negotiation of an agreement was completed.

Zambia was a relatively poor risk for foreign investment. A major obstacle, despite its natural resources, was the country's appalling lack of business organization and management. Yet how can foreigners who are guests in the country for but a short time expect more from a ten-year-old government with only one hundred or so high school graduates and perhaps ten university graduates when it started up as a nation in 1963? The story may be apocryphal but it was said that when the Zambians sought to diversify their agriculture by going into fruit orchards, they sent a truck to South Africa for planting and breeding stock. It was reported to have returned filled with young trees, their roots pointing skyward in the hot tropical sun, their branches mashed into the flatbed of the truck. Whether this was a bad joke that the white South Africans played on the black Africans or the Zambian importer's mistake is not known. The idea of fruit orchards was abandoned.

Although the Zambians began as a nation of humble, largely rural people eager to learn, they were also a very proud people, and their president was perhaps the proudest of them all. But in defending his country from occasional accusations of poor organization and management, Kaunda would heatedly reply, "We will build our country, but we will do it *our way*, and the mistakes we will make will be *our* mistakes." Indeed, there were many costly mistakes as the country was attaining its growing legs in the early years when I was there. One example concerned the national brewery—the country's crown jewel, given the people's love of beer. The brewery was started up with foreign capital and management and was said to have turned in an annual profit of some $5 million in its early years. When the brewery was nationalized and under Zambian government's management, it is said to have *lost* $4 million a year and had to be heavily subsidized by the government.

Zambia was far more interesting politically to the United States and other foreign observers for a number of reasons. Located near the heart of Africa, it was considered the key borderline state between black- and white-ruled Africa, the latter at that time being Rhodesia (later Zimbabwe) and South Africa. Most important, Zambia was the exile base of choice for the heads of liberation leaders in the southern African states of Namibia, Angola, Rhodesia, Mozambique, and South Africa and thus an important political listening post, as Senator Fulbright had so astutely observed during my confirmation hearing. Although Nelson Mandela was imprisoned on Robben Island off the coast of Cape Town in South Africa, his principal deputy and former law partner, Oliver Tambo, was a refugee in Lusaka at the time I was stationed there.

Another factor underlying U.S. interest in Zambia was the political importance—nationally and internationally—of President Kenneth Kaunda, known as the George Washington of his country for leading the fight for independence from Great Britain. Kaunda became Zambia's first president within a one-party, socialist-oriented state. His political stature, prestige, and influence in Africa and in the broader, worldwide Non-Aligned Movement were also significant. Kaunda was at the center of the political ferment over liberation and majority rule in southern Africa. The more I came to know him, his character and his personality, the more I thought of him as the heart and soul of Black Africa. He maintained strong, political links with his good and close friend, President Julius Nyerere of neighboring Tanzania. The latter seemed a more sophisticated and perhaps more studious man than Kaunda, so I viewed him more as the brains of the region. Together, Kaunda and Nyerere were a remarkable team and models to whom the liberation leaders in exile went for advice and support. Their views were sought and carefully listened to not only by the liberation movement leaders but by the diplomats of countries following the political evolution of southern Africa. The United States was one of these, but hardly as much in the forefront in following developments as the British, Zambia's former colonial rulers.

Zambian Attitudes toward the United States

I always found it curious that despite the fact that a few Zambian leaders in business and government had been schooled in the United States (though many, many more had studied in Britain), this sector of society made a deliberate effort to keep its distance from U.S. diplomatic representatives, at least in the 1970s when I was there. Part of this attitude was the Zambian government's socialist orientation as well as its great depth of animosity toward the United States for its involvement in Vietnam, strongly and repeatedly criticized by President Kaunda, and echoed by the political faithful. His socialistic philosophy of humanism, clearly anti-capitalist, also condemned any deliberate taking of human life. Kaunda mixed this philosophy with a missionary zeal to condemn the powerful who oppress the weak and the poor.

The faithful of Kaunda's one-party state strongly avoided doing anything out of line with the president's humanist philosophy or in any way displeasing to the nation's leader. At times it appeared almost sycophantic. Of minor significance but noteworthy, a small coterie of Fabian Socialists from England had hung on in Zambia after Independence to help steer the country's social and economic policies. Their influence was not always very deep, but undoubtedly they did influence the sporadically nonfriendly attitude toward the United States among some officials and in the local press.

Yet President Kaunda could not have been more courteous or genuinely friendly toward me; he was even gallant at times, on both an official and personal basis. When I left the country, he sent me a large autographed picture of himself, urging me to "keep up the good work of the Lord, which you have done so well in Zambia!" That was typical of his manner of speaking, missionary-born and raised as he was. But it mistakenly cast my official mission in religious terms, which it certainly was not.

The generally cool but correct public attitude toward the United States took a radical shift on the occasion of former president Lyndon Johnson's death. President Kaunda immediately phoned me to invite himself over to the U.S. Embassy to "sign the book," a hangover British custom of expressing condolences. I had received the cabled announcement from Washington only minutes before and immediately dispatched the administrative officer to the local bookstore to get a proper book for signing. "And don't forget the black ribbon," I added.

Kaunda arrived a few hours later with a large entourage from his government to sign the condolence book. They filled the Embassy's small entrance lobby. I was overwhelmed by this official show of sympathy for the United States and its former president. The exchange of remarks that followed between President Kaunda and myself marked a decided turning point for the better in official and public relations. As Kaunda made clear in his remarks, he was motivated because of Johnson's stand on peace, the poor and underprivileged, as well as by the U.S. exit from Vietnam that led him—indeed the entire body politic of his small country— to a public show of condolence and a hand of friendship. Also, during my tour in Zambia, Kaunda had always maintained an open door for me to meet with him on official business, despite his occasional public outbursts on the Vietnam issue and his delay in receiving me to present credentials.

Dealing Mostly with Men

My official dealings in Zambia were almost exclusively with men, mainly President Kaunda. There were no women except secretaries in the Foreign

Ministry or other government offices, and I encountered only a few in social work, hospitals, and welfare agencies. Of course I met any number of women on social occasions. However, about the second year I was in Zambia, I was surprised and pleased to learn that the government was appointing a woman to a top post in the Foreign Ministry; later the same woman, Gwen Konie, was named Zambia's first woman ambassador and posted to Japan. Still another woman was given a leadership post in one of Zambia's missions to the United Nations. It was not until 2003, some twenty-seven years after I had left Zambia, that that country named its first woman ambassador to the United States, Dr. Inoge Mbikusita-Lewanika.

Very near the close of my tour in Zambia I received a phone call from a woman who was becoming prominent in local politics. She did not ask for an appointment (Zambian security was tight and she surely would have had to seek permission and explain). She merely wanted a brief moment to express her personal views. She said she spoke for herself but also for a number of other Zambian women, saying she was grateful to me personally and to the United States for naming a woman to head its diplomatic mission to her country, as it was proving a model and example in her own government. Had I noticed the changes being made? I sensed that she and the others may well have cited me when lobbying for higher jobs and more participation in their government and its international affairs. I thanked her for her thoughtfulness in calling me and wished her success in the future.

Embarrassing Moments

Early in my assignment, when medical reasons caused my return to the United States for surgery, Kaunda insisted he see me immediately upon my return and privately. When I returned to Zambia after an absence of some six weeks, I was greeted with a message that the president expected me at a private dinner for two at State House. I had to explain to his aides that I was hardly in any shape to dine in public. I had abdominal surgery in Washington and thought it bad taste to discuss the details. Yet Kaunda insisted I accept his dinner invitation; he "understood." So I summoned my courage and accepted somewhat conditionally, praying nothing would go amiss with my physical condition. Fortunately, the evening passed without my disgracing myself with abdominal rumblings.

Dinner was informal—just the two of us, with places set at a small card table in the middle of one of the vast great rooms overlooking the broad, formal terraced gardens laid out by the English colonial government. There was little to suggest Africa in the setting; the British had so mimicked their formal country estates—a bit like *Brideshead Revisited*. The peacocks were still strutting about emitting those wild, unsettling shrieks to signal their domineering presence, as they had the day I presented credentials. Fortunately, by sheer dint of willpower and eating sparingly of the chicken and rice set before me, I was able to control my abominable abdominal condition. President Kaunda thoughtfully wanted to bring me up to date on political and military developments in the liberation struggle in southern Africa. I somehow managed to get a reporting cable off to Washington.

Kaunda's compassion and courtliness helped the evening along. He did understand. The entire experience reminded me of a foolish childhood limerick that went something like this: "Yesterday I sat next to the Duchess at tea. Her rumblings abdominal were simply phenomenal, and everyone thought it was me!" God was good; I played no symphony at the president's command performance.

More Embarrassment—Golf with the President

Perhaps the biggest gaffe during my service in Zambia came about as a result of a golf game. The time was well into the second year of my assignment, when I had fully recovered from my earlier abdominal surgery. I was pleased yet mildly surprised one day when President Kaunda extended an invitation for me to join him in a game of golf on his executive course within the extensive, beautifully landscaped grounds surrounding his residence and office at State House. The British had done well in providing a palatial Georgian mansion of red brick, complete with two-story-high white columns for their governors when then Northern Rhodesia belonged to the British Crown.

I say I was only mildly surprised because I had been deliberately dropping large hints to the caddies at Lusaka's major golf club just across the road from State House, knowing that they worked at the president's course as well. I seldom missed prodding the caddies for information about the president's game. I am confident one of them made a direct suggestion to the president while assuring him I was not so strong I might beat him if we played a game together. So I accepted when the president invited me to a game. We were joined by one of his ministers of state, who was an extraordinarily good player, having won a blue in golf at Oxford, where he had studied anthropology. He was clearly President Kaunda's personal golf pro and coach.

We were a strange assembly: a threesome of two black men and a white woman surrounded by a bevy of caddies, personal and forward, plus scorekeeper and assorted hangers-on. It looked rather like a troop movement across a field. I was told that the Oxford Blue's wife had to care for the children and was unable to join us. So on we went, with the score-keeper carefully announcing results after each hole. As we played the president and I managed to stay quite even on the score. After nine holes, I thought the game was over when the scorekeeper announced rather formally: Zambia 45, United States of America 46. We then repaired to the shade of a grove of trees on the lawn just down from the grand terraces fronting State House. Instead of appropriate lawn furniture, the help had pulled out some rather formal high-backed and totally inappropriate mahogany chairs from the state dining room and a few coffee tables. We sat there awkwardly sipping tea.

Having mentally kept my own score, I was certain the scorekeeper had reversed the totals. But then I had enough common sense to know one should never claim to beat a head of state at any game, especially when one is a guest. So I just smiled. After at least forty-five minutes of small talk about the weather, the beauties of the place, and the fun of outdoor sport, I thanked my host profusely ("how generous and kind of him . . ."), bade all goodbye, and left the grounds for my car. The next day at my office, I got a call from the Oxford Blue, scolding the daylights out of me, after starting out, "Your Excellency . . ." He wanted to know why I had left after only nine holes, saying they always played eighteen. I explained that this was not clear either from the conversation or body language at the end of nine holes. The tea party was so extended that I thought it was the end of the outing. I was never invited back to play with Kaunda. Perhaps

Lusaka, Zambia, 1972–76

it was just as well. We were both too competitive and too closely matched.
I assumed that he had never played golf with a woman before. I gave him
credit for taking me on.

The Liberation Struggle in Southern Africa

Shortly after my arrival in Zambia, I realized that my Washington briefings had not fully prepared me for the reality that my daily work would be
far less on bilateral issues—of which there were few—than on regional
matters. This was largely because President Kaunda was playing such a
pivotal role in the politics of the armed liberation struggle under way
in five of the eight countries of southern Africa—Angola, Mozambique,
Namibia, Rhodesia, and South Africa (excluding independent Botswana,
Lesotho, and Swaziland). Moreover, visitors to Zambia from the U.S.
public and private sectors, representatives of international institutions,
and academics were all taking an increasing interest in the regional liberation struggles.

By the mid-1970s Zambia had become a center for exiles and refugees
of the liberation movements in the region, as well as the site of military
training and R&R for the insurgents fighting these wars. The Zambian
government was actively lending material, financial, and moral support
to these movements. Indeed, many regarded Kaunda, along with his friend
and neighbor, President Julius Nyerere of Tanzania, as their inspiration
and champions.

Lusaka had clearly become a key political listening post in southern
Africa. The Zambians, I learned, thought that the United States hardly
knew or little understood what was going on in that part of the world nor
did they seem to care. I saw this negative image of the United States as
a diplomatic challenge. I realized that it was only occasionally that the
State Department issued some low-key statement in a "me-too" sort of
vein, favoring free peoples and majority rule in southern Africa. From
the perspective of the average Zambian, the United States was "just another country out there," big and remote—not an unusual view, given the
country's colonial links to Great Britain, its Socialist sympathies, and most
Zambians' limited education and travel.

It was China, with its large foreign aid program and future trade prospects, and to a lesser extent the Soviet Union that were well regarded by Zambian officialdom and urban elites, albeit with some reservations. These two countries and the Nordics, especially the Swedes, were perhaps the most appreciated and respected countries represented in Zambia.

Besides President Kaunda's never-ending public criticism of U.S. involvement in Vietnam, he would privately urge me to inform my government to "wake up" to the problems of southern Africa and to remember American history and independence from England and its "morally correct" abolition of slavery. He seldom hesitated to repeat this same advice to visiting U.S. officials, urging the United States to take a more active, less rhetorical stance toward the region. After dutifully listening, I always assured Kaunda I would continue to report his views to Washington. Often I would add my recommendation that the State Department give serious consideration to a more sympathetic policy, as I failed to see how it would carry unreasonable risks or burdens.

Friends in the Department of State who were privy to Secretary of State Henry Kissinger's staff meetings jokingly told me of his reactions to our cables. Once when a message came in from Lusaka, Kissinger is reported to have said in his familiar accent, "Oh, no, no, not dot voman from Afreeka *again!*"

Yet Embassy Lusaka and Embassy Dar es Salaam soon became an antiphonal chorus, reporting the pleas of Presidents Kaunda and Nyerere that the United States change to a more engaged and principled policy toward southern Africa. But there always seemed to be the higher priorities of the Cold War in the foreign policy agendas of both the Nixon and Ford administrations—that is, until the civil war in Angola intensified soon after the Portuguese ceded independence to that country in 1975, bringing increased foreign involvement.

Even before this turn of events, visitors from the U.S. public and private sectors and international organizations sought information on regional matters, expecting Embassy Lusaka to be knowledgeable. Although we had easy access to the Zambian government, it was only a secondary source. I believed we had to broaden and deepen direct contacts with the liberation movements but without being able to offer any material support in their armed struggle.

Lying to the west of Zambia and bordering the Atlantic Ocean, Angola had little in common with Zambia other than a border. It had been a Portuguese possession for 500 years. The two countries had no major road, rail, or air links; no common language; and no trade connections of any significance. Thus it was all the more strange that Angola's most notorious guerrilla, Jonas Savimbi, would occasionally turn up in Lusaka, either with his entourage of bodyguards or alone in a chauffeur-driven car. Savimbi was the insurgent leader of UNITA, the National Union for the Total Liberation of Angola, who waged war for liberation against the Portuguese government. It seemed less strange when one realized that Savimbi was supported in his quest for political power by both the Chinese and the South Africans. South Africa had no diplomatic relations or presence in Zambia other than indirectly, through some tenuous links to the Anglo American (South African) copper company in Zambia. But China's diplomatic mission in Lusaka was available to him.

It thus made sense for Savimbi to pay his closest benefactors the occasional business call. Less comprehensible was why Savimbi, a dashing figure in camouflage fatigues and red beret, would appear from time to time at the U.S. Embassy in Lusaka, without advance notice or prior request, asking "to see the ambassador." I must have met with him three or four times, but the purpose of his visits was never clear. I came to think he was trailed on his Zambia visits by his foreign backers or by Zambian security wanting to keep track of all his contacts, never mind exactly what business he might be transacting. Some American scholars considered Savimbi odd to the point of psychotic, or certainly enigmatic. I think his "game" was pretending to any "tails" that the United States was also supporting him, though we were not providing him any overt assistance at the time. I was under no instructions from Washington either to agree or to refuse to see Savimbi, despite my regular reports to Washington on each of his inconsequential visits.

Finally in 1975, after years of guerrilla warfare, the Portuguese gave up their colonial government in Angola and granted independence to the insurgents, but not to Savimbi's UNITA. Rather they ceded power to a rival insurgent faction, the Popular Movement for the Liberation of Angola

(MPLA), led by Dr. Agostinho Neto, but, to Neto's chagrin, without recognizing the MPLA as the "sole legitimate representative" of the Angolan people. To Savimbi, it must have been exceedingly galling not to obtain his country's leadership, after all those years of guerrilla warfare. UNITA promptly joined forces with another liberation movement to form a national council that would "act as Angola's government." More strife ensued, intensifying civil war and inviting even more foreign involvement. The Soviet Union and Cuba supported Neto's MPLA; the United States and South Africa openly backed Savimbi's UNITA.

I was not privy to the full story of the buildup toward U.S. involvement except for one tense moment when one of my own embassy officers (the one representing "another U.S. government agency") bluntly told me, but only to inform me, that he had been instructed to see Kaunda by Washington ("back channels involving Kissinger himself").

"Not alone," I replied. "I am the U.S. representative here; I was appointed by the U.S. president, and I am the one who deals with the president of Zambia. I am going with you."

The officer was furious but did not argue; he was under time constraints because of an imminent air shipment of arms through Zambia to Savimbi's forces in a remote area of northeast Angola bordering on northwest Zambia. It seems the Cuban involvement in Angola under Soviet auspices was more than the United States and Kissinger could tolerate. The Cold War had come to southern Africa.

When I went with this officer to see Kaunda at State House, I merely informed the president that my embassy officer had a message for him, sat down, and waited for their business to be transacted. I am not sure I did the right thing in such an awkward situation not of my own making. Fortunately for me, I received no reprimand from Washington for my "interference" in the secretary's back-channel business, though I was later told it was intended that I be "bypassed" so that I might be able to deny knowledge of the operation. Certainly my insistence on ambassadorial prerogatives did not endear me to Henry Kissinger, as subsequent events would suggest.

Hoping I was not being paranoid, and with time to reflect, I came to wonder if my subsequent assignment to the United Nations rather than to another post of my own in Europe or Latin America, for which I was qualified, might have been punishment for interference in the secretary's secret business in the field. But I was probably just one of a number of Foreign Service officers who, while following their best lights trying to do their assigned job, fell out of Henry's good graces, if ever I or they had been in them.

My problems were nothing compared to Savimbi's. After sixteen years of fighting, in which, according to a BBC report, up to 300,000 had died, a peace deal made it possible for elections to be held in Angola. UNITA lost the election, rejected that outcome, and continued its brutal war. Eventually, the war brought Savimbi to his death on the battlefield, but not until February 2002, twenty-seven years after I first met him. UNITA then accepted the inevitable and two months later signed a formal cease-fire with the Angolan army.

Hindsight can be a gift or a curse. But if anyone in Washington had asked for my advice on Savimbi, based on my limited acquaintance with him and my even more limited knowledge of military affairs, I would not have placed even a two-dollar bet on his winning a war against Soviet-backed Cubans in Africa. At this point, one can do little more than pray that Savimbi's very troubled soul now rests in peace.

Namibia

A surprisingly large and mineral-rich country bordering the Atlantic Ocean, Namibia was under a United Nations trusteeship, ignored by the white South African government's occupation and administration. It is not surprising that many black Namibians fled to Zambia seeking refuge. Their opposition group called itself the Southwest Africa People's Organization (SWAPO) and was led by Sam Nujoma, the president-designate of a free and independent Namibia. Nujoma was a youthful, carefree figure who could often be seen around Lusaka in a black leather jacket astride a high-speed motorcycle.

Embassy Lusaka had occasional contact with a number of Namibians, who seemed less interested in guerrilla warfare than in obtaining scholarship and leadership grants and visas to the United States. I met Nujoma at an informal family supper at the U.S. consul's home and wondered how so young and unsophisticated a person was prepared to be his country's first president—as indeed he became in 1990. He undoubtedly matured in the ensuing fifteen years, but I obviously failed to see his leadership qualities, or perhaps he was holding out on me for some obscure reason.

Yet it was to their credit and perhaps Nujoma's leadership that the exiled Namibians in Lusaka—with the help of the United Nations—set up a shadow administration composed of all the major ministries necessary to running a government. They actually spent their exile practicing how to do each job once they had obtained freedom (which they did in March 1990). I was impressed with their imagination and industry when I visited the site at their invitation.

The Namibians in exile were not without sophistication. Their foreign minister–designate, Theo-Ben Gurirab, who was director of the Namibian Institute in Zambia, was tall and good-looking, with a stylish American wife. His elegant dress and manner were hardly typical of the main group of Namibian exiles. I speculated that some of the exiles might have been supported beyond UN grants by Namibia's rich diamond trade. It was not mine to wonder if and how. Just before I left Zambia, Gurirab or one of his official colleagues bought my private car, a sporty-looking, low-mileage Ford Capri, which I had shipped to Zambia from Italy.

Mozambique

The other Portuguese colony in southern Africa, Mozambique, on the Pacific coast, had its own liberation struggle, but our embassy in Dar es Salaam followed this action for the most part. Samora Machel, the leader of the main opposition movement, the Front for the Liberation of Mozambique (FRELIMO), was an admirer of Kaunda and visited him frequently in Lusaka.

As we had publicized the fact that U.S. Assistant Secretary of State for African Affairs Donald Easum would be visiting Zambia, Machel asked the Zambians to intercede for him in gaining an appointment with Easum. I received a call from Mark Chona asking me to facilitate such a meeting. I agreed to meet with this black liberation leader, and the Zambians provided a safe house for our meeting, which I found rather amusing.

No thought had been given to the language we might use, which turned out to be awkward when I discovered that Machel claimed to speak only

Portuguese. Yet we managed as best we could. Machel spoke slowly, and I listened carefully, answering in a strange mixture of Italian and Spanish. However, for the little business we had to transact, it worked well enough. A date, time, and place were set for Machel to meet Assistant Secretary Easum. Subsequently, I wondered if Machel hadn't been playing some sort of "macho" game with me when I heard that he had an English mistress— or was she really his political advisor (as publicly claimed)—and was perhaps bilingual in Portuguese and English. I never learned the truth of the matter.

Machel was killed in an airplane crash in 1986, which some thought an act of sabotage by the white South African government. Machel's widow later married Nelson Mandela after his African National Congress (ANC) won victory and majority rule and Mandela had become South Africa's president.

South Africa

Zambia also hosted exiles from South Africa, but they were far fewer than the others and not in an armed status. The imprisonment of Nelson Mandela and others on Robben Island off the coast of Cape Town had debilitated the leadership of the ANC political opposition in South Africa. Mandela's main deputy and former law partner, Oliver Tambo, had escaped imprisonment and sought safe haven with his wife and family in Zambia. I invited them to tea at the residence one day, both out of sympathy for their situation and also with a bit of curiosity about their political connections. I wanted to underscore that U.S. policy was generally supportive of majority rule in white-ruled South Africa. The Tambos were grateful for this interest in their situation, which notwithstanding its hardships was not comparable with the rougher life of the armed insurgents hiding out in Zambia.

About ten years later, when I was retired and living in Washington, my phone rang and a voice said, "This is Oliver." As this was during the days of the Oliver North scandal involving Iran and Central America, I was instantly thrown off until the voice announced, "This is Oliver of South Africa." He was in the United States on business for the Mandela government. I was pleased by his personal kindness in remembering me and calling, as I was then totally unconnected with the U.S. government. Like so many Africans, he was warmhearted, caring, and friendly.

Zambia shared its Zambezi River border with Rhodesia to the south. Rhodesia had broken away from the United Kingdom with its Unilateral Declaration of Independence in 1965, when it was led by the white "rebel" government of Ian Smith. Smith's leadership was heavy-handed in controlling a restive black majority that sought full and legal independence and majority rule.

The two major black Rhodesian opposition groups remained separate and distinct, mainly reflecting the differing personalities and aspirations of their leaders. Each maintained large, armed militias, some of whom remained in Rhodesia as insurgents, while others sought refuge in Zambia for a variety of purposes, from training to a base for attacks on Rhodesia to R&R. The Zambian border along the Zambezi thus became a dangerous place, with the local press reporting border skirmishes between black and white Rhodesians, especially when poor, unfortunate Zambian farmers got caught in the occasional crossfire of hot pursuit.

Rhodesia's main opposition political parties were known by their acronyms, ZAPU and ZANU. The Zimbabwe African People's Union (ZAPU) was led by Joshua Nkomo and supported financially and militarily by the Zambians and Chinese and perhaps others. The Zambians urged me "to know Nkomo better," when he made Lusaka his political base in 1974.

A giant of a man, Nkomo seemed shy and taciturn on the few social occasions when we met by chance. Given his background in white Rhodesia, he was probably uncomfortable in the presence of a white woman, and a foreign diplomat at that. I made no effort to cultivate him, as I could offer him no hope of help. Again, I was under no instructions from Washington, nor did I think it appropriate to request such instructions.

Nkomo's political opponent for the presidency of a truly independent country was Robert Mugabe of the Zimbabwe African National Union (ZANU), who was backed mainly by the Soviets. Though Mugabe visited Zambia once while I was there, I did not meet him. He was never made to feel welcome by the Kaunda government and presumably did not return, unless clandestinely, to support his loosely controlled exiles based there. As it turned out, Mugabe finally won the prize of the presidency of a free Zimbabwe. His authoritarian tenure and abysmal economic management have been bumpy, with some daring publicly to assert that "life was better under the whites!"

During my time in Lusaka, one had to be extremely cautious about excursions on the Zambezi River. Yet early in my tour, I made a weekend safari into Botswana via the quadripoint in southwest Zambia, where the tips of the borders of Rhodesia, Zambia, Botswana, and Namibia's Caprivi Strip converged along the Zambezi. I invited the wife of my DCM, Harvey Nelson, to accompany me on the weekend excursion, and Saul drove us down in my car. When we reached the quadripoint, we found we had to drive onto a primitive flatboard ferry to cross the Zambezi. Directly opposite the crossing point and a bit to the left was a Rhodesian machine gun nest, with an armed soldier in ready position, his weapon aimed directly at us! The Zambian ferryman casually told us to ignore the soldier, and then guided us up the ramp, reminded us to brake the car, and told us to get out and stand where we could be seen.

The sight of the Rhodesian soldier aiming directly at us frightened the daylights out of Saul. I told him to remain calm, put the flags up on the car fenders, and stand alongside us, hands down and empty, to indicate we bore no weapons. Frankly, we all stood absolutely frozen until we reached the Botswana side, reentered the car, and drove down the ramp and off on the road to the Chobe National Game Park. The park later became famous as the site of a honeymoon visit by actors Richard Burton and Elizabeth Taylor. Our experience with the armed Rhodesian sentry increased my dislike of "the rebel Ian Smith" and his hateful white regime. But the trip to Chobe and its broad swamps was worth it. We had never seen such large herds of elephants nor gotten so close to them as we did at Chobe.

Back in Lusaka I busied myself in following developments among the exiled Rhodesians. I had heard of but never met Herbert Chitepo, one of the pre-Mugabe leaders of ZANU. Chitepo seemed better liked by the Zambians than Mugabe, and so it came as a shock when he was mysteriously assassinated in Zambia. It was never clear who committed the crime. Surprisingly, the Zambian Ministry of Foreign Affairs invited the entire diplomatic corps to Chitepo's funeral, presumably to show general sympathy for the Rhodesian cause without necessarily showing political party preferences.

I was conflicted, not wanting to be conspicuous by my absence nor to have my presence misinterpreted. I attended, more out of curiosity but also in humanitarian recognition of a man who had fought for a just cause. I received a few questioning looks from some Zambians and others, but I ignored them. I had learned that trying to interpret the gestures and arched eyebrows of others can be pointless and time-consuming, except in critical diplomatic situations.

American Citizens under Attack

Precisely how Zambia was guarding its borders from Rhodesian and South African military incursions and reprisals against guerrillas was never clear. Recurring border clashes did not reach very serious levels until it was reported in the local press that "spies trying to infiltrate Zambia had been shot and killed near Victoria Falls by a vigilant Zambian Army sentry." It was not long before the Canadian High Commissioner called me at the U.S. Embassy, having been contacted by some of the Canadian survivors, that we began to learn the truth. Three of the Canadians had been shot and killed alongside the Zambezi River near Livingstone, their bodies toppling into the water and left as prey for the crocodiles. Several other Canadians and some Americans in the tourist party had promptly taken refuge behind large boulders and spent a terrifying night in hiding while waiting for the chance to escape to safer ground. They eventually made their way out to a telephone from which they called the Canadian High Commissioner in Zambia.

My Canadian colleague had only recently arrived at post and was still not fully installed in his office, nor did he have confidential cable communications with Ottawa. He asked for U.S. assistance, which we readily provided. His account to Ottawa was cause for outrage in the Canadian government, with cries from the Parliament for an immediate cut-off of Canada's rather significant foreign assistance program to Zambia. The High Commissioner was able to put a temporary hold on such drastic action pending an approach to the Zambian Foreign Ministry.

A few days later I received news of the Americans who had been shot along with the Canadians. The news came in a handwritten, hand-delivered letter through the foreign missionary network. It was from the American couple, both schoolteachers, who had become separated from the Canadians during their escape from the river bank. Just before dawn the injured couple had made their way to the main road. There they hitched a ride to the nearby coal-mining town of Wankie, where they gained admittance to the hospital. They wrote that they would need several weeks of care in Rhodesia before returning to the States for more extended treatment.

Their eyewitness account of the experience refuted and clarified local press reports. I faced a dilemma: how and to whom in Zambia I should reveal the truth of the shooting—that American and Canadian tourists had been mistaken for spies and shot by a Zambian border guard? And what should I do about representations to the Zambians for damages? The couple were very explicit in their appeal to the U.S. government for help in pressing an official claim. The couple claimed losses on their round-the-world trip, which had to be canceled, their medical treatment, and anticipated losses in time and salaries from their teaching jobs. Naturally I reported the facts to Washington, as required when the interests of American citizens are affected and families at home need to know. I urged discretion because the Zambian government's integrity and responsibility were in question.

Given the delicacy of the situation, I promptly sought an appointment with the president's special assistant, Mark Chona, and went to State House to explain the facts to him. I hardly expected nor did I request the Zambian government to publish the truth and admit their error in the shooting, though I suggested it might be useful. Here again, my Tanzanian diplomatic colleague and informal advisor on things African, whom I consulted, advised me that any such public admission of error could hardly be expected. However, I made it clear to Chona and later to the foreign minister that some sort of indemnity might be required. I also informed him that I was in consultation with the Department of State on the matter. I left it to the Zambians to deal with whatever public relations problems they might encounter, giving them my word that I intended to keep confidential the letter the Americans had sent me.

I collaborated closely with my Canadian colleague, as his was the graver of the two cases, with deaths involved. I felt because he had the more compelling case, he should go first in filing a claim for indemnity. Indeed, if he did, I thought it would make the American case easier, should we decide to file.

The Zambian officials were shaken by the thought that they might be faced with monetary payment for damages and injuries. Forgive the comparison, but it was like a parent dealing with teenage children who had done something horrible after borrowing dad's gun or car during summer vacation. I laboriously spelled out for the host country the consequences of violations of international law, kept reminding them of their obligations, and insisted on the need for reparations. I believe the whole incident was a first for the Zambian government during its first decade of independence.

In time, the injured Americans healed enough to return home. Their case was fully documented, their losses quantified, and a financial claim for damages formally lodged with the Zambian government through its Foreign Ministry. Eventually, reparations were paid, and the case was closed. The Canadians seem to have had a lengthier and more complicated settlement.

The Prime Minister and the American Nuns

My golf game with President Kaunda was not to be the only misunderstanding or mixed signals with ranking officials of the host government. Fortunately, neither involved official business nor was it serious—only curious. It was mostly an experience in learning that Zambian ways are not American ways, sometimes requiring fast footwork as well as fast thinking.

One evening while in my official residence entertaining at a dinner for a mixed group of some fourteen or so Zambian officials and foreign diplomats, I was called to the telephone by a rather uneasy looking houseman. He whispered to me that the caller was Prime Minister Mainza Chona, a rather eccentric but powerful member of President Kaunda's inner circle. Where was I, Chona asked rather insistently, though laughing throughout as was his playful manner. He had expected me for dinner and I hadn't arrived. While saying I was terribly sorry, I explained that the date was never entered in my calendar nor confirmed by my secretary, nor was I aware that I was expected. Oh yes you were, he insisted, and he was still waiting dinner, expecting me to come right over. I realized it was not a time to play games and so I came right out and explained that I had a dining room full of guests and could not leave. He ignored my explanation, saying he was expecting me; that I must come straightaway to his house. End of conversation. He had studied law at Gray's Inn in London—though briefly—and occasionally resorted to a clipped British way of speaking.

Fortunately Nelson, my very able deputy chief of mission, and his wife were among my guests. I signaled him away from the table, explained the dilemma, and said I believed I had to heed the PM's call and leave. He should offer no explanations to the guests, just to please carry on for me as though nothing had happened. Because my driver, Saul, was off for the evening, I drove myself in my own car the short three blocks to the PM's house. On entering I was shocked to find no party and no other guests. Indeed I had interrupted an entirely domestic scene with only the PM, his wife, and their children playing about the living room.

I was offered a drink, which helped take the edge off my surprise and chagrin. In short order we moved into the dining room. I kept waiting for the PM to impart some urgent or critical news or information. But there was none—nothing but small talk centered mainly around the children and their domestic life. I began to wonder if I had lost my mind. Or if the PM had lost his. What was up? Was this simply a display of power? Was he offended because he and his wife had not been invited to my dinner party? Or was there someone at my dinner party whom the PM disapproved of? It wasn't difficult, I had learned, for the Zambians, through their carefully structured intelligence network (set up and partly maintained by the British colonial "hangovers"), to know who was where and who was doing what.

I ate my main course of chicken with the PM and family. By dessert time I felt I had played the game (whatever it was) long enough. Total elapsed time: just under an hour. So I mumbled something like "not having anything urgent or critical to review," I felt I had to return to my residence and guests. Strangely enough neither the PM nor his wife raised any strong objections so I withdrew as gracefully as I could and

Lusaka, Zambia, 1972–76

returned to my residence. Even though I ended up at home in time for dessert, I felt I might have lost a few pounds that evening from the stress.

The PM could be mysterious to the point of buffoonery. But the "dinner" experience topped them all. There was something distinctly odd about the man—his infernal laughter and pointless small talk. Yet his brother, Mark Chona, was the intelligent, well-educated, competent, no-nonsense special assistant to the president. Did the PM have an illness that no one would discuss?

This was not the first time the PM had surprised me. On a visit to California, he somehow met up with a group of Poor Clare nuns. Impetuously he invited them to open a mission in Zambia. More surprisingly, they came only to find that no provision had been made to receive them. The small band of eight Americans had to build their convent and chapel in farmland between Lusaka and the airport and try to scratch out a living with plantings and chickens.

They encountered any number of hardships, from robbers and vandals to snakes and wild animals, plus extreme weather. One by one they dropped out and returned to the United States. Gradually they were replaced by Poor Clare sister missionaries from South Africa, Kenya, as well as from Europe. I never learned to what extent they might have been supported either privately or officially by the PM or the Zambian government.

One day after Mass at the Church of St. Ignatius, run by Irish Jesuit Missionaries in Lusaka, I saw a tall, middle-aged, blonde woman dressed in an attractive blue print dress and wondered if she was perhaps an Irish or English visitor. To my surprise, she turned out to be yet another American nun, a Sister of Charity from the Ohio Province. She was on voluntary assignment as chief matron at the Zambia University Teaching Hospital, which meant she was the chief administrative officer. Before long we became friends, occasionally having meals together, as she was leading a rather lonely life in a tiny apartment on the hospital grounds and had to cook her own meals, something she was not accustomed to from her community life in the States.

Occasionally I would send my driver, Saul, to pick her up or take her home. Then one day I learned she took childish delight—as did Saul—in having him fly the American and ambassadorial flags on the car's fenders as they drove around town! Once I realized what was going on, I had a little talk with Saul and the high jinks stopped. I suppose I should not have been such a killjoy. Here was another American nun trying to make the most of life in Zambia.

The Jolly Chief Justice

A single woman in a foreign country, regardless of status, age, place, or century, is bound to have interesting experiences whether in her work or personal capacity. Frankly I had little time for the latter—but there were moments, some good, some very bad.

I had never paid much attention to the somewhat remote but sly-eyed chief justice, a short white-haired Irishman, one of a number of the ten-year holdovers form Northern Rhodesia colonial days. They figured in Zambian officialdom, because indigenous replacements had not yet completed their education or were not sufficiently experienced to take over senior Zambian government posts. Like so many of the ex-colonials from the previous government, the chief justice lived alone, with a good-sized domestic staff, in one of the nicer garden neighborhoods in an attractive, British-style house of some distinction.

I understood the CJ entertained often, generally within the holdover ex-colonial community, especially, I was told (with raised eyebrows), some of the former British female secretaries, mostly "of an age." Having thus been forewarned, I was invited some months after my arrival to one of his rather formal dinner parties for eight. Had I passed a test? Or was I just something new and worth exploring? Following cocktails we moved into the dining room where I found myself seated to the CJ's left (the wife of the British high commissioner was on his right), but blessedly close to a door to the hall, just in case.

The case wasn't long in coming. I felt a few minor nudges through the first course, but discounted them as either accidental or a clumsy waiter. But toward the end of the main course, after much wine had flowed and the conversation was reaching crescendo, I distinctly felt a hand on my knees and some tentative groping. The CJ remained seated upright, almost sedate—dare I say sober as a judge? With one hand attending to a semblance of eating above the table, he used the other to engage in a flirtation below the table. I gave him my steeliest of looks and a shove, excused myself, and quickly slipped away from the table, through the door, and out into the hall.

Like a greyhound after a rabbit, the CJ sped after me, grabbing me in the hall with a full body press. "Excuse me, the ladies' room?" I asked, pushing him away with the full strength of both my arms; then followed his nod toward the loo. He had the good grace to return to the dining room. None of the other guests seemed the wiser, judging from the din of the conversation reaching the hall.

Inside the ladies' room I took my sweet time. Having had too many glasses of excellent wine, I decided I would not return to the table and whatever seemed inevitably to be in store after dinner. Rather I would slink quietly down the hall and even more quietly out the front door. Which I did. Outside I found a dozing Saul waiting at the curb. I knocked lightly on the car window and didn't wait for him to open the door, slid in, and told him to take me home immediately. He did, no questions asked, no confidences revealed. I think he understood.

The other guests were no doubt accustomed to the CJ's dinners and his routine "home entertainment" in lieu of concerts, theater, or ballet, of which we had none in Africa. I speculated it was all part of a long life of Empire in the tropics and that I was either out of touch or excessively uptight and Victorian. But I preferred to live with my American Puritanism. Besides, something must have been wrong with the CJ's eyesight. We were definitely mismatched—he at 5'5" without his white judge's wig, I at 5'11" or more with curly high-rising hair. Also, he had made a wrong assumption, or at least too quick a call.

Visitors, Visitors, Visitors

There are times when the U.S. ambassador, whatever the capital, country, or continent, begins to feel like a hotel concierge or local manager of American Express—booking and receiving tourists as well as receiving cables, phone calls, and faxes from Washington that "so and so will be visiting your post; please extend all appropriate courtesies," or "Mr. and Mrs. Bigwig (campaign contributors) or Congressman So-and-So will be arriving and wish an appointment with the president of the host country." Surprisingly, Zambia proved to be far from a sleepy outpost in southern Africa where only a few visitors might come on safari looking for big game. Visitors to Embassy Lusaka in my time of assignment included American businessmen scouting trade and investment opportunities, Duke Ellington for two concerts, Coretta Scott King and Congressman Andy Young to open a new Cultural Center, Governor William Scranton of Pennsylvania and his wife, and finally Secretary of State Kissinger on U.S. foreign policy business. Kissinger was preceded by an advance planning and security team from the State Department. Other visitors included ranking officials like assistant secretaries of state for African affairs and only one really— thank heavens—troublesome member of Congress and his assistant.

There was also an unexpected visit from representatives of a major American computer company on an important sales mission to the Zambian government. The embassy received no advance notice or request for assistance; rather it was the Zambians at the very last minute who asked us "to help out with the U.S. corporate visitors so they would be properly welcomed." The group included about twelve people, from the CEO on through the corporate lawyer and a wife or two. They arrived in two executive jets. Entertainment was always a major challenge in Africa. The local food shops offered only the bare minimum, and we had no Embassy commissary.

So when the VIP corporate executives arrived (one had been a high official in the State Department), I cabled my colleague in Dar es Salaam and asked him to throw some bags of lobsters and shrimp on the next day's plane to Lusaka. We arranged a respectable luncheon at the residence. Wine never seemed to be a problem. It may well have been contraband from South Africa. After the lunch one of the wives observed how well we seemed to dine on seafood in landlocked Zambia. I didn't divulge my secret and unconventional supply line, just smiled and thanked her for the compliment.

As it developed, meal planning and playing hostess became a regular part of Madam Ambassador's work. It was not uncommon to start the day with a fifteen-minute stop-off in the kitchen, a brief discussion with the cook, and a quick check of the contents of the refrigerator and storeroom. In the first days of my assignment, I would go with Saul to the open market, to train him to select and buy fresh produce for the official residence. Eventually Saul performed this chore on his own, and quite well, indeed. These housekeeping activities were hardly a normal part of either of our job descriptions. Nor did I imagine that many ambassadors started their day this way, certainly not in developed countries. But it can happen, and did, to this single woman ambassador in a developing country.

When I complained to a visiting U.S. government inspector, arrangements were made to engage a local housekeeper who was said to have suitable "experience" at one of the mining camps. She proved more of a burden, even an annoyance, than it was worth. Once when I returned from consultation in the States, I found that she had used Bon Ami or some such cleanser to scrub down a hand-painted fake antique Venetian desk (a prized gift from my family). The delicate floral design and antiquing, which she claimed were "dirty smudges," were totally obliterated. Too distressed to wonder what else her poor eyesight missed, I said she had to go. We then had to return to my rather haphazard supervision of the all-male domestic staff and household operations.

When an old friend, a retired Foreign Service officer, came to Zambia for a visit, we offered her the job as she wanted to gain some Social Security "quarters." However, her background was markedly European and she had had little personal experience in direct management of domestic staff, much less male or African. So our second try at alternative household management of the residence had to be abandoned and I again returned to double duty—residence and office.

Duke Ellington

Thank heavens for the Duke Ellington visit—it lifted spirits at Embassy Lusaka to an all-time high, provided excellent entertainment, much good-hearted laughter, and excellent public relations. The visit came about quite by accident. Ellington had been booked by our Embassy in Nairobi, Kenya, to celebrate that country's tenth Independence Day. But at the last minute the Kenyans feared Ellington would overshadow their own national orchestra, perhaps even to the point of public embarrassment. Kenya's loss proved Zambia's gain.

Lusaka, Zambia, 1972–76

Our very alert and energetic public affairs officer, John Burns, quickly arranged with Washington for the change in venue. Suddenly we were given the social event of the year, if not the decade since Zambian Independence. It was indeed a public diplomacy coup. The host government was welcoming and cooperative, allowing Ellington and his band to play in the spacious auditorium of the National Assembly, which was not only beautifully decorated, with walls sheathed in dark and light shades of tropical woods, but equipped with comfortable chairs and excellent acoustics. When Ellington's "A Train" rolled out over our distinguished Zambian guests and the entire diplomatic corps, I had to hold myself in check to keep from dancing in the aisles, the music was so moving and I was so hungry for a taste of the USA. It was a rare treat in an otherwise entertainment-starved, remote African post.

Before Ellington arrived, he had cabled the embassy that he would be receiving a very important air express parcel from Europe and would the embassy be so kind as to keep it refrigerated until he arrived and took delivery. I took personal responsibility and promptly delivered it to him upon his arrival. He immediately placed it in a sort of doctor's black bag, which was always at his side. Hmmm. Some sort of medicine? I wondered.

The next day after Ellington's sensational performance at the National Assembly in Lusaka, I flew with him and his band up to the copper-belt town of Ndola for an afternoon performance. Ellington was clutching his black doctor's bag, and of course I kept wondering what kind of medicine or special tonic he might be taking to keep up the heat and beat of his phenomenal jazz playing. Who knows. I didn't ask.

Ndola proved a strange experience. We went immediately from the airport to the local hotel so the Duke could rest up for an hour before the performance. He was mobbed by admirers in the hotel lobby. Then the hotel manager got a grip on things and escorted him up to the Presidential Suite. There was no dismissing the admirers who surrounded him. After all, here was an internationally famous black musician visiting a tiny, insignificant town in northern Zambia. It, too, was starved for good entertainment. Meanwhile I was escorted by a bellhop down a long hall to a dingy little room with a concrete floor, no carpets, just a single iron frame bed in the corner for my "rest" before the performance. But rest was out of the question with the racket going on down the hall in homage

Lusaka, Zambia, 1972–76

to the Great Ellington. Beer and talk flowed freely. After an hour or so we met up and left for the theater. I took the stage and did the introductions. The concert that followed, though good, was not the blockbuster affair it had been in Lusaka. It seemed to lack dynamism. And some of the Duke's magnetism was missing. Was the man tired, or sick?

On the return flight to Lusaka, Ellington pulled up the black leather doctor's satchel he was holding between his feet and placed it on his lap. He was still wearing that high rising brown bowler hat with the rakish feathers on the side, real dude style. I was in the aisle seat beside him and was pretending to be totally absorbed in my magazine while not taking my eyes off the satchel. Oh, oh, I thought, he is in a downer so here comes the fix.

Slowly he opened the satchel and carefully began unwrapping a white paper parcel within. Then he turned to me and asked, "Would you like a piece?"

"A piece?" I repeated dumbly. It turned out to be THE most elegant piece of Danish pastry I had seen in sometime. I was dumbfounded. Why did the man have these parcels air expressed to him all over the world, as he claimed? So much for misjudging people and their physical and emotional needs. I never shared so much as a crumb of his well-traveled Danish pastry, so I was none the wiser as to its special appeal. Ellington's secret died with him, but before that and not long after his visit to Zambia, he sent me a personal photo, inscribed with effusive thanks for the visit.

Martin Luther King's Widow Comes to Africa

Next to Ellington, the most important African American visitors from the States were Coretta Scott King, widow of the Reverend Dr. Martin Luther King, and Georgia politician U.S. Representative Andrew Young, later U.S. ambassador to the United Nations. The King visit was on and off several times because of news during the planning that the FBI had some derogatory and controversial information in its files on the deceased Dr. King. His widow was indignant over the publicity and wanted nothing to do with a U.S. government-sponsored visit to Zambia, however much good the visit might do for U.S. public diplomacy in that disturbed part of the world to which the United States was paying so little attention.

Finally the visit was back on and Mrs. King decided to include her three children, two sons and a daughter. Suddenly I had the prospect of putting up the two King women in my residence and billeting the two boys at my administrative officer's home across the street. Andy Young chose to stay at the local Intercontinental Hotel. The housing worked out reasonably well, but feeding and scheduling our visitors presented challenges. Because the adults' schedule held little interest or suitability for the children, my domestic staff found itself preparing several sets of meals almost to the point of mutiny. I remember a couple of tense situations when I was obliged to pitch in and serve the family during the break times of the cook and two housemen. Then I would hustle Coretta off to adhere to our tight official schedule. It was useful that I had had previous experience as a short-order cook when I was working my way through graduate school at the University of Wisconsin, though I never dreamed it would later be part of my job as an ambassador in Africa!

On her visit to Zambia Coretta Scott King suffered from a leg ailment that required tedious and time-consuming dressings. As a result, we were very, very late for our first official meeting. Fearing the worst when we were to meet with the president and first lady and later to open the Martin Luther King Cultural Center in downtown Lusaka, I simply rejiggered her schedule, moving all the remaining engagements up three-quarters of an hour so we would be on time. It worked out well, and I don't think she ever suspected my deception unless she read the official programs.

Besides minor KP duty and waiting on table for the Kings, my only other ventures into domestic service during my Zambian tour occurred when we celebrated America's 200th Independence Day—the Bicentennial. We had invited about 250 guests, whom we crowded into the garden, because the Residence was too small to contain them all. The embassy wives had been doing yeoman service making canapés by the dozen. They needed an extra hand, so I rolled up my sleeves to pitch in. But it wasn't long before I realized that my more important job was to mingle with the multitudes in the garden rather than make tiny ham sandwiches. "Let them go hungry!" I muttered as I wiped my hands and set off to chat up the hordes of guests.

CODEL Dick Clark, U.S. Senator

One of the joys, or headaches, at U.S. Embassies the world over are CODELs, the acronym for visits by Congressional Delegations. It could be one representative or senator or a group of members and some of their staffs. The rationale for the trip is usually a "need to know"—to gather on-the-ground information to sharpen and enrich the discourse of committee work in the U.S. Congress.

Certainly the most memorable yet hardly most pleasant CODEL was the visit of Senator Dick Clark of Iowa, accompanied by his hard-driving staffer, Richard Moose of Arkansas, who later became under secretary of state for administrative affairs. Our advisory from the Department of State indicated Clark wanted a meeting and discussion on the increasingly volatile political situation in southern Africa. No problem. I would arrange it and accompany him, "standard operating procedure" in the Foreign Service. The Zambians always welcomed outside attention to this their favorite political issue, always hopeful the United States might take a deeper policy interest in the twin subjects of independence and majority rule in southern Africa.

A problem arose after Clark and Moose arrived and made it known they wanted to meet with President Kaunda alone, that is, without the resident ambassador. This might not be an extraordinary request if it were the president of the United States visiting. Even Secretary of State Henry Kissinger was known to have sought to exclude resident ambassadors. But a senator from Iowa? Clark and Moose allowed as how I might accompany them as far as State House, in my own limo, but not join them for the meeting! I immediately phoned the president's special assistant, Mark Chona, who heard me out about the requested private meeting that would exclude me. Chona responded crisply, "We will expect you and your guests as previously arranged—no changes."

The timing of the meeting coincided with President Kaunda's historic meeting the next day with South African President John Vorster, who had been making noises about the need for "détente in southern Africa." Kaunda was intrigued with the political prospects for his meeting with Vorster, which was to take place in a railway car near Victoria Falls, alongside the Zambezi River in Rhodesia. I thought it important that the

American ambassador hear out and report Kaunda's thoughts in preparation for that meeting.

Diplomats and political observers of the armed struggle for independence and majority rule in the region were keen to learn what Vorster was proposing. It could be a rare opportunity for a political breakthrough. Were I to have ceded to Clark and Moose in their insistence on exclusivity with Kaunda, I am certain the State Department would have thought I'd fallen down on the job. Besides, since when does a senator take precedence over an ambassador trying to carry out his or her job with a chief of state in a foreign country? I was affronted by their request for a "private meeting" and beside myself with wonder that Moose would think his wife, who was accompanying the party, had more right than the resident ambassador to take part in the meeting!

Despite the awkwardness of the whole situation, all four of us eventually arrived at State House in my limo. Chona greeted us cordially at the door and ushered us into a waiting room. We were left to cool our heels for longer than usual, and then Chona led us into a small reception room where Kaunda received us. After exchanging the briefest of pleasantries, Moose suddenly rose from his seat, turned to Kaunda, and said he was sure the president wanted to speak with Clark privately and alone, thus he, Moose, and his wife, would absent themselves and wait outside. Then he shot me a look as though he expected me to join them!

Before Moose took a step toward the door, President Kaunda replied in the firmest of voices, saying directly to Clark and Moose, "We have no secrets from the American ambassador, do we, Madam?" Then to Moose and his wife, he said, "You may leave." I shot a sneaky half-smile of relief in Chona's direction. Well done, Zambia.

Following Moose's departure, I took the lead to say how grateful we were to see the president on the eve of such an important and historic meeting in southern Africa. Would the president be so kind as to tell us about his hopes for the meeting so that I might report them to the secretary of state, who was personally interested in the peaceful resolution of the armed conflict in the region? I was hoping my rank and position might have some effect on the senator. Kaunda then briefed us on the suggestions for action he intended to lay before the South African prime minister the next day. He hoped to nudge Vorster further in the direction of early concessions toward majority rule in the region. Kaunda again made his favorite point that he felt nations like the United States should support these efforts beyond mere rhetoric.

Clark raised a few appropriate questions without revealing why an exclusive meeting was important to him. The interview made for an informative cable back to Washington. I don't recall asking Clark if he wished to review the cable. Frankly I didn't think he deserved it, nor did Clark ask for a copy, though I must assume he picked one up off the cable traffic at his next stop, which was in Kinshasa. I never heard from Clark again on the issue, nor did I want to. Much later I encountered Moose after he had moved from Capitol Hill to a high position in the State Department. I never learned whether or how our encounter in Zambia may have affected me professionally for better or worse. I only hope Clark and Moose came to see their own behavior in a more mature, professional light.

A few years were to pass between Vorster's historic meeting with Kaunda and the decision by Washington to follow a slightly more engaged policy in southern Africa following the visit by Kissinger. In the interim Kaunda kept reminding the United States that its cool and reserved policy was hard for Africans to understand, given America's history.

President Kaunda Comes to Washington

I was pleased when Washington decided in the early months of 1975 that it was time to send an official U.S. invitation to President Kenneth Kaunda to visit the United States. After ignoring the growing insurgency problems in southern Africa for far too long, U.S. officials wanted to hear firsthand what was happening from a heroic father figure and historic independence role model for the liberation leaders in southern Africa, and Kaunda fit the bill perfectly. In addition, the armed threats to peace and development in southern Africa were growing apace.

Kaunda's strategic position in the heart of southern Africa, with insurgencies raging on three sides, and his regular contacts with the leaders of these independence movements made him the ideal person to clarify and describe the situation, as we had been insisting in our reports from

Lusaka. The decision to invite Kaunda to Washington reflected much credit on the political wisdom of those in the Bureau of African Affairs at the State Department and on their bureaucratic skills in convincing Secretary of State Henry Kissinger to take a personal interest and to upgrade Africa's priority on America's foreign policy agenda. Certainly a motivating factor was the growing interest and involvement of the Soviets, Chinese, and South Africans in the troubled countries of the region. The increasing danger of the situation must have piqued Kissinger's interest in preventing the Cold War from spreading to the continent.

Moreover, Cuba's interest in playing a role in the region was growing, though it was not until October 1975 that the Cubans would actually send troops into Angola, with materiel support from the Russians. Throughout 1975, rumors persisted of Cuban intervention, made even more credible by reports that Che Guevara was operating out of Zaire. After all, it would not be the first time Cuba had intervened in Africa, starting with Libya in the 1960s and later with Guinea Bissau and the Congo.

While giving hospitality and other help to insurgents in exile in his country, Kaunda was nonetheless surely uncomfortable with his central geographic position. On Zambia's border to the south was Rhodesia (now Zimbabwe), to the east, Mozambique, and to the west, Angola. Kaunda was obviously concerned lest his country be dragged more deeply into conflicts which had already attracted the Soviets, South Africans, and Chinese. So the United States and Zambia had common political interests.

The United States could hardly stand by and watch the spread of the Cold War into southern Africa. That would certainly not be in the *realpolitik* style or interest of Henry Kissinger. Nor would it suit President Gerald Ford, a man deeply committed to justice and peace.

The resulting invitation for a visit and exchange of views brought President Kenneth Kaunda, his wife, Betty, and their official entourage to Andrews Air Force Base in mid-April 1975 for what was basically a two-day "good friendship" visit. Nothing earthshaking occurred at the Oval Office meeting with President Gerald Ford or at Kaunda's press conference at Blair House, where the Kaundas were guests. It is possible that a private meeting occurred, with specific assurances between principals, from which I and Kaunda's close assistants were excluded; but I rather doubt it, given the tight schedule of the visit.

It was at the State dinner at the White House that views were exchanged and general assurances given. Ford's speech was bland and flattering—". . . delighted to have you . . . friendship since Zambia gained independence in 1964. . . . America knows and respects you . . . admiration of the world. . . . We support self-determination . . . are ready to help. . . . We look to your wise counsel . . . (and finally) we have been following developments in southern Africa with great, great interest." Ford recalled his recent speech to the U.S. Congress to assure Kaunda of America's interest in Africa.

Kaunda's reply was about four times the length of Ford's and, regrettably, not just in bad taste but contentious. After the usual pleasantries Kaunda became far too critical of the United States for its previously lukewarm policy, "or lack of it," toward Africa. He bluntly charged, "America has not fulfilled our expectations . . . in the struggle for independence . . . and building peace in southern Africa." He warned of the threat of escalating violence and deplored "low-layer" American policy, which had "given psychological comfort to the forces of evil." He contrasted America's "good" Africa policy in the days of G. Mennen "Soapy" Williams to current policy (under Kissinger, but not naming him). Then Kaunda blatantly asked if American principles had changed at a time when "America should be in the vanguard of democratic revolution in southern Africa." Finally, "We call upon America to support our efforts in achieving majority rule in Rhodesia and Namibia immediately and in the ending of apartheid in South Africa."

Trying to soften his admittedly "candid" remarks, Kaunda concluded by accepting President Ford's challenge to a round of golf! However, the damage had been done—Kaunda had undiplomatically overstepped White House hospitality by implying that a Democratic Party's foreign policy on Africa was more sympathetic and preferable to Africans than that of the current Republican administration. Unfortunately, it was a clumsy tack to take, bad-mannered and hardly diplomatic. It could have been far subtler and less blunt, especially in his host's own home and country.

Secretary of State Kissinger was extremely displeased and quick to take offense. Right after the speech, he summoned me to appear at his office in the State Department the next morning. He suggested that I had a hand in helping the Zambians draft Kaunda's offending speech! He made me feel like a traitor to my country. I could not help but wonder if the man suffered from paranoia. True, the Zambians had asked me for models of White House dinner speeches. And I had provided them with a few State Department *Bulletins* so they could see how other chiefs of state had handled them, in length and substance. But never did we discuss content, nor did I offer any advice whatsoever. If I had been a man, I might have been tempted to take a swing at the secretary, superior or no superior.

The next day in his office, Kissinger repeated his accusations, and again I denied any influence on Kaunda's ill-chosen remarks. I slowly followed Kissinger out of his office to his personal secretary's desk. There he self-consciously started rifling through papers in her in-box. I stood very close, my near-six feet towering over him, without speaking for a minute or two. Then I inquired in a sarcastic and harsh tone, "Is that ALL, Mr. Secretary?" He merely grunted, signifying the conversation was over.

Clumsy as Kaunda had been at the White House, he made his point that Zambia was proud and independent and nobody's patsy. Yet, it needed America's concern and interest in southern Africa. Later, Kissinger was to put any personal grievances aside and work with Zambia both to check Soviet power and help the independence struggle in Angola.

Guerrilla Encounter at Gunpoint

It wasn't until Secretary of State Henry Kissinger was persuaded to visit Africa for the first time in 1976 that U.S. policy on southern Africa began to change. Kissinger's planned visit was top secret. The Department of State ordered me to join colleagues in the region for a secret planning session in Kinshasa, Zaire (now the Democratic Republic of the Congo). Little thought was given to how I would get there, given the lack of any direct air or road links between Lusaka and Kinshasa. This meant I would have to go in my own car up through the northern Copper Belt of Zambia and across the border into Zaire, to the town of Lubumbashi, and from there by plane to Kinshasa. Surprisingly we had a U.S. Consulate there, the rationale for which was probably the existence in the area of an extensive mining industry, which employed some Americans.

The trip turned out to be a real adventure, albeit a bit harrowing. Saul and I set out into unknown territory, made pretty good time up to the border, passed easily through Customs and official inspections, and proceeded into Zaire. There the problems began. The roads were incredibly bad. We had about an eighty-mile stretch to our destination through uninhabited bush and scrub forest. The two-lane road had at one time in the distant past been blacktopped, only to be torn up and heavily pockmarked from shelling during the civil war ten or so years before. Obviously, there had been no discernible repairs to it in the interim.

We hadn't been a half hour into this hazardous drive when a man in shabby, dirty camouflage suddenly exploded out of the bush on the dead run, brandishing a machine gun and headed straight for our car shouting "ALT." Scared, Saul slammed the car to a screeching halt. I ordered him to lower the window so I could try to understand what the grimacing gunman was saying. Saul had his hands off the wheel and up into the air.

In something resembling basic French the gunman was asking us who we were and where we were going. I wasn't sure who he was, or his mission, given his shabby attire. It never occurred to me that he might be trying to shake us down for money or food, but something seemed fishy about the holdup. The guerrilla didn't ask for credentials, nor did he show any. He seemed nervous and uptight, perhaps at the mere sight of a white woman and a uniformed black man. No time to wonder or even converse. I just shouted to Saul, "Let's get out of here. Floor it!" and then to the gunman, "*Mission diplomatique, très importante; nous sommes bien pressés; laissez passer; laissez passer!*"

When had this poor dumbfounded gunman ever seen a shouting white woman in the African bush? Perhaps it was only out of sheer shock and astonishment that he refrained from shooting. I kept shaking official-looking paper and shouting "*Laissez passer, laissez passer. Très importante.*"

As he backed off a step, I shoved Saul with a piercing "GO!" then ducked down in the back seat and prayed. But nary a shot was fired as we bumped and swerved ahead on that unbelievably bad road.

As soon as we made it over the next rise in the road and were out of sight, I asked Saul to stop. Accredited to Zaire or not, I told him we were mounting the flags on the fenders (American and ambassadorial) to make us look a little more important should another guerrilla burst out of the bush. I prayed it might keep us from getting killed, as I was not confident that my rusty French would suffice.

Lusaka, Zambia, 1972–76

Then I had the mad idea to switch places with Saul. He would be the uniformed black potentate in the back seat, and I would be his special, French-speaking driver. But I had no intention of stopping should we be accosted again. Saul was too dazed to argue and went along with the switch. We hadn't gone more than five miles when yet another guerrilla came out of the woods holding a semiautomatic pointed at us! Rather than slow down or stop, I simply gunned the motor, signaling a sort of "All OK" as we bounced furiously forward over the potholes. We continued without further incident and without sighting a single other car on the rest of the journey. I was overjoyed that our ruse had worked, although I wasn't at all sure that Saul had weathered it without some personal accident.

Before long we were climbing a fair-sized hill overlooking a wide plain of barren countryside. In the distance we could make out the foggy outlines of a town we thought must be Lubumbashi. Then far ahead, out on the long stretch of road, we sighted a good-sized vehicle coming toward us at some speed, kicking up dust at the occasional break in the awful road. I feared the worst—that it might be the U.S. consular staff coming to escort us in. So I ducked low in my seat as we rushed past them! I told Saul that at the next dip in the road we would stop, rip off the flags, and exchange places again. We were still standing by the roadside when our escorts—sure enough—came back to greet us. Where were you when we needed you, I wanted to say. Instead we exchanged pleasantries and assured them we were delighted to follow them into Lubumbashi and put up overnight at the consul's residence. Neither party said a word about the flags or the driver switch.

Later, during the course of supper at the consul's home, I learned that there were indeed some ragtag elements of the army, even some lingering insurgents, trying to make a living shaking down unsuspecting travelers (of which were few) on the roads. We were lucky to have gotten off unscathed and without having to pay our way. I made no reference to our reverse role-playing.

The next morning I was taken to a surprisingly busy airport where I boarded a plane for Kinshasa. Never had I experienced such a flight. But then it was the middle of Africa. The local travelers—and they were in the majority—thought nothing of bringing their animals on board with them.

Lusaka, Zambia, 1972–76

So we had chickens and rabbits in crates and goats on tether as we flew over the rivers and jungle to the capital city of Kinshasa. I pitied the flight attendants and service people who had to clean the plane at turnaround. Perhaps they were given a chicken or two to put up with the mess.

The Kinshasa planning meeting for the Kissinger visit lasted but a day and a night and the resident American ambassador, Walter L. Cutler, and his wife were most hospitable to our little group. I was glad when it was all over and I could get back to Lusaka, where life would be a bit more normal. The return trip proved mercifully without incident. Two experiences with shakedown guerrillas were more than enough.

The Kissinger Visit and U.S. Policy Change

All went surprisingly well with Secretary Kissinger's visit to Africa, beginning with his short stopover on UN business in Kenya, followed by his visit to Zambia of two half days and one overnight. The Lusaka visit turned out to be far more low-key and effective than anticipated, centering mainly around an office visit and informal lunch with Kaunda and no formal dinners or receptions. The highlight came with the press conference announcing the extraordinarily welcome change in U.S. policy toward southern Africa.

Kissinger's arrival at the Lusaka airport was not without the awe factor. He and his party arrived in not one but two huge, gleaming 747s with "United States of America" emblazoned in blue and silver across the fuselage. I never fathomed why it was necessary for a bulletproof limousine to be air freighted in a cargo jet across the Atlantic and down into the heart of Africa for a couple of trips from airport to town center and back again, first in Lusaka and then in Livingstone for the visit to Victoria Falls. But then he also visited Nairobi, Kenya, although this was years before terrorism hit the continent and before the Embassy bombings in East Africa. Nonetheless, it took two jets to land Kissinger in Zambia.

The entire diplomatic corps turned out, together with President Kaunda and ranking Zambian officials, to welcome the secretary at the airport in Lusaka. He was then driven in his own offloaded limo to the Intercontinental Hotel in downtown Lusaka, where he checked in, freshened up, and proceeded to State House for a small, informal lunch hosted by President Kaunda.

Following lunch, Kissinger held a press conference at which he delivered the historic speech changing U.S. policy on southern Africa. It was understandable and right that Kissinger chose Zambia for this speech, given the country's strategic location in the heart of southern Africa and the central role Kaunda was playing in support of liberation and majority rule in the region. The speech was directly responsive to the African appeals and policy recommendations that Embassy Lusaka, Embassy Dar es Salaam, and others had pressed on Washington. The new policy moved the United States from an ambiguous, lukewarm rhetorical position to one of clear commitment to cooperate and help in advancing liberation and majority rule and to help with economic development.

As I listened to the speech at State House, I was pleased with its vindication of the boldly challenging position Embassy Lusaka and others (especially Ambassador Carter in Dar es Salaam) had taken over the past few years. The speech was understanding of the grave injustices in the region and the need for the United States to seek higher moral ground in its political stance. Department of State support staff had ably crafted an eloquent, balanced, and measured response, even though the secretary was reportedly personally annoyed at times with the field's advocacy for change. Perhaps it was our persistence.

Kissinger's speech rightly discouraged further debate on "whether in the past America has neglected Africa or been insufficiently committed to African goals. . . . No good can come from mutual recrimination." In this "new era in American policy," slogans would be put aside and practical solutions sought for common ends. The secretary promised that the United States was prepared to help with the evolving process in Angola, Mozambique, Namibia, South Africa, and Rhodesia.

Kissinger recognized that Zambia had been "directly and grievously affected by strife in southern Africa . . . yet stood by its principles by closing the border with Rhodesia and enduring the economic consequences." He described these actions as "testimony to . . . the statesmanship of its great leader, President Kaunda."

Kissinger declared that the United States would strongly oppose the illegal Rhodesian government of Ian Smith with economic sanctions until a negotiated settlement was reached and majority rule promptly implemented. The U.S. government would urge the Congress to repeal the Byrd Amendment, which had allowed chrome imports to the United States, and would withhold U.S. diplomatic representation to Rhodesia and advise Americans not to travel there.

Furthermore, the United States would press for humanitarian assistance and support through UN agencies for refugees from Rhodesia; give technical and economic aid to an independent Zimbabwe (Rhodesia) and assistance to ensure civil rights for both blacks and whites in an independent Zimbabwe. In addition, the United States would give financial assistance to Mozambique to close its borders with Rhodesia.

The secretary called upon the South African government to permit all people and groups in Namibia to freely express their views, under UN supervision, on the political future and constitutional structure of their country. He recommended a timetable for actions toward Namibian self-determination, offered U.S. collaboration to expedite urgent transition to Namibian independence, and direct economic and technical assistance to Namibia. South Africa was strongly condemned by the secretary for "the extent to which racial discrimination has been institutionalized, enshrined in law and made all-pervasive. This must end," he said. South Africa must also help promote a "rapid, negotiated settlement in Rhodesia."

Secretary Kissinger showed sensitivity in recognizing that the fall in copper prices had "a devastating impact" on the economies of Zambia and Zaire. To help remedy this, he promised bilateral assistance and help through the World Bank and other international institutions.

Two prominent African scholars, Dr. Pauline Baker, formerly of the Aspen Institute and the Carnegie Endowment for International Peace, and Ambassador Princeton Lyman, formerly of the Council on Foreign Relations, both told me they looked back at Kissinger's 1976 Lusaka speech as marking a major turning point in U.S. policy toward Africa.

I was pleased to have played a diplomatic role in the change. The routine of Foreign Service work—regardless of post, country, or continent—is generally such that few can claim a share, however small, in any major advance in U.S. foreign policy. But Secretary Kissinger's policy shift enabled me to believe that my Zambia tour was one of genuine, professional accomplishment, notwithstanding the many superficialities and inanities of my isolated life there. I was proud that my government finally took the high moral ground and announced a policy more clearly in line with our democratic traditions and beliefs, one also offering help in delivering tangibles in response to the political and economic needs and aspirations of other, poorer people.

Following the speech, Kaunda was overwhelmed with joy, convinced, I am sure, that all his pushing for change in U.S. policy had borne fruit. After heartfelt expressions of appreciation from Kaunda and a few of his closest government advisors and ministers present, Kissinger returned to his hotel to enjoy a quiet and restful evening. The next day he would fly out early as a tourist in his private plane, heading for Livingstone to see Victoria Falls. On the trip he took his own personal staff and Press Secretary Robert Funseth. He also graciously included me and my niece, who was visiting from the States.

On the short half-hour flight to Livingstone, I unctuously assured the secretary that he was in for a real treat. Victoria Falls was indeed one of the wonders of the world; moreover, there were immense hippopotamuses to be seen in the Zambezi above the falls. "Why, when Governor Scranton of Pennsylvania visited just a few weeks back," I gushed, "he spotted nineteen hippos on his safari." I never pictured Kissinger as the outdoor type, but his appetite for big game had obviously been whetted. I might better have kept the advance hype to myself.

Once landed in Livingstone we drove the short distance from the airport to a landing site on the Zambezi River about five miles upriver from Victoria Falls. Unfortunately the large fifteen-passenger launch the embassy had hired accidentally sprang a leak the night before, so we were reduced to putting the secretary in a small boat with a pilot. Naturally I accompanied him together with my niece. The Secret Service detachment had been assigned to small motorboats, which took to circling around us in the stream above the falls, hardly the place for an armed terrorist attack or a kidnapping; but ours not to question security arrangements. Our little flotilla of some six to eight boats combined to function as a huge turbine in the river, causing crosscurrents and much spray. No hippos would be sighted in such turgid waters. The outing was a disaster.

When it appeared that all hope of sighting animals was futile, Secretary Kissinger turned to me and above the roar of the boats said in his inimitable accent, "Dare are too many Foreign Services officers in dis boat!" What could I say? There were only my rather shy eighteen-year-old niece and myself! I suppose it was the secretary's way of laying the blame for the safari fiasco on me, the woman ambassador whose cables to Washington he had never liked. My niece was controlling her hysterical laughter with a scarf to her face.

After less than an hour of this waterworks party, we gave up and docked in favor of a short walk over the Victoria Falls Bridge, which offered a superb view of the roaring, cascading Zambezi, truly one of the wonders of the world. No one had told us that for security reasons the rail tracks and cross beams on the bridge had been removed and there was only one very narrow two-plank foot path on the north side of the bridge, with a rather flimsy handrail along it. Nor had anyone mentioned that Kissinger was acrophobic. Although surrounded and well protected by the Secret Service, he moved hesitantly and seemed far too nervous to move very far along the path, so his viewing was limited. Yet even a partial view of the falls is powerful. The volume of water is perhaps double or triple that of Niagara, and the roar is deafening. The Zambians call it Musiotugna, or the Thunder that Roars. So much for the secretary's safari.

We had laid on lunch at the hotel near the falls, where Kissinger made a little speech to an assorted group of officials and tourists who applauded. We were not very talkative on the flight back to Lusaka, and I was not the least disappointed when we landed back in Lusaka at the point on the schedule where the secretary bade a brief planeside farewell to the assembled dignitaries at the airport before departing immediately for Zaire.

Lessons learned the hard way: put all African safaris—on water or land—in the hands of professional guides and do not expect the impossible of the embassy's administrative staff. Leave your houseguests at home (beloved family or not), and don't promise animal viewing when the critters have not the faintest interest in foreign affairs or visiting dignitaries.

For some never fully explained reason, on the day of Kissinger's arrival in Zambia the *New York Times* had a two-column article on the front page (albeit at the bottom of the page) reporting that the American ambassador to Zambia (who, me?) had resigned upon Kissinger's arrival there. It implied that I had some sort of grievance against the secretary and was showing my animus. While privately I harbored less than positive feelings for the man—and he for me—I hardly considered my putative departure front-page news. As it happened, the State Department's personnel people—after frequent delays surrounding Kissinger's planned trip to Africa—had arranged for me to remain at post beyond the normal tour of duty and to depart only *after* Kissinger had come and gone. I learned later that some misunderstanding of this arrangement had arisen from the press interview Under Secretary of State Lawrence Eagleburger had given concerning the Africa trip. Kissinger later kidded Eagleburger about the incident and told him if Eagleburger, while acting secretary, ever "recalled" Kissinger himself, the least Eagleburger could do was to leave the U.S. government airplane to facilitate Kissinger's return to the United States. All I could think was how "boys will be boys," especially when they are big boys and have BIG toys.

South Africa—A Different Perspective

Though my work and associations in Lusaka were both stimulating and interesting, at times a sense of claustrophobia would overtake me and I had to get away. After a few game parks and sorties into Tanzania, Malawi, and Botswana—for yet another game park—there were few places nearby where one could go for the weekend, without being known or recognized, or just for a break that rejuvenates. So in between official consultations back in the States (I had about six of these over four years), I managed to get away for medical checkups, once to Nairobi and another time to Johannesburg, South Africa. The United States had regional medical offices in both locations. The change of scenery and opportunities to learn more about Africa and other Africans were welcome.

The visit to South Africa was noteworthy not only for the extraordinary contrast with Zambia in living and in development—a truly modern economy—but also for providing a wholly different perspective on the ongoing liberation struggle in the region. I had heard much about the country from the many South Africans in Zambia, most of them connected with copper mining, such as the Anglo American Mining Company and the Roan Selection Trust. Those in Zambia and visiting South Africans would often ask me, "How long do you think we have?" They meant before apartheid gives way to majority rule. I hardly thought myself a prophet but intuitively would reply, "At least 20–25 years." That proved to be near the mark, as it was not until 1994 that Nelson Mandela became the first black president of South Africa.

I was especially friendly with the South African managing director of one of the mining companies in Zambia, Zach de Beer. He and his wife, Mona, felt I should visit South Africa and should meet his boss, none other than the amazing Harry Oppenheimer, chairman of the board of the world-famous De Beers mining conglomerate. Books had been written about him, and internationally, the man was considered the world's diamond king. Oppenheimer was also a leading member of South Africa's political opposition party, the Progressives, which had taken a strong stand against the apartheid regime of the Boers and did much philanthropic work to advance the status of the black majority. My South African friend in Zambia suggested a specific date for the visit, because the Oppenheimers wished me to be their guest for dinner. Flattered, I accepted.

Relations between Zambia and South Africa were murky. There were no formal diplomatic links, though obviously because of the mining connections there were many subtle, below-the-surface economic relations between these white and black governments, including rail connections, though not commercial air links. To get to South Africa (if you were not a high official in a mining company with private jets), one had to drive by car from Lusaka to Blantyre, Malawi, and there board a South African commercial flight to Johannesburg, which is what I did. But before I made the trip (as the Zambian government was sure to learn of it), I thought it prudent and courteous to inform President Kaunda in the course of other business that I was flying to South Africa for medical reasons. He smiled and understood. In fact, he even gave me a message to deliver to someone in South Africa's government! Contact between white and black governments in southern Africa reminded me a bit of touch football.

When the cable announcing my visit reached the U.S. ambassador in Pretoria, John Hurd, he promptly and very kindly invited me to be a guest at his residence. I accepted only to find after my arrival that it presented a rather awkward situation. When we met, Ambassador Hurd and his wife explained that he would not be accompanying me to the Oppenheimers as he had not been invited. But he wanted me to use his car and driver to make the round trip from Pretoria, the capital and seat of government, to Johannesburg, the business and financial center of the country.

It was not until I met up with my South African friends at the dinner that I learned the reason for the ambassador's exclusion. As leaders of the anti-apartheid political party, the Oppenheimers were appalled by the behavior of the ambassador, an American businessman and political appointee. They considered him politically ignorant, socially offensive, and indiscreet for having gone game hunting with leaders of the Boer government in no less a place than Robben Island, where Nelson Mandela had been held a political prisoner for years. Whether the ambassador ever got the message, I do not know. He certainly never heard it from me.

Dining with the Oppenheimers was nothing short of awesome. The home itself in the most fashionable enclave of Johannesburg revealed regal architecture and furnishings. I was ushered in from the front door by a liveried servant, who announced my arrival from the top of the stairs leading to the main drawing room. I was immediately received by my elegantly gowned hostess standing in the middle of the room. As we spoke, I noticed her perfect image in a beautiful oil painting over the mantelpiece—an identical pose but minus the greyhounds straining at the leash by her side.

The dining room was another study in elegance, its walls of some sort of chocolate-colored heavy fabric, with matching high-backed chairs in soft brown upholstery. Several uniformed butlers stood in attendance behind our places at table. The lighting was soft, and the candles glowed. The walls provided a perfect backdrop for three—or was it four—individually illuminated paintings, which appeared to be Impressionists. I was seated at Oppenheimer's right, wondering just how I was going to carry on an appropriate conversation. This was Africa?

Sophisticated as he was, with his British education, rearing, and world travel, Oppenheimer wisely chose to open on a personal note. He admired my diamond ring! Here was the little girl from Rhinelander, Wisconsin, hardly feeling like an ambassador in a strange land, talking diamonds with the best known diamond dealer in the world! I was wearing "the family jewels." Mine was indeed an unusual ring, designed by an excellent jeweler in Rome who had set my mother's diamonds, not all large but impressive because there were eleven of them plus another stone, taken from a lion's mouth ring my father had worn. The diamonds were set on the points of entwined golden wires. Of course, I was flattered and made to feel very much at ease in my new surroundings by this perfect, sophisticated host.

Then Oppenheimer called my attention to the diamonds his wife was wearing. He explained they were yellow diamonds and somewhat rare—certainly never heard of in Rhinelander, Wisconsin, I might have added but didn't. Oppenheimer might have thought it was some place in Germany.

I tried to relax a bit on the wine and filet mignon or whatever it was we were eating. Then another question from Oppenheimer: "How do you like my Sisleys?" I noted his use of the plural and remembered hearing he had bought his first one for under $20,000 while still a student at Oxford. I also remembered seeing Sisleys in a gallery in London—perhaps the Tate. I managed a very appreciative sounding, "Impressionists are my favorite artwork"; so he moved on to more mundane topics. What a pity. At that point I think my host may have concluded that he had exhausted his guest's supply of small talk.

Had I done some homework beforehand, I might have mentioned a few things that I later learned we had in common. Both our paternal ancestors had originated in Germany, and both had at one time been in the cigar-making business. In both families the paternal German side had married Irish women, in Oppenheimer's case his own wife, one Bridget McCall. Typically Irish, she was reported to be a great horse fancier, indeed, almost an addict at the race track in Durban. Another common thread was that both our fathers were named Ernest, his with a knighthood from the British Crown. I would not have mentioned religion, though, because his was German Jewish, mine German Lutheran, until converted to Catholicism. Here comparisons ended. How many such missed opportunities do we experience in life?

By the time dinner ended and the driver had taken me back through the dark night to Pretoria, I was totally exhausted from the heady evening. Zambian society certainly had nothing to compare. I began to realize how easy it could be for an American corporate executive—like our U.S. ambassador there (poor soul)—to blunder in the eyes of this highly sophisticated segment of South African society. I hope I at least earned a passing grade, though it was tough sledding.

Lusaka, Zambia, 1972–76

I had thought my assignment to Africa was the high point of my career and the off-track assignment at the Occidental College that followed something rather special, allowing me to relive the African experience and speak widely on the subject. But more diplomatic surprises lay ahead for me, with an assignment to the United Nations, where I would conclude my thirty-five years in the Foreign Service on a high note.

Lusaka, Zambia, 1972–76

Eleven

To State and the United Nations, 1977–80
(Father Ted, China, and Vienna)

Toward the end of my academic year at Oxy, I received a phone call from Ambassador Carol Laise, then director general of the Foreign Service. "How would you like to work with Father Theodore Hesburgh of the University of Notre Dame?" she inquired, adding, "The President [Jimmy Carter] has just appointed Hesburgh to head up the U.S. delegation to the United Nations Conference on Science and Technology for Development, which will take place in Vienna three years hence. The preparatory work will be long and complicated, and you will have negotiations on the domestic and international fronts, but we believe you can handle the necessary support work for Hesburgh."

"Thanks for the confidence, Carol. While I am thrilled with the prospect of working for such a prominent national figure, the idea of tackling such a complex subject as science and technology is a bit daunting."

Carol assured me that there were scientists, engineers, and specialized institutions both in government and private industry to provide me with all the professional help I needed. My task would be largely organization and management of all the needed players to keep them on course in formulating a national policy for negotiation.

It sounded like a great opportunity, but I knew I would miss not being assigned to another country and having my own embassy again. However, the prospect of working closely with Hesburgh on such a broad-gauged subject and retaining my title of ambassador was intriguing.

To give me and my new operations at State the authority and image deemed necessary to be effective with my colleagues at the United Nations and with Washington embassies, I was told I would be located in the Office of the Under Secretary of State. While there was no space on the prestigious seventh floor of the department, I was assigned the transition suite of several offices and conference rooms (with private bathroom—almost unheard of in government!) on the first floor of State, normally used for the secretary of state–designate during political transitions.

I came to realize that the assignment made sense in relation to my background in economic and commercial work and in developing countries. It was also another leadership opportunity, with new and broader horizons, though a relatively small staff. So it was settled. I was to become the U.S. coordinator for the UN Conference on Science and Technology for Development (UNCSTD), with the title of ambassador and offices in both Washington and New York and with considerable overseas travel for preparatory conferences outside the United States. A huge and impressive sign bearing this new and awkward title was affixed above the main entrance to my offices.

Setting Up Shop in the Department

I had never been in charge of preparations for a world conference so I had to learn by doing, as is often the case in diplomacy. Whoever had the administrative good sense to include my office in that of the under secretary of state had the right foresight.

The incumbent under secretary for security assistance, science, and technology, Lucy Wilson Benson, was a political appointee, a businesswoman from Massachusetts new to the federal government. We got along well, although I had to take care to show proper deference to her ranking position and not to appear as a "know-it-all" career person. My office benefited greatly from the guidance and wisdom provided by the under secretary's principal counselor, Professor Joseph Nye, a highly regarded political scientist on loan from Harvard to State who had government experience and connections.

The U.S. Congress had appropriated $3 million for U.S. participation in this international conference. The money was assigned to the National Science Foundation with the understanding they would act as our bankers. My office would simply make the necessary drawdowns from that special budget.

To help me on the administrative side, State assigned me a budget and fiscal officer whose Foreign Service background was not entirely clear. Indeed, I was horrified when someone hinted that he might have acted as "a bag man for Imelda Marcos" during an assignment in the Philippines. It was never clear whether that implied money or shoes, but I had neither the time nor interest to run down any such rumor—at least not unless he stumbled or failed to serve us well, which he did not. He was the only one in my office who somehow managed a private line and answering service, but he was seldom at his desk and never easy to find. Still, he got things done.

My suspicions were again aroused when one fine day the U.S. Government Accounting Office (the dreaded GAO) suddenly turned up on my doorstep to run an audit on our brand new and temporary operation, which had hardly gotten off the mark. I was dismayed and regarded it as time-consuming interference. Fortunately, they turned up nothing untoward in any phase of our new operations. And so we proceeded on our merry way to get ready for Vienna under tight deadlines. It was probably that $3 million grant to NSF for my office's exclusive use that had raised eyebrows at GAO.

As we moved along in our preparations, another surprise was the frequency of requests for me and occasionally Father Ted and the under secretary to appear before various congressional committees to explain our preparatory work and objectives at the upcoming UN conference. Occasionally some members on the Hill would focus singlemindedly on advancing science and technology so as to benefit U.S. interests in the private sector. It was our job to try to bring balance to expectations for the conference, underscoring the critical significance of the words "for development" in the conference title, namely, assisting poor countries, and how this could benefit broader U.S. interests. We even had members of Congress wanting to accompany us to New York for our meetings, and later to our conference in Vienna, both of which they did.

To State and the United Nations, 1977–80

My office's attachment to the under secretary's office helped significantly in our relations with the U.S. Congress. It was also helpful in gaining entrée and support around the State Department and in getting things done within the broader Washington bureaucracy. I was surprised to learn how many and varied were the bureaucratic interests in science and technology, from NASA to the U.S. Geological Survey and a host of others who insisted on a voice in our operations.

With the help of an experienced political infighter in the State Department Personnel Division, I succeeded in "stealing" a first-class Foreign Service officer, James Stromayer, to be my deputy. Assigned to the National War College as a lecturer, Stromayer was mature, seasoned, and wise. He was also tall and handsome with straight black hair. Some of our opposite numbers at the UN, especially the Gucci-shod and Hermes-scarfed young beauties from some of the developing countries, took to calling him "Superman," even asking why he didn't wear his S-labeled shirt and cape! He proved to be the perfect deputy, helping balance my sometimes overeager and overly determined ideas with a casual "Have you thought of this . . . or that?" Together I think we provided sound professional leadership to a hurriedly recruited staff that blended in short order to become a strong and effective team on temporary assignment.

In addition to our Washington location, we were fortunate to obtain good office space at the U.S. Mission to the United Nations in New York for our frequent meetings and contacts with the United Nations Secretariat and the Conference Secretariat.

I also engaged in a little nepotism. A young graduate from Johns Hopkins School of Advanced International Studies, Jimmie Pagano, was the son of U.S. Army Col. Stephen Pagano, who, prior to his premature death, had been on the embassy staff in Honduras when I was DCM there. Absent the father to help him get a toehold in the Washington bureaucracy, the widowed mother asked if I could help the son get started on a career in international affairs. So my office took him on as an unpaid intern until he qualified and got on State's payroll. He proved to be an excellent note-taker and rapporteur, though understandably a bit shy at taking initiatives. But he learned quickly. Indeed I had such confidence in him that when we were in Panama for a regional preparatory meeting and I had to go to Honduras briefly, I put him behind the "United States of America" placard to carry on. He did, I was later told, with some help from the Canadian delegate who sat next to him. When the Vienna conference was over, he moved on to become a line officer in USAID.

Although we were indeed a motley crew and hardly like an embassy staff, we were soundly organized with two seasoned diplomats in charge; a senior bureaucrat formerly with the National Research Council, Simon Bourgin; a few extremely able "borrowed bodies" from the U.S. Agency for International Development with expertise in agriculture and small industry; and some excellent secretaries with top-level experience. Bourgin knew the U.S. science community inside and out and brought an incredible range of contacts and a wealth of information. The heart and soul of our small staff was a USAID professional, Lois Hobson, a single mother, skilled writer, and modest, subtle intermediary who smoothed over many a rough edge in our operations.

Our Man for Vienna — Hesburgh

We were all slicked up and ready to march when Father Theodore M. Hesburgh, president of the University of Notre Dame and head of our U.S. delegation, made the first of his quarterly appearances in Washington. We soon became acquainted with his unique, laid-back style—warm, friendly, and extremely kind with everyone he met, yet powerfully effective in making his way through the bureaucratic maze and achieving desired results.

Father Hesburgh was not new to government, having carried out any number of previous presidential appointments under different administrations, of which our science and technology conference was probably the eighth on his long list. He was adroit and knowledgeable in dealing with both the executive and legislative branches. Yet he was very much at home in the private sector among high-ranking corporate executives whose collaboration we also needed to forge a credible and negotiable national policy. Respected both nationally and internationally, Hesburgh was the perfect choice to head our delegation to Vienna. I felt honored to be his deputy and alternate.

An outstanding figure in academe, Hesburgh had achieved something of a record in having received well over 150 honorary degrees from U.S.

and foreign colleges and universities. He was also a member of the Vatican's international Scientific Commission. Although he had once served as head of a Vatican mission to international atomic energy meetings, in Vienna he was strictly a U.S. government man on his science and technology assignment with us.

It certainly helped that he had been chairman of the board of the U.S. National Science Foundation as a young cleric, in one of his earliest ventures onto the government stage. It also helped that he was on the boards of major corporations like the Chase Manhattan Bank and had close personal relations with men like David Rockefeller. Father Ted was also on a first-name basis with such prominent government figures as Joseph Califano, secretary of Health and Human Services; Robert McNamara, president of the World Bank; "Tip" O'Neill, Speaker of the House; and countless other leading figures in the executive and legislative branches of the government. Access to these power centers within and outside government was useful in supporting the policy and positions we would take at the UN.

The first directive Father Ted laid on his small Washington staff was: "Let's organize an Advisory Council." Whereupon, with pen in hand over a yellow legal pad, he drew up a list of leading figures in the industrial and business world, from IBM, Bell Laboratories, General Electric, the Overseas Development Council, engineering associations, and others of his close acquaintances who would help us through the bureaucratic maze and put a highly professional face on our preparations. Father Ted's list of names would in time make up the core of the official U.S. delegation we would take to Vienna to help us negotiate a realistic outcome to the conference. Listening to Father Ted draw from his wealth of knowledge and professional connections and experience was a revelation. I had never known or worked with anyone who seemed to know so much, including where to go or whom to see for answers to the many questions our conference preparations posed.

There was another remarkable side to his knowledge and memory. As he would stride down Connecticut Avenue from one appointment to another, or on his return to the Mayflower Hotel, where he always stayed, he would invariably encounter University of Notre Dame graduates. They would hail him to stop and chat about this or that campus experience or memory. I would kid him by asking, "Is this going to be a six- or twelve-man Notre Dame day?" Par was usually four or five such daily encounters.

Those three years working with Father Ted on the United Nations Conference were for me a rare opportunity and unique education. Before each quarterly visit to Washington and New York, Father Ted would phone to list the Washington bureaucrats or UN officials whom he wanted to meet with and for what purposes to advance our planning. I was at liberty to add other "must sees." Once he arrived in D.C., it was a whirlwind of calls, luncheons, and dinners, making one-on-one contacts. Because Father Ted disliked long, formal bureaucratic meetings, we tried to keep them few and brief.

Meanwhile, our small and enterprising staff set to work contracting for the kinds of required research and documentation we needed to support our case at the United Nations. We drew upon excellent in-house writing talent to put together a required national paper on science and technology. It turned into a clear and comprehensive brief, outlining past U.S. achievements and planned future programs in science and technology for development. And it was innovative. No such statement had ever been done before in the U.S. government.

We contracted with the National Academy of Sciences, just across the street from the State Department, for a multisector study on a wide range of potentially beneficial science and technology projects for practical implementation in developing countries. The academy called upon nearly one hundred of its leading physicists, agronomists, biologists, engineers, and others to come to Washington for meetings. They discussed their ideas and made recommendations for specific scientific and technological applications that could accelerate development in the poorer countries of the world. These recommendations were recorded and compiled into a book, which the academy published.[1] The book was widely distributed to member states at the UN. They were impressed. No other developed country had comparable resources nor was organized to deliver such a

---

1. *U.S. Science and Technology for Development: A Contribution to the 1979 UN Conference,* Background Study . . . prepared by National Research Council, National Academy of Sciences, National Academy of Engineering, Institute of Medicine (Washington, D.C.: U.S. Government Printing Office, 1978).

carefully conceived, rich choice of initiatives to guide the international conference in its program of action or to help member countries in their national development plans.

To broaden its informational contribution to the conference and to stimulate greater public awareness, our coordinating office at State organized some thirty-five meetings in various cities throughout the United States to draw further on the talents and recommendations of the private sector, including prominent scholars at colleges and universities as well as corporate and industrial leaders. This process produced yet another broad range of options.

Father Ted's commanding figure gained respect for our preparatory work not only on the domestic front but also with foreign missions in Washington and at the United Nations in New York. We made our first trip to New York for protocol reasons, to meet first with UN Secretary General Kurt Waldheim, later with Dr. João Frank da Costa, the Brazilian who had been chosen secretary general of the Conference on Science and Technology for Development, and finally, the Austrian hosts of the conference. Father Ted expressed certain reservations about Waldheim, on which he did not wish to elaborate. Subsequent events in later years proved him correct in his misgivings about UN leadership at the time. This university president from the Midwest had a keen and unerring sense of people and could read their characters perfectly, from the pretentious and officious to the knowledgeable, hard working, and trustworthy. He did not suffer fools gladly and would immediately advise me when he thought we could work productively with someone or when he doubted others would be helpful. He was always on target.

Preparing for Vienna by Way of China

One day Father Ted told me that he did not think it advisable for the U.S. delegation to go to Vienna without knowing more about how science and technology figured in the policies and economy of the largest developing country in the world, the Peoples Republic of China, with a population at the time of over 1 billion, or one-fourth the world's population. He proposed a visit to China with a small, hand-picked delegation of experienced professionals from the Rockefeller Foundation, Overseas Development Council, Harvard University, and the State Department's Office of Asian affairs. I was to make all arrangements for the trip.

I took up the matter simultaneously with the science attaché of the Chinese embassy in Washington and our ambassador in Beijing, Leonard Woodcock. In no time we were invited to be official guests of the People's Republic of China. This was a rare opportunity; we would be the first American delegation to be visiting the country since normalization of bi-lateral relations between the United States and China six months earlier in January 1979. The Chinese reacted positively to our proposed visit, be-cause science was beginning to play an important role as they developed contacts with the outside world.

Our ten-person delegation to China (including wives—at Hesburgh's suggestion) was to meet in New York an hour before scheduled departure from Kennedy International Airport. I spotted Father Ted as he came striding toward me in the airport lounge dressed in a very unclerical blue and white striped seersucker suit with white shoes that looked more like snowshoes. Perhaps it was his large size, but the shoes were spotlessly white and stood out. He looked more like a tourist than a university presi-dent. He held up his hand, saying, "Don't kiss me; I have a bad head cold!" This was worrying. People usually come back with head colds from overseas trips, especially to Asia, but they don't usually start off with them. I hoped it would not retard him or our mission—we needed his brisk and enthusiastic leadership.

We then met up with James Grant and his wife. At the time he headed the private Overseas Development Council; later, with Father Ted's per-sonal support, he became the head of UNICEF. The Grants were the linchpins of the delegation that Father Ted had carefully chosen. Jim had not only been born in China and spoke Chinese; he and his wife had lived there years later after World War II. Other Chinese speakers in the group were the desk officer from State, Lynn Pascoe (later to become Under-secretary General for Political Affairs at the UN), who came with his wife, and the executive director of Harvard's International Institute for Devel-opment, Dwight Perkins, and his wife.

From Grant I learned the art of boarding a plane in a way that assured oneself plenty of space. Boarding with a load of books, he would dump some of his books on three or four unoccupied seats together to create the impression the seats were occupied, thus discouraging other travelers from spreading out on them. I soon realized he was doing this to ensure that Father Ted would have a choice of four seats in a row to stretch out and sleep off his cold. I happened to have the aisle seat in the row Father Ted eventually moved to. Soon after we were airborne, the stewardess came by, saw our leader stretched out, and said, "You'll just have to tell your husband he cannot occupy all those inside seats." I smiled sweetly as though I understood and did absolutely nothing to disturb our leader's rest and recovery.

Soon after we landed in Beijing, the Chinese picked up on this same mistaken notion of matching up Father Ted and me, as we were the only singles along with the four couples accompanying us. While clarifications were tactfully made, hotels tended to put us in adjoining rooms. Amused, the other members of the delegation playfully took to calling me "Mrs. Hesburgh," but only behind Father Ted's back. Sometimes before turning in, Father Ted would open his door, stick his head out, and in a very loud voice say, "Jean, what time would you like me to say Mass in the morning?"

One of our first stops was to the nearby central hospital in Beijing. It had been founded, partly staffed, and furnished by the Rockefeller Foundation in the early part of the twentieth century. It was where Jim Grant's father had practiced medicine and where Jim was born. We met the lady commissar in charge of the place, and Jim asked if he might see his birth certificate and if a Chinese woman doctor who had been a close friend of the family was still practicing there.

The commissar showed some hesitation, then excused herself to go deeper into the hospital. She finally returned with an ancient Chinese woman, small and shuffling (her feet had once been bound), whom Jim had known as a child. She was carrying his birth certificate, which she presented to him with an emotional embrace. Jim's baby footprint was on the certificate. We were all deeply touched.

Getting Around China

The Chinese provided a limousine and interpreter for Father Hesburgh and a small bus for the rest of the delegation. Because I was his deputy and kept track of the schedule, Father Ted tended to invite me to ride with him in the limo. But as time went on he felt this was neither necessary nor egalitarian. And so the wives would take turns riding with him, or sometimes their husbands. Meanwhile Father Ted was busy learning Chinese from our hosts. Before the trip was over he had acquired a vocabulary of close to a thousand Chinese words, which he used at appropriate moments.

On the boat trip down the Yangtze River, we were the only foreigners on board except for a German photographer. I drew the Chinese woman interpreter as my roommate. Father Ted, as was becoming the rule, had the cabin next door. At that point some on the delegation began to assume the interpreter was also a spy of sorts. I demurred because I did not think she was bright enough, nor were the people who might have given her this extra chore. We had absolutely nothing to hide, carried no weapons, and had no intention to perform dangerous acts. Nor did we have a hidden agenda. We merely sought a genuine exchange of information on our respective countries' economic and political policies and interest in science and technology, at a time when China was just beginning to come out of its Communist shell and broaden its international relations. The Chinese seemed as curious about us as we were about them. They proved to be excellent hosts, generous and gracious.

At the start in Beijing, we held numerous exchanges with ranking government officials in science and technology, discussing their plans and ours for the Vienna conference. Then we did a lot of sightseeing, first in Beijing, then on to the Great Wall, the Ming Tombs, typical rural farms and communes, and universities, lots of universities. We visited Xian, Chengdu, Wuhan, and Chungking before returning to the States.

Father Ted took copious notes on the most obscure revelations, amassing reams of facts and figures, and reading them back every night into his Dictaphone. I understand that his notes on the China trip were transcribed into reports that were later contained in some of his published works.

Religion in China

Father Ted brought up religion only twice on our tour that I recall—once casually in an aside, the other time by design. From his hotel room in Beijing he could see the steeple of a former Catholic Church, which we were told was being used for grain storage. Father Ted wisely avoided political debate on principle; but over many years of Communist rule, time and weather had half-toppled the cross at the peak of the church's steeple, leaving it askew. We might have meditated on that and its possible significance for the future. But we didn't. Instead, as we passed the church yet again, Father Ted turned to the government official accompanying us that day and said rather sternly, "Do me a favor, please; either straighten that cross or tear it down completely, but don't leave it crooked like that." The very next day the cross was set aright atop the steeple. I knew then that Father Ted was the right man for Vienna.

The other occasion on which Father Ted brought up religion was when he asked our hosts to allow time for him to visit the church in Beijing where the seventeenth-century Jesuit missionary, Matteo Ricci, had lived and worked. We were taken to a rather run-down neighborhood and an even more run-down small chapel with adjoining buildings where a group of three or four priests and their assistants lived. Preferring not to involve the official translator, Father Ted spoke to them in Latin. Surprisingly they managed a conversation at some length. Later he gave us a rough outline of his exchange, confirming much of what he already knew: that Christian evangelization in China had not been easy since Ricci's time, let alone much earlier, as far back as the seventh century, and it was no easier at the time of our visit in the late 1970s.

Ricci had found a measure of success, however, by immersing himself in the local culture, dressing like a member of the Chinese intellectual class, speaking and even writing in the local language—but was still only barely tolerated by his hosts. At the time of our visit there were no official ties between the Vatican and the People's Republic of China; even so, the Catholic bishops in China were recognized by the Vatican, and priests had the Vatican's approval to administer the church's sacraments.

Floating down the Yangtze River on the Fourth of July

Perhaps the most memorable of our experiences in China was our boat trip down the Yangtze River from Chunking to Wuhan through the three gorges. As we moved downriver, we traced the worn path that had been carved out of sheer stone cliffs rising out of the water. We were told the narrow and dangerous-looking path allowed the crewmen just enough space to tow the barges with their long hawsers. Someone in our party recalled the scene as depicted in John Hershey's memorable book, *A Single Pebble,* which delineates different cultures and differing human talents and gifts.

We happened to be navigating the river on the 4th of July. Though the men had stocked up on firecrackers, they hesitated to light and toss them overboard for fear of disturbing the boat's captain—not that he couldn't have navigated the shoals in his sleep, but we all thought it might be disconcerting.

Somehow the Chinese learned it was our National Day. So that evening at dinner aboard ship they surprised us with a special dessert — an enormous white cake topped with candles and a single word inscribed: "Happy." How very Chinese, we thought. They hadn't known quite what words should follow to help us celebrate our national day, so they left it at that. We all thought the gesture very dear and our Chinese-speakers thanked the captain and the chef profusely for their thoughtfulness.

We saved the firecrackers for dry land at Ychang, where we ended our Yangtze journey and where a huge dam was being built. Our hosts insisted we visit the construction site and listen to endless and elaborate explanations of engineering matters that few of us fully understood. But we thought we knew enough to fear an environmental disaster in the making that would not only flood and destroy entire villages but alter thousands of people's lives beyond repair. So much for science and technology for development. It left us with more questions than answers.

Once docked at Ychang we were lodged mainly in separate bungalows, in something of a small, gated village that had been a free trade compound in the days long before Communism. Some drew the French domain, others like me, a room in what had been a small hotel. Father Ted was billeted in solitary splendor in a large white Georgian villa, obviously once owned by the British, with a front terrace boasting white pillars topped by Ionic capitals.

Father Ted sat on the villa's steps, lighted up a cigar, and said, "Bring on the fireworks." So we all took turns handing him one thing or another to light with his cigar and hurl into the garden separating us from the main drive. It wasn't long before the fancy ironwork main gate and the stone walls surrounding our compound filled with fascinated locals, who took perches as high as they could climb, including trees, all wanting to join us and celebrate whatever it was we were celebrating. If they had been let in, they would have mobbed the grounds. It was a festive evening of cross-cultural fun: our holiday and their firecrackers. The next day as some of us walked through the town of Ychang, smiling people would stop us, nod, and ask in Chinese dialect, a few words of pidgin English, or simply by gestures what we had been celebrating. As I was ignorant of their national holiday for comparison, I simply smiled back.

We had many more official stops to make, and tourist sights to see, before we completed our visit. At yet another hospital, in one of the most startling experiences of the trip, we were invited to observe brain surgery using only acupuncture for anesthesia! We didn't linger long at that demonstration of medical prowess, nor were we sure it would be a best seller at Vienna.

In addition to buses, cars, and the riverboat, we rode ancient airplanes on one leg of the journey and a fairly modern train on another. I privately wondered but did not ponder long about Chinese air safety records. The only way of dealing with the situation seemed to be to continue saying the rosary throughout the flight. The main drawback on the train ride— not unlike its U.S. counterparts—was the difficulty of sleeping with the clickety-clack of the iron wheels on the iron rails. The second biggest drawback of the train ride was not having good strong coffee for breakfast, but instead having to face steaming chicken noodle soup with thick noodles and chopsticks. China already needed Starbucks then and surely has it now, some 25 years after our visit.

Our meals were generally excellent, from the shabbiest hotel at Chengdu, in the province of Sichuan, to the one and only first-class hotel in Beijing. We usually stuck to bottled beer or tea with our meals, the quality of both, especially the beer, being excellent. None of our party took ill on the trip.

Our memories of China were perhaps "prehistoric," in the sense of seeing the last remnants of Communist China in its relatively pure form. There were no modern skyscrapers, no copycat foreign hotels, not even the first wave of the tourist avalanche that was to come in the late 1980s and 1990s. Except for ranking government officials, no one but official visitors like ourselves rode in automobiles. Indeed, it seemed as though the entire capital of Beijing rolled past our hotel each morning on bicycles or on foot, all dressed in those anonymous gray or beige Mao suits, even the women. Since then the country has grown and developed at a phenomenal pace that none of us could have predicted or imagined at the time of our visit in the late 1970s. Nor could we have guessed that the country would come to hold a large part of the U.S. debt!

We were invited to a reception at the Residence of Ambassador Leonard Woodcock, a political appointee who had been president of the United Auto Workers. He had been sent to Beijing first as a special envoy to negotiate U.S. diplomatic recognition of the People's Republic directly with Vice Premier Deng Xiaoping. After succeeding at that, President Carter named him our first ambassador there. Present at the reception were none other than Bob Hope, the entertainer, and his wife, Dolores, who were on a private sightseeing tour. Both were old friends of Father Ted and surprised to meet up with him in China.

Near the end of our visit, we encountered a monsoon in Guangzhou, in the southern province of Guangdong. Transportation came to a standstill, and we could not fly back to Beijing to catch our return flight to the States. While most of our group welcomed the monsoon-enforced rest stop, Father Ted was anxious to stay on schedule and return to the United States, as he had a family wedding to perform in California. So he proposed to skip the return to Beijing in favor of departing on a hydrofoil boat along the Pearl River from Guangzhou to Hong Kong, and I chose to accompany him. After an overnight in Hong Kong, we departed the next morning on our respective planes back to the United States, he to Los Angeles and I to Washington.

On to Vienna for the UN Finale

Not long after our return from China, it was time to prepare for our trip to Vienna for the grand finale of the UN Conference on Science and Technology for Development. The gathering would draw over five thousand people from all over the world. Having visited the largest developing country in the world and acquired considerable information on Chinese science and technology policy, plans, and operations, Father Ted suggested some political balance. Arriving in Vienna, he proposed we lose no time in meeting with the Soviet representatives to the UN conference. I was assigned to invite the Russian delegation and arrange a luncheon at the leading restaurant in the Vienna Woods, which he remembered from previous international meetings in Vienna. Hesburgh was pleased to find that some of his old science buddies from earlier meetings were on the Russian delegation to UNCSTD. It immediately facilitated relations.

Hesburgh's political theater was clear—he wanted the stage well set should the United States need to approach Russia or China or both to sort out any serious differences between or among developing countries and their patrons, whether East or West. Fortunately the conference stayed fairly clear of big power political rivalry or rigid positions. India's representatives, experienced in brokering deals in complicated multilateral settings, worked effectively behind the scenes to help bridge differences.

Following his openings to China and Russia, Father Ted shrewdly held several small luncheons in his hotel suite to consult with the leading Europeans and representatives of key developing countries of Asia, Africa, and Latin America. Talk about a professional diplomat! I realized I had yet to meet a man or woman, American or foreign, who could resist Father Ted's natural charms or match his political acuity, all the while conveying the impression of a just-plain-folks prelate.

Although a few heads of UN delegations from New York came to Vienna, the burden of work at the conference was carried on by their designated negotiators, whom we had come to know from our many preparatory meetings at UN Headquarters and regional meetings. Also present at Vienna were high-level political delegates, such as cabinet-level economic and development ministers, and even foreign ministers in the case of smaller, developing countries.

The more we worked to organize the U.S. delegation along tight, practical lines, the more it got out of control for political reasons, within and outside the U.S. bureaucracy. In the end we had seventy-eight in our official delegation! But there was a silver lining: a number of the delegates, while gratified at being named, could not make the trip; moreover, some who did stayed less than the full week.

Father Ted and I functioned as chair and vice chair of the delegation for internal purposes, and as U.S. representative and deputy representative in our external conference dealings. There were four alternate representatives, at the under secretary and assistant secretary levels. In addition our delegation had two special advisors, my own deputy from State and one from the Bureau of International Organizations. There were sixteen other mainly U.S. government advisors, twenty-two advisors from the private sector, and twenty-two delegates from the U.S. Congress, including both House and Senate.

Our delegation was in daily cable and phone contact with the Department of State and the White House to report on the direction of the negotiations and to obtain authorization, when needed, as new proposals arose or others needed modifying. The weeklong Vienna negotiations followed a highly stylized United Nations ritual. Various committees assembled along agreed subject lines. They reviewed, revised, and provisionally approved language that would constitute the final Agreement and Plan of Action. Then heads of delegations made the political commitment by signing for their respective governments. The daily proceedings often went far into the night.

Despite simultaneous interpretation and printed texts in several languages, differences arose over the simplest of language choices or punctuation, requiring patience and time to settle. One major sticking point that had long dogged the preparations and nearly sabotaged the Vienna meeting was the strong political desire of the developing countries (the "Group of 77") to establish and gain control of an international fund of more than a billion dollars. The fund would be set up to make grants for specific science and technology needs in developing countries, implying huge financial contributions from industrialized nations while minimizing their management control. In its initial and exaggerated form, it was thus unacceptable to potential funders. Even when scaled down to more reasonable dimensions, it failed to win the necessary support. In the end, agreement was reached on the most general language possible, committing individual governments to fund and execute a variety of well-defined, specific areas of development needs.

I recall one moment at Vienna when my head was swimming to such a degree that I had to sign myself in at the nearest first aid station, where I fell flat on a narrow infirmary cot between temporary partitions to shut out the bedlam. I even feared I might be having a heart attack in exasperation over some minor language differences: was it to be an "a" or a "the" in a particular sentence?

In another incident in one of the plenary sessions, with thousands of people present, the Austrian economy minister, the woman who was chairing the conference, leaned over to one of her deputies, not knowing she was speaking before an open microphone, and asked, "Vaht doo vee doo next?" It brought down the entire house.

Once when a break occurred in the proceedings and it was feared the conference might go on beyond its allotted time in the facility we were occupying, our Austrian hosts reminded those present that the conference had to conclude and delegates had to move out of the building because the national circus needed the space the following week. At that point I privately wondered if anyone could have distinguished the difference between our conference and the circus had we been forced to extend beyond the allotted time.

To ease the tensions of the conference our Austrian hosts provided receptions and galas at their leading tourist attractions. At one such event at the Imperial Hofburg Palace, I found myself too tired and unsteady with a blood sugar episode to enjoy the elegant buffet and choice Austrian wines, though I remember the architecture was stunning. At another event, a formal affair at the Schönbrun Palace, one of Austria's top orchestras played endless Strauss waltzes in the enormous ballroom. When the head of the British delegation approached me for a dance, he soon made clear he was anxious to learn what the U.S. position would be at a delicate negotiation meeting the next day. Normally, I love to dance, having grown up in the Swing Era of the 1940s, but I was totally unschooled and, worse, unpracticed in Viennese waltzes. I hung on to my Brit partner for dear life, twirled as best I could, but was out of step with the music most of the dance. The poor Brit learned far more about my awful waltzing than about U.S. strategy for the upcoming session.

The Vienna conference finally came mercifully to an end. It was a rather hollow conclusion, despite what many observers said had been excellent preparations, with the technical knowledge base richly deepened.[2] The U.S. delegation disbanded and returned to Washington and other points; a few of us stayed on in Europe for a day or two to see the Lipizzaner horses and a few other attractions. When I arrived back in Washington near midnight after a long trans-Atlantic flight, I found my visiting cousins still lingering on in my apartment, the door firmly locked, and no answer to my continued knocking. Dog-tired and weary beyond words, I made my way across the street to the condo of a friend whom I knew to be on vacation; there I sweet-talked the clerk on duty into letting me use her vacant apartment. The next morning I returned to work at the Department of State to write up my final conference report and inquire as to my next assignment.

---

2. For a more scholarly treatment of the Vienna Conference, see Jean M. Wilkowski, *Conference Diplomacy II—A Case Study: The UN Conference on Technology For Development* (Washington, D.C.: Institute for the Study of Diplomacy, Edmund A. Walsh School of Foreign Service, Georgetown University, 1982); U.S. Department of State, U.S. National Paper, "Science and Technology for Development," UN Conference on Science and Technology for Development, 1979; and Congressional Research Service, Library of Congress, "United Nations Conference on Science and Technology for Development—A Background Paper Prepared for the Committee on Foreign Relations, U.S. House of Representatives, February 12, 1979" (Washington, D.C.: U.S. Government Printing Office, 1979).

TWELVE

Later Years, 1980–2000

With the Vienna conference over, my three-year stint in multilateral diplomacy with the United Nations was completed. So I made an appointment with the director general of the Foreign Service, Ambassador Harry Barnes, to see what my next assignment might be. The morning I called at his office, the *Washington Post* reported that the U.S. Congress had voted to lower the mandatory retirement age of Foreign Service officers from 65 to 60 years of age, given the hardship of repeated overseas assignments or some such reason. Or was it because of overall budget constraints? Was the State Department an easy target for reductions and savings that might be allocated to domestic rather than foreign affairs needs? On budgetary matters it was seldom easy to get a straight answer.

I had turned 60 in Vienna and celebrated by crossing the Danube into Budapest for dinner with friends and a thousand violins (well, not quite a thousand—it only seemed that way, what with all the champagne). Memories of that historic birthday eased the anxiety I felt en route to see Ambassador Barnes in mid-October 1979. I greeted Harry, saying, "I fear this meeting may be academic having read today's *Post*."

His reply was blunt: "I'm afraid you're right, Jean."

"What a way to end my life in the Foreign Service after 35 years of loyal and dedicated service!" I blurted out, just short of tears. I was too numb to question if the congressional ruling would hold or be reversed, or even to ask Harry if there might be some temporary job that would give me time to plan next steps toward retirement. No such devices or dodges for a softer landing seemed available, and other retirees were in the same boat.

Retired on Age!!!!

Damn the U.S. Congress, I thought, especially as some of its members would be comfortably lodged in their jobs well into their nineties while they handed out harsh rulings for ending Foreign Service careers. There was nothing further I could say to Barnes, nor he to me. So I dragged myself back to my office to stare at the four walls until I regained my composure, cleared my head, and started to make plans. I was to damn the Congress yet again when a few months later in 1980 it reversed itself and reinstated the 65-year age limit for the Foreign Service! By then I had been mustered out of the Service and any dreams of a third ambassadorial assignment (not unreasonable) had been dashed.

Before I took my leave, a formal farewell and expression of gratitude took place in the elegant eighth floor reception room of the main State Department building, presided over by the kindly and gentlemanly secretary of state, Cyrus Vance. I remember looking and feeling pretty tatty without even a prior stop at the hairdresser or any thought of dressing up. The photo of the event reflects my depressed emotions. My facial expression said it all: upturned jaw with sad, inquiring eyes, bad angle that exaggerated my nose, a pose I always regretted and characterized as my "Polly-want-a-cracker" look.

A few folks from my small staff were present. Most everyone was under the impression that retirement was of my own choosing. It hardly seemed appropriate to invite a wide range of old colleagues, some of whom must have known that the real reason for my leaving was AGE(!), thanks to the fickle actions of the U.S. Congress. Later, when I began to bless the rascals in their legislative sinecures rather than continuing to damn them for putting me out of a job, I knew I must be mellowing with age. It was time to stop feeling sorry for myself and begin thinking positively about new job possibilities with as much dignity as I could muster.

Looking for a Job

A few organizations with which I had been associated might, I thought, offer leads. These included the Ford Latin American Group (FLAG), a Latin American luncheon and study group, and possibly DACOR, Diplomatic and Consular Officers, Retired. I was proud to have been named the first woman Foreign Service officer on DACOR's board of directors and was playing an active role on its education and welfare committees. DACOR included any number of Foreign Service officers who had gracefully retired and moved on to worthwhile occupations. And no one seemed to inquire about the reasons for their retirement. So stop the brooding and get on with it, Jean.

My church, which had various humanitarian assistance programs throughout the world, also presented potential opportunities. I soon made it onto a short list of candidates for executive director of one of the largest such groups. Headquartered in the United States, it was an organization I had worked closely with in Rome. Though I had what I thought was a good interview, the organization's board eventually decided—and rightly—on another Foreign Service officer, a male former ambassador whose strengths were in the administrative area. In time the organization even chose a high-ranking retired woman executive from the armed services to be the director's deputy. Good for the church!

I considered other avenues of approach. One was in academe. I had been honored beyond dreams by six honorary degrees, one from the University of Notre Dame in the mid-1980s as a thank-you from Father Ted Hesburgh for service with the UN conference, as well as to recognize women in the Foreign Service.

There was something else which looked promising. During the 1970s and 1980s, I was engaged in a vibrant program at the University of Notre Dame called Multinational Corporations and Third World Poverty. The group was composed of corporate executives, academics, and people in and out of government with economic development interests and expertise. We carried out research and analysis on successful corporate social responsibility projects in developing countries. While work with the study group could hardly be considered a full-time job, I had done field research and writing on some of the group's projects in the Caribbean. Here was another avenue for contacts and leads.

Meanwhile, I was keeping busy on academic boards, such as my own college in Indiana and Barry University in Miami, Florida. The latter had given me my first job out of college, both teaching and doing public relations. That job was in the dim past, but my current work on the board offered a wide range of important contacts that might be helpful.

About the same time, I was attending meetings of a group called Women in Foreign Affairs, sponsored by the Carnegie Endowment for International Peace. It held periodic supper meetings at which members spoke of their work and experiences. One of the prominent speakers, who regaled us with stories of her friendship with Vaclav Havel, was Georgetown University professor Madeleine Albright (well before her stints as U.S. ambassador to the United Nations and secretary of state). The Carnegie group enabled members to keep current on international affairs in the public and private sectors.

At the time I did not fully appreciate how helpful this "sisterhood" could be until Jean Newsom, professional editor and wife of retired ambassador David Newsom, approached me. She had suggested my name to an organization engaged in technology transfer to Third World countries. They were searching for a chairman of their board. Jean felt it offered a good fit for me, given my work with the UN Conference on Science and Technology for Development and my Foreign Service background. I thanked her for her thoughtfulness and immediately followed up on the lead.

New Life at VITA

The organization, Volunteers in Technical Assistance, or VITA, was a highly respected group of some 3,000 volunteer scientists and engineers, with Washington area headquarters offices and staff. It had begun some thirty years previously through the initiative of a few General Electric employees who voluntarily took to answering mail addressed to GE that was outside the scope of the company's normal business operations. From these humble beginnings and with hard-won assistance from the U.S. government, corporations, foundations, and other private entities, VITA vastly expanded the number of its volunteers and their activities to become a respected nongovernmental organization (NGO). With an annual budget of $10 million and a dozen or so employees, it served in effect as a mail-order house providing "how-to" technical literature to developing countries and also ran a few overseas technical assistance projects.

Over its thirty-odd years of existence VITA built up a considerable body of documentation on a wide range of technologies. It was constantly expanding this information bank in the course of answering inquiries from all over the world, with the help of both its volunteer scientists and engineers and its in-house technical staff. To learn more about the organization I decided to see for myself.

In Mt. Rainier, a low-rent district in northeast Washington, D.C., VITA had taken over an old convent next to a church in a neighborhood where I had been told crime was on the rise. But wasn't that true of many parts of Washington? I drove the Alfa Romeo out Rhode Island Avenue to Mt. Rainier and prayed the hub caps wouldn't be stolen during my call on VITA's executive director, Henry Norman, an experienced Peace Corps veteran with commendable service in West Africa. His office was the former bedroom of the Mother Superior on the old convent's second floor. I found him seated leisurely in the nun's old rocking chair, planning some technical assistance foray in Africa. There was one spindly, straight-backed chair for visitors but no proper board room or reception area for a prospective chairman to sit or hang a hat—all in all, rather Spartan.

Although appearances can be deceiving, I realized from my visit that the operation might have possibilities. Certainly Norman, a lawyer with city management experience preceding his Peace Corps experience, was a dedicated professional. I felt that, with the proper encouragement and financial support, he could probably make the major organizational and operating improvements that VITA seemed to need. I decided to go through with the formal interview with VITA's departing chairman.

I was impressed. He was Arthur Taylor, CEO of CBS Broadcasting, with offices in Rockefeller Center in New York City. He and Norman scheduled their meeting with me in Taylor's offices in New York. It was an appropriate offset to the Mt. Rainier site. Taylor's affinity to VITA—like that of many of its board members, I was to learn—was clearly his common touch and his do-good humanitarian contribution to society, characteristic of some corporate leaders in those days.

I knew I was on VITA's short list of candidates and felt the interview went well. I had the leadership as well as the economic development experience they were looking for. That I was a woman with the title of ambassador seemed also in my favor, given the growing emphasis on women in the developing world and the increasing number of women heading up NGOs and foundations working in the Third World. With little delay Taylor and Norman chose me to be the new "chair" of VITA's board. I learned that the board was composed exclusively of men from the corporate, academic, and government world, a situation I remedied in the course of my tenure by adding some experienced women.

VITA's board members offered impressive résumés. Some had worked on the Manhattan Project during World War II; one was an acclaimed astronaut (Buzz Aldrin) who had flown on the Apollo 11 mission. Still others headed up advanced research laboratories associated with universities and corporations. All were dedicated volunteers and humanitarians. Despite VITA's quaint, homespun offices and far-out location, it was getting the job done, though in a limited way. Nonetheless, its reputation in the NGO community of private voluntary organizations and with the U.S. government was first class.

The position of chair was nonremunerative, but it offered psychic value in matters of prestige, entrée into the corporate and public sectors, and as much travel to the developing world as I was up to. During my twelve-year tenure with VITA, I made a few trips to Africa and two exploratory trips to the People's Republic of China. Though very interesting as a prospective field of operations, China was also fiercely independent and proud. VITA managed to pick up one or two volunteer scientists and engineers from China but no projects of any significance. Yet we continued to answer the mail from that country and sell our "How To" publications there.

As my stint with VITA evolved, I found I was participating in almost as many domestic and international conferences and making nearly as many speeches on economic development and technical assistance as I did while working for the U.S. government. I finally called a halt to the wearisome overseas travel, whose cost-benefit ratio I came to doubt. I preferred to concentrate on VITA's modernization needs, including total computerization of its technical information center. The time was the early 1980s, when computers were becoming the *sine qua non* and central operating focus of every respectable organization, whether in the public or private sector.

Moreover, I was not the top manager; Norman was, and he had the necessary conviction, vision, and energy to revolutionize and update VITA's operations, along with the finesse to deal with his primary supporters in the U.S. government, with occasional help from me. Indeed, government funding enabled VITA to "go uptown" and relocate in Roslyn, Virginia, in the heart of USAID and the international assistance community.

My working relationship with Norman was good, especially when he realized that despite my previous leadership experience in government I had not come to VITA "to run the place." That was his job. Mine was to provide policy guidance and management oversight. We got along exceptionally well, even had fun traveling overseas looking for new opportunities to employ VITA's resources.

During our trip to China I may have jinxed our business prospects by falling down half a flight of stairs in an old Shanghai office. Norman turned pale and speechless at the sight of his board leader now a "fallen woman." I am sure he must have wondered if he would be shipping a body back to the United States. Despite a few bruises I escaped any broken bones, experienced just a loss of balance and dignity, and survived the trip. To ease the awkwardness of my experience, I told him the story of a Princeton professor who had asked his students to write an essay using the word "prostrate." When one turned in a paper saying "the woman descended from the train and fell prostitute upon her face," the professor explained how important it was to distinguish between a fallen woman and one who has only temporarily lost her balance.

As time went on and VITA grew and prospered in the heady atmosphere of the new information age and even took some innovative leads, my first and slightly unfavorable impressions of the organization receded— especially the farther away we got from days in the old convent in Mt. Rainier. Norman's intelligent move to Roslyn and his eagerness to computerize both enhanced VITA's image and brought greater efficiency. We modernized quickly. Every desk had a computer on it; the entire documentation center was computerized; and the old stacks of bulky subject files in manila folders were junked. A large conference room was available to the board, and its members were booked into nearby hotels for VITA's regular meetings. The chairman was even given an office with a computer, located next to the director. There were elevators and no stairways to stumble down. Although everyone on the VITA staff soon became proficient on the computer, the lady chairman was a slow learner.

VITA's board assumed a forward-looking posture in the mid-1980s, acknowledging the critical need to reevaluate the organization's basic purposes and future directions. The board remained committed to VITA's central mission of transferring technology to developing countries by answering the mail and fielding on-site projects. It also explored various ways of improving efficiency in deliveries. Yet some board members felt the organization should go into manufacturing, for example, turning out low-cost, easily assembled windmills to solve energy and water problems, especially in Southeast Asia. Still others felt VITA should go more high-tech and get into the information transmission business, possibly using satellites!

VITA Takes to the Air

I found the thought of moving from a convent rocking chair into outer space not only a stretch of the imagination, but breathtaking. Yet the clearest and most compelling idea came about quite by accident. A VITA staff physicist, Gary Garriott, and I were invited to testify before the House Committee on Science and Technology. Its chairman, George E. Brown Jr. from California, had been on the U.S. delegation to UNCSTD in Vienna. He asked VITA to suggest practical applications of some of the conference's recommendations. Garriott threw out a few blue-sky possibilities, including satellites.

Later at lunch together we explored this idea further. Garriott believed a low-earth-orbiting communications satellite might prove practical for transmitting technical information to developing countries. His detailed explanation went far over my head so I merely asked, "Can it really work?" He assured me it could. "Then let's sell it to Norman," I urged. We returned to VITA headquarters, where Garriott again outlined the idea. Norman immediately said, "Lets' go for it." At its next meeting VITA's board of directors bought into the idea and the imaginative project was on its way.

The earlier and questionable notion of manufacturing windmills (with or without help from a Sancho Panza!) was clearly out the window. VITA threw itself into intensive research and planning to see if it could build or buy and launch a low-earth-orbiting satellite to prove the scientific concept. An experiment was tried on a Delta rocket in California, which successfully demonstrated the utility of store-and-forward communications with radio amateurs worldwide.

Work progressed further, and VITA helped fund and design a communications experiment (PACSAT) aboard the UoSAT-3 launched from French Guyana on an Ariane rocket in January 1990. For its work in the design and development of this low-earth-orbiting satellite technology, specifically to meet communication needs of nonprofit and humanitarian organizations, VITA received the Pioneer's Preference Award from the U.S. Federal Communications Agency. This was no small achievement. It pleased VITA staff and board and greatly enhanced its reputation in the development community in the United States and abroad. Unfortunately, after I had retired from VITA in the 1990s, the project encountered technical, financial, and organizational problems, forcing its advanced expansion plans in satellites to be put on hold, where they have remained.

This disappointing situation detracts nothing from VITA's basic achievement and pride of leadership. The satellite concept was proven for VITA's purposes and those of other development organizations. As with so many business ideas, the basic need for adequate venture capital proved insurmountable. The story also illustrates how new life can and did rise from the ashes of a not-very-successful Vienna-based international conference, though the route was accidental and circuitous and the achievement limited.

Going Corporate in a Big Way

I had been with VITA only a couple of years when I was invited in the early 1980s to be on the board of a Fortune 500 multinational corporation, CPC Best Foods. I was told I never would have been invited had I not had the leadership experience in the Foreign Service or as the chairman of VITA's board of scientists and engineers. The invitation came about through a chance encounter, and one thing led to another. While at the United Nations I had met the head of CPC's research and development unit, who was part of an industry advisory group. By chance this same CPC official whom I had met in New York at the UN turned up on a flight I was making to Thailand for a regional UN meeting.

In the ensuing conversation he asked what I planned to do following the UN conference. Recalling my years of Foreign Service economic and commercial work with American business firms, I boldly told him I would like to have a corporate connection—be on a board, if possible. He reminded me that one of my American business associates in Milan, James McKee (a young accountant at the time), had risen up through CPC's ranks and was now its CEO. He promised to call my interest to the CEO's attention.

My knowledge of CPC was only the vaguest, dating back forty years or so when I first heard of Corn Products Company in Milan, Italy. The company was just getting back on its feet after World War II; its farm holdings and corn wet-milling facilities had been left relatively intact. The company had been unable to remit profits during the war years, but it had wisely invested them in real estate in Italy. Moreover, it had extended its European holdings well beyond Italy into Switzerland, Germany, France, and elsewhere. Indeed the company's presence had become worldwide, with headquarters in Englewood Cliffs, New Jersey.

It was many weeks later when I got a phone call from the CEO's secretary inviting me to visit corporate headquarters. It was good to see Jim McKee, my old acquaintance from Milan, impressively ensconced in the CEO office of a multibillion-dollar multinational corporation. We talked briefly about old times in Italy; then he made reference to my VITA connection, saying that CPC was aware of the organization through one of its engineers, a VITA volunteer and supporter. Later McKee introduced me to his deputy, and the two of them invited me to the corporate dining room for lunch. The deputy, Jim Eisner, was an accomplished chemical engineer who eventually succeeded my friend as CEO.

I lacked familiarity with internal corporate affairs, notwithstanding 35 years in the Foreign Service and many social occasions with corporate officials (including that famous night at Versailles outside Paris). I behaved shamefully like an awkward schoolgirl at the CPC lunch. Maybe it was because I so much wanted to be a corporate director and to prove I still had professional value after my forced retirement from the Foreign Service. It certainly was out of character for me to be intimidated by new people, places, or circumstances. Being conscious of my discomfort made me all the more nervous, but I forged on.

As I studied the luncheon menu my companions pressed me to have the full meal, saying how good everything was, including their own chocolate cake made with their own Hellman's Real mayonnaise! I followed their advice and ordered the biggest lunch I had faced in years. How could I decline their products when I was being asked to approve, even rave over them! When they both ordered sandwiches, which might well have contained Skippy peanut butter (another of their products), I was made to feel even more foolish. They both claimed to be on diets. I returned to Washington believing that my awkward behavior at lunch, including rather silly small talk from me, had quashed my chances.

My reflections on the interview convinced me I had failed CPC's test to replace a woman Navy captain, Winifred Quick Collins, who was leaving the board after a full term. She had been among the pioneer women on corporate boards; indeed, she was CPC's first. I had met her earlier in Washington at her invitation. At the time I felt I compared favorably and was qualified to succeed her. She had been a prominent and effective leader in the U.S. Navy and faced many challenges. She recalled the time her superior, Admiral Hyman Rickover, had questioned her about the appropriateness of a new WAVES uniform she had helped design. She was curt in her reply to him: "Admiral, I don't know a damn thing about nuclear submarines!" Rickover was taken aback, but quick with a reply: "Message received." And so the WAVES' new summer uniform remained unaltered.

I told Captain Collins about my own nemesis, Henry Kissinger, who also questioned my work and failed to understand any number of things about me, most of all my frequent policy recommendations from Lusaka to Washington on the liberation struggle in southern Africa. Kissinger's greatest misgivings may have related to my failure (in his view) to track down hippos for his safari on the Zambezi River.

My new Navy friend from the CPC board advised me to relax, saying all would go well in the end. But self-doubt persisted regarding my conduct at CPC corporate headquarters, followed by silence from the company. I finally stopped worrying and went off to enjoy Christmas with friends in Florida. It was there several weeks later that I received a surprise telephone call from Jim McKee, my old friend, the CEO, inviting me to join the CPC board. All my misgivings disappeared. It was a wonderful

Christmas present and restored my self-confidence. I could forget my mandated retirement from the Foreign Service.

Navigating Corporate Waters

Being on the board of directors, on the inside of a major multinational corporation, opened a whole new world and a new culture to me. Even though I thought I knew corporations from consulting with them on trade and investment during my Foreign Service days and those seven years on the Notre Dame corporate project, I was in truth a complete outsider in those days.

Among the basics I learned were that the CPC was divided between manufacturing for industrial purposes such products as corn starches and sweeteners and producing a wide variety of brand name consumer products, such as Hellman's mayonnaise, Skippy Peanut Butter, Mueller's Spaghetti, Arnold Breads, and Thomas's English Muffins, to mention but a few. The two parts of the company were always being compared in terms of profitability, and there was the perennial question of whether CPC had the right balance or ratio. Being a woman and a homemaker, I intuitively felt the company should aim for greater depth in the consumer side of the business. But being new, I remained discreet and guarded about my views until I learned the ropes better. Eventually that is the direction the company took, but I can claim no influence on that move, though my intuition was on the mark.

CPC boasted operations in more than sixty countries around the world. To gain a feel for these operations and how they might vary from country to country, with different cultures, laws, and markets, among other factors, I visited England, Ireland, France, Germany, Switzerland, and Turkey, as well as Kenya and South Africa. Having invariably encountered health problems (read Montezuma's Revenge) on government assignments to Latin America, I chose to imagine rather than travel to see firsthand what CPC's corporate operations might be like in such major installations as Brazil, Argentina, and Mexico.

In the Far East the company was in a state of phenomenal growth, but the thoughts of a fifteen-hour plane ride and what it could do to my back and joints was too daunting. So I concentrated on meeting and talking with our country and regional directors when they were back in the States on consultation at corporate headquarters in Englewood Cliffs. Each month a corporate briefing book would be sent to my home in anticipation of the regularly scheduled board meetings. It required careful study and annotation as to questions that might arise at board meetings.

There was only one other woman on the board of directors, Jewell Plummer Cobb, a black professor of biology from Rutgers University, who by strange coincidence had been on the U.S. delegation to Vienna, being also on the National Science Board. The other ten or so directors were impressive men, mainly CEOs from other corporations such as McGraw-Hill, Western Electric, Chemical Bank, NYNEX, Readers' Digest, and Goodyear Tire and Rubber. I found them all interesting, well traveled, and good company. I got to know them and their families during meetings throughout the year and at annual meetings held at varying locations, including San Francisco, Los Angeles, Chicago, Boston, and Palm Beach.

During an annual meeting in Chicago my colleagues had a good laugh at my expense. They noted that in shareholder voting for board members I had received the least number of votes among my colleagues, although not few enough to remove me from the board, thank heavens! Corporate staff attributed this to alleged local prejudice against "Polish-Americans" despite their high numbers in the Chicago area.

Yet despite the Polish construction of my surname, there is not the least bit of Polish in my background. My great-great-grandfather had come to the United State speaking German in the mid-1840s from a town on the Wisla river west of Berlin and south of Gdansk in what was then Germany. Indeed the German family traditions were strictly passed through three generations to my father, who was required to speak German as a young boy in Watertown, Wisconsin. He refused to pass the language on to his children born in the early part of the twentieth century, even though I had a deep interest in foreign languages. Little did my father dream that his daughter would enter the upper echelons of corporate America with all of its perquisites, including the Washington-to-New York air shuttle once a month. In addition, I would be met by a big black limousine and driven to corporate headquarters just above the Hudson with overnights at hotels of my choice in the Big Apple. Foolishly, I seldom stayed over to see Broadway shows or do the museums. Eventually, I became so hardened to the monthly meetings that I could do them in one day on a round trip. Perhaps it was the lack of companionship.

I recall one very heady corporate meeting that featured Henry Kissinger as guest speaker, which drew in the managers from CPC's branches throughout the world to the Windows Conference Center and Restaurant atop the World Trade Center, mercifully some years before September 11, 2001. I still have a souvenir Windows umbrella from the occasion, though I find it too eerie to use.

Takeover Threat

Perhaps the most memorable of my corporate experiences was when CPC came under a hostile takeover attack from none other than Ronald O. Perelman, Revlon's chairman and well-known corporate raider. It was never clear to me why a company that dealt mostly in cosmetics wanted to buy out a multinational food corporation. Perhaps the price may have seemed right at the time, but it was probably the nature of CPC's global reach that attracted Perelman. Or perhaps we looked like a pear ripe for the picking.

The takeover attempt put the fear of God into CPC's management and board. We all gathered together in relative secrecy at a central Manhattan bank boardroom not far from Rockefeller Center. I don't think I have ever seen a group of mature business leaders under so much emotional stress as during the telephone negotiations and the talk of white knights, as we proceeded nervously over an appropriate stock price that would preserve shareholder value. Late in the afternoon, the deal was suddenly off, things calmed down, and we returned to our respective homes, greatly relieved.

But that was not to be the end of the affair. There was the usual Securities and Exchange Commission inquiry into the takeover attempt. Together with three other board members I was named to a special committee that would review our corporate actions and prepare a legal defense. Throughout the following hot summer months we met with our legal counsel, former secretary of state Cyrus Vance, in the Manhattan offices of the McGraw-Hill company, Harold McGraw being one of the other board members on the special committee. We could not have had better counsel than Vance. It was all pretty heady, complicated stuff, but Vance and his staff did the basic legal thinking and writing, which we then reviewed, commented on, and finally approved. The case was finally settled, with CPC fully cleared of any wrongdoing.

My strongest memory of that special committee assignment was a secret little game I played with Harold McGraw, the host of our meetings, who provided us with morning coffee and Danish. The tray offered several kinds of Danish but, strangely enough only one of the kind I liked best: cinnamon-raisin-nut, which always seemed to be placed nearest our host. I think I managed to outmaneuver him only once during our hot summer's work.

I also served as chair of the CPC board's corporate affairs and audit committees, which afforded deeper insights into the company's private affairs but nothing that presented serious oversight problems. Indeed, the staff work was so carefully drafted and presented that I sometimes felt I was on automatic pilot when chairing the committee.

The one little ripple during my tenure with CPC occurred when I argued against the company's pulling out of South Africa simply because of the noisy political stance taken by U.S. church groups opposed to apartheid. I thought it more important that the company stay and continue giving employment and training to the less advantaged blacks in that country, for which it had a very good record there and elsewhere. But the majority on the board believed it would be difficult for the company to stand up against any church-led demonstrations and related boycotts of its products in the United States. Both the majority who favored the pullout and the few who dissented recognized that once apartheid ended the company would return to South Africa and resume operations, which it eventually did.

All in all, my corporate experience was immensely positive as well as remunerative, and I felt sad when my tenure at CPC ended, as required, after ten years. The corporate world knew how to conclude things with grace and largess, presenting gifts targeted at the departing board member's current hobby. At the time mine was birdwatching, having shifted from golf following joint surgery. This was obviously a mistake, for a full set of golf clubs (as was the company's custom) would have been welcome and usable in time. But I did appreciate the definitive and comprehensive bird book, which seemed to weigh nearly ten pounds and the fancy, imported binoculars presented to me.

There were few negatives during my experiences in the private sector, although there were times during my work with VITA and CPC when I awoke in the middle of the night wondering what would happen if either of these private institutions failed and went bankrupt. My involvement and legal obligations would be great, and I could lose my life's savings and more. Although this was before Martha Stewart and Enron, I did not need their experiences to understand the personal risks. So my prayer list, which had always been lengthy during dicey situations in government, was expanded during my twelve years of corporate service. To be honest, though, I always had trouble praying for President Nixon and Secretary of State Kissinger.

The end of my affair with the corporate world was not final; bonds of friendship had been established. What followed were reunions and anniversaries even after CPC Bestfoods was bought out by Unilever in 2000. There have been CPC get-togethers in Florida, to which some of the company's management and board members retired and to which others come for reunions from as far away as Argentina, Switzerland, and Hong Kong.

Foreign Service Cup

Fifteen years after I retired from the State Department, my former colleagues surprised and honored me by choosing me to receive the Foreign Service Cup, awarded annually for distinction. The citation read:

> For fifty years of service to the Nation in governmental and private capacities.
>
> Diplomat, voluntary agency leader, private corporation executive and educator, Ambassador Wilkowski served as economic officer in numerous European and Latin American posts before being named Ambassador to Zambia and later ambassadorial head of the U.S. delegation to the United Nations Conference on Science and Technology for Development.

After retiring in 1980, she chaired for twelve years the Board of Volunteers in Technical Assistance (VITA) and concurrently held senior positions in CPC International, Inc., advising on corporate operations abroad. Honored by the Order of Malta for humanitarian service to Central American refugees, she remains active in various international relief organizations. Her lifelong interest in education has been demonstrated as college teacher, trustee, Woodrow Wilson Foundation Fellow, and scholarly author.

Creativity, selflessness, and leadership have marked her distinguished career, and she has contributed significantly to international understanding and cooperation.

The award was made in the Loy Henderson Auditorium of the State Department on Foreign Service Day, May 5, 1995. It certainly did much to dim some of the bad memories of my mandatory retirement fifteen years earlier. Implicit in the award was recognition that the private sector believed that sixty-year-olds still had sufficient intelligence and competence to perform professionally even though the U.S. government did not so believe for a time in 1980. I was especially pleased that the recognition came from DACOR—Diplomatic and Consular Officers, Retired—an organization of professional diplomats.

In my public acceptance remarks, I ignored the reason for my retirement in favor of light references to the ups and downs of my career and my "jolly times" serving Henry Kissinger in Africa, especially as his safari guide. Immediately following my termination at State in 1980 at age 60, I came to understand and appreciate that old adage, "A woman who tells you her age will tell you anything." I certainly did not reveal even to my closest friends exactly why I had left the Foreign Service after thirty-five years, a reasonably long period. As things turned out, it may well have been the right decision at the right time.

I had been hurt because the decision was not mine but one that was imposed and because the regulation that removed me was reversed so quickly. Receiving the Foreign Service Cup and my positive experience in the private sector went a long way toward making up for the unwelcome exit ramp from government. I thank and bless DACOR for the award and wish it continued success.

Following the Faith

While I remained interested in international business in my two post-retirement jobs with VITA and CPC, I realized there was more to life than

work and that mine needed better balance. Having worked for government the better part of my life, I deliberately pursued constructive work for the church and its related institutions. During the 1980s and 1990s I successively served on two Catholic college boards, Saint Mary-of-the-Woods College in Indiana and Barry University in Miami, Florida. At both these institutions I established faculty fellowship programs to encourage faculty to travel abroad and expand the global dimensions of their curricula. These programs are achieving the ends for which they were designed and I hope they will continue for years to come.

During my active retirement I was named international consultant to the Association of Catholic Colleges and Universities, which serves about 220 institutions throughout the United States. Among my vague assignments I was asked to help on an overseas evaluation of Bethlehem University in the Middle East, then under consideration for extension of its U.S. government operating grant. The evaluation group was made up of professors and administrators from several U.S. Catholic colleges, with strong representation from the University of Notre Dame. It was my special task on this trip to ensure that matters ran smoothly and that there were no international problems. Yet, through carelessness, I myself became an international problem. After an overnight in Amman, as our bus pulled out to take us through the country and across the border to Israel, a Jordanian army guard stopped us at an intersection and came aboard to see our passports. He ended up pointing to me and saying, "You, OUT!"

What was one member of the group en route to Israel doing with a diplomatic passport when the group's mission was private education? What was my specific mission? My stumbling excuse for carrying the diplomatic passport, which was perfectly legitimate, was not readily understood by the Jordanian guard who stopped us. So while I stood on a street curb in a strange city in a foreign land, the chartered bus rumbled on to the border with the entire delegation minus me.

I was taken to the Jordanian Ministry of Foreign Affairs and detained there in a dirty, hot, fly-infested room without ready telephone access to the U.S. embassy. When I finally got through to the embassy and explained my position, I was released and returned to the hotel where we had spent the previous night. A local travel agent suggested I hire a taxi to take me to the border at the Jordan River and from there another taxi into Jerusalem to our hotel. It seemed preposterous, but it worked. I finally made it by taxi to Bethlehem University. When I arrived, I went immediately to the conference hall where the meeting with our delegation was still in session. I was greeted by loud guffaws and smart remarks from the team about my "diplomatic immunity."

I realized that the ridicule the group directed at me was small relief from the strain of the setting. The conference room's large windows looked out across the street to a garage rooftop on which three Israeli troops with machine guns were positioned, aimed directly at the conference room. While our academic hosts were probably accustomed to such public threats, I was doubtful that foreign visitors should be taking such chances.

Indeed the very next day our visit was cut short when Palestinian students demonstrated in celebration of their National Day. The Israelis responded by tossing tear gas bombs over the walls; the students bravely flung them back, and the university was promptly closed. However, we managed to gather sufficient on-site information the first day plus a few home visits with faculty to make a usable evaluation. The university eventually got its million-dollar U.S. government assistance grant, and no doubt similar incidents kept occurring at the university over the following years.

Also while in retirement I became a member of the Sovereign Military Order of Malta, one of the church's oldest orders, dating back to the twelfth century and dedicated to serving the poor and sick throughout the world. I conducted several humanitarian missions for the Order to Colombia, the Dominican Republic, Honduras, and Cuba. Cuba was especially interesting, albeit difficult. With the Order's support and encouragement, I organized a private mission made up of a small team of health and education professionals to work with single mothers and their children. But under existing Cuban government controls, the effort was limited mainly to small contributions of food, clothing, and financial aid. This area of single mothers' needs had been described by Cuba's Cardinal Jaime Ortega to Pope John Paul II during his visit to Cuba in 1998 as one of Cuba's greatest social deficiencies.

Believing that further grounding in my faith might be useful after being out of college for more years that I wished to remember, I did two things. First, I signed up for the Spiritual Exercise of St. Ignatius Loyola at my parish in Georgetown, Holy Trinity Church, where I learned a lot about theological reflection on the Scriptures. Later, I pursued a four-year religious education course in a program called "Education + Parish + Service," out of Trinity College in Washington at its winter site in Naples, Florida. It was designed to prepare people to serve as lay volunteers in the church following the dictates of Vatican II. Eventually I became a member of its board of directors and chair of its Development Committee. I have since worked with this program and a former affiliate in Rome—at the Lay Centre there on the Pontifical Irish College campus—to sponsor some lectures in memory of my maternal Irish grandparents, who brought their faith to the United States from the Dingle area of County Kerry in Ireland.

Friends have chided me for "faking my Irish heritage and connections," which they contend are completely disguised by the "ski" ending of my obviously Polish-appearing surname. I have since researched my genealogical connections and satisfied myself that, despite the Polish-looking name, my German connections are genuine. Moreover, I learned that I have a legitimate right to a distinguished coat of arms (Jelita Arms) and a corresponding signet ring. At this stage in life, my fingers are too arthritic to burden them with yet another ring. Maybe the grand nieces and nephews will do that.

The general design of the coat of arms is impressive, but I am not sure I like that part of the description which reads: "*a destra:* goat rampant out of a ducal coronet." In addition, the design carries three lances, which are supposed to signify royal status from ancient times. But to claim all this would only raise more questions from friends who already have doubts regarding my true background and heritage. Best perhaps to let sleeping dogs, or goats, lie and lay down the spears. My Irish mother had often counseled, "Hang up your gloves!"

As I look back over the years of my life growing up in Wisconsin and Florida, being educated in Indiana, Wisconsin, California, and Washington, D.C., beginning my first real job in Florida, then later working in eight countries on three continents, then at the United Nations, retiring from government, and ultimately entering a new chapter in the corporate sector, I recognize how good this long life has been. Although there were some hard choices, personal sacrifices, and trying days and nights, I do believe that any success I may have enjoyed has been through the generosity and mercy of a loving God.

Epilogue

1 Corinthians 3:6–9

I planted, Apollos watered, but God caused the growth.
Therefore, neither the one who plants nor the one who waters is anything,
but only God, who causes the growth.
The one who plants and the one who waters are equal,
and each will receive wages in proportion to his labor.
For we are God's coworkers; you are God's field, God's building.

—*The New American Bible,* 1970

Index

Acosta Bonilla, Manuel, 221
Air Force Academy, visit to, 161
Albright, Madeleine, 322
Alessandri, Jorge, 142
Ambassador's Seminar (Occidental
   College), 167–68
ambassadorship. *See also* Lusaka,
   Zambia; UN Conference on
   Science and Technology for
   Development
   confirmation hearings, 238–40
   presentation of credentials in
      Lusaka, 246–47
   swearing-in ceremony, 240
Angola, 263–65
anti-American demonstrations
   in Bogotá, 53
   in Tegucigalpa, 209–10, 212–15
Appling, Hugh, 160
Armour, Norman, 58
Armstrong, Louis, 94
Asociación Colombiana de los
   Cafeteros, 51–52
Association of Catholic Colleges and
   Universities, 336

Atlantic crossings
   Ile de France, 99
   SS *Saturnia*, 71–74
   aviation, U.S.-Italian negotiations on,
      184–85

Baker, Pauline, 292
Ball, George, 155
ballet lessons, 95–96
Barnes, Harry, 319
Barry, William, 12, 13
Barry College (later University)
   on the board of, 336
   teaching at, 12–13
Bartlett, Jimmy and Madeleine, 65–67
Beaulac, Willard, 56, 58
Begin, Menachem, 166
Benson, Lucy Wilson, 301
Bethlehem University, evaluation of,
   336–37
Black, Shirley Temple, 165
Bogotá, Colombia, 47–70
   diplomatic courier in, 57–58, 60
   housing, 48, 50, 63–64
   job, 51–52

Bogotá, Colombia (*continued*)
  lessons learned, 63–64
  revolution, 55–63
  social life, 50–51, 66–67
Bogotázo, 55–63
bombing at Embassy Rome, 173–74
Bourgin, Simon, 304
Bowdler, William, 226, 227–28
Bradley, Tom, 165
British diplomats, officials
  in Lusaka, 248
  in Trinidad, 36–37
Brown, George E., Jr., 326
Brown, Robert Lyle, 159
Buenos Aires, visit to, 146
Bunker, Ellsworth, 65
Burns, John, 279

Califano, Joseph, 305
calypso singers, 32
Cape Canaveral, 162
Capone, Al, Jr. (Sonny), 6
career, importance of, 100
Carnegie Endowment for
    International Peace, 322
cars
  Bella Yella Studebaker, 84–87
  in Chile, 143
  Hillman Minx, 113–14, 119–20
Carter, Beverly, 238
Carter, Jimmy, 314
Castro, Fidel
  admired in Chile, 139
  in Colombia, 55
Catholic Church, in China, 311
Catholic students (Sorbonne), 129
Catholic University (Washington),
    job at, 17
Chargé d'Affaires a.i. See Tegucigalpa,
    Honduras
Chartres, student pilgrimage to,
    128–30

Chesterton, G. K., 13
Chevalier, Elizabeth Pickett, 169
Chile. See Santiago, Chile
China
  diplomats in Lusaka, 250–52
  and southern Africa, 285
  trips to
  —in preparation for UN
      Conference, 307–14
  —for VITA, 324
  and Zambia, 262
Chitepo, Herbert, 269–70
Chobe National Game Park, 269
Chona, Mainza, 272–74
Chona, Mark, 266, 271, 274
  at presentation of credentials, 246
  and visit of Clark and Moose, 282,
      283
Christopher, Warren, 170
Clark, Dick, 282–83
Claxton, Philander Priestly, Jr., 159,
    160
Clifford, Bede, 27
Cobb, Jewell Plummer, 331
COCOM, training for, 98, 99
CODELs (Congressional Delegations)
  in Lusaka, 282–84
  in Rome, 192–93
coffee industry, 51
Collins, Winifred Quick, 329
Colombia, assignment to. See Bogotá,
    Colombia
commerce
  Chilean fruit exports to the U.S.,
      140
  Colombian fresh flower exports,
      54
  commercial negotiations, 184–86
  entrepreneurs in Bogotá, 54–55
  export controls in Italy, 87–88
  government as sources of trade
      information, 82

Honduran exports to the United
States, 207–8
promoting U.S. economic and
commercial interest in Italy,
183–84
Santiago job and, 139–41
trade and investment, 80–81
U.S. exports of poultry and
oranges to Italy, 184
Commerce, Department of
Export Control Division, 98
International Trade Division,
European Section, Italian
Desk, 96–97
Commercial Counselor. See Rome, Italy
Connally, John, 192–93
Console, Il (Menotti), 93–94
Corry, Andrew V., 158, 160
Costa, João Frank da, 307
CPC Best Foods, 327–34
board member of, 330–34
takeover threat, 332–34
Cuba
Angola and, 264
Order of Malta's mission to, 337
and southern Africa, 285
visits to, 14
cultural exchange programs, 94–95
Cunard, Edward, 27
Cutler, Walter L., 290

DACOR (Diplomatic and Consular
Officers, Retired), 321
Foreign Service Cup, 334–35
dating
in Bogotá, 64–65, 67–70
in Trinidad, 38
Daughters of Charity convent (Paris),
109
De Beer, Zach and Mona, 296
delegating, learning, 210
Dempsey, Jack, 7

Deputy Chief of Mission. See
Tegucigalpa, Honduras
Deputy Commercial Attaché. See
Paris, France
Dillon, Douglas, 152
Dillon Round. See GATT tariff
negotiations
Dimetrieva, Eva, 102–3
diplomacy, person-to-person contacts
and, 144–46
Diplomat in Residence at Occidental
College, 164–71
Ambassador's Seminar, 167–68
speaking invitations, 166
Disneyland, in France, 101
driving
in Paris, 114
in Rome, 175

Eagleburger, Lawrence, 295
Easum, Donald, 266, 267
education. See also Foreign Service
Institute
college, 10–11, 19
grade school, 3–5
high school, 9–10
Eisner, Jim, 328
Ellington, Duke, 278–80
El Salvador. See Soccer War
entertaining
in Bogotá, 50–51
importance of, in diplomacy, 24
in Lusaka, 137, 241, 272, 277–78,
281
in Rome, 181, 182–83
in Santiago, 138
in Trinidad, 39–40
at the Tuscan farmhouse, 189
European Economic Community
(EEC)
GATT and, 152, 154
U.S. multilateral issues with, 184

Fabian Socialists, 256
faith, 336–39
    college education and, 11
    convent retreat, 127–28
    deepening, 108–9, 127
    pilgrimage to Chartres, 128–30
    in retirement, 336–39
    romantic relationship and, 68
family
    brother
    —and father's death, 125
    —and flying, 45–46
    —meeting in Switzerland,
        88–89
    father's funeral, 125–26
    mother
    —funeral, 179
    —in Rome, 178–79
    —in Santiago, 132–35
    parents' visit to Paris, 117–19,
        123–24
Feminist Revolution, 202
Fidel, E. Allen, 159
financial reporting, 51
Florida, 6–8
food, Italian, 72, 199
    after-dinner drinks, 73–74
Ford, Gerald, 285
Ford Foundation, 167, 168
Ford Latin American Group, 321
Foreign Service
    application, 16
    considering a career in, 14–15
    mandatory retirement age, 319
    on marriage of women officers,
        42, 100
Foreign Service Cup, 334–35
Foreign Service Institute
    language classes, 46–47, 71
    Senior Seminar in Foreign Policy,
        157–64
Francis of Assisi, Saint, 196, 215

FRELIMO (Front for the Liberation of
        Mozambique), 266–67
friends. See also social life
    in Bogotá, 48–50, 54, 65–67
    missionaries as, 150
    in Paris, 116–17
    in Santiago, 150
Fulbright, William, 238, 255
Funseth, Robert, 293

Gaitán, Jorge Eliécer, 55
game parks, 269, 295
Garriott, Gary, 326
GATT tariff negotiations, Geneva,
        Switzerland
    interim assignment, 151–57
    temporary assignment, 121–23
General Agreements on Tariffs
        and Trade. See GATT tariff
        negotiations
Genoa, Italy, 74
George, Mishell, 98
Giacometti, 83
gifts and regulations, 143–44, 183–84
    Vatican gold medallions, 198
Gilman, Richard C., 164, 170
    and Ambassador Seminar, 167,
        168
    "His Magnificence," 169
golf
    in California, 164–65
    in Lusaka, 259–61
    in Milan, 84–85, 96
    in Paris, 115–16
    in Rome, 194
    in Santiago, 146–47
    in Tegucigalpa, 231
Government House, Trinidad, 36–37
Graef, Hilda, 127–28
Grant, James, 308–9
Guevara, Che, 285
Gurirab, Theo-Ben, 266

Haiti negotiator at GATT, 122–23
Harriman, W. Averell, 251
Hart, William, 153
Hershey, John, 312
Herz, Martin F., 159, 160
Hesburgh, Theodore M., 300, 304–7
    in Vienna, 315
    during visit to China, 310–11
hiking, 156–57
Hobson, Lois, 304
Honduras. *See also* Soccer War
    agrarian reform program, 217
    anti-American demonstrations,
        209–10, 212–15
    assignment to. *See* Tegucigalpa,
        Honduras
    immigrant population, 208–9
    military dictatorship, 208
    Peace Corps, 207
    U.S. corporations in, 208
Hope, Bob, 314
horseback riding, 231–32
Houghton, Armory, 105
housing
    in Bogotá, 48, 50, 63–64
    in Lusaka, 242–43
    in Milan, 75–78
    in Paris, 112–13
    in Rome, 177–78, 181–83
    in Santiago, 133–34, 137–38
    in Tegucigalpa, 205
    in Trinidad, 24, 38, 39
Howe, Walter, 142
Hudson, Joel, 95
Hurd, John, 296

Ile de France, 99
India, at UN Conference in Vienna,
    315
Indians in Zambia, 252
interim assignments. *See* Diplomat
    in Residence at Occidental

College; GATT tariff negotia-
    tions; Senior Seminar in
    Foreign Policy
invoices, consular, 83
Italian businessmen, 82
Italian language course, 71
Italian Rice Growers and Exporters
    Association, 83
Italy, assignments to. *See* Milan, Italy;
    Rome, Italy

Jacks, Sidney, 98
jobs, descriptions of
    in Bogotá, 51–52
    as CPC board member, 330–34
    at the Department of Commerce,
        96–98
    at GATT in Geneva, 121–23
    in Milan, 80–81
    in Paris, 101–3, 104–6
    in Rome, 183–86
    in Santiago, 139–41
    in Trinidad, 29, 31–34
    VITA chairman, 322–27
John Paul II, 337
Johnson, Lyndon
    death of, 257
    visit to Honduras, 211–12
Johnson, U. Alexis, 240
John XXIII, 199
Jova, Joseph J., 214
    choice of a woman deputy, 206
    learning from, 232–33
    transfer before Soccer War,
        218
    welcome by, 205

Kaunda, Kenneth
    criticism of United States, 246,
        262, 286
    friendliness, 257
    golf with, 259–61

Kaunda, Kenneth (*continued*)
  and liberation struggle in southern
    Africa, 261
  meeting with Clark and Moose,
    283–84
  meeting with John Vorster, 282–83
  political importance of, 255–56
  presentation of credentials to,
    246–47
  and tribal dialects, 236
  visit to Washington, 284–87
Kennedy, John F., 159
King, Coretta Scott, 277, 280–81
Kissinger, Henry, 169, 264, 277, 329
  Bureau of African Affairs and, 285
  cables from Zambia and, 262
  excluding ambassadors, 282
  guest speaker at CPC corporate
    meeting, 332
  lecturer during Senior Seminar,
    160
  reaction to Kaunda's speech in
    Washington, 286–87
  at Victoria Falls, 293–94
  visit to southern Africa, 290–95
  —1976 Lusaka policy speech,
    291–92
  —planning session in Kinshasa,
    Zaire, 287–90
Klein Saks, 139
Konie, Gwen, 258
Kreig, William, 142
Krol, John Cardinal, 194

Laboure, Catherine de, 110
Laise, Carol, 300
La Scala Opera House (Milan), 93–94
Latin America
  men, 63
  portrayal of United States in the
    press, 53–54
  women, 141–42

lessons learned
  in Bogotá, 63–64
  in Paris, 127–31
  in Rome, 199–200
  in Santiago, 148–50
Levitt & Sons Company, 101
Lewis, Samuel, 154
liberation leaders of southern Africa,
  255
liberation theology, 150
López Arellano, Gloria, 223
López Arellano, Oswaldo, 208, 213,
  214–15
  on possible black U.S. ambassa-
    dor, 231
  reception for Somoza, 229
  during Soccer War, 219–20
Los Angeles Times, 165, 171
Lusaka, Zambia, 241–99. *See also*
  Kaunda, Kenneth
  attacks on American citizens,
    270–72
  diplomatic colleagues, 247–50
  entertaining, 137, 241, 272,
    277–78, 281
  Kissinger's visit, 290–95
  —planning for, 287–90
  political listening post, 239, 255,
    261
  presentation of credentials, 246–47
  security of embassy, 248–49
  visiting a shebeen, 244–45
Lydman, Jack, 159
Lyman, Princeton, 292
Lyon, Cecil B., 142

Machel, Samora, 266–67
Madrid, Spain, 126
Magnani, Anna, 83
male environment
  on board merchant vessel, 35
  in Latin America, 141–42

in meeting at Vatican, 197
in reporting on Soccer War, 228
during Senior Seminar, 158, 162,
163
during sensitivity training, 201
during Spanish classes, 47
Malta, Sovereign Military Order of,
337
Mandela, Nelson, 255, 267
Marcinkus, Paul, 194–95
Marian shrines (Paris), 108–9
Marillac, Louise de, 110
market surveys, 80, 101
marriage
career versus, 42–43
Foreign Service on marriage of
women officers, 100
Marshall, George Catlett, 58
Martin, Graham, 172, 192–93, 195,
235
Mary Basil, Sister, 109–12, 127
Mbikusita-Lewanika, Inoge, 258
McGraw, Harold, 332, 333
McKee, James, 328, 329
McNamara, Robert, 305
Meloy, Francis, 198
men. *See also* dating; male
environment
Chief Justice in Zambia, 275–76
Italian, 72, 79–80
Latin, 63
and women equals, 202
in Zambia, 257–58
Menotti, Gian Carlo, 93–94
merchant vessel, free ride on, 34–35
Miami Herald, 13
Milan, Italy, 74–96
culture, 93–95
housing, 75–78
job, 80–81, 87–88
walking to work, 78–80
Milan Trade Fair, 81–82, 184

Minges, Bob, 223
Minister/Counselor for Economic
Affairs. *See* Rome, Italy
Ministry of Foreign Affairs
(Colombia), 52–53
missionaries
in Chile, 150
in Zambia, 253
Moose, Richard, 282–83
Morabia, Alberto, 85–86
Mozambique, 266–67
United States and, 292
MPLA (Popular Movement for the
Liberation of Angola),
263–64
Mugabe, Robert, 268–69
Multinational Corporations and
Third World Poverty, 321
Mutemba, Saul, 243–45

Namibia, 265–66
United States and, 292
Narvaez, Agostine, 167, 171
Narvaez, Alicia, 167, 171
National Academy of Sciences, 306
National Science Foundation, 302
Hesburgh and, 305
National Union for the Total
Liberation of Angola (UNITA),
263, 264
Nelson, Harvey, 237, 246, 249, 269
Neto, Agostinho, 264
Newsom, Jean, 322
New York, office in, 303
New York City Ballet, 94–95
New York Times, 294
Nigerian High Commissioner in
Lusaka, 248, 252
Nixon, Richard, 247
Nkomo, Joshua, 268
Noel, Cleo, 234
NORAD, 161

Nordic countries, Zambia and, 262
Norman, Henry, 323, 324–25
Nujoma, Sam, 265–66
nuns
    in Argentina, 146
    in Paris, 109–11
    in Zambia, 274–75
Nye, Joseph, 301
Nyerere, Julius, 249, 256

Occidental College, 164–71
O'Neill, Thomas, "Tip," 305
Oppenheimer, Harry, 296, 297–98
Organization of American States
    (OAS), 221–22
Ortega, Jaime Cardinal, 337

PACSAT, VITA and, 327
Pagano, Jimmie, 303
Pagano, Stephen, 223, 303
Paris, France, 99–131
    Bois de Boulogne, 108
    father's funeral, 125–26
    housing, 112–13
    job, 99, 101–3, 104–6
    lessons learned, 127–31
    parents' visit, 117–19, 123–24
    return trip from, 126–27
    social life, 107, 108–9, 114–17
Pascoe, Lynn, 308
Peace Corps, 207
Péguy, Charles, 129
Perelman, Ronald O., 332
Perkins, Dwight, 308
Pioneer's Preference Award, 327
PL-480 Food for Peace
    closing in Italy, 195, 196–98
    in Zambia, 254
Popular Movement for the Liberation
    of Angola (MPLA), 263–64
Port of Spain (Trinidad), 22–23
Prohibition, 8–9

protocol, learning, 24–28, 102
Puerto Rico, 162

race in Trinidad, 26, 27
Ramirez, Roberto, 221
Rennert, Murray, 98
reports, 84
    on French housing, 104–5, 108
    on Italian rice production and
        exports, 83
    World Trade Directory Reports, 101
retirement job, looking for, 321–22
Rhodesia, 268–70. See also
    Zimbabwe
    United States and, 291–92
Rickover, Hyman, 329
Riso Amaro (film), 83
Rockefeller, Nelson, 209–11
Rome, Italy, 172–200
    bombing at embassy, 173–74
    Borghese Gardens, 176–77
    entertaining, 181, 182–83
    farewell dinner with Zambians,
        235–36
    farmhouse in Tuscany, 186–92
    housing, 177–78, 181–83
    job, 183–86
    lessons learned, 199–200
    stray bullet, 177
Rome, Italy, visits to, 84
    with parents, 119–21
Roosevelt, Franklin D., memorial
    service for, 31
Rose Society (Italy), 82
Rotberg, Robert, 238
Rumsfeld, Donald, 182
Ryan, Finbar, 39
Ryan, Hewson A., 149

Saint Mary-of-the-Woods College
    on the board of, 336
    student at, 10–11

Sandoval, Rigoberto, 217
Santiago, Chile, 132–50
    car, 143
    entertaining, 138
    house fire, 135–37
    housing, 133–34, 137–38
    job, 139–41
    lessons learned, 148–50
    political and social setting in, 148
    sports in, 146–48
    trip to doctor's farm, 144–46
Sarich, Robert, 153
satellites, VITA and, 326–27
Savimbi, Jonas, 263, 265
Scelba, Mario, 180
Scranton, William, 277
Second Secretary. See Rome, Italy;
    Santiago, Chile
security
    in Lusaka, 248–49
    at U.S. posts, 174–75
Senior Seminar in Foreign Policy,
    157–64
sensitivity training, 201–4
shipping, 32–34
shoes, commercial negotiations on,
    185–86
Siegel, "Bugsy," 7
Single Pebble, A (Hershey), 312
skiing
    in Chile, 147–48
    in Italy, 90–93
Smith, Ian, 268
Soccer War (El Salvador and
    Honduras), 215–27
    causes of, 216–17
    consequences, 222–27
    events, 218–21
    human rights abuse, 225
    reporting to Washington on,
        227–29
    U.S. relief mission, 223–24

social life. See also friends
    in Africa, 295–98
    in Bogotá, 50–51, 66–67
    in Paris, 107, 108–9, 114–17
    in Tegucigalpa, 229
    in Trinidad, 36–37
Societa Immobiliari, 76
Somoza, Anastasio "Tachito," 229
South Africa, 267–68
    Angola and, 264
    relations with Zambia, 296
    visit to, 295–98
southern Africa, liberation struggle
    in, 261–70
Southwest Africa People's
    Organization (SWAPO), 265
Sovereign Military Order of Malta,
    337
Soviet Union
    Angola and, 264
    diplomats in Lusaka, 250
    and southern Africa, 285
    at UN Conference in Vienna, 315
    Zambia and, 262
Spain and GATT tariff negotiations,
    155
Spanish language course, 46–47
Spiritual Exercise of St. Ignatius
    Loyola, 338
sports. See also golf; skiing
    in Santiago, 146–48
    in Tegucigalpa, 231–32
SS Santa Rosa, 132
SS Saturnia, 71–74
State, Department of
    applying at, 15–16
    Bureau of African Affairs, 283
    Office of European Affairs, 153
    preparation for the UN Confer-
        ence on Science and Tech-
        nology for Development, 301–7
    security at, 175

Stein, Edith, 128
Stettinius, Edward, 15
Stromayer, James, 303
SWAPO (Southwest Africa People's
    Organization), 265
swearing-in ceremony, 240
Swett, Darwin, 212
Switzerland, visit to, 88–90

Tambo, Oliver, 255, 267
Taylor, Arthur, 323
Tegucigalpa, Honduras, 204–33.
    See also Soccer War
    anti-American demonstrations,
        209–10, 212–15
    arrival, 204–5
    housing, 205
    social life, 229
    visit of Lyndon Johnson, 211–12
Temple, Shirley, 165
tennis, 231
Thérèse de Lisieux, Saint, 99
Third Secretary—Economic. See
    Bogotá, Colombia
Time magazine, 140
Tinken, Art, 242, 243
traveling
    Atlantic crossings, 71–74, 99
    as a child, 5–6, 9
    on a freighter from Trinidad to
        Alabama, 34–35
    from Genoa to Milan, 74–75
    to Lusaka, 241–43
    from Lusaka to Kinshasa,
        287–90
    in the Middle East, 336–37
    return trip from Paris, 126–27
    to Santiago, 132
    with the Senior Seminar, 161–62
    to Trinidad, 19–20
    on vacation in Italy, 119–21
    for VITA, 324

Trinidad, BWI, 18–43
    arrival, 20–22
    Consul in, 28–31
    job, 28–31
    learning protocol, 24–28
    leaving, 41–42, 44–46
    Pan American Airways Clipper
        crash, 35–36
    Port of Spain, 22–23
    social life, 36–37
    society, 25–26
Trinity College, religious education
    course, 338
Trowbridge, Alexander, 186
Troxel, Oliver L., Jr., 237
Tuscany, farmhouse in, 186–92
    absentee landlord, 190–91
    entertaining at, 189
    selling, 191–92
Two Hundred Fifteen Days in the Life
    of an American Ambassador
    (Herz), 159

Ugolini, Cardinal, 196
UN Conference on Science and
    Technology for Development,
    300–318
    preparations, 301–14
    U.S. Advisory Council, 305
    U.S. coordinator for, 301
    in Vienna, 314–18
Underraga (Chilean wine producer),
    140
Unilateral Declaration of
    Independence (Rhodesia,
    1965), 268
UNITA (National Union for the Total
    Liberation of Angola), 263, 264
United States
    Angola and, 264
    armed forces in Trinidad, 26–27,
        28–29

policy toward southern Africa,
287, 290–92
portrayal in Latin American press,
53–54
University of Nebraska, 166
University of Wisconsin, 14
Untener, Ken, ix–x
U.S. Congress
confirmation hearings, 238–40
and UN Conference on Science
and Technology, 303
U.S. Information Service (USIS), 149
U.S. Machine Tool Association, 103
U.S. Southern Military Command,
223
USAID. *See also* PL-480 Food for
Peace
in Honduras, 207

Valobra, Veronica, 38–41
Vance, Cyrus, 320, 332–33
Vanderbilt University, 166
Vatican, 196–98
Bank, 194–95
Vekeman, Roger, 149–50
Versailles, dinner at, 103–4
Vice Consul. *See* Milan, Italy;
Trinidad, BWI
Victoria Falls, Kissinger at, 293–94
Vienna, 314–18
Vietnam War
Honduran supply mission, 214
Zambia and, 246, 256, 262
Vincent de Paul, Saint, 110
violence
anti-American demonstrations in
Honduras, 209–10, 212–15
bombing at Embassy Rome,
173–74
revolution in Bogotá, 55–63
in Zambia, 270–72
visas, issuing, 31–32, 81

visitors to embassies, 192. *See also*
CODELs; Ellington, Duke;
Johnson, Lyndon B.; King,
Coretta Scott; Kissinger, Henry;
Rockefeller, Nelson; Young,
Andrew
in Lusaka, 276–78
VITA (Volunteers in Technical
Assistance), 322–27
Vorster, John, 282–83

Waldheim, Kurt, 307
Walker, Herman, Jr., 153, 154, 155,
156
wardrobe
for Africa, 240–41
in Paris, 106–7
for swearing-in ceremony, 240
in Trinidad, 37
Washington, D.C.
at the Department of Commerce,
96–98
job at Catholic University, 17
Kaunda in, 284–87
preparation for GATT tariff
negotiations, 153
preparation for Lusaka, 236–38
preparation of UN Conference,
301–3
Washington Post, 319
Williams, G. Mennen "Soapy," 286
winery, 188–89
Wisconsin, 3–5
women
in Latin America, 141–42
wives of diplomats, 206, 209
Women in Foreign Affairs, 322
women's liberation, 202
Woodcock, Leonard, 308, 314
World Cup (1969), 217

Xiaoping, Deng, 314

Young, Andrew, 277, 280, 281

Zaire, trip to Kinshasa, 287–90
Zambia
    agriculture, 254
    attitude toward the United States,
      256–57
    beer drinking in, 235–36, 237
    copper mining, 253
    national brewery, 255
    organization and management
      skills in, 254
    relations with South Africa, 296
    U.S. relations with, 253–56
    Vietnam War and, 246, 256

Zambia, assignment to. *See* Lusaka,
    Zambia
ZANU (Zimbabwe African National
    Union), 268–69
ZAPU (Zimbabwe African People's
    Union), 268
Zimbabwe. *See also* Rhodesia
    United States and, 292
Zucca, Albert, 207, 216, 224
    during Rockefeller's visit, 210
    during Soccer War, 218, 220, 221,
      222
    Somoza and, 229
Zuñiga, Ricardo, 215, 219, 221

JEAN M. WILKOWSKI

entered the U.S. Foreign Service in 1944, accepting career assignments to nine countries on three continents before retiring in 1980. She has received six honorary degrees and is the only woman to receive the Foreign Service Cup from the Diplomatic and Consular Officers, Retired (DACOR).